THEORY AND INTERPRETATION OF NARRATIVE
James Phelan, Peter J. Rabinowitz, and Robyn Warhol, Series Editors

READING CONRAD

~

J. Hillis Miller

Edited by John G. Peters and Jakob Lothe

THE OHIO STATE UNIVERSITY PRESS
COLUMBUS

Copyright © 2017 by The Ohio State University.
All rights reserved.

Library of Congress Cataloging-in-Publication Data
Names: Miller, J. Hillis (Joseph Hillis), 1928– author. | Peters, John G. (John Gerard), editor. | Lothe, Jakob, editor.
Title: Reading Conrad / J. Hillis Miller ; edited by John G. Peters and Jakob Lothe.
Other titles: Theory and interpretation of narrative series.
Description: Columbus : The Ohio State University Press, [2017] | Series: Theory and interpretation of narrative | Includes bibliographical references and index.
Identifiers: LCCN 2017029074 | ISBN 9780814213483 (cloth ; alk. paper) | ISBN 0814213480 (cloth ; alk. paper)
Subjects: LCSH: Conrad, Joseph, 1857–1924—Criticism and interpretation.
Classification: LCC PR6005.O4 Z7787 2017 | DDC 823/.912—dc23
LC record available at https://lccn.loc.gov/2017029074

Cover design by Andrew Brozyna
Text design by Juliet Williams
Type set in Adobe Minion Pro

♾ The paper used in this publication meets the minimum requirements of the American National Standard for Information Sciences—Permanence of Paper for Printed Library Materials. ANSI Z39.48-1992.

9 8 7 6 5 4 3 2 1

CONTENTS

Foreword	JAKOB LOTHE AND JOHN G. PETERS	vii
Acknowledgments		xxiii
Note on the Text and Abbreviations		xxv
INTRODUCTION	Conrad and Me J. HILLIS MILLER	1
CHAPTER 1	Joseph Conrad: The Darkness and *The Secret Agent*	4
CHAPTER 2	*Lord Jim*: Repetition as Subversion of Organic Form	57
CHAPTER 3	*Heart of Darkness* Revisited	74
CHAPTER 4	Joseph Conrad: Should We Read *Heart of Darkness*?	88
CHAPTER 5	Conrad's Secret	122
CHAPTER 6	Revisiting "*Heart of Darkness* Revisited" (in the company of Philippe Lacoue-Labarthe)	156
CHAPTER 7	Conrad's Colonial (Non)Community: *Nostromo*	172
Index		260

FOREWORD

MOST SCHOLARS, even some Conrad scholars, are unaware of how much J. Hillis Miller has written about the work of Joseph Conrad and how influential that commentary has been. Miller is regularly cited in Conrad criticism, and his impact on Conrad studies and on literary studies in general—through his discussion of Conrad's fiction—is significant. There is a close, and revealing, connection between Miller's important contribution to Conrad studies and his invaluable contributions to literary studies overall, including his thoughtful and thought-provoking discussions of the role of, and challenges to, literature and literary studies in the modern world. It is as though, returning to Conrad at different stages of his long career, and reading and rereading Conrad in the light of new critical trends (to whose formation, particularly that of deconstruction, he also contributed) and modern history, Miller keeps discovering new aspects of Conrad's fiction. As he puts it in his introduction to this volume, "it is possible to go back again and again to the same work by Conrad and always find something new to say about it" (p. 1). For Miller, Conrad is one of those authors whose fiction, read in the light of different critical theories, provides rich and varied responses from the reader. But the key point for Miller is that this can only happen if the critic has the ability, and patience, to engage in close reading of the literary text under consideration. Reading literature, especially when the author is

Conrad, is for Miller a demanding and potentially rewarding act possessed of a distinctly ethical dimension.

Miller's first consideration of Joseph Conrad's fiction appeared as two chapters in his *Poets of Reality* (1965), in which he posited a nihilism in Conrad's works—a claim that directly influenced, for example, Royal Roussel's *The Metaphysics of Darkness: A Study in the Unity and Development of Conrad's Fiction* (1971) and later William W. Bonney's *Thorns & Arabesques: Contexts for Conrad's Fiction* (1980). But these are only the most extended works that were directly influenced by Miller's view of nihilism as it relates to Conrad's works. An entire thread of Conrad commentary that sees some degree of nihilism at the core of Conrad's fiction undoubtedly has Miller's *Poets of Reality* as its ultimate source, and any other critics who have seen nihilism in Conrad's works have, directly or indirectly, knowingly or unknowingly, drawn upon Miller's original views in *Poets of Reality*. Rereading those chapters on Conrad, we have been struck by just how far ahead of his time Miller was. No contemporary of Miller's was writing on Conrad in anything close to those terms, and as critical history has shown, Miller's views in that book have remained relevant. Had these chapters in *Poets of Reality* been Miller's sole contribution to Conrad commentary, this contribution would have been significant, but they were just the beginning of his contributions to Conrad scholarship.

Miller's identification and discussion of nihilism in Conrad's fiction is linked to, and inspired by, his strong and lasting interest in the relationship between philosophy and literature. In *Poets of Reality* he takes a particular interest in the trend within twentieth-century philosophy commonly referred to as phenomenology, with Edmund Husserl as a main representative. For Husserl and his successors, it is essential to study "structures of consciousness as experienced from the first-person point of view."[1] Concomitantly, in so-called phenomenological criticism a consideration of the author's consciousness plays a key role. Miller was, and in one sense continues to be, inspired by the Geneva School of literary theorists and critics, and particularly by Georges Poulet as a critic associated with that school. Born in Belgium in 1902, Poulet became a professor of French literature at Johns Hopkins University in 1952. When Miller started to teach at the same university the following year,[2] the two became colleagues.

---

1. "Phenomenology," *Stanford Encyclopedia of Philosophy*, last modified December 16, 2013, accessed November 1, 2016, http://plato.stanford.edu/entries/phenomenology/.

2. Miller taught at the Johns Hopkins University from 1953 to 1972. See J. Hillis Miller, "Should We Read or Teach Literature Now?," in *Narrative Ethics*, ed. Jakob Lothe and Jeremy Hawthorn (New York: Rodopi, 2013), 13.

Miller succinctly presents the constituent elements of Poulet's criticism of consciousness when he writes that, for critics such as Poulet, literature is

> neither an objective structure of meanings in the words of a poem or novel, nor the tissue of self-references or "message" turned in on itself, nor the unwitting expression of the hidden complexities of a writer's unconscious, nor a revelation of the latent structures of exchange or symbolization which integrate a society. Literature, for them, is the embodiment of a state of mind.[3]

Although Miller does not understand literature exactly in this way in *Poets of Reality*, Poulet's ideas no doubt exerted a strong influence on him. When he writes that "many twentieth-century poets begin with an experience of the nihilism which is one of the possible consequences of romanticism," he relates nihilism to the author's consciousness. Importantly, when he then goes on to note, "My chapter on Conrad attempts to identify this nihilism by analysis of a writer who follows it into its darkness and so prepares the way beyond it,"[4] he suggests that, in common with Poulet, he does not understand a facet of consciousness such as nihilism as a static or stable quality. Rather, Conrad's nihilism, and by implication his consciousness as an author, is imbued with a dynamic aspect furthered by elements of narrative and plot formation. In later commentaries Miller would study these elements more carefully, but it does not follow that the idea of the author's consciousness is rejected completely.

Miller's next commentary on Conrad is similar and yet also different. In "The Interpretation of *Lord Jim*" (1970), he focuses on the impossibility of ever providing an ending to the novel because the process of interpretation similarly lacks an ending, always moving "toward a light which always remains hidden." Although James Guetti, in *The Limits of Metaphor* (1967), had previously argued that the indeterminacy of language leads to the indeterminacy of Conrad's works, Miller goes beyond Guetti to suggest that not only the indeterminacy of language but the very nature of interpretive activity itself makes Conrad's works curiously indeterminate and open-ended. One reason is that, as Miller convincingly shows in his analysis of *Lord Jim*, Conrad's narration incorporates, and in the case of *Lord Jim* even necessitates, elements of interpretation as Marlow and the other narrators attempt to understand the enigma of Jim. Miller's ideas here are linked to those he presents in *Poets of*

---

3. J. Hillis Miller, "The Geneva School: The Criticism of Marcel Raymond, Albert Béguin, Georges Poulet, Jean Rousset, Jean-Pierre Richard, and Jean Starobinski," *The Critical Quarterly* 8 (Winter 1966): 306–7. See also J. Hillis Miller, "The Literary Criticism of George Poulet," *MLN* 78 (December 1963): 471–88.

4. J. Hillis Miller, *Poets of Reality* (Cambridge, MA: Harvard University Press, 1965), 1.

Reality, but they also move in a different direction: toward the emphasis on language and interpretation and the role of the reader that would become a prominent aspect of Conrad scholarship some years later.

Although it would be misleading to claim that Miller's 1970 essay on *Lord Jim* marks a dramatic turn in his commentaries on Conrad, it is significant that this essay appeared just a few years after the publication of Jacques Derrida's *De la grammatologie* (1967).[5] Miller's relationship with Derrida is much more complex and multifaceted than we can show in a brief foreword, but we would like to highlight one aspect of this relationship that Miller himself has emphasized. In order to do this, we first need to point out that while Poulet's criticism of consciousness exerted a considerable influence on Miller's thought and writing in the 1950s and '60s, including his discussion of Conrad in *Poets of Reality*, that influence was linked to the input of New Criticism. An important trend of literary studies in the United States in the first couple of decades after the Second World War, and gradually also becoming influential in Europe, New Criticism advocated a kind of close reading that would aim to demonstrate the literary text's "organic unity."[6] While Miller, who throughout his career has insisted on the need for careful attention to textual detail, was attracted to the idea of close reading, he had, as he states in an interview in 2004, problems with the idea of a literary text's "organic unity."[7] For this reason he became, he says in the interview, particularly interested in the work of critics admired by the New Critics, such as Edmund Burke and William Empson. For example, Empson's *Seven Types of Ambiguity* (1930; revised editions 1947 and 1953) does not unproblematically support the idea of a literary text's "unity" since Empson discusses literary texts in a way that, not least by identifying different *types* of ambiguity, puts emphasis on textual complexity and thematic heterogeneity.[8] This kind of critical openness appealed to Miller. A

---

5. Jacques Derrida, *De la grammatologie* (Paris: Les Éditions de Minuit, 1967); English translation: *Of Grammatology*, trans. Gayatri Chakravorty Spivak (Baltimore: Johns Hopkins University Press, 1976).

6. The term is often linked to Cleanth Brooks, a leading representative of New Criticism, in whose influential *The Well Wrought Urn: Studies in the Structure of Poetry* (1947) it plays a key role. Emphasizing the importance of Brooks's study, Miller notes that for the New Critics, "a good poem . . . was assumed to be an 'organic unity' bringing disparate materials together in a complex ironic harmony of opposites in tension." "Theory in the Development of Literary Studies," in *An Innocent Abroad: Lectures in China* (Evanston: Northwestern University Press, 2015), 12.

7. Julian Wolfreys, ed., *The J. Hillis Miller Reader* (Edinburgh: Edinburgh University Press, 2005), 413.

8. In the interview with Wolfreys, Miller refers to Burke's claim that "a literary work . . . is motivated by some kind of problem the writer has, perhaps an Empsonian contradiction. . . . Writing the work is a way of working through the problem. I found Burke's paradigm produc-

key aspect here is his readiness to take the fictional text seriously in the sense of allowing, even inviting, the text to challenge the reader's critical approach. This is, for him, an essential part of the ethics of reading.

Because of his interest in French literature and in the work of French philosophers and critics, particularly Poulet, Miller taught himself French and started to read Derrida and other French critics in their original language. In the 2004 interview he says, "My reading of *De la grammatologie* and of Derrida's other early work was a turning point for me.[9] . . . Derrida liberated me to recognize that a work can be a great work and nevertheless be contradictory."[10] This kind of "liberation" is observable in Miller's 1970 essay on *Lord Jim*. For Miller, this novel's apparent lack of an "organic unity" makes it more, not less, interesting. In a way, it also makes it more important: Miller is intrigued by, and carefully explores, the various ways in which the literary text's narrative form and metaphoric patterns generate, and blend into, a complex thematics that cannot, and should not, be summarized as, or misleadingly condensed into, a unifying theme.

Although there may be no direct connection between Miller's 1970 essay on *Lord Jim* and his major study of Hardy, *Thomas Hardy: Distance and Desire*, that appeared in the same year, both signal a new direction in his literary criticism. In the period from 1970 to 1982, Miller published relatively few book-length studies. However, in a string of important essays that appeared over the course of this decade, he responded to, tried out, and gradually implemented significant aspects of deconstruction.[11] We write "significant aspects" in order to stress that Miller did not uncritically appropriate the main tenets of deconstruction, including Derrida's theoretical formulations of a key concept such as *la différance*. The aspect of deconstruction that became particularly important for Miller was, as indicated already, the combination of insistence on careful close reading and the realization that careful reading and rereading

---

tive. My dissertation on Dickens is strongly influenced by Burke." Wolfreys, *J. Hillis Miller Reader*, 413.

9. Derrida's "other early work" includes *L'écriture et la différance* (Paris: Éditions du Seul, 1967; English translation 1978) and *Le Voix et la Phènoméne* (Paris: Presses Universitaires de France, 1967; English translation 1973).

10. Miller specifies that "Derrida's work combines in a quite singular way the two traditions that had influenced me until then, the New Criticism and so-called phenomenological criticism," Wolfreys, *J. Hillis Miller Reader*, 415.

11. Several of these articles later formed the basis for full-length studies. Thus there are, for instance, important links between "The Linguistic Moment in 'The Wreck of the Deutschland'" (in *The New Criticism and After*, ed. Thomas D. Young [Charlotteville: University of Virginia Press, 1976, 47–60]) and *The Linguistic Moment: From Wordsworth to Stevens* (Princeton: Princeton University Press, 1985).

does not necessarily resolve the formal and thematic tensions and contradictions of which a literary text may be possessed.

This aspect of deconstruction is striking in the chapter on Conrad in *Fiction and Repetition* (1981). Developing the ideas in "The Interpretation of *Lord Jim*," Miller here revises and expands his 1970 essay, producing his extremely influential "Repetition as Subversion of Organic Form in *Lord Jim*." Focusing on the issue of repetition, the chapter on *Lord Jim* in *Fiction and Repetition* explores the ways in which the repetition of, for instance, words, images, and episodes both generates meaning and complicates meaning by suggesting interpretive possibilities that may be incompatible. For example, the novel's variations of perspective as well as voice both follow from and generate its repetitive narrative movement, slowly spiraling toward a possible understanding of Jim, who, however, "passes away under a cloud" (312). Thus, although the presentation of narrative seems to suggest that its repetition will result in comprehension, in fact it works in the opposite direction, with the novel leaving readers with questions rather than answers at its conclusion. Miller links the first aspect of the novel's repetition to what he calls the "first" form of repetition, a kind of Platonic repetition associated with the idea of origin and direction toward some kind of goal. The second aspect, that which prompts questions rather than providing answers, he relates to a different, Nietzschean form of repetition that, though linked to the first form, is actually very different as it furthers different kinds of doubt and uncertainty about, and postponement of, answers that might suggest a stable meaning or purpose. Significantly, however, as Miller shows in his analysis of *Lord Jim*, the second form does not eliminate the first; rather, the two forms of repetition curiously coexist, thus leading to, even necessitating, the continuation of Marlow's, and Conrad's, narrative exploration of the enigma of Jim. That this kind of exploration—which, Miller demonstrates, also becomes the reader's—is never concluded makes the experience of reading and rereading the novel more, not less, rewarding.

Unquestionably one of Miller's most influential essays, "Repetition as Subversion of Organic Form in *Lord Jim*" helped to usher in the influx of commentary that availed itself of the innovations of contemporary critical theory of the time. A few years later, Miller contributed to an important collection of essays on Conrad edited by Ross C. Murfin, *Conrad Revisited: Essays for the Eighties* (1985). Miller's "*Heart of Darkness* Revisited" is possibly the most original essay in this excellent volume. Taking his cue from Francis Ford Coppola's *Apocalypse Now* (1979), the classic Vietnam film strongly indebted to Conrad's *Heart of Darkness*, Miller asks whether—and if so, how—there is already something apocalyptic about Conrad's novella itself. This question prompts a wide-ranging, thoughtful, and thought-provoking discussion in which Miller, describing *Heart of Darkness* as "a cacophony of dissonant voices" (45; 84 this volume), argues that a full exploration of the possible ways in which the novella is an apocalypse would involve consideration of the converging figures of irony, antithesis, catachresis, synecdoche, aletheia, and prosopopoeia. While elements of these rhetorical figures had been identified and discussed by other critics, Miller was the first to interlink the six figures in a critically productive manner, relating all of them not only to one other but also to constituent aspects of an apocalypse.[12]

Noting that the word "apocalypse" means unveiling or aletheia, Miller suggests that the narration in *Heart of Darkness* assumes the form of an "unveiling [that] unveils unveiling" (43; 82 this volume). This point about *Heart of Darkness* bears a significant relation to a theoretical point argued by Miller in *The Ethics of Reading*, an important book published two years later: "Narrative can be defined as the indefinite postponement of that ultimate direct confrontation of the law that narrative is nevertheless instituted to make happen in an example worthy of respect."[13] Miller's understanding of "the law" is inspired by Kant's idea of a moral law that "exercises over me an implacable necessity, a categorical imperative."[14] It is also linked to Miller's understanding of the promise as a particular kind of performative language: "In the space between the promise and the perpetually deferred fulfillment of the promise the story takes place."[15] Using Marlow and the frame narrator as narrative instruments that enable him to construct a fictional narrative, Conrad promises a story, and in one sense he gives readers one. And yet, for the reader, as for Marlow and his listeners aboard the *Nellie*, this story proves inconclusive, leading into "an immense darkness."[16]

Although not all readers of "*Heart of Darkness* Revisited" have been convinced by Miller's description of the novella as a narrative process of "unveiling [that] unveils unveiling" (43; 82 this volume), there is no doubt that the essay has proved thought-provoking and influential. The analysis presented in this essay is consonant with Miller's view of literature as "the creation or

---

12. Although we need to be cognizant of the generic difference between poetry and narrative fiction, it is worth noting that Miller also pays close attention to, and emphasizes the importance of, rhetorical figures in *The Linguistic Moment* (see note 10 in this chapter), a major study of poetry that appeared in the same year as the Conrad essay.

13. J. Hillis Miller, *The Ethics of Reading: Kant, de Man, Eliot, Trollope, James, and Benjamin* (New York: Columbia University Press, 1987), 33.

14. Ibid., 32.

15. Ibid., 33.

16. Joseph Conrad, *Youth, Heart of Darkness, The End of the Tether*, ed. Owen Knowles (Cambridge: Cambridge University Press, 2010), 126; hereafter cited as *HD*.

discovery of a new, supplementary world, a metaworld, a hyper-reality."[17] "Literature," Miller goes on to argue in *On Literature,* "makes exorbitant and large-scale use of the propensity words possess to go on having meaning even in the absence of any ascertainable, phenomenally verifiable, referent."[18] Yet it does not follow that, for Miller, Conrad's novella is not anchored in historical reality, including that of the empirical reader. Moreover, that literary language's reference to historical reality is indirect, complicated (and in the case of *Heart of Darkness* "parabolic") in its deferral of meaning and resistance to closure, does not make it less important. Rather, for Miller, it enhances the value of literature in the real world.

Notable in the 1985 essay, this recognition of, and emphasis on, the value of literature as an indirect reference system is even more pronounced in Miller's "Should We Read *Heart of Darkness*?" This 2002 essay, a revised version of a keynote lecture that Miller gave at an international conference arranged in South Africa a few years earlier to mark the centenary of *Heart of Darkness,* elaborates the discussion of irony as a key narrative strategy in the novella. Finding that Conrad's novella is "ironic through and through" (466; 106 this volume), Miller here too links the text's irony to the other figures mentioned above. More explicitly than in the earlier essay, however, the combined effects of these figures lead Miller to consider *Heart of Darkness* as "a powerful exemplary revelation of the ideology of capitalist imperialism" (474; 121 this volume).

Miller's concluding observation on *Heart of Darkness* establishes an important link to key points argued in two significant essays on *Nostromo*. In common with the two essays on *Heart of Darkness,* these are also remarkably original. In "'Material Interests': *Nostromo* as a Critique of Global Capitalism" (2008), Miller shows how the novel's narrative discourse recovers the ways in which individuals are related, each in a different way, to their surrounding community as it evolves through time. If, for Miller, *Lord Jim* aims to recover a single life story, *Nostromo* is about "an imagined community" (161). There is a sense in which this essay anticipates his discussion of community in *The Conflagration of Community: Fiction before and after Auschwitz* (2012).[19] While

---

17. J. Hillis Miller, *On Literature* (London: Routledge, 2002), 18.
18. Ibid., 19.
19. *The Conflagration of Community: Fiction before and after Auschwitz* (Chicago: Chicago University Press, 2012). Interestingly, this is the only book title that links "fiction" directly to a geographical name, and to a historical event (the Holocaust) of which that name has become a symbol. As is often the case with Miller, this study is also an extended, refined version of previously published essays, including, in this particular case, his contribution to *After Testimony: The Ethics and Aesthetics of Holocaust Narrative for the Future,* ed. Jakob Lothe, Susan Rubin Suleiman, and James Phelan (Columbus: Ohio State University Press, 2012), 23–51.

emphasizing that the community of *Nostromo* is fictional, Miller also stresses that it is based on, and inspired by, Conrad's reading about South American history. Still insisting that a literary work is "the creation or discovery of a new, supplementary world,"[20] both the 2008 essay and his recently published "Text; Action; Space; Emotion in Conrad's *Nostromo*" (2014) relate the fictional world of the novel more closely to history and context.

These essays show that Miller reacts not just to critical theories in literary studies, but also to what he observes in his contemporary world. His criticism is thus informed both by theory and, broadly understood, politics—and his politics has a distinctly ethical component. Among the most original features of the latter essay are Miller's observations, aided by earlier works of his such as *Ariadne's Thread* (1992), *Topographies* (1995), and *Reading Narrative* (1998),[21] on the ways in which spatial and temporal elements are intertwined in *Nostromo*; these observations are then very interestingly linked to an extended discussion of the novel's narration seen in the light of Kant's notion of the sublime. Miller has recently incorporated both of these essays on *Nostromo* into his "Conrad's Colonial (Non)Community," a lengthy chapter from his *Communities in Fiction* (2014), in which he considers the issues raised in his earlier essays on the novel in the broader context of the relationship between the individual and the larger community, concluding that for "the Conrad of *Nostromo* there is only the immense indifference of things" (231; 259 this volume).

Ultimately, bringing together Miller's various commentaries on Conrad will not only demonstrate how important a commentator he has been but will also provide an easy access to this commentary, which will allow one to see how Miller's commentary on Conrad has developed over time.

Perhaps it is the fact that Miller has been a leading figure within different trends of literary theory, especially (but not only) deconstruction, that has allowed us to overlook the significance of his contribution to Conrad studies. In fact, there is a close link between these two areas of his extraordinary achievement as a critic, one who started to publish important works of criticism fifty years ago and who is still active as a writer. While Miller has been influenced by critical trends such as phenomenology, New Criticism, deconstruction, narrative theory, and narrative ethics, he has also influenced these trends. When linked to his work on Conrad, we can see how his evolving theoretical orientation colors his different Conrad essays and studies published

---

20. Miller, *On Literature*, 18.

21. *Ariadne's Thread: Story Lines* (New Haven: Yale University Press, 1992); *Topographies* (Stanford: Stanford University Press, 1985); *Reading Narrative* (Norman: University of Oklahoma Press, 1998).

over the years. Yet this critical activity is reciprocal: for Miller, theory and analysis are closely related. This is an interesting example of how literary theory and literary analysis can interact: although Miller's analyses are informed by theory, the theories are also informed—modified, refined, and sometimes challenged—by his analyses and close readings. This kind of critical practice is in concert with a main point argued in the first chapter of *Fiction and Repetition,* where Miller claims that the profession of literary criticism "is nothing if it is not philology, the love of words, the teaching of reading, and the attempt in written criticism to facilitate the act of reading."[22] Approximating to a program, this statement signals not only Miller's commitment to close reading of literary texts but also his readiness to make the literary texts challenge aspects of theory, thus encouraging the critic to modify or even change his or her approach. At the center of Miller's critical attention remains, as his work on Conrad shows, the literary text and the experiences it inspires in readers.

This combination of careful, sustained attention to the literary text and an equally sustained readiness to let himself be surprised by the text is a characteristic feature of Miller's work. As he notes at the end of the chapter on Wallace Stevens in *Topographies,*

> I did not know where [this chapter] was going to go when I began writing it.... Things have happened through the act of writing that no amount of simple thinking or silent reading could have achieved. Writing this chapter ... has taken me to a place I did not even know existed, much less intend to reach, before I started writing.[23]

As such writing is effectively an extension of the reading process, this comment applies equally to the trajectories of Miller's readings in this volume. Over and over again, Miller's careful studies of Conrad take him to unknown places; his reading of a Conrad text—including a chapter, a passage, or even a phrase from that text—puts him, to appropriate the title of a poem by Thomas Hardy, "In Front of a Landscape." While Miller has written a brilliant analysis of this masterly poem,[24] his reading of a narrative text by Conrad also takes him to a landscape, a place, that is a complex literary universe. As the following chapters show, Miller is intrigued by the literary qualities of this universe,

---

22. J. Hillis Miller, *Fiction and Repetition: Seven English Novels* (Cambridge, MA: Harvard University Press, 1982), 21.

23. Miller, *Topographies,* 290.

24. "Topography and Tropography in Thomas Hardy's 'In Front of a Landscape,'" in *Post-Structuralist Readings of English Poetry,* ed. Richard Machin and Christopher Norris (Cambridge: Cambridge University Press, 1987), 332–48.

including Conrad's use of language, the fictional texts' narrative structure, their characters and plot formations, and their metaphoric and symbolic patterns. As indicated already, he is also fascinated by the ways in which, as literature, the fictional texts that make up Conrad's literary universe represent historical reality and historical processes. As we have suggested, the fact that this representation is characteristically oblique does not make it less interesting or less important. On the contrary, as Miller's extended discussion of *Nostromo* at the end of this volume demonstrates, Conrad's fiction is significant precisely because of the ways in which, as literary form, it tells us something about the world, and about us and the way we live and interact in this world, that we would not or could not otherwise have known.

It would be oversimplified, however, to suggest that Miller's 2002 essay on *Heart of Darkness* signals a "political turn" in his literary criticism. Rather, its political elements become, from the publication of *The Ethics of Reading* in 1987 onwards, more pronounced and more explicit—but it does not follow that other constituent elements of his criticism, the way he reads literature, are abolished or left behind. Nor does it follow that there was no political element in his criticism earlier. Since writers of fiction use literary language to describe constituent elements of a fictional universe that is inspired by, and indirectly represents, the real world, there is a sense in which all fiction is political, and one premise for Miller's criticism is that fictional narratives cannot, and should not, be ideologically or politically "neutral." Nor is the reading of literature an ideologically or ethically neutral activity. The writer of fiction describes the world as he or she knows it from a certain perspective—a perspective linked to, and influenced by, his or her experiences, attitudes, values, and priorities. This kind of perspectival limitation—which, however, is not just a problem but also a gain or advantage—applies to the reader too. Importantly, though, the creative writer has the privilege of making his or her perspective more nuanced and multifaceted by linking it to those of the fiction's characters and narrators. Moreover, perspectives may change over the course of the narrative, thus becoming more multifaceted; they may also change over an author's writing career.

That few authors illustrate these characteristic features of fiction better than Joseph Conrad may partly explain Miller's lasting fascination with this writer. Although all of Conrad's fictional texts are possessed of a political dimension, this dimension cannot be reduced to a stable position or perspective. This distinctive feature of Conrad's fiction strengthens its political facet: even textual passages that on a first reading seem relatively "apolitical"—for instance, descriptions of landscape and setting—may on a second or third reading turn out to be possessed of thematic elements that are ideological and political. As Miller shows in his discussion of *Nostromo,* the opening of that novel is a revealing example. Linked to this characteristic feature are two further aspects that are also important to Miller. First, the tensions, conflicts, inequalities, and power struggles of Conrad's fictional world are closely linked to issues of gender, class, and ethnic affiliation. Second, they are not limited to characters and narrators but also include communities and nations, and the complex relationships between these can also be tense and unstable.

This observation highlights the strong interest in ethics that is also a distinctive feature of Miller's work as a literary critic and scholar. In addition to his seminal contribution to critical trends as varied as phenomenology, New Criticism, deconstruction, and narrative theory, he has also played a key role in initiating the "ethical turn" of literary studies. In actual fact, the phrase "in addition to" is somewhat misleading, for narrative ethics has been an integral part of Miller's readings all along; it is strikingly apparent, for example, in the 1957 essay entitled "Franz Kafka and the Metaphysics of Alienation."[25] In the first chapter of *The Ethics of Reading* (1987), Miller claims that "there is a necessary ethical moment in the act of reading as such, a moment neither cognitive, nor political, nor social, nor interpersonal, but properly and independently ethical" (1). If, for Miller, the "ethical moment" is inseparable from the act of reading, it is also indistinguishable from literary form—and especially narrative form. "Ethics," he goes on to note in *The Ethics of Reading,* "has a peculiar relation to that form of language we call narrative" (3).

If the ethical moment is a response to something in the text—for example, the presentation of a character's or narrator's moral dilemma or test-like experience—it also "leads to an act. It enters into the social, institutional, political realms" (4). Taking literature seriously and emphasizing its rhetorical and performative power, Miller finds that it "must be in some way a cause and not merely an effect" (5). In the narrative texts studied in this book, literature emerges as both cause and effect, and this is a main reason why Miller's readings of Conrad are unfailingly engaged and engaging, thoughtful as well as thought-provoking. While narrative fiction is undeniably an effect of a series of complex phenomena in society and in the human psyche, as literary language it can also contribute to the formation of history from within.

Since Miller is, in the best sense of the word, a student of narrative, it is actually somewhat misleading to refer, as we have done, to his contributions to "narrative theory." The reason is not that these contributions are not significant—books such as *Fiction and Repetition, Ariadne's Thread,* and *Reading Narrative* have surely influenced the development of this field of literary

---

25. In *The Tragic Vision and the Christian Faith,* ed. Nathan A. Scott (New York: Association Press, 1957), 281–305.

studies. The reason is that, as indicated already, for Miller narrative theory is closely affiliated with, and in a way dependent on, narrative analysis—both narrative analysis generally and the analyses of Conrad's fiction that he presents in this book. Thus, for example, while the first chapter of *Fiction and Repetition* is an important contribution to narrative theories of repetition in fiction, the range, suggestiveness, and interpretative potential of that theory depend on the following analysis, not least that of *Lord Jim*.[26] A second illustrative example is an essay on Franz Kafka published in 2002.[27] While Miller's comments on aspects of J. L. Austin's speech act theory in this essay are theoretically interesting, its critical value for narrative theory is increased by his carefully developed argument that, when applied to Kafka, speech act theory can explain some, but not all, constituent elements of this author's strange, and for Miller appealing and critically challenging, fictional discourse.[28]

There is one more aspect of Miller's criticism that needs to be mentioned since this aspect too is associated with, and arguably to some extent furthered by, his lasting interest in Conrad. This is Miller's concern with the state of the academy in general and of literary studies in particular. "Should We Read or Teach Literature Now?" is an important essay in this regard. In this essay, first published in *Narrative Ethics* (2013) and then, in different versions, in *An Innocent Abroad: Lectures in China* (2015) and *Thinking Literature across Continents* (2016),[29] Miller reflects on the diminished role of the humanities in higher education, noting that "it is extremely difficult to demonstrate that humanities departments bring any financial return at all."[30] Toward the end of the essay, however, he demonstrates a different, and potentially more valuable, kind of "return": choosing W. B. Yeats's poem "The Cold Heaven" as an example, he lists fifteen "things that might need to be explained not only, for example, to a

---

26. It is hardly coincidental that the chapter on *Lord Jim* is the first narrative analysis in *Fiction and Repetition*, as it not only illustrates but in some ways also challenges theoretical points made in the preceding, introductory chapter. Significantly, the chapter is entitled "*Lord Jim*: Repetition as Subversion of Organic Form."

27. "Geglückte und misslungene Sprechakte in Kafkas *Der Process*," in *Franz Kafka. Zur ethischen und ästhetischen Rechtfertigung*, ed. Beatrice Sandberg and Jakob Lothe (Freiburg: Rombach Verlag, 2002), 233–46.

28. Miller's rich response to this kind of critical challenge is also striking in his narrative analysis of Kafka's *The Castle* in *Franz Kafka: Narration, Rhetoric, and Reading*, ed. Jakob Lothe, Beatrice Sandberg, and Ronald Speirs (Columbus: Ohio State University Press, 2011), 108–22.

29. "Should We Read or Teach Literature Now?," in Lothe and Hawthorn, *Narrative Ethics*, 13–24; "Cold Heaven, Cold Comfort: Should We Read or Teach Literature Now?," in Miller, *An Innocent Abroad*, 227–41; "Should We Read or Teach Literature Now?," in Ranjan Ghosh and J. Hillis Miller, *Thinking Literature across Continents* (Durham: Duke University Press, 2016), 177–203.

30. Ghosh and Miller, *Thinking Literature across Continents*, 183.

Chinese reader, but also . . . to a video-games-playing Western young person ignorant of European poetry, or to a student in an Indian classroom . . . to lead them to respond to the poem as enthusiastically as I do."[31] Unsurprisingly, these "things" turn out to be perceptive, thoughtful, and thought-provoking comments—observations that present the reader of the essay with the rich critical rewards of Miller's close reading of Yeats's poem.[32] It is also characteristic of Miller's criticism that what he writes about the poem, stressing the need to account for what the text says (and what it does not say), is closely linked to the challenge of teaching the poem; here Miller's strong interest in pedagogy blends into his lasting commitment to literary studies, and vice versa. Given that "Should We Read or Teach Literature Now?" is inspired by, and builds on, Miller's "Should We Read *Heart of Darkness*?," there is a strong sense in which his concern with the profession of literary studies is importantly related to his reading of Conrad. As Miller's interest in politics in a broad sense expands, so does his interest in the politics of the profession and of literary criticism.

The reader of this volume will notice that although Miller discusses a range of Conrad's most important fictional texts, there is much in Conrad that gets little or no discussion (e.g., *Almayer's Folly, Under Western Eyes, Victory*, short stories, and autobiographical writings). Conrad scholars are familiar with books that have a similarly narrow focus within the corpus of Conrad works as Miller has. While in recent years Conrad scholars have begun to pay more attention to Conrad's works outside what Jacques Berthoud termed Conrad's "major phase,"[33] many book-length studies over the years have tended to focus on the major works Conrad wrote between roughly 1900 and 1911, which include all of the works Miller considers except *Under Western Eyes*. Recently, however, more attention has been paid to those Conrad works that fall outside his "major phase," and Conrad scholars as well as nonspecialists in Conrad studies might well wonder about Miller's views when reading other works by Conrad than those discussed in this volume.

---

31. Ibid., 198. While the example of "a Chinese reader" alludes to *An Innocent Abroad*, that of "a student in an Indian classroom" may indirectly refer to the fact that his coauthor of *Teaching Literature across Continents*, Ranjan Ghosh, teaches in the Department of English, University of North Bengal.

32. For example, observation six: "An explanation of oxymorons (burning ice) and of the history in Western poetry of this particular one." Ghosh and Miller, *Thinking Literature across Continents*, 199. See also J. Hillis Miller, "Yeats: The Cold Heaven," in *Others* (Princeton: Princeton University Press, 2001), 170–82.

33. Jacques Berthoud, *Joseph Conrad: The Major Phase* (Cambridge: Cambridge University Press, 1978).

The essential point to make here is twofold. First, remarkably original, Miller's readings of major works by Conrad have proved hugely influential; this influence, not least on new generations of Conrad scholars, is likely to continue. Second, one facet of the originality of Miller's readings is suggested by the way in which several of the issues he raises in the works he investigates are relevant to other works in Conrad's corpus. For example, a number of Miller's views on *Nostromo* are potentially very interesting if linked to Conrad's other great revolutionary novel, *Under Western Eyes*. Similarly, several of the points Miller makes about *Heart of Darkness* are relevant not only to a novel such as *Lord Jim,* which he discusses, but also, albeit in different ways, to *Almayer's Folly* (1895), Conrad's first novel, and to "An Outpost of Progress" (1897), one of his most important short stories. Linked to this characteristic feature of Miller's Conrad commentaries is an attractive kind of generosity assuming the form of an invitation to the reader of this volume to read and reread the works of Conrad that he himself has read and reread—and, as a consequence, chosen to subject to critical scrutiny.

Miller's combined interest in narrative form and narrative ethics may partly explain why he has continued to read, reread, and write about Conrad, for Conrad's fiction gives rich and varied response to this kind of dual focus. Conrad's complexity, including his biographical complexity, is perhaps best illustrated by the phrase *homo duplex,* "the double man." "Homo duplex has in my case more than one meaning," Conrad wrote to a Polish friend.[34] Relating this quality of Conrad's ethos to his fictional work, it is striking to what extent his narratives are characterized by paradoxes, tensions, and conflicts that, at least in large part, remain unresolved. Although there are links between the ideological fissures of Conrad's life and the political dimension of his fiction, however, it would, as Miller shows, be reductive to explain the latter by referring to the former. Yet as Miller also demonstrates, it would also be reductive, even misleading, to claim that no such connection exists: Conrad's fiction is a forceful reminder that no literary text is written or read in a historical and cultural vacuum.

The blend of skeptical detachment and moral involvement that Miller identifies and discusses in Conrad's narratives is central to Conrad's achievement as a writer. This is one reason why—indirectly, as fictional texts—the stories and novels discussed by Miller may present not just a different, but in one sense also a more complete, account of a given phase or period of history

---

34. *The Collected Letters of Joseph Conrad,* ed. Frederick R. Karl and Laurence Davis, vol. 3 (Cambridge: Cambridge University Press, 1988), 89.

than a historical rendering of the same period could have done. Conrad, to paraphrase Aristotle, narrates what "might occur,"[35] and he demonstrates that human beings' experience of history varies, not least because of our different positions, diverse interests, and dissimilar perspectives. *Nostromo* is an illustrative example. The history of the men whom Giorgio sees fighting on the plain below Higuerota is very different from that of Charles Gould or Holroyd. Conrad's empathy gravitates towards the former group. As *Reading Conrad* shows, so does Miller's.

Jakob Lothe and John G. Peters

---

35. Aristotle, *Poetics*, ed. and trans. Stephen Halliwell (Cambridge, MA: Harvard University Press, 1995), 59.

ACKNOWLEDGMENTS

JOHN PETERS would like to thank the University of North Texas for their financial support of this volume by way of grants they provided. He would also like to thank the many Conrad scholars who expressed enthusiastic interest in seeing J. Hillis Miller's work on Joseph Conrad brought together in one volume. Furthermore, he greatly appreciates Miller's help and willingness to see these commentaries appear in this volume. Finally, he would like to express his great appreciation to Jakob Lothe for offering to coedit this volume and for the effort he spent in making it a far better volume than it would have been had he not been involved.

Jakob Lothe would like to thank J. Hillis Miller for his seminal contributions to literary studies, including Conrad studies. He would also like to express his gratitude to Miller for his inspired and inspiring participation in the research project "Narrative Theory and Analysis" at the Centre for Advanced Study, Oslo, in 2005–2006. Miller made significant contributions to all three books in which this project resulted, *Joseph Conrad* (2008), *Franz Kafka* (2011), and *After Testimony* (2012) (all published by The Ohio State University Press). Lothe would also like to thank Jeremy Hawthorn for his support and wise advice.

J. Hillis Miller would like to thank Ross Murfin of Southern Methodist University warmly for many Conrad kindnesses, especially for encouraging me to bring my reading of *Heart of Darkness* up to date for Conrad volumes he put together and published in several forms over a number of years.

We would like to express our appreciation to The Ohio State University Press for their help and interest in this volume, and we are also very grateful to the various publishers who have granted permission to reprint these commentaries. The details are as follow: "Joseph Conrad: Should We Read *Heart of Darkness*?" (pp. 104–34) and "Conrad's Secret" (pp. 137–69) are from *Others* by J. Hillis Miller. Copyright © 2001 by Princeton University Press. Reprinted by permission. "Revisiting '*Heart of Darkness* Revisited' (in the Company of Philippe Lacoue-Labarthe)" (pp. 17–35) is from *Conrad's Heart of Darkness and Contemporary Thought*, ed. Nidesh Lawtoo. Copyright © 2012 by Bloomsbury Publishing. Reprinted by permission. Fordham University Press has also been kind enough to grant us permission to reprint "Conrad's Colonial (Non)Community: *Nostromo*," which originally appeared in J. Hillis Miller's *Communities of Fiction* (Fordham University Press, 2015). Finally, we would like to acknowledge that "*Heart of Darkness* Revisited" originally appeared in *Conrad Revisited*, ed. Ross C. Murfin (The University of Alabama Press, 1985), and "Joseph Conrad: The Darkness and *The Secret Agent*" originally appeared in J. Hillis Miller's *Poets of Reality* (Harvard University Press, 1965).

NOTE ON THE TEXT AND ABBREVIATIONS

FOR THE SAKE of consistency and for the ease of the reader, we have substituted the Cambridge University Press editions of Conrad's works (where available) or the Doubleday Uniform edition of Conrad's works (when there was no Cambridge University Press edition yet available) for the original editions that J. Hillis Miller used. Where there were variations between the Cambridge University Press or Doubleday editions and the edition Miller originally cited, we have silently changed the cited passage to the language of the new edition. The only exception to this policy was in the case of *Nostromo*, where Miller preferred the Modern Library edition over the Doubleday Uniform edition. We have also changed all references to Conrad's correspondence to Cambridge University Press's *The Collected Letters of Joseph Conrad*.

In cases of obvious typographical or other such errors in the original essays, we have silently corrected those errors, and where there were occasional quoted passages in the original essay that included no citation or page reference, we have supplied these in square brackets. Furthermore, we have differentiated our notes from those of J. Hillis Miller with "[Editors]" following such notes.

Citations of Conrad's works subsequent to the initial citation will appear parenthetically with an abbreviated title (when the work cited is not apparent from context) and the appropriate page reference; the abbreviations are as follows:

HD   *Heart of Darkness*
     Youth, Heart of Darkness, The End of the Tether, ed. Owen Knowles. Cambridge: Cambridge University Press, 2010.

N   *Nostromo*
     Nostromo, ed. Robert Penn Warrren. New York: Modern Library, 1951.

LJ   *Lord Jim*
     Lord Jim, ed. J. H. Stape and Ernest W. Sullivan II. Cambridge: Cambridge University Press, 2012.

Re   *The Rescue*
     The Rescue. Garden City, NY: Doubleday, Page & Co., 1924.

PR   *A Personal Record*
     A Personal Record, ed. Zdzisław Najder and J. H. Stape. Cambridge: Cambridge University Press, 2008.

NN   *The Nigger of the "Narcissus"*
     The Nigger of the "Narcissus." Garden City, NY: Doubleday, Page & Co., 1924.

SA   *The Secret Agent*
     The Secret Agent, ed. Bruce Harkness and S.W. Reid. Cambridge: Cambridge Univeristy Press, 1990.

SL   *The Shadow-Line*
     The Shadow-Line, ed. J. H. Stupe and Allan H. Simmons. Cambridge: Cambridge Univeristy Press, 2013.

V   *Victory*
     Victory, ed. J. H. Stape and Alexandre Fachard. Cambridge: Cambridge University Press, 2016.

CL   *The Collected Letters of Joseph Conrad*
     The Collected Letters of Joseph Conrad, ed. Laurence Davies et al. 9 vols. Cambridge: Cambridge University Press, 1983–2007.

INTRODUCTION

Conrad and Me

IT IS a great honor for me to have my essays over the years on Conrad's fictions gathered and edited by such distinguished Conrad scholars as John Peters and Jakob Lothe. Lothe is an old friend from the University of Oslo whom I first met long ago at a conference on Conrad's *Heart of Darkness* in South Africa. We have been engaged together on many projects, Conradian and otherwise, since then. I also know and admire John G. Peters's work on Conrad. He is from the University of North Texas. I am deeply grateful to them both.

This introduction is not the place to recapitulate my readings of Conrad works over the years. Readers of this book can find that out for themselves. I want to stress here, however, two features of Conrad's work that my essays demonstrate. One is that it is possible to go back again and again to the same work by Conrad and always find something new to say about it. My several essays on *Heart of Darkness*, or *Lord Jim*, or *Nostromo*, are quite different from one another, though I would not claim they form a progression toward ever-better readings. They just differ. Second, Conrad's novels and stories are markedly diverse. It is difficult if not impossible to make generalizations about Conrad's works that apply to all of them. One striking example is the disappearance of the theme of a personified transcendent and immanent spiritual power that is so important in *Heart of Darkness*: "The horror! The horror!"; "The inner truth is hidden—luckily, luckily. But I felt it all the same; I felt often its mysterious stillness watching me at my monkey tricks." That theme does not, as my careful reading indicates, appear at all in *Nostromo* except in an extremely attenuated and ambiguous way that I discuss in one of my essays on that novel. This is true even though the two novels were published only a few years apart (1899 and 1904, respectively). In *Nostromo,* nature is for the most part just a material backdrop for the actions of the characters. That is really strange. I have no explanation for this striking difference.

Now a word about how I came to be an avid reader of Conrad. I first read Conrad when I was in high school, back in the early 1940s. I came quite by accident, as well as I can remember, when I was thirteen or so, upon a copy of *Typhoon* (first published in 1902, just between *Heart of Darkness* and *Nostromo*). I found it among my father's theology and psychology books on the shelves in his study at our home. We lived at that time in Delmar, New York, outside of Albany, where he was associate commissioner for higher and professional education for the State of New York. His books for the most part did not interest me when I tried to read them, but I found *Typhoon* absolutely absorbing, and still do. It was like entering the world of that great storm in the China Sea. I rediscovered what a wonderful novel *Typhoon* is when I recently read it once more to write this introduction. It still holds a magic power over me.

My father was Southern Baptist minister, a farmer's son from Virginia, who eventually took a PhD in philosophy with a learned dissertation, of which I have copies, on *The Practice of Public Prayer* (Columbia University Press, 1934). His title refers primarily to the traditions of prayer in church services of various kinds. I had always thought that John Dewey directed the dissertation, but he is nowhere mentioned in the dissertation. My father was the real J. Hillis Miller. I am J. Hillis Miller Jr., though I dropped the Jr. when my father died. He became a distinguished educator and a gifted administrator, with a special interest in the higher education of women. He died in his early fifties while president of the University of Florida in Gainesville. Those old books were the ones he collected for his work, a good portion I believe in connection with preparing his dissertation.

What was *Typhoon* doing among books like William James's *The Varieties of Religious Experiences*? I thought I was onto something when I imagined the sailors on Captain MacWhirr's *Nan-Shan* may have prayed together in the midst of the great storm the circumstantial description of which is the center of *Typhoon*. That was the aspect of the novel that so moved me when I first read it, more than the psychologies of the main characters that interest me now as much as the storm. If the crew do pray together publicly, that would make *Typhoon* an appropriate item among the books used by my father to write his dissertation. No such public prayer happens, however, in *Typhoon,* nor does my father mention the novel in his dissertation. Jukes, the first mate of the *Nan-Shan*, does pray silently, if you can call it that, when the great storm first strikes and inundates the ship. He would not have been audible to Captain MacWhirr in any case, even if he had spoken aloud, so tremendous is the noise. A great wall of water throws Jukes and Captain MacWhirr across the deck of the wheelhouse and into the railing: "All the time he was being tossed, flung, and rolled in great volumes of water, he kept on repeating mentally, with the utmost precipitation, the words: 'My God! My God! My God! My God!'"[1] One "precipitation" here responds to another, the rain and water accompanying the storm, in a characteristic, though perhaps unintentional, Conradian play on words.

My great idea of a connection between *Typhoon* and my father's dissertation was a completely false lead. Great hypothesis, but no evidence to support it. There is scholarship for you—mine, at least! I conclude that I haven't the slightest idea how Conrad's novel found its way among my father's books. There were no other works of fiction among them, so far as I remember. I do recall, though, that he told me once that William James was famous for writing philosophical works that read like novels, while his brother Henry was famous for writing novels that read like philosophical works.

In any case, that early reading of *Typhoon* was the beginning of the lifelong fascination with Conrad's fictions that has led over the years to the essays that are collected in this volume. I have in those essays attempted to do justice to various of Conrad's fictions. The essays have been generally written on specific occasions, mostly as commissioned essays. My admiration for Conrad's work may also have something to do with my lifelong love of small boat sailing, something I still do at the age of eighty-seven, just as I still read Conrad with delight and with abiding admiration for his genius at creating imaginary worlds on the basis of his experiences and, in the case of *Nostromo* and some others, on the basis of his reading too. Or perhaps it is the other way around, since my interest in sailing, encouraged by my father, predates my reading of *Typhoon*.

J. Hillis Miller

---

1. Joseph Conrad, *Typhoon and Other Stories* (London & Toronto: J. M. Dent & Sons Ltd., 1923), 42. My set of the standard collected Dent edition was bought online from a small bookshop in Amsterdam. As I believe I have mentioned in one of the essays in this volume, the set has bookplates of one Thomas Niemeyer. The bookseller emailed me that Niemeyer was a tobacco merchant. He no doubt had dealings with the East Indies. Therefore he bought Conrad's books, though there is no evidence that he ever read them, just sun-fading from sitting too long in the same place on the bookshelves.

CHAPTER 1

Joseph Conrad

The Darkness and The Secret Agent

THE POETRY OF REALITY[1]

Reality is not that external scene but the life that is lived in it. Reality is things as they are. The general sense of the word proliferates its special senses. It is a jungle in itself.[2]

A change in literature as dramatic as the appearance of romanticism in the late eighteenth century has been taking place during the last fifty years. This book tries to explore the change through a study of six writers who have participated in it.[3] . . .

My interpretation of these writers questions the assumption that twentieth-century poetry is merely an extension of romanticism. A new kind of poetry

---

This essay originally appeared in *Poets of Reality: Six Twentieth-Century Writers* (Cambridge, MA: Harvard University Press, 1965), 1, 5–8, 13–67.

1. "The Poetry of Reality" is the first chapter of the book, which serves as its introduction. This excerpt is particularly relevant to Miller's chapter "Joseph Conrad," which follows herewith [Editors].

2. Wallace Stevens, *The Necessary Angel: Essays on Reality and the Imagination* (New York: Alfred A. Knopf, 1951), 25–26.

3. Joseph Conrad, William Butler Yeats, T. S. Eliot, Dylan Thomas, Wallace Stevens, and William Carlos Williams [Editors].

has appeared in our day, a poetry which grows out of romanticism, but goes beyond it. Many twentieth-century poets begin with an experience of the nihilism which is one of the possible consequences of romanticism. My chapter on Conrad attempts to identify this nihilism by analysis of a writer who follows it into its darkness and so prepares the way beyond it. Each succeeding chapter describes one version of the journey beyond nihilism toward a poetry of reality. . . .

Only if the nihilism latent in our culture would appear as nihilism would it be possible to go beyond it by understanding it. In spite of two world wars, and the shadow of world annihilation, this is a course which our civilization has not yet chosen, or had chosen for it. Nevertheless, a central tradition of modern literature has been a countercurrent moving against the direction of history. In this literature, if not in our culture as a whole, nihilism has gradually been exposed, experienced in its implications, and, in some cases, transcended.

The special place of Joseph Conrad in English literature lies in the fact that in him the nihilism covertly dominant in modern culture is brought to the surface and shown for what it is. Conrad can best be understood as the culmination of a development within the novel, a development particularly well-marked in England, though of course it also exists on the continent and in America. After the attempt to recover an absent God in nineteenth-century poetry, a subsequent stage in man's spiritual history is expressed more fully in fiction than in poetry. The novel shows man attempting to establish a human world based on interpersonal relations. In the novel man comes more and more to be defined in terms of the strength of his will, and the secret nihilism resulting from his new place as the source of all value is slowly revealed.

Conrad is part of European literature and takes his place with Dostoevsky, Mann, Gide, Proust, and Camus as an explorer of modern perspectivism and nihilism. Within the narrower limits of the English novel, however, he comes at the end of a native tradition. From Dickens and George Eliot through Trollope, Meredith, and Hardy the negative implications of subjectivism become more and more apparent. It remained for Conrad to explore nihilism to its depths, and, in doing so, to point the way toward the transcendence of nihilism by the poets of the twentieth century.

In Conrad's fiction the focus of the novel turns outward from its concentration on relations between man and man within civilized society to a concern for the world-wide expansion of Western man's will to power. Conrad is the novelist not of the city but of imperialism. Several consequences follow from this. He is able to show that society is an arbitrary set of rules and judgments, a house of cards built over an abyss. It was relatively easy for characters in Victorian fiction to be shown taking English society for granted as permanent and right. The fact that Western culture has the fragility of an edifice which might have been constructed differently is brought to light when Conrad sets the "masquerade" of imperialism against the alien jungle. With this revelation, the nature of man's will to power begins to emerge, and at the same time there is a glimpse of an escape from nihilism.

The will to power seemed a subjective thing, a private possession of each separate ego. Though the struggle for dominance of mind against mind might lead to an impasse, nonhuman nature seemed to yield passively to man's sovereign will. Everything, it seemed, could be turned into an object of man's calculation, control, or evaluation. In *Heart of Darkness* (1899) Conrad shows how imperialism becomes the expansion of the will toward unlimited dominion over existence. What begins as greed, the desire for ivory, and as altruism, the desire to carry the torch of civilization to the jungle, becomes the longing to "wring the heart" of the wilderness[4] and "Exterminate all the brutes!" [95]. The benign project of civilizing the dark places of the world becomes the conscious desire to annihilate everything which opposes man's absolute will. Kurtz's megalomania finally becomes limitless. There is "nothing either above or below him." He has "kicked himself loose of the earth," and in doing so has "kicked the very earth to pieces" [113].

It is just here, in the moment of its triumph, that nihilism reverses itself, as, in Mann's *Doktor Faustus*, Leverkühn's last and most diabolical composition leads through the abyss to the sound of children's voices singing. Conrad's work does not yet turn the malign into the benign, but it leads to a reversal which prepares for the daylight of later literature. When Kurtz's will has expanded to boundless dimensions, it reveals itself to be what it has secretly been all along: nothing. Kurtz is "hollow at the core" [104]. Into his emptiness comes the darkness. The darkness is in the heart of each man, but it is in the heart of nature too, and transcends both man and nature as their hidden substance and foundation.

---

4. Joseph Conrad, *Youth, Heart of Darkness, The End of the Tether*, ed. Owen Knowles (Cambridge: Cambridge University Press, 2010), 116; hereafter cited parenthetically.

When the wilderness finds Kurtz out and takes "a terrible vengeance for the fantastic invasion" [104], then the dawn of an escape from nihilism appears, an escape through the darkness. By following the path of nihilism to the end, man confronts once again a spiritual power external to himself. Though this power appears as an inexpressibly threatening horror, still it is something beyond the self. It offers the possibility of an escape from subjectivism.

The strategy of this escape will appear from the point of view of the tradition it reverses the most dangerous of choices, a leap into the abyss. It will mean giving up the most cherished certainties. The act by which man turns the world inside-out into his mind leads to nihilism. This can be escaped only by a counterrevolution in which man turns himself inside-out and steps, as Wallace Stevens puts it, "barefoot into reality."[5] This leap into the world characterizes the reversal enacted in one way or another by the five poets studied here.

To walk barefoot into reality means abandoning the independence of the ego. Instead of making everything an object for the self, the mind must efface itself before reality, or plunge into the density of an exterior world, dispersing itself in a milieu which exceeds it and which it has not made. The effacement of the ego before reality means abandoning the will to power over things. This is the most difficult of acts for a modern man to perform. It goes counter to all the penchants of our culture. To abandon its project of dominion the will must will not to will. Only through an abnegation of the will can objects begin to manifest themselves as they are, in the integrity of their presence. When man is willing to let things be then they appear in a space which is no longer that of an objective world opposed to the mind. In this new space the mind is dispersed everywhere in things and forms one with them.

This new space is the realm of the twentieth-century poem. It is a space in which things, the mind, and words coincide in closest intimacy. . . .

JOSEPH CONRAD: THE DARKNESS

> When near the buildings I met a white man in such an unexpected elegance of get up that in the first moment I took him for a sort of vision. I saw a high, starched collar, white cuffs, a light alpaca jacket, snowy trousers, a clean necktie and varnished boots. No hat. Hair parted, brushed, oiled, under a green lined parasol held in a big white hand. He was amazing and had a penholder behind his ear. . . . I respected the fellow. . . . His appearance was

---

5. Wallace Stevens, "Large Red Man Reading," in *The Collected Poems* (New York: Alfred A. Knopf, 1954), 423.

certainly that of a hairdresser's dummy but in the great demoralization of the land he kept up his appearance. That's backbone! [*HD* 59]

Conrad respected those who could keep up appearances in a wilderness. He admired people who could keep their heads clear in any circumstances and remain single-mindedly faithful to a job to be done. The elegantly dressed accountant at a trading station halfway to the heart of darkness is a symbol of this equilibrium in the midst of demoralization. His artificiality of dress and manner is the exact correlative of the artificiality of his accounts. The precision and enumeration of the latter stand against the blur of the surrounding jungle as light stands against darkness in the dominant symbolism of the novel. The accountant represents the triumph of an unceasing act of will, a will to keep the darkness out and to keep what is within the charmed circle of civilization clear, distinct, and inventoried.

The starched and scented accountant is not only an example of one kind of human life. He represents the human enterprise generally as it appeared to Conrad at a certain stage of history. That stage was not the mid-nineteenth century, the time of the triumph, in the Western world, of the middle class, industrialism, and the scientific interpretation of nature. Nor was it our darker time when these forces have reached out to dominate the world, and seem about to reverse themselves and destroy their makers. It was the time of imperialism, when the middle class and the commercial spirit, having conquered the countries of their birth, were spreading outward to conquer the world. In that time "brave young England," in Charles Kingsley's words, was "longing to wing its way out of its island prison, to discover and to traffic, to colonise and to civilise, until no wind can sweep the earth which does not bear the echoes of an English voice."[6] There were still blank places on the map, *terrae incognitae* offering themselves to man's greed for power and knowledge, as the white patch of the Congo fascinated Conrad's Marlow. In the imperialist epoch European countries were still aware of the existence of areas which had not yet submitted to their ideals. Primitive places and primitive peoples still existed, and one would not yet have expected to find a jukebox or a Coca-Cola sign in the midst of every jungle. It was still possible to write a pamphlet on "The Suppression of Savage Customs," because there were still savage customs to suppress.

As a consequence of his vantage point in time, Conrad was able to see, better than we can today, the nature of the historical process unfolding before his eyes. For us the process is more or less complete. There are scarcely any

---

6. *Westward Ho!*, chapter 2, quoted in Walter Houghton, *The Victorian Frame of Mind: 1830–1870* (New Haven: Yale University Press, 1957), 122.

white patches on the map, few dark, savage corners of the world. Enlightenment and progress have triumphed, or seem about to triumph, and one homogeneous civilization has spread almost everywhere. It is difficult for man now to see his civilization clearly because there is nothing to set it against for purposes of comparison, but Conrad could put imperialism against the backdrop of the darkness it was about to conquer.

In Conrad's view civilization is the metamorphosis of darkness into light. It is a process of transforming everything unknown, irrational, or indistinct into clear forms, named and ordered, given a meaning and use by man. Civilization has two sides, curiously in contradiction. To be safe, civilized man must have a blind devotion to immediate practical tasks, a devotion which recalls the Victorian cult of work. For Conrad as for Carlyle work is protection against unwholesome doubt or neurotic paralysis of will. "A man is a worker," says Conrad. "If he is not that he is nothing. . . . For the great mass of mankind the only saving grace that is needed is steady fidelity to what is nearest to hand and heart in the short moment of each human effort."[7] In *The Nigger of the "Narcissus"* he praises the "everlasting children of the mysterious sea."[8] remaining innocent and inarticulate, faithful to the sailor's code of obedience and devotion to duty, and in *Chance* he speaks of "the peace of the sea,"[9] a peace which derives from the fact that the sailors have time only for work and sleep. So Marlow in *Heart of Darkness* is protected from the wilderness by the hard work necessary to keep his river steamer going: "I had to watch the steering, and circumvent those snags, and get the tin-pot along by hook or by crook. There was surface-truth enough in these things to save a wiser man" (80). When Marlow finds in a jungle hut a battered copy of *An Inquiry into Some Points of Seamanship*, the book seems to him an expression of man's power to keep possession of himself through concentrated attention on practical problems: "The simple old sailor with his talk of chains and purchases made me forget the jungle and the pilgrims in a delicious sensation of having come upon something unmistakably real" (81–82).

Devotion to work is real, with a specifically human reality and sanity, but there is more to the humanizing of the world than "devotion to efficiency" (47). Behind the efficiency and directing it must be "the idea" [47]. Sometimes this idea is the simple one of obedience and fidelity, as when Conrad

---

7. Joseph Conrad, "'Well Done!,'" in *Notes on Life and Letters*, ed. J. H. Stape (Cambridge: Cambridge University Press, 2004), 150.

8. Joseph Conrad, *The Nigger of the "Narcissus"* (Garden City, NY: Doubleday, Page & Co., 1926), 25; hereafter cited parenthetically.

9. Joseph Conrad, *Chance* (Garden City, NY: Doubleday, Page & Co., 1926), 31; hereafter cited parenthetically.

speaks of his "belief in the solidarity of all mankind in simple ideas and in sincere emotions" (*C* xi), or when he affirms his "conviction that the world, the temporal world, rests on a few very simple ideas; so simple that they must be as old as the hills. It rests notably, among others, on the idea of Fidelity."[10] Sometimes Conrad means by the idea the grandiose goal of bringing light and civilization to the unillumined peoples of the earth. The idea is civilized man's protection against the anarchic power of atavistic ways of life. It is the guide of devoted work, directing that work as it transforms the world to man's measure. The idea gives meaning to what is wrested from the wilderness, and it builds a barrier making the circle of civilization secure, as the crew of the *Narcissus* triumphs over the formless might of the great storm, or as Kurtz is an "emissary of light" [*HD* 53] imposing his "ideas," his "plans" on the jungle, or as Marlow's voice, "the speech that cannot be silenced," protects him against the "fiendish row" of the savages (80). The idea is man's armor against the darkness, and it is the source of the form and the meaning he gives the world.

Civilization is at once a social ideal and an ideal of personal life. The ideal society is imaged in the relation among men on board a well-ordered ship: a hierarchical structure, with those at the bottom owing obedience to those above, and the whole forming a perfect organism. As a personal ideal, submission to civilization may mean being one of the stolid, unimaginative people, like Captain MacWhirr in *Typhoon*. It may also mean setting up for oneself an ideal of glory, the winning of power and fame for the accomplishment of some difficult project. A man who does this accepts as the meaning of his life the value he has in the eyes of other people. "A man's real life," says Conrad, "is that accorded to him in the thoughts of other men by reason of respect or natural love."[11]

To live in this way means substituting some goal in the future for gratification in the present. A man who makes glory his aim makes of the present a means to an end, and lives always beyond himself. So Lord Jim hopes for some act of bravery which will make up for his cowardice; Lingard, in *The Rescue*, wants to win renown by reinstating his native friends to power; Razumov, in *Under Western Eyes*, proposes to himself a career as a professor; Nostromo centers all his life on an egotistic dream of personal glory; and Kurtz's goal is the power he will win in Europe for the successful conquering of the jungle. He wants "to have kings meet him at railway stations on his

---

10. Joseph Conrad, *A Personal Record*, ed. Zdizsław Najder and J. H. Stape (Cambridge: Cambridge University Press, 2008), 17; hereafter cited parenthetically.

11. Joseph Conrad, *Under Western Eyes*, ed. Roger Osborne and Paul Eggert (Cambridge: Cambridge University Press, 2013), 19.

return from some ghastly Nowhere where he intend[s] to accomplish great things" (*HD* 116). There is more than a nominal form of speech in the way Kurtz refers to his fiancée as his "Intended." That lady, with her "pure brow," "smooth and white, . . . illumined by the unextinguishable light of belief and love" (122, 123), and her "soul as translucently pure as a cliff of crystal" (118), is a symbol of the orientation of Kurtz's life. He faces toward an ideal intention which depends on the faith and respect of other people. He lives in terms of an expectation.

Perhaps the intention can never be fulfilled. Perhaps a society based on progress can never reach the far-off divine event when all the darkness will be turned to light. Nevertheless, the project of humanizing the world has in some places been successful, and to dwell in such a place means, as Marlow says, living "with solid pavement under your feet, surrounded by kind neighbours ready to cheer you or to fall on you, stepping delicately between the butcher and the policeman, in the holy terror of scandal and gallows, and lunatic asylums" (94). All the strangeness and danger has been removed or covered up. Everything has been labeled, transformed into a utensil or a significance. The lower regions of human consciousness have been forgotten or buried deep out of sight. The rational mind of man matches the lucid distinctness of forms in a daylight world, and together they form a closed circuit of reciprocal interchanges, each confirming the other. A man's relations to his neighbor are assimilated into the clarity of this world. The strangeness of other people is hidden behind forms, clothes, institutions, and some convention always stands between man and man. Civilization is the triumph of the human, of the all too human. There is nothing, says Conrad in *The Nigger of the "Narcissus,"* which holds people together like the "strong, effective and respectable bond of a sentimental lie" (155).

The human world is a lie. All human ideals, even the ideal of fidelity, are lies. They are lies in the sense that they are human fabrications. They derive from man himself and are supported by nothing outside him. There is a gap between man and the world, and what remains isolated within the human realm is illusory and insubstantial. Nostromo's goal in life is an egotistic sham, as is Lord Jim's, Lingard's, or Razumov's. Kurtz is not really devoted to a worthy ideal. He is "avid of lying fame, of sham distinction, of all the appearances of success and power" (*HD* 116).

Collective social ideals are no less unreal. Each is, like the idea of international fraternity, *"un très beau phantôme," "les ombres d'une éloquence qui est morte, justement parce qu'elle n'a pas de corps.*"[12] This dark truth is the source of Conrad's pessimism, of his *"desespoir plus sombre que la nuit"* (*CL* 2:160). A crucial moment in his experience is the time when he must recognize the impossibility of man's hope "for the laying of what is the most obstinate ghost of man's creation, of the uneasy doubt uprising like a mist, secret and gnawing like a worm and more chilling than the certitude of death—the doubt of the sovereign power enthroned in a fixed standard of conduct."[13]

Conrad's pessimism has a double source. It is a recognition that ethical terms have no meaning because they do not refer to something outside man which tells him what he ought to do: "The ethical view of the universe involves us at last in so many cruel and absurd contradictions, where the last vestiges of faith, hope, charity and even of reason itself, seem ready to perish, that I have come to suspect that the aim of creation cannot be ethical at all" (*PR* 86). A fixed standard of conduct is not a sovereign power enthroned above man. It is his own creation. A man obeying an ethical code is trying to lift himself by his own bootstraps, and by bootstraps which have only an imaginary existence. On the other hand, the tragedy of man's existence lies in the fact that he is cut off irrevocably from the truth of the universe. As long as he remains human he will remain exiled in a nightmarish realm of illusion. "A man that is born," says Stein in *Lord Jim*, "falls into a dream like a man who falls into the sea" (162). No passage by Conrad expresses more completely this double tragedy of imprisonment within the factitious and exclusion from the truth than a letter of 1898 to R. B. Cunninghame Graham: "Of course reason is hateful—but why? Because it demonstrates (to those who have the courage) that we, living, are out of life—utterly out of it. The mysteries of a universe made of drops of fire and clods of mud do not concern us in the least. . . . Life knows us not and we do not know life" (*CL* 2:16–17).

If civilization and each man in it move farther from reality the more completely the humanizing of the world succeeds, is there any chance to escape from the falsity of the human? How can man be liberated from his dream? The aim of all Conrad's fiction is to destroy in the reader his bondage to illusion, and to give him a glimpse of the truth, however dark and disquieting that truth may be. His work might be called an effort of demystification. It attempts to rescue man from his alienation. His problem in reaching this goal is double: to lift the veil of illusion, and to make the truth appear. The second aim is especially difficult, for Conrad's truth is the exact opposite of precise images and events. It is *"une ombre sinistre et fuyante dont it est impossible de*

---

12. Joseph Conrad, *The Collected Letters of Joseph Conrad*, ed. Laurence Davies et al., 9 vols. (Cambridge: Cambridge University Press, 1983–2007), 2:158, 159; hereafter cited parenthetically.

13. Joseph Conrad, *Lord Jim*, ed. J. H. Stape and Ernest W. Sullivan II (Cambridge: Cambridge University Press, 2012), 43; hereafter cited parenthetically.

fixer l'image" (*CL* 2:160). Yet fiction must deal in clear and vivid images. How can Conrad use fiction to make the reader see things as they are?

The first step in his method of demystification consists, strangely enough, in accentuating the lucidity of vision typical of civilized man. The characteristic stance of Conrad's narrators is one of cold, clearheaded, ironic objectivity, what he calls in *A Personal Record* "the detached curiosity of a subtle mind" (87), or what Henry James in his review of *Chance* calls "a prolonged hovering flight of the subjective over the outstretched ground of the case exposed."[14] James's splendid phrase defines exactly the somber intensity with which Conrad's narrators brood over their stories as they tell and retell them, seeking to reach the elusive truth behind superficial facts. James's image also expresses the distance between Conrad's narrators and the action of the stories. His habit of multiplying narrators and points of view, so that sometimes an event is told filtered through several consciousnesses, his reconstruction of the chronological sequence to make a pattern of progressive revelation, his use of a framing story—all these techniques increase the distance between the reader and the events as they were lived by the characters.

The avowed purpose of this detachment is to permit a clarity of vision which will reach the truth of things, but detachment has, in Conrad's most striking and characteristic passages, another surprising effect. It leads the reader to experience the story with a dreamlike and hallucinatory intensity, to see things as irreducibly strange, separated from their usual meaning. Conrad, more than any other English novelist, is a master of this way of showing things, and the narrators of all his novels could say what Marlow says in *Heart of Darkness*: "It seems to me I am trying to tell you a dream—making a vain attempt—because no relation of a dream can convey the dream-sensation, that commingling of absurdity, surprise and bewilderment in a tremor of struggling revolt, that notion of being captured by the incredible which is of the very essence of dreams" (70).

To recognize the dreamlike quality of the waking world does not mean a distortion of civilized man's usual clarity of vision. Tables, chairs, trees, and people are still seen as definite objects, with names, meanings, and forms. The difference lies in a change in the liaison between perceiver and perceived. Ordinarily things are assumed into the process of living and so taken for granted that they are scarcely noticed, only used, as a man does not notice the

---

14. Henry James, "The New Novel," in *The Art of Fiction and Other Essays* (New York: Oxford University Press, 1948), 204.

doorknob he turns a dozen times a day. Conrad shows such things wrested from their context in daily life and put before the spectator as mute, static presences. The interpretations ordinarily connecting man to things are broken, and the world is put in parentheses, seen as pure phenomenon.

Though all men live in a dream, many people are lucky enough to go on with their illusions untouched, in the serene and peaceful state of being deceived. "Of course," says Marlow, "a fool, what with sheer fright and fine sentiments, is always safe" (*HD* 80). Some men, like Conrad himself and like most of his heroes, are not so lucky. An experience of solitude, of failure, of adventure, of intense emotion, or simply of unfortunate perspicuity breaks the illusion, and leads such people to see that the dream is a dream.

The most extraordinary aspect of this experience is the deceptive ease with which it occurs. No great catastrophe is necessary. A momentary absence of mind, a new way of looking at a familiar object, a slight change of routine may be enough to shatter the structure of a life. "There are often in men's affairs," says the narrator of "Falk," "unexpectedly—even irrationally—illuminating moments when an otherwise insignificant sound, perhaps only some perfectly commonplace gesture, suffices to reveal to us all the unreason, all the fatuous unreason, of our complacency."[15] Man's fatuous complacency is his assumption that his world is organically unified. The meanings of things, he believes, are identified with the things themselves; all things are bound together in a coherent system; the mind of man forms an integral part of this system. An interpretation of the world of this sort is so fragile that a touch suffices to destroy it. It is as if man were "a tight-rope dancer who in the midst of his performance should suddenly discover that he knows nothing about tight-rope dancing." A "broken neck is the result of such untimely wisdom" (*CL* 2:90).

This unfortunate fall is often brought about by some insignificant event which detaches the mind ever so slightly from its surroundings. The initial moment of self-consciousness in Conrad is a seemingly benign experience of perplexity or puzzlement, a tiny fissure of separation from the everyday pattern of things. This often takes place when an object is detached from the fabric of its relations to other things. Such an "unexpectedly illuminating" experience causes a double division of the world. The experienced thing is separated from what seemed connected to it by an unbreakable web of relations. When this happens the mind recognizes its isolation from things. The detachment of the object from its surroundings is matched by man's loss of his unthinking engagement in the world. The moment of puzzled detachment

---

15. Joseph Conrad, "Falk," in *Typhoon and Other Stories* (Garden City, NY: Doubleday, Page & Co., 1926), 169.

rapidly expands to become the recognition that "we, living, are out of life—utterly out of it" [*CL* 2:16–17]. Man discovers that he is an outcast.

Examples of this disastrous moment of self-awareness occur throughout Conrad's work. Willems, in *An Outcast of the Islands*, first understands that his old life has come to an end when he notices the odd look of his house: "He looked at it with a vague surprise to find it there. His past was so utterly gone from him that the dwelling which belonged to it appeared to him incongruous standing there intact, neat, and cheerful in the sunshine of the hot afternoon."[16]

The irony of *Typhoon* lies in the fact that the huge storm produces only a gentle ripple on the surface of Captain MacWhirr's stolid complacency: "The hurricane, with its power to madden the seas, to sink ships, to uproot trees, to overturn strong walls and dash the very birds of the air, to the ground, had found this taciturn man in its path, and, doing its utmost, had managed to wring out a few words."[17] The climax of the novel comes not at the height of the storm, but during the calm in the middle of it. The Captain returns to his cabin and is irrationally annoyed when he sees how things there have been slightly disarranged. The right placing of his matchbox is "the symbol of all these little habits that chain us to the weary round of life" (85). Here too the moment of awareness is connected with the sight of objects detached from their usual positions in an orderly world:

> He had not consciously looked at anything by the light of the matches except at the barometer; and yet somehow he had seen that his water-bottle and the two tumblers had been flung out of their stand. It seemed to give him a more intimate knowledge of the tossing the ship had gone through. "I wouldn't have believed it," he thought. And his table had been cleared, too; his rulers, his pencils, the inkstand—all the things that had their safe appointed places—they were gone, as if a mischievous hand had plucked them out one by one and flung them on the wet floor. The hurricane had broken in upon the orderly arrangements of his privacy. This had never happened before, and the feeling of dismay reached the very seat of his composure. (84–85)

The detachment of things from one another and from man, so rarely glimpsed by a man like MacWhirr, is expressed throughout Conrad's novels by a precise description of what is there to be seen or heard. A good example

---

16. Joseph Conrad, *An Outcast of the Islands*, ed. Allan H. Simmons (Cambridge: Cambridge University Press, 2016), 28.

17. Joseph Conrad, *Typhoon*, in *Typhoon and Other Stories* (Garden City, NY: Doubleday, Page & Co., 1926), 90; hereafter cited parenthetically.

of this is Verloc's hat in the murder scene of *The Secret Agent*: "A round hat disclosed in the middle of the floor by the moving of the table rocked slightly on its crown in the wind of her flight."[18] The hat here has ceased to be Verloc's hat, a useful object in his life. It is simply *a* hat, and its normal motion is in violent contrast to the abnormality of the situation. Such glimpses of the oddity of inanimate things reveal the gap between human passions and the ineluctable "thingness" of external objects. When a man is in a situation of extreme danger or emotional tension, and it seems as if everything should be in an uproar, an everyday object, being itself, impassible and indifferent, often catches the eye. Subjective intensity, by a kind of negative causality, makes the alien quality of the physical world appear.

The same transformation can also affect the way human beings appear. Sometimes people will momentarily seem like sleepwalking actors in an implausible drama, acting out their parts without consciousness or volition. These visions are often expressed by Conrad in dehumanizing metaphors which recall those of Dickens. Marlow, in *Lord Jim*, sees the grotesquely fat captain of the *Patna* as "a trained baby elephant walking on hindlegs" (*LJ* 34), or as "something round and enormous, resembling a sixteen hundred weight sugar-hogshead wrapped in striped flannelette, up-ended in the middle of the . . . floor" (34–35). The captain's entrance into a small gharry is described in a way that makes it seem like a nightmare or hallucination: "The little machine shook and rocked tumultuously, and the crimson nape of that lowered neck, the size of those straining thighs, the immense heaving of that dingy, striped green and orange back, the whole burrowing effort of that gaudy and sordid mass, troubled one's sense of probability with a droll and fearsome effect, like one of those grotesque and distinct visions that scare and fascinate one in a fever" (41). In *Chance*, as Marlow sits with two ordinary people, the Fynes, he suddenly sees the scene as inexplicably strange, like a solemn but senseless masquerade: "We three looked at each other as if on the brink of a disclosure. . . . Nothing more absurd could be conceived. It was delicious. . . . I don't know that I am liable to fits of delirium, but by a sudden and alarming aberration while waiting for her answer I became mentally aware of three trained dogs dancing on their hind legs. I don't know why. Perhaps because of the pervading solemnity. There's nothing more solemn on earth than a dance of trained dogs" (57–58).

In all his novels Conrad makes images of things and people which cause them to appear mysterious, but perhaps no novel makes a more strategic use

---

18. Joseph Conrad, *The Secret Agent*, ed. Bruce Harkness and S. W. Reid (Cambridge: Cambridge University Press, 1990), 119; hereafter cited parenthetically.

of this technique than *Heart of Darkness*. That novel is structured as a passing of portals, a traveling through states which leads the reader ever deeper into the darkness. The method of this presentation is to put in question whatever Marlow reaches, to show it as a misleading illusion, something which must be rejected for the sake of the truth behind it. Conrad succeeds in this way in showing civilization as a "fantastic invasion" directed by a "flabby devil," as a "sordid farce acted in front of a sinister back-cloth" (65, 62, 54). The two silent women knitting in the office of the company in Belgium, "introducing, introducing continuously to the unknown" (51); the French ship firing shells one after another into the immensity of Africa; the disorder of the first station Marlow reaches, with its dying natives, its aimless dynamiting, its machinery lying broken and useless in ditches; the perfectly dressed accountant keeping up appearances in the jungle; the stout man with mustaches trying to put out a blazing warehouse fire with water carried in a tin pail with a hole in it; the Eldorado expedition with its "absurd air of disorderly flight with the loot of innumerable outfit shops and provision stores" (73)—each of these is another example of the absurdity of the imperialist invasion.

The first stage in the reader's liberation from his customary dream is a way of presenting human activities and intentions which holds them at arm's length and shows each one as "a mournful and senseless delusion" (54). What is uncovered when the veil of forms is lifted?

To see the world without interpretations is to see it reduced to pure quality. Instead of namable things, only patches of dark or light are seen. These can be given no meaning. They are simply there, mute presences. In place of articulate speech, or sounds which can be interpreted, only the duration, timbre, and tone of sounds can be heard. This recognition of the qualitative aspect of sense experience is an ultimate point reached through the vision of the world as dreamlike. A stage of seeing the everyday world as a waking nightmare leads to a moment when the significance is drained out of things, as when a man stares at some familiar object until it suddenly becomes strange, or as when a phrase is repeated over and over until it is emptied of meaning and becomes senseless sound, or as when something is seen too close to the eyes or too highly magnified, and can no longer be identified. What the thing is can no longer be said because the attention is absorbed and fascinated by how it is.[19]

---

19. The best discussion of this aspect of Conrad's work is in Ramón Fernández, "L'Art de Conrad," *Messages, premiere sine* (Paris: Gallimard, 1926), 110–19.

Conrad habitually calls attention to the conflict between the qualitative aspect of things and the interpretation of what is seen into recognizable objects. The world is often perceived simultaneously as colors or incomprehensible sounds and as things which can be identified. The reader is balanced precariously between two ways of being related to the world:

> Something like a small white flame in the sky was the carved white coral finial on the gable of the mosque which had caught full the rays of the sun.[20]

> a few small islets, black spots in the great blaze, swimming before my troubled eyes.[21]

> I became bothered by curious irregular sounds of faint tapping on the deck. They could be heard single, in pairs, in groups. While I wondered at this mysterious devilry I received a slight blow under the left eye and felt an enormous tear run down my cheek. Rain-drops. Enormous. Forerunners of something. Tap. Tap. Tap. (*SL* 91)

In such passages the work of interpretation is successful, and the spots of color or the inexplicable sound are translated into recognizable objects. The raindrops are identified, fled, the islets are seen as islets, the white flame is resolved into the finial on the mosque. In other texts the process of interpretation, though successful at first, fails in the end, and the reader is left face to face with a qualitative spectacle. Often this failure is accompanied by the appearance of metaphors. The patches of color are susceptible of alternative explanations. They may be one thing. They may be another:

> I beheld him as one sees a fish in an aquarium by the light of an electric bulb, an elusive, phosphorescent shape. (*SL* 91–92)

> ... the sun, all red in a cloudless sky raked the yacht with a parting salvo of crimson rays that shattered themselves into sparks of fire upon the crystal and silver of the dinner-service, put a short flame into the blades of knives, and spread a rosy tint over the white of plates. A trail of purple, like a smear of blood on a blue shield, lay over the sea. (*Re* 146)

---

20. Joseph Conrad, *The Rescue* (Garden City, NY: Doubleday, Page & Co., 1926), 251; hereafter cited parenthetically.

21. Joseph Conrad, *The Shadow-Line*, ed. J. H. Stape and Allan H. Simmons (Cambridge: Cambridge University Press, 2013), 77; hereafter cited parenthetically.

in the still streak of very bright pale orange light I saw the land profiled flatly as if cut out of black paper and seeming to float on the water as light as cork. But the rising sun turned it into mere dark vapour, a doubtful, massive shadow trembling in the hot glare. (*SL* 64)

In these texts fish and man, fire and dinner-service, shield and sea, cork, black paper, and land are superimposed. The hovering of the mind between these possibilities leads the spectator to see impressions without interpretation: a phosphorescent shape, a trail of purple, a massive shadow trembling in the glare. Sometimes, however, there is no transition from the perception of things to the sensation of qualities. From the first glimpse nothing is seen but areas of color, light, or dark, and these are never resolved into significant forms. The reader sees nothing but a "belt of orange light" which "faded quickly to gold that melted soon into a blinding and colourless glare" (*Re* 466), or "a mere stir of black and white in the gathering dusk" (*Re* 449), or "a black smudge in the darkness" (*C* 29).

This sensitivity to the qualitative dimension of experience is conscious as well as instinctive. Conrad articulates it in his theory of impressionism. When he says that the aim of his fiction is above all to make us see [*NN* xiv], he means that he wants the reader to see the true world "buried under the growth of centuries" (*Re* 153), and behind man's ordinary perception of things. To see things in this way is to see them as they appear to a detached spectator who registers not perceptions but sensations, as the impressionist painters tried to catch the very forms of light. So Conrad defines his aim as a writer as a "scrupulous fidelity to the truth of [his] own sensations,"[22] and in another place asserts that "the unwearied self-forgetful attention to every phase of the living universe reflected in our consciousness may be our appointed task on this earth" (*PR* 87).

Such a technique of impressionism is the deliberate method of *Heart of Darkness*. "You must remember," says Conrad in a letter about this novel, "that I don't start with an abstract notion. I start with definite images and as their rendering is true some little effect is produced" (*CL* 2:157–58). One aim of the novel is to make it possible for the reader to see the wilderness outside the frail fences guarding the outposts of imperialism, the "silent wilderness surrounding this cleared speck on the earth . . . something great and invincible, like evil or truth, waiting patiently for the passing away of this fantastic invasion" (*HD* 65).

---

22. Joseph Conrad, *Within the Tides*, ed. Alexandre Fachard (Cambridge: Cambridge University Press, 2012), 6; hereafter cited parenthetically.

The culmination of the vision of the world as pure quality is the recognition that behind "the overwhelming realities of this strange world of plants and water and silence" (*HD* 77) is something else, something more than human and more than natural, an "implacable force brooding over an inscrutable intention" (*HD* 77). This is the darkness. The impressions things make on the senses are no more ultimate reality than their interpretation into meanings and objects. Qualities are a thin layer of scintillating light spread over the formless stuff of things, like the moonlight's silvery glitter on the jungle river or on the primeval mud. The famous sentence in the preface to *The Nigger of the "Narcissus"* about making the reader see is followed by another text not so often quoted: "If I succeed, you shall find there according to your deserts: encouragement, consolation, fear, charm—all you demand—and, perhaps, also that glimpse of truth for which you have forgotten to ask" (xiv). The attempt to render the exact appearances of things is not an end in itself. Its aim is to make the truth of life, something different from any impression or quality, momentarily visible. Not colors or light, but the darkness behind them, is the true reality. What does Conrad mean by the "darkness"?

The darkness is first of all a sensible experience. Like its opposite, white light, darkness is the vanishing point of visual sensation. It is the blurring of clear forms in an all-engulfing sensation of the fact that there is nothing to sense. A darkness of this sort is experienced by the captain in *The Shadow-Line*: "Such must have been the darkness before creation. It had closed behind me. . . . I was alone, every man was alone where he stood. And every form was gone, too, spar, sail, fittings, rails everything was blotted out in the dreadful smoothness of that absolute night" (90).

Again and again in Conrad's novels anything distinct, anything colored or light, shows itself as a scintillating flash against a black background. All things appear as "iridescent gleams on a hard and dark surface" (*Re* 411). But the darkness is not just a neutral background for intelligible forms or gleams of light. These have come from the darkness, as Ransome appears to the captain in *The Shadow-Line*, "stepping out of the darkness into visibility, suddenly as if just created with his composed face and pleasant voice" (90), and as the people and scenes of Conrad's stories seem to come out of a darkness within him: "my mind goes wandering through great spaces filled with vague forms.

Everything is still chaos, but, slowly, ghosts are transformed into living flesh, floating vapours turn solid" (*CL* 1:151).[23]

If the darkness is the original chaos, it is also, even more frighteningly, the end toward which things hurry to return, "the night that waits for its time to move forward upon the glitter, the splendour, the men, the women" (*Re* 139). In *The Shadow-Line* the young captain has a special experience of darkness as the end of all creation:

> When the time came the blackness would overwhelm silently the bit of starlight falling upon the ship and the end of all things would come without a sigh, stir, or murmur of any kind, and all our hearts would cease to beat like run-down clocks.
>
> It was impossible to shake off that sense of finality. The quietness that came over me was like a foretaste of annihilation. It gave me a sort of comfort, as though my soul had become suddenly reconciled to an eternity of blind stillness. (87)

The universe exists for Conrad, as for Dylan Thomas, as a process of the birth of things out of a genetic darkness and their return to that darkness. Each thing or person has a precarious hold on existence, and is constantly coming out of the darkness and being engulfed by it, as the shore appears and disappears to Lingard in *The Rescue* during a violent thunderstorm: "at every dazzling flash, Hassim's native land seemed to leap nearer at the brig—and disappear instantly as though it had crouched low for the next spring out of an impenetrable darkness" (*Re* 79). But darkness is more than the origin from which things come, and the end toward which they go. It is a metaphysical entity. The blackness of any night is "the shadow of the outer darkness, the shadow of the uninterrupted, of the everlasting night that fills the universe, the shadow of the night so profound and so vast that the blazing suns lost in it are only like sparks, like pin-points of fire, the restless shadow that like a suspicion of an evil truth darkens everything upon the earth on its passage" (*Re* 151). The darkness is present at every moment and in every thing and person, underlying them as their secret substance, but also denying them as formlessness denies form, or as impersonality denies personality.

It would be an error to identify Conrad's darkness with Sartrean nothingness, just as it would be an error to identify it with the Freudian uncon-

---

23. "La pensée s'en va vagaboundant dans des grands éspaces remplis des formes vagues. Tout e[s]t chaos encore mais—lentement—les spectres se changent en chair vivante, les vapeurs flottantes se solidifient" (*CL* 1:150) [Editors].

scious, or with evil, if that implies the existence of some opposing principle of good. The darkness is not nothingness, and it is not limited to the depths of human nature. It is the basic stuff of the universe, the uninterrupted. It is what remains, horrifyingly, when every thing or color has disappeared. In *The Shadow-Line* Conrad describes such an "impenetrable blackness," a darkness which "beset the ship so close that it seemed that by thrusting one's hand over the side one could touch some unearthly substance. There was in it an effect of inconceivable terror and of inexpressible mystery" (87).

The crucial experience for Conrad's characters is the moment when they escape from their enclosures in the sane bounds of everyday life and encounter the heart of darkness which beats at the center of the earth and in the breast of every human being on earth. The darkness is everywhere, like Kurtz's last words, which Marlow hears whispered in the air even when he is back in Europe and safe in a city: "The dusk was repeating them in a persistent whisper all around us, in a whisper that seemed to swell menacingly like the first whisper of a rising wind. 'The horror! The horror!'" (*HD* 117). The experience of knowing the darkness takes many forms in Conrad's work, but the darkness remains the same in all its manifestations, as a point reached by diverse radii remains the same center. In any of its forms the darkness causes the collapse of daylight intentions and ideals, the rational forms by which civilized man lives.

The darkness is present in the sheer materiality of things, in the primeval mud of the jungle, but also in the "asphalt and bricks, . . . blind houses and unfeeling stones" (*SA* 207) of the city. It is the wild animal clamor of the wilderness or of savagery, which modern man has gone beyond to become civilized. In one way the scrawled note ("Exterminate all the brutes!" [*HD* 95]) at the bottom of Kurtz's pamphlet on "The Suppression of Savage Customs" does not reverse his former eloquence but only states it in another way. The civilizing of the world is the transformation of brute men into restrained human beings. Primitive man and civilized man are related to one another as are, in *The Rescue*, Immada and Edith Travers, who are "the beginning and the end, the flower and the leaf, the phrase and the cry" (148). The human world is made by the extermination of its source, the substitution of Marlow's clarity for the irrational emotion of the native life he sees on the shore.

The darkness is the present nature of man, too, for no man has outgrown his beginning. The heart of darkness exists beneath Apollonian clarity, ready to burst out and change the most civilized man into a savage, as, at the deepest point of his penetration of the darkness, Marlow "confound[s] the beat of the drum with the beating of [his] heart" (*HD* 112). The shock to Marlow of his sight of the dancing, howling natives is "the thought of your remote kinship with this wild and passionate uproar," "just the faintest trace of a response to the terrible frankness of that noise, a dim suspicion of there being a meaning in it which you—you so remote from the night of first ages—could comprehend" (*HD* 79). At this moment Marlow must recognize that "the mind of man is capable of anything—because everything is in it, all the past as well as all the future" (*HD* 79–80).

Kurtz's return to savagery is striking proof of this terrible law of Conrad's universe. With his plans, his genius, his eloquence, his ideals, he is an example of civilized man at his highest point of development. In spite of this he is swallowed up by the jungle. The fantastic invader is himself invaded and destroyed by the wilderness.

This invasion takes a number of forms, forms which reveal Conrad's sense of what the darkness means as a possible condition of even the most civilized man. Kurtz is driven to substitute the immediate moment of self-forgetful gratification for the satisfaction he has sought in dreams of fame and power. The native woman, apparently Kurtz's mistress, who stands on the shore with her arms upraised, "like the wilderness itself with an air of brooding over an inscrutable purpose" (*HD* 107), is a symbol of the present as Kurtz's Intended with her crystalline brow is a symbol of the future. Sexual abandon, as opposed to spiritualized love, belongs to the darkness. Conrad's misogyny, present in his work from *An Outcast of the Islands* and *Almayer's Folly* onward, derives from his identification of sexual experience with the loss of mental clearness and self-possession. Sex is descent into the darkness of irrational emotion, the blurring of consciousness or its extinction. It is not surprising to find that Conrad identifies sex with the jungle.[24] Both mean the same thing to him: the destruction of lucid consciousness. Kurtz's return to the jungle is "the awakening of forgotten and brutal instincts" (*HD* 113). He becomes a god in the wilderness, and is worshiped by his native followers. This means putting absolute sovereignty in place of submission to any law or authority. Religious experience, like sex, is for Conrad a loss of rationality. Kurtz's willingness to think of himself as a god is a special form of that perversion. He replaces reasonable dreams of political or commercial power with a desire for the omnipotence of a god. The riotous dances and unspeakable rites offered to him are forms of the Dionysiac abandon to which he has succumbed.

Kurtz has even unleashed the power of death. Marlow's first understanding of Kurtz's condition comes through his view of the shrunken heads on poles around Kurtz's hut, each "smiling continuously at some endless and

---

24. See Thomas Moser, *Joseph Conrad: Achievement and Decline* (Cambridge, MA: Harvard University Press, 1957), 53–54.

jocose dream of that eternal slumber" (*HD* 104). If the mind of man is capable of anything this is because it contains all the future as well as the past. The future is death, the return of created things to the night from which they have sprung. To say that the darkness is the end of all things is to identify the darkness with death, and to realize that the truth of the universe can only be recognized by those who have entered the realm of death. In *The Rescue* Jörgenson has come back into the world of action from a deathlike disengagement from life. He understands the triviality of all earthly projects, and is at the beginning of the novel where the hero, Lingard, is going to be at the end. He sees everything as mere appearance because he sees everything from the point of view of death:

> Jörgenson, standing by the taffrail, noted the faint reddish glow in the massive blackness of the further shore. Jörgenson noted things quickly, cursorily, perfunctorily, as phenomena unrelated to his own apparitional existence of a visiting ghost. They were but passages in the game of men who were still playing at life. He knew too well how much that game was worth to be concerned about its course. . . . In that world of eternal oblivion, of which he had tasted before Lingard made him step back into the life of men, all things were settled once for all. (382)

In *Heart of Darkness*, too, death is another form of the darkness. Kurtz's victory comes at the moment of his death and depends on his proximity to death. So Marlow compares his own inconclusive "wrestle with death" to Kurtz's: "True, he had made that last stride, he had stepped over the edge while I had been permitted to draw back my hesitating foot. And perhaps this is the whole difference; perhaps all the wisdom and all truth and all sincerity are just compressed into that inappreciable moment of time in which we step over the threshold of the Invisible" (118).

The deepest experience of truth is a moment which is neither past, present, nor future, but out of time altogether, like death itself. Many of Conrad's characters reach this state, but not necessarily by dying. The crucial experience for many of them is a moment which hovers on the threshold of the invisible. *The Rescue* offers important examples of this. At different times, but in ways which have to do with their relation to each other, Lingard and Mrs. Travers reach a state in which their awareness of themselves as separate individuals is lost, a state in which the ordinary qualities of time and space disappear, a state in which they are no one and nowhere because they are everywhere at once, simultaneously motionless and moving with infinite velocity. Such a place makes "this moment of time and . . . this spot on the earth's surface" a location where the laws of exclusion and succession are no longer obeyed, and "the moving shadow of the unbroken night [stands] still to remain . . . forever" (152). Twice Mrs. Travers reaches, through the combination of physical tension and the perception of a dark silent night, such a place:

> After a time this absolute silence which she almost could feel pressing upon her on all sides induced in Mrs. Travers a state of hallucination. She saw herself standing alone, at the end of time, on the brink of days. All was unmoving as if the dawn would never come, the stars would never fade, the sun would never rise any more . . . (151)

> And all this—the wan burst of light, the faint shock as of something remote and immense falling into ruins, was taking place outside the limits of her life which remained encircled by an impenetrable darkness and by an impenetrable silence. Puffs of wind blew about her head and expired; the sail collapsed, shivered audibly, stood full and still in turn; and again the sensation of vertiginous speed and of absolute immobility succeeding each other with increasing swiftness merged at last into a bizarre state of headlong motion and profound peace. The darkness enfolded her like the enervating caress of a sombre universe. It was gentle and destructive. Its languor seduced her soul into surrender. Nothing existed and even all her memories vanished into space. She was content that nothing should exist. (244–45)

In the same way, Lingard, through his love for Mrs. Travers, is put in the condition of "a man who, having cast his eyes through the open gates of Paradise, is rendered insensible by that moment's vision to all the forms and matters of the earth" (415). He is driven by his love to abandon his habitual relation to the world. He has been actively engaged in "the visible surface of life open in the sun to the conquering tread of an unfettered will" (210). Now he is taken by his hopeless love into a strange realm of "wavering gloom" (210). Conrad finds terms to define these two forms of being: "existence" and "life." Existence corresponds to the all-embracing night, to a world of flashes of light, impalpable shapes in the fog. Life corresponds to the vision of things as significant objects projected in broad daylight:

> It was as to being alive that he felt not so sure. He had no doubt of his existence; but was this life—this profound indifference, this strange contempt for what his eyes could see, this distaste for words, this unbelief in the importance of things and men? He tried to regain possession of himself, his old self which had things to do, words to speak as well as to hear. But it was too difficult. He was seduced away by the tense feeling of existence far superior

to the mere consciousness of life, and which in its immensity of contradictions, delight, dread, exultation and despair could not be faced and yet was not to be evaded. There was no peace in it. But who wanted peace? Surrender was better, the dreadful ease of slack limbs in the sweep of an enormous tide and in a divine emptiness of mind. If this was existence then he knew that he existed. (431–32)

Life is the voluntary commitment of one's energies to the fulfillment of a noble idea, in Lingard's case his promise to get Hassim and Immada back on their thrones. But life is only an unreal scene performed before a black curtain, and the curtain negates the play acted before it. Black is the color which absorbs all colors, the place where contradictions meet, the force that turns all forms and judgments into nothing, but there is a way of being which is not separate from it: existence. Lingard's love for Mrs. Travers brings him to this state. Existence is passivity, inaction, as opposed to volition and energy. It is an impersonal awareness of an impersonal darkness, rather than the affirmation of personality. Having reached such a condition, Lingard betrays his friends, and abandons his "idea" and all its careful preparation.

People in Conrad's world are in an intolerable situation. The Apollonian realm of reason and intention is a lie. The heart of darkness is the truth, but it is a truth which makes ordinary human life impossible. It is the absorption of all forms in the shapeless night from which they have come. A man who reaches the truth is swallowed up by a force which invades his reason and destroys his awareness of his individuality. To know the darkness is to know the falsity of life, and to understand the leap into emptiness man made when he separated himself from the wild clamor of primitive life.

Throughout his career Conrad recognized that there is no way to relate existence and life, no way to evade the tragic contradictions of the human situation. Captain MacWhirr, after a moment of insight, returns to his imperturbable calm, but most of Conrad's heroes are not so fortunate. Their moments of puzzled detachment lead them step by step into the darkness. There is no return from that interior to the fatuous unreason of their complacency. "The habit of profound reflection," says Conrad, "is the most pernicious of all the habits formed by the civilized man."[25] Heyst's "fine detachment," in *Victory*, leads him to lose "the habit of asserting himself" [8], and separates him from life. Decoud, in *Nostromo*, is driven to suicide not by some overwhelming experience, but by a few hours alone on the Golfo Placido. His solitude, "from mere outward condition of existence becomes very swiftly a state of

---

25. Joseph Conrad, *Victory*, ed. J. H. Stape and Alexandre Fachard (Cambridge: Cambridge University Press, 2016), 8; hereafter cited parenthetically.

soul in which the affectations of irony and scepticism have no place. It takes possession of the mind, and drives forth the thought into the exile of utter unbelief."[26] In novel after novel Conrad presents characters driven to passivity or death by a confrontation with the darkness: Marlow, with his Buddha's pose, Winnie Verloc, driven to suicide by "madness and despair" [SA 230], Lingard, Razumov, Kurtz, and many others.

Is there no way to remain in touch with the darkness without being engulfed by it, no way to be actively engaged in life without becoming part of an empty masquerade?

Apparently there is no way. Even those who are not destroyed by their recognition of the darkness seem to have no satisfactory course open to them. Marlow comes back from the darkness. Now he can look down on the citizens of the sepulchral city because, as he says, "I felt so sure they could not possibly know the things I knew" (HD 119). What good does his wisdom do him? He knows that the lie is a lie, and confirms his allegiance to civilization by the lie he tells Kurtz's Intended. Action which is taken with awareness that the lie is a lie is the only action which is not a mournful and somber delusion, but this authenticity is based on a contradiction. Action is authentic only insofar as it is recognized that no action is authentic. True action must be based on that which denies it. Its hope is its despair, its meaning its meaninglessness, its reality its proximity to the uninterrupted night, the horror. It is a mistake to define Conrad's solution to the ethical problem by the phrase the "true lie."[27] There is nothing true about any action or judgment except their relation to the darkness, and the darkness makes any positive action impossible. Marlow, in a moment of insight, recognizes the pointlessness of life: "it occurred to me that my speech or my silence, indeed any action of mine would be a mere futility. What did it matter what any one knew—or ignored? What did it matter who was Manager? One gets sometimes such a flash of insight. The essentials of this affair lay deep under the surface, beyond my reach and beyond my power of meddling" (HD 82). The basis of this somber pessimism is formulated in an early letter to Edward Garnett: "When once the truth is grasped that one's own personality is only a ridiculous and aimless masquerade of something hopelessly unknown, the attainment of serenity is not very far off" (CL 1:267). It

---

26. Joseph Conrad, *Nostromo* (New York: The Modern Library, 1951), 556; hereafter cited parenthetically.

27. See, for example, Robert Penn Warren, "*Nostromo*," *Sewanee Review* 59, no. 3 (Summer 1951): 377–78.

was, no doubt, an understanding of this attitude in Conrad which led the Polish critic Stefan Napierski to ask: "Do they not feel the despair lurking behind these truly nihilistic books?"[28]

Nevertheless, there is someone else present in *Heart of Darkness*, someone besides Kurtz, even someone besides Marlow who has come back from the darkness to sit like a dreaming Buddha, contemplating his empty truth and preaching it. There is the narrator, one of those on board the *Nellie*, a passive listener whose understanding of the world, it may be, is radically transformed by the story he hears.[29] And there is Conrad himself, the author of the book, the man who after years of active life at sea settled down to decades of solitude, covering thousands upon thousands of blank sheets of paper with words. As he said of himself, remembering Flaubert's *Salammbô*: "Et le misérable écrivait toujours!" (*CL* 4:8).

To devote oneself to writing, however, is to engage in the most unreal action of all. Conrad was always tormented by his task, partly by what he called, echoing Baudelaire, "les stérilités des écrivains nerveux" (*CL* 3:224), but more painfully still by the sheer unreality of writing: "I have often suffered in connection with my work from a sense of unreality, from intellectual doubt of the ground I stood upon. This has occurred especially in the periods of difficult production" (*CL* 3:224):

> It is strange. The unreality of it seems to enter one's real life, penetrate into the bones, make the very heartbeats pulsate illusions through the arteries. One's will becomes the slave of hallucinations, responds only to shadowy impulses, waits on imagination alone. A strange state, a trying experience, a kind of fiery trial of untruthfulness. And one goes through it with an exaltation as false as all the rest of it. One goes through it—and there's nothing to show at the end. Nothing! Nothing! Nothing! (*CL* 2:205)

Words, the medium of fiction, are a fabrication of man's intellect. They are part of the human lie. One way to define the darkness is to say that it is incompatible with language. As Marlow gets closer to the heart of darkness he also gets further from it, for he more and more recognizes the gap between words and the darkness they can never express. The expression of Kurtz's genius is his eloquence: "Kurtz discoursed. A voice! A voice! It rang deep to the very last. It survived his strength to hide in the magnificent folds of eloquence the barren darkness of his heart" (*HD* 115). The hollowness of Kurtz's eloquence

---

28. Quoted in Albert Guerard Jr., *Joseph Conrad* (New York: New Directions, 1947), 77.
29. See Seymour Gross, "A Further Note on the Function of the Frame in 'Heart of Darkness,'" *Modern Fiction Studies* 3, no. 2 (Summer 1957): 167–70.

exposes the incompatibility between language and truth, and shows that of all the superficial films putting a glittering surface between man and the darkness, language is the most ephemeral. So Conrad is tormented not only by the unreality of words, but also by a sense of guilt for the mendacity of language. He feels that he is "not half as decent or half as useful" as "the gentlemen in gray who live in Dartmoor [Prison]" (*CL* 4:309).

In spite of this, the separation from the daylight world involved in the act of writing, its forgetting of life in order to penetrate into a realm which does not exist, is the only safe means of reaching truth. Language faces two ways. Words are a sign of man's imprisonment within illusions, but the language of fiction is the substance of a story which has no existence outside words. This detachment of words from their utilitarian function as signs puts language in touch with the unworded darkness. It brings to light the fact that words have always been detached from the everyday world. Language is that which is most intimate to man and therefore flows from the profound dark rather than from the daylight of rationality. The "gift of expression" is double. It is "the bewildering, the illuminating, the most exalted and the most contemptible, the pulsating stream of light or the deceitful flow from the heart of an impenetrable darkness" (*HD* 92).

How, in a novel, can words flow from the darkness and name the nameless? The form of Conrad's fiction gives the answer. Words can name the darkness by describing a double motion of descent into the darkness and return from it. To descend directly into the dark is to be destroyed. The writer must structure the experience of some surrogate in such a way as to reveal its truth. This truth will either destroy that other self, as Kurtz and Decoud are destroyed, or will be hidden from them, as it is hidden from Lord Jim or from Flora de Barral in *Chance*. Conrad's novels are an elaborate manipulation of data in order to make the truth behind the facts appear, and the relation of Marlow to Kurtz may be seen as a dramatization of the writer's relation to his subject. Marlow's real experience, he says, is not his own, but Kurtz's: "It is his extremity that I seem to have lived through" (*HD* 118). Each writer must bring the truth back from the darkness, as Marlow carries Kurtz away from the midnight revelry of the natives and bears him toward civilization like a sacred burden.

But Kurtz cannot be rescued. Like Eurydice, he is claimed by the darkness and soon dies, after delivering his terrifying judgment on the universe. Like a new Orpheus, Marlow can only rescue Kurtz indirectly, by transforming his life into words. Writing gives a form to the indefinable. By a return, through language, to the heart of darkness, the writer affirms himself as the power which breaks down the frontier between man and the darkness, and makes the darkness enter for a moment the daylight world. Writing is a dangerous hovering between two realms which are incompatible. Through literature they are brought together and yet kept at a distance. The writer can create a film of words which detaches man from the falsely human by making images of it, and puts him in possession of truth while still protecting him from it. By expressing the experience of someone who has been swallowed up in the darkness, the writer creates a fragile web of narrative between himself and the horror. This web gives the reader a knowledge in no other way available, and at the same time it keeps the devouring darkness at a distance. Writing is the only kind of authentic action. It is in the world and in the darkness at once.

Conrad deliberately uses the precise description of events to reach what is opposed to all visible things. The key to his aesthetic theory is a sentence in *Lord Jim*: "only a meticulous precision of statement would bring out the true horror behind the appalling face of things" (29). Through exactly described scenes the horror appears, called by the magical incantation of words, though it is something which cannot be directly defined in words. It is the halo which appears around the reflected light of the moon. In Conrad's fiction an invisible haze is lit up by the glow of bright light, the definite facts, reflected in meticulous words, which make up the action. This, I take it, is the meaning of the famous declaration of the narrator of *Heart of Darkness* when he says that, for Marlow, "the meaning of an episode was not inside like a kernel but outside, enveloping the tale which brought it out only as a glow brings out a haze, in the likeness of one of those misty halos that, sometimes, are made visible by the spectral illumination of moonshine" (45). The haze is everywhere, at all times, in the air, everywhere in nature, and at the heart of each human being, like a darkness which is seemingly dissipated by light. The goal of writing is to make darkness visible by means of the light. All words belong to the light, yet for a moment, if the story is successful, they reveal the darkness, for words belong to the darkness too.

But this is not really so. Writing can only oscillate perpetually between truth and falsehood, and endure endlessly its failure to bring what is real, the darkness, permanently into what is human, the light. Every story is necessarily a failure. In the moment that the darkness is caressed into appearing by the words of the story, it disappears. Though writing is the only action which escapes the imposture of the merely human, at the same time all literature is necessarily a sham. It captures in its subtle pages not the reality of the darkness but its verbal image.

Nevertheless, this momentary glimpse of truth is the highest human accomplishment, and it is the aim of all authentic writing. Such is Conrad's claim in the concluding sentences of the preface to *The Nigger of the "Narcissus,"* in a text which recapitulates in brief all the stages of his thought. True art, he says, must shift the gaze of the reader from the unreal dream of the future to the immediate moment of sensation. A meticulous description of the appearances of that moment will lead to a brief glimpse of the truth behind appearance, and that glimpse is the goal of art:

> To arrest, for the space of a breath, the hands busy about the work of the earth, and compel men entranced by the sight of distant goals to glance for a moment at the surrounding vision of form and colour, of sunshine and shadows; to make them pause for a look, for a sigh, for a smile—such is the aim, difficult and evanescent, and reserved only for a very few to achieve. But sometimes, by the deserving and the fortunate, even that task is accomplished. And when it is accomplished—behold!—all the truth of life is there: a moment of vision, a sigh, a smile and the return to an eternal rest. (*NN* xvi)

This return to an eternal rest is the inevitable aftermath of the moment of vision. It is a double return, the return of the darkness to its uninterrupted repose in the flux at the heart of things, and the return of man, after his evanescent glimpse of truth, to the forgetful sleep of everyday life. "Rare moments of awakening when we see, hear, understand ever so much—everything—in a flash" are always followed by a "fall back again into our agreeable somnolence" (*LJ* 111). This forgetting of truth after a brief vision of it is the denouement of the Conradian adventure. It is also the most somber moment of all in Conrad's long dialogue with the darkness.

THE SECRET AGENT

> And in those days shall men seek death, and shall not find it; and shall desire to die, and death shall flee from them. (*Revelation* 9:6)

In *The Secret Agent* Conrad's voice and the voice of the darkness most nearly become one. To explore the meaning of this novel will be to approach as close as possible to the dark heart of Conrad's universe. Its starting place is a certain conception of modern society. Against this background the events of what Conrad, in his dedication to H. G. Wells, calls "This Simple Tale of the XIX Century" (2), enact themselves. Apparently Conrad's notion of modern society is the one implied by the germ idea of the story. That germ was a discussion of anarchist activities, particularly of "the already old story of the attempt to blow up the Greenwich Observatory; a blood-stained inanity of so fatuous a kind that it was impossible to fathom its origin by any reasonable or even unreasonable process of thought" (5). Conrad's attitude is not merely one of "pity and contempt" for the "criminal futility" of anarchism, "doctrine, action, mentality," mixed with "indignation" (5, 4) deriving from his sense of the threat the anarchists pose to a good society kept stable by fidelity to duty. Conrad is not a conservative of this sort at all. Another element had to be added to the story of the Greenwich explosion before the events and characters of the novel began to take shape in the indistinction of Conrad's "quieted down imagination" (6). That process he explains by "the analogy of the addition of the tiniest little drop of the right kind, precipitating the process of crystallisation in a test tube containing some colourless solution" (6). The metaphor recalls T. S. Eliot's more famous description of the imagination as the neutral catalyst which, without itself taking part in the reaction, causes elements otherwise independent to combine in a chemical fusion. Conrad's metaphor, however, does not contain Eliot's notion of the detachment and neutrality of the imagination. The writer's mind, for Conrad, is both the test tube and its contents. When the right elements were brought together there, "strange forms, sharp in outline but imperfectly apprehended appeared and claimed attention as crystals will do by their bizarre and unexpected shapes" (6). The tiny drop that crystallized Conrad's imagination was a passage in a book of reminiscences by a man who had been Assistant Commissioner of Police during the dynamite outrages of the eighties.[30] The passage described the Home Secretary's angry distrust of the police: "your idea of secrecy over there," he had said, "seems to consist of keeping the Home Secretary in the dark" (*SA* 6). This anecdote, along with the Greenwich incident, gave Conrad the combination he wanted: the vision of an entire society linked in a chain of complicity with the anarchists, and yet keeping such relations hidden from one another. Mr. Verloc, secret agent, at once respectable bourgeois shopkeeper and family man, member of various revolutionary societies, *agent provocateur* for a reactionary foreign power, and unofficial spy for the British police, is a perfect example of the sinister connectedness of all levels of society from bottom to top, from the far left to the far right. The vision of society which informs *The Secret Agent* is not that of a stable civilization threatened by the absurd criminality of a lot of "half crazy" (5) anarchists. Conrad sees all society as rotten at the core, as a vast half-deliberate conspiracy of police, thieves, anarchists, tradesmen, aristocratic bluestockings, ministers of state, and ambassadors of foreign powers.

---

30. For an excellent brief discussion of anarchist activities at this time, see Lionel Trilling, "*The Princess Casamassima*," in *The Liberal Imagination* (New York: Viking Press, 1950), 68–74.

Conrad's symbol for this web of secret connections is London itself, the enormous commercial and industrial city. Within the city everyone is related to everyone else, often in hidden and unlawful ways, and at the same time each person is cut off from his neighbors in a solitude "as lonely and unsafe as though [he] had been situated in the midst of a forest" (201). When the elements which quickened Conrad's imagination combined, there first rose before his mind a picture of London, the greatest city on earth. That image was the dark background from which the characters and events of the story "disengaged" themselves: "Then the vision of an enormous town presented itself, of a monstrous town more populous than some continents and in its man-made might as if indifferent to heaven's frowns and smiles, a cruel devourer of the world's light. There was room enough there to place any story, depth enough there for any passion, variety enough there for any setting, darkness enough to bury five millions of lives" (6).

The city is the place imposing the mode of human relationship peculiar to modern life. It is also "man-made," a monstrous human construction which surrounds man with his own image, and hides from him the light and truth of nature. The city generates its own darkness, an especially human one, not the transhuman blackness of *Heart of Darkness*, but an obscurity made of illusion, fatuity, and blindness, the blindness of five million people who agree, with Winnie Verloc, that "life doesn't stand much looking into" (7).

Enclosed within this comfortable darkness, all men—anarchist, policeman, tradesman, and thief—accept certain assumptions. They agree that life is a game with rules everyone must obey, that many of these conventions cannot be talked about openly, and that nothing must be done to upset the delicate balance between thief and policeman, anarchist and reactionary ambassador. All of these classes of men deny their cooperation with the others. All are more or less consciously living a lie. They are alike in their refusal to look for the truth behind the surface of things, and in their determination to maintain the status quo. Like Winnie Verloc, they waste "no portion of this transient life in seeking for fundamental information" (130). Their instinct is not to question themselves or the world, but to be and let be. They remain as little conscious as possible, and as much as possible bound by unthinking habits. Chief Inspector Heat, forced to deal with anarchists, regrets "the world of thieves—sane, without morbid ideals, working by routine, respectful of constituted authorities, free from all taint of hate and despair" (75):

> he could understand the mind of a burglar, because, as a matter of fact, the mind and the instincts of a burglar are of the same kind as the mind and the instincts of a police officer. Both recognise the same conventions, and

have a working knowledge of each other's methods and of the routine of their respective trades. . . . Products of the same machine, . . . they take the machine for granted in different ways, but with a seriousness essentially the same. (74–75)

Society is a machine, a man-made system of conventions obeyed as much by thief as by policeman. The man-made machine has ended by making men, and by determining their existence within a framework of which many of them are not aware and which they do not wish to question.

What of the revolutionists? Are they not examples of a critical detachment from society? They want to destroy injustice in order to make way for the reign of peace, fraternity, and the triumph of science over nature. Inspector Heat, however, is right about thieves, but wrong about anarchists. With the exception of the Professor, the revolutionists in *The Secret Agent* are as much bound by respectability as any policeman, tradesman, or thief. Conrad is careful to distinguish among them, and to make them form a spectrum of the shades of revolutionary belief in his day, from the dialectical materialism of Michaelis, through Comrade Ossipon's faith in science, to the "terrorism" of Yundt. Nevertheless, all are alike in being completely impotent, and in being parasitically dependent on society. Of each of them Conrad could say what he says of Yundt: "The famous terrorist had never in his life raised personally as much as his little finger against the social edifice" (42). Each is in one way or another fed, clothed, cherished, and comforted by women. Strangely enough, the "mission in life" of Verloc, as of the other revolutionists, is "the protection of the social mechanism, not its perfectionment or even its criticism" (17). The trouble with the anarchists is that they are not anarchistic enough. There is more than simple irony in Conrad's boast that "there had been moments during the writing of the book when I was an extreme revolutionist, I won't say more convinced than they but certainly cherishing a more concentrated purpose than any of them had ever done in the whole course of his life" (8).

The Professor is the only true anarchist in *The Secret Agent*, the only one who stands outside society and is free of its infatuations. It is the Professor who most explicitly identifies the attitude of the revolutionists with that of respectable people. "You revolutionists," he says, "are the slaves of the social convention, which is afraid of you; slaves of it as much as the very police that stands up in the defence of that convention. Clearly you are, since you want to revolutionise it. . . . You plan the future, you lose yourselves in reveries of economical systems derived from what is; whereas what's wanted is a clean sweep and a clear start for a new conception of life" (60–61).

A clean sweep and a clear start—the only hope would be to escape altogether from the darkness of the city, but this would be possible only through the "destruction of what is" (228). All ways of living short of that are the same, whether they seek to maintain things exactly as they are, or whether, like the Marxism of Michaelis, they foresee an inevitable development, governed by the material laws of production, from the present state of things to a better one in the future. Anything derived from what is could only be a rearrangement of elements which suffer from a fatal weakness. They are a human creation, as tools, as money, as laws, as the bricks and stones of the city are shaped by man and therefore without authenticity. Conrad in *The Secret Agent* is not unfaithful to the somber picture of modern civilization which he presents in *Heart of Darkness*, in *Nostromo*, and elsewhere. He still sees civilization as an arbitrary creation, resting on no source of value outside humanity. His picture of the sinister cooperation of policemen, anarchists, and ministers of state within the brooding darkness of the enormous town is one of his most impressive dramatizations of this black view of civilized society.

Only if man were in some way liberated from the darkness could he be freed from his fatuous complacency. The purpose of the novel is to bring about such a liberation for the reader by effecting it for the chief characters of the novel, and the objects of Conrad's "inspiring indignation and underlying pity and contempt" [SA 4] are not only the revolutionists of the story, but all men, his readers too, trapped, like the characters of the story, in a blind belief in what is a human fabrication and a lie.

Since *The Secret Agent* is a work of literature, its power to liberate the reader from his infatuation must derive from a certain use of words. Since it is a novel, words must be used in it to describe the appearances of an imagined scene, and to dramatize human actions within that scene. What the scene is we know: the enormous town, generator of its own darkness and devourer of the world's light. To describe this town from the point of view of someone blindly enclosed in it would be no way out of the darkness. The nature of the collective dream is invisible to the dreamers because it determines what is seen and how it is judged. If society is to be exposed there must be a withdrawal to some vantage point outside it. Some dreamers must waken and be able to compare the waking world to the dream.

Conrad chooses two ways of separating his readers from the dark city. The first of these is the point of view of the narrator. His stance is one of ironic detachment. The "purely artistic purpose" of the novel, Conrad says, is "that of applying an ironic method to a subject of that kind" (7). The detachment of an ironic perspective is necessary because the clear vision of an uninvolved spectator is the mode of seeing of the waking sleeper, the man who knows all he sees is permeated by the unreality of dreams. Such a man is both inside and outside his dream at once, and can describe it with meticulous precision, while knowing that it is a dream. It is not surprising that Conrad should have said that *The Secret Agent* was written "in the earnest belief that ironic treatment alone would enable me to say all I felt I would have to say in scorn as well as in pity" (7).

Conrad wants to do more than show the dream as dream. He also wants to show what is outside it, to reveal the light which is swallowed up by the city's darkness. In a good novel, the narrator, even if he is omniscient, is limited by the mode of vision possible to the characters in the story. He may present characters as deluded, but it is difficult to show the truth which is hidden from them unless the scales fall from their eyes too. What is not presented as the experience of a character is not properly presented, and "Dramatize! Dramatize!" is the first law of fiction. Conrad must therefore use another method of separating his readers from the urban dream. He must show characters whose enclosure in the dream is destroyed. Only because such people exist in the novel can the narrator describe not only the dream, but what the dream hides.

The plot of *The Secret Agent* is a chain reaction, a sequence of disenchantments started by M. Vladimir's demand that Verloc create a sensational anarchist demonstration. The chain leads from Verloc eventually to Winnie Verloc, and then to the man who survives her and must live on with the terrible knowledge of her death, Comrade Ossipon. One by one these characters are wrested from their complacency and put in a situation which is outside everything they have known, a situation which is, one might say, out of this world. Conrad's ways of describing these cataclysmic experiences are necessarily hyperbolic. Winnie Verloc, after she learns of Stevie's death, is a "free woman." Her freedom is of such a terrifying completeness that she cannot see "what there [is] to keep her in the world at all" (189). Her "moral nature" has been "subjected to a shock of which, in the physical order, the most violent earthquake of history could only be a faint and languid rendering" (192). Similar shocks destroy the unthinking insulation of other characters. Winnie is the central figure only because she goes from the most complete innocence to the most shattering knowledge of what lies beyond the world. Because she moves so far beyond her initial assumptions Conrad can say of her story that it is related reciprocally to its background. It draws its tenebrous gloom from the monstrous town, but it also illuminates the darkness of the city, and shows it as what it is: "Slowly the dawning conviction of Mrs. Verloc's maternal passion grew up to a flame between me and that background, tingeing it with its secret ardour and receiving from it in exchange some of its own sombre colouring. At last the story of Winnie Verloc stood out complete from the days of her childhood to . . . its anarchistic end of utter desolation, madness and despair" (6–7, 8).

A narrator who sees the story with clearheaded pity and contempt, and characters who move toward this detachment—these are the two modes of vision which Conrad uses to "make us *see*" the conditions of life in the city.

When the comfortable dream of a humanized world is rudely shattered, man sees what has been there all along. Reality is always present, but is usually hidden behind the façade of meanings which has been spread over the world. Through the detachment of the ironic narrator and through the experience of the characters the reader is brought to see this dissimulated reality. Such seeing takes several forms, each corresponding to a stage of penetration into reality.

All the levels of this penetration are unobtrusively introduced in an admirable passage at the beginning of the second chapter. This text describes the progress of Mr. Verloc through the streets of London as he walks one spring morning toward the embassy which houses one of his employers:

> The very pavement under Mr Verloc's feet had an old gold tinge in that diffused light, in which neither wall, nor tree, nor beast, nor man cast a shadow. Mr Verloc was going westward through a town without shadows in an atmosphere of powdered old gold. There were red, coppery gleams on the roofs of houses, on the corners of walls, on the panels of carriages, on the very coats of the horses, and on the broad back of Mr Verloc's overcoat, where they produced a dull effect of rustiness. . . . The polished knockers of the doors gleamed as far as the eye could reach, the clean windows shone with a dark opaque lustre. And all was still. But a milk-cart rattled noisily across the distant perspective; a butcher boy, driving with the noble recklessness of a charioteer at Olympic Games, dashed round the corner sitting high above a pair of red wheels. . . . With a turn to the left Mr Verloc pursued his way along a narrow street by the side of a yellow wall . . . (15, 17)[31]

---

31. My attention was originally called to this passage by Avrom Fleishman. See his essay, "The Symbolic World of *The Secret Agent*," *ELH* 32, no. 2 (June 1965): 196–219.

Conrad has here made use of the fact that weather of a particular sort brings about a startling transformation of the usual look of things. The diffused light makes everything look alien. Instead of seeing houses, walls, carriages, and people as distinct objects, the spectator also sees the identical gleams which the diffused light casts on each indiscriminately. It may be, in fact, that nothing exists except these gleams, since one evidence of the solidity of objects, the fact that they interrupt the light and cast shadows, is missing. No thing or person has a shadow, and it is as if they did not exist as massive forms, but had been dissolved into scintillations of light. To see things in this way is to understand how little of what is seen derives from objects themselves, and how much is a reflection of the pervasive light which makes things visible. The spectator sees that the world is composed of splotches and blobs and gleams, gleams which his intelligence distorts by fitting them into its pre-existent concepts. Such a way of seeing shows that there is an identity of all red or yellow things which merges them into cases of a single mode of sensation. What the observer experiences in this scene, Conrad suggests, is not doors, windows, a wall, the wheels of a butcher boy's cart, but a "gleam," "a dark opaque lustre," the color yellow, the color red. He is always sensitive to the colors of things, and can often persuade the reader of the strangeness of the visible world by insisting on the unlikely colors things have, as when he describes Winnie's mother during her last cab ride to the poorhouse: "In the gas-light of the low-fronted shops her big cheeks glowed with an orange hue under a black and mauve bonnet" (123).

To see the world as areas of color or flashes of light is no longer to feel certain of the names man has applied to things. These identifying labels seem to have detached themselves from things, and to be wandering around in a sort of limbo halfway between the spectator and the world, or perhaps to have got attached by accident to the wrong things. It may be that solid things, obscured from view by a screen of colors, have, in this unnatural and rarefied world, begun to stray here and there, defying the law of gravity. As Mr. Verloc approaches the embassy which is his goal he reaches a place where all signs are misleading. It is significant that this approach goes by way of a visible object whose color is its only identifying characteristic:

> Mr Verloc pursued his way along a narrow street by the side of a yellow wall which, for some inscrutable reason, had No. 1 Chesham Square written on it in black letters. Chesham Square was at least sixty yards away, and Mr Verloc, cosmopolitan enough not to be deceived by London's topographical mysteries, held on steadily, without a sign of surprise or indignation. At last, with business-like persistency, he reached the Square, and made diago-

nally for the number 10. This belonged to an imposing carriage gate in a high, clean wall between two houses, of which one rationally enough bore the number 9 and the other was numbered 37; but the fact that this last belonged to Porthill Street, a street well known in the neighbourhood, was proclaimed by an inscription placed above the ground floor windows by whatever highly efficient authority is charged with the duty of keeping track of London's strayed houses. Why powers are not asked of Parliament (a short act would do) for compelling those edifices to return where they belong is one of the mysteries of municipal administration. (17)

In this passage, as elsewhere in *The Secret Agent,* the spectator comes to see how familiar objects exceed the mind's grasp and dwell beyond human meanings. The milk cart and the butcher boy's chariot which appear before Mr. Verloc's eyes have no connection with each other, and no special meaning for Mr. Verloc. They appear one after the other against the drab background of the silent street, and are followed by "a guilty looking cat issuing from under the stones," and a "thick police constable" who surges "apparently out of a lamppost" (17). These objects exist with three-dimensional solidity between the spectator and the veil of light which forms the background of the scene. They can be identified, but nothing more can be said of them. Recognitions of the intrinsic absurdity of things most often occur in moments of violence, danger, or surprise, times when man's ordinary engagement in the world is broken. Such moments occur in *The Secret Agent* when Verloc's complacent life is endangered by M. Vladimir, and when the reader first hears of the violent death of Stevie:

He was, in truth, startled and alarmed. . . . And in the silence Mr. Verloc heard against a windowpane the faint buzzing of a fly—his first fly of the year. . . . The useless fussing of that tiny, energetic organism affected unpleasantly this big man threatened in his indolence. (6)

An upright semi-grand piano near the door, flanked by two palms in pots, executed suddenly all by itself a valse tune with aggressive virtuosity. The din it raised was deafening. [Then] it ceased, as abruptly as it had started. . . . (52)

∽

Apparently the shapes and colors of things, their appearance as mute presences, have a quality of firstness before which it is impossible to go. Behind the visible qualities of things, however, is something else: the substance of which they are made. Behind the gleams of colors or light as Mr. Verloc makes his way through the street, behind the houses, walls, carriages, and trees which these gleams reveal and hide, is "the majesty of inorganic nature, of matter that never dies" (17). All things have this in common: they are made of immortal matter.[32] This may be more important, in determining each thing, than the fact that one particular bit of matter has been given just this shape or structure. Repeatedly in *The Secret Agent* Conrad reminds the reader that the forms which man imposes on matter effect only a precarious transformation. At any moment a change in his way of looking at things or a change in the things themselves will force him to see the reality behind surface colors or shapes. This chthonic substance is prior to what had seemed irreducible qualities and is far more alien to man than they. Like the recognition of the strangeness of things, insight into the hostility of matter is brought about by a collapse of man's normal relation to the world. Often this substance, the cold, wet stuff of which London is made, is seen through a window. It seems as though it would be dangerous to face it unprotected:

> he pulled up violently the venetian blind, and leaned his forehead against the cold window-pane—a fragile film of glass stretched between him and the enormity of cold, black, wet, muddy, inhospitable accumulation of bricks, slates, and stones, things in themselves unlovely and unfriendly to man. Mr Verloc felt the latent unfriendliness of all out of doors with a force approaching to positive bodily anguish. (48)

Though man's great cities are the expression of his dominion over nature, even there the unfriendliness of the out-of-doors is ready at any moment to appear. This unfriendliness is a stubborn recalcitrance in matter, a passive resistance to man's shapings or valuings. The "majesty of inorganic nature" appears in the solidity, immobility, and inertia of matter. Whatever may be done to it, it remains fundamentally the same. It is outside time, since time cannot change it, and it transcends all attempts to understand or control it. Matter is static and perdurable, and therefore alien to man, that creature of time and change.

Man in one way participates in the majesty of matter that never dies. Though his body is organic rather than inorganic, it comes from matter and returns to it. Even while a man is alive his body is as inertly passive as are rocks and bricks. Mr. Verloc marches along the street "steady like a rock—a

---

32. Conrad did not know that $E = mc^2$, but energy, after all, is another form of substance. It does not have the insubstantiality of spirit or consciousness.

soft kind of rock" (17), and the thick police constable surges out of a lamppost "as if he too were part of inorganic nature" (17). From the point of view of consciousness, the fact that men are in one sense part of nature is the most shocking evidence of the strangeness of matter. If a man exceeds his body by reason of his knowledge, his intentions, memories, and thoughts, in another way he is trapped in his body. He is just this piece of matter here, so many pounds of flesh and blood, like a soft rock, and, like a rock, enclosed within his own bounds. Ordinarily the grossness, or, one might say, the obscenity of a man's enclosure in a thick envelope of flesh is not noticed, so powerful are the evidences of his spirituality, but fat men remind us of the scandal of our incarnation, just as does the sight of a corpse. It is this fact as much as the evidence it gives of gluttony which, it may be, makes obesity seem morally wrong. A fat man seems in danger of ceasing to have a soul and becoming simply a body, and this recalls the grotesque absurdity of our own incarnation. Mr. Verloc can more justly be called "a soft kind of rock" because he is fat than if he were thin. He is "undemonstrative and burly in a fat pig style" (16), and the police constable who looks as if he had just surged out of a lamppost is "thick."

With something of a shock the reader realizes how many of the characters in *The Secret Agent* are fat. Conrad seems to be insisting on their gross bodies, as if their fatness were connected with the central themes of the novel. Winnie Verloc is "a young woman with a full bust, in a tight bodice, and with broad hips" (10). Her mother is "a stout, wheezy woman, with a large brown face.... Her swollen legs rendered her inactive" (11). M. Vladimir has "a large, white, plump hand" (22). Inspector Heat's "determined character" is "marred by too much flesh" (91), a cabman has an "enormous and unwashed countenance" which flames "red in the muddy stretch of the street" (121), and the obesity of the "great personage," a minister of state whom the Assistant Commissioner interviews, is insisted upon at length. He is "vast in bulk and stature," "an expanding man" (105). The most striking example of grotesque fatness in *The Secret Agent* is someone at the other end of the social scale: Michaelis, the ticket-of-leave apostle. This man weighs eighteen stone, has legs like bolsters, and a voice that wheezes "as if deadened and oppressed by the layer of fat on his chest" (37). He has "come out of a highly hygienic prison round like a tub, with an enormous stomach and distended cheeks of a pale, semitransparent complexion" (37).

A clue to the reason why there are so many fat characters in *The Secret Agent* is given by what happens to Stevie, one of the few characters who is not fat. Stevie is blown to bits when he stumbles with a can of explosives on his way to destroy the Greenwich Observatory. The disappearance of this half-witted boy is the central event of the novel, but it is never directly described. Stevie's end is hinted at, imagined, and approached from various perspectives. It is recounted by various people, but remains hidden, a blank place in the center of the narrative. Stevie's death is proof that human beings are radically different from the majesty of matter that never dies. A man can come to an abrupt end. So a "doctor's brougham arrested in august solitude close to the curbstone" is the "only reminder of mortality" (17) as Mr. Verloc walks to the embassy on the morning which starts the chain of events leading to Stevie's death.

Stevie is dead, but in another sense he is not dead at all. Conrad insists on this other sense. He returns to it, and broods over it, as though it were an important fact in the story. Stevie is not annihilated. He is transformed into "a heap of rags, scorched and bloodstained, half concealing what might have been an accumulation of raw material for a cannibal feast" (70). He is "blown to small bits: limbs, gravel, clothing, bones, splinters—all mixed up together" (159). He becomes "a heap of nameless fragments," like "the by-products of a butcher's shop" (71). Stevie's death is shocking proof of man's incarnation. It proves that a man cannot, even after death, escape from his identification with so many pounds of inorganic nature that never dies. When Stevie dies his consciousness vanishes, but he does not leave a vacuum behind him. He leaves an "enormous hole in the ground under a tree filled with smashed roots and broken branches. All round fragments of a man's body blown to pieces" (59).

Man's identification with his body has another meaning for Conrad. This meaning is dramatized in the character of the Professor. "Exterminate, exterminate!" he says, echoing the note at the bottom of Kurtz's pamphlet in *Heart of Darkness*. "That is the only way of progress.... Every taint, every vice, every prejudice, every convention must meet its doom" (226). For this reason he gives explosives to anyone who asks for them. "The condemned social order," as the Professor says, "has not been built up on paper and ink, and I don't fancy that a combination of paper and ink will ever put an end to it" (59). Though the social edifice is made up of a vast system of institutions based on an "idealistic conception of legality" (60), nevertheless these intangible ideals have got themselves embodied in a very tangible form. They exist not only in the bricks and stones of London, but also in the stolid inertia of the citizens of London, shopkeepers, lazy, fat revolutionists, and "thick" policemen alike. Incarnation means more than the imprisonment of spirit in a body. It also means the imprisonment of spirit within the narrow bounds of a set of imperfect assumptions about law and morality. For this reason the Professor's bombs must destroy more than the buildings of modern civilization. They must destroy people too, for in them history is embodied as much as in stones and inscriptions. The Professor's bombs must kill people without killing them. They must "destroy public faith in legality" (66), clear men's minds of the inert residue of traditional beliefs, and yet leave men still alive. The clean sweep and a clear start for a new conception of life must take place in the minds of men. The Professor makes explicit the focus of his destructive aim when, comparing himself to the guardians of law and order, he says that, whereas they depend on life, he depends on death:

> Their character is built upon conventional morality. It leans on the social order. Mine stands free from everything artificial. They are bound in all sorts of conventions. They depend on life, which, in this connection, is a historical fact surrounded by all sorts of restraints and considerations, a complex organised fact open to attack at every point; whereas I depend on death, which knows no restraint and cannot be attacked. My superiority is evident. (57)

The Professor wants to employ the power of death in a special way. By using it as the erasure and forgetting of history, he believes he can make the minds of all men pure and empty. Mankind will then be possessors, like himself, of a "sinister freedom" [67]. With this freedom will begin a new era in human history, an era of justice and truth.

The Professor fails. He remains poised indefinitely in the moment between the discovery of his sinister freedom and the act which would use that freedom to liberate mankind. The failure of the Professor is as exemplary for our time as was the failure of Chamfort at the time of the French Revolution. Chamfort too sought a spiritual purification, but he died in the frenzies of the Terror. The Professor's failure is strikingly symbolized in his search for a perfect detonator, and in the bomb which he carries on his own person as the expression of his "force of personality" (56). Rather than be captured, he will press the india-rubber ball in his pocket and blow himself and those around him to bits. The only flaw in this "supreme guarantee of his sinister freedom" (67) is the full twenty seconds which must elapse from the moment he presses the detonator until the explosion takes place. The failure of the detonator expresses the contradiction which keeps the Professor hovering interminably in the infinite moment between the decision to bring about the "destruction of what is" and the moment of the explosion. Death is too powerful to be used as an instrument. It is always an end, in more senses than one. The man who tries to bring death into the human world as a means of purification will find that he has committed the world to death. He cannot destroy men's beliefs without actually killing them. To perform such a delicate operation of purification would require infinite time, whereas the Professor's time is finite. One slip, one tiny error, and, instead of bringing death into the world, he will send that world, or part of it, into eternity, and eternity, as Ossipon says, is "a damned hole." "It's time that you need. You—if you met a man who could give you for certain ten years of time, you would call him your master. . . . Wait till you are lying flat on your back at the end of your time. . . . Your scurvy, shabby, mangy little bit of time" (227, 227–28). Time, in Ossipon's speech, is opposed to eternity, in a juxtaposition which recurs throughout the novel. Time can be measured by man, as it is in the Greenwich Observatory. It can be employed as a dimension within which man fulfills his intentions. Eternity, the realm of death, is a damned hole, of no use to man. The imperfection of the Professor's detonator is a symptom of his inability to reconcile time and eternity.

His failure can be defined in another way. He cannot make a large enough blank place to bring into existence his new conception of life. His bombs are not big enough to make a clean sweep. Mankind is "as numerous as the sands of the seashore, as indestructible, as difficult to handle," and the sound of exploding bombs will be "lost in their immensity of passive grains without an echo" (228). Only if the Professor could destroy mankind at the same moment as he killed himself would he be justified in pressing the india-rubber ball. A vacuum less than total will still leave some men tied to history, believing in the old conventions and laws, and ready to continue the old rather than to initiate the new. The Professor's bombs are too weak, and this weakness alone keeps him from suicide.

The impasse of the Professor explains Conrad's insistence that an explosion does not leave a vacuum but what was there before in a different form. The indestructibility of inorganic nature is identified with the stolid obduracy of human personality. The "constitutional indolence" (130) of so many of the characters in the novel is the exact moral correlative of their obesity. People insist on being themselves in the same way that a grain of sand resists destruction, and the world is dominated by a law of individuality. Each thing or person is just the thing or person it is and no other. This habit of selfhood resists the Professor's attempts to return it to anonymity in order to make a new start. The Professor cannot make a big enough hole. In fact he cannot make any hole at all. Mankind as much resists destruction as do the passive sands of the seashore, which have reached their limit of pulverization, or as do bricks, which are the atomic units of buildings:

> After a while he became disagreeably affected by the sight of the roadway thronged with vehicles and of the pavement crowded with men and women. He was in a long, straight street, peopled by a mere fraction of an immense

multitude; but all round him, on and on, even to the limits of the horizon hidden by the enormous piles of bricks, he felt the mass of mankind mighty in its numbers.... Often while walking abroad, when he happened also to come out of himself, he had such moments of dreadful and sane mistrust of mankind. What if nothing could move them? (67)

"Often while walking abroad"—the Professor's suspicion that nothing can move mankind comes when he himself is moving. To be outside the refuge of his room, that "hermitage of the perfect anarchist" (67), is to be in danger of recognizing "the resisting power of numbers, the unattackable stolidity of a great multitude" (77). It is to be in danger of seeing the heavy weight of history as it is embodied in the present. This happens only occasionally, when the Professor happens to come out of himself as well as out of his room. It is possible for him to go through the streets in complete separation from the surrounding world, as when he walks "with the nerveless gait of a tramp going on, still going on, indifferent to rain or sun in a sinister detachment from the aspects of sky and earth" (77). Verloc walks back from his disastrous interview at the embassy in the same state: "This detachment from the material world was so complete that, though the mortal envelope of Mr Verloc had not hastened unduly along the streets, that part of him to which it would be unwarrantably rude to refuse immortality, found itself at the shop door all at once, as borne from west to east on the wings of a great wind" (33). Mr. Verloc participates in the majesty of inorganic nature by means of his "mortal envelope," with its paradoxical immortality. He is also able to detach himself from the material world and dwell alone in his mind. If matter is immovable and out of time, consciousness is evanescent and dwells in time. The expression of this insubstantiality is motion. Even a heavy body which is moving is lightened and spiritualized by its motion. It is in one place only for an instant, and the place where it was a moment ago is empty. This emptiness seems to transfer itself to the body and hollow it out. A body in motion slides athwart the solidity of motionless matter like a meteor across the night sky, and seems, like the meteor, to have little in common with its stationary background. Mr. Verloc's detachment from what he sees is expressed in the fact that he is not standing immobile like a lump of matter or a thick police constable, and the stillness of the immobile street, which has the majesty of inorganic nature, is broken, as he walks toward the embassy, by the motion of the milk cart and the butcher.

The effect of motion on an inorganic mass exactly parallels the effect of the presence of mind within a human body. A body inhabited by consciousness is freed from its materiality and seems detached from the surrounding world, just as a man who is walking seems more alive than a motionless one. John Hagan, Jr. has shown the importance of the motif of the interview in *The Secret Agent*.[33] Equally important is the image of walking. It expresses a "sinister freedom" [67] rather than attempts at communication. Verloc, the Professor, the Assistant Commissioner, Inspector Heat, Winnie Verloc, and Comrade Ossipon are at different times shown walking through the streets of London, and an entire chapter is given to an apparently irrelevant description of a journey by cab to the poorhouse. The purpose of this extraordinary chapter is to create a dreamlike atmosphere dramatizing the paradox of man's ability to move himself through the world and thereby escape from it:

> In the narrow streets the progress of the journey was made sensible to those within by the near fronts of the houses gliding past slowly and shakily, with a great rattle and jingling of glass, as if about to collapse behind the cab; and the infirm horse, with the harness hung over his sharp backbone flapping very loose about his thighs, appeared to be dancing mincingly on his toes with infinite patience.... And for a time the walls of St Stephen's, with its towers and pinnacles, contemplated in immobility and silence a cab that jingled. It rolled, too, however.... The cab rattled, jingled, jolted; in fact, the last was quite extraordinary. By its disproportionate violence and magnitude it obliterated every sensation of onward movement; and the effect was of being shaken in a stationary apparatus.... (121, 122, 126)

From inside the cab the buildings seem to be moving, while the cab vibrates up and down without getting anywhere. The horse appears to be executing a stationary dance. The rarefying of matter through its motion appears only to someone who watches the moving object from a stationary point. From the perspective of the moving object, the cab and its passengers remain as solid as ever, and the cab carries its weight as an inescapable burden, however fast and far it goes. Conrad insists on the obesity of Winnie, her mother, and the cabman, and on the immense efforts necessary on the part of the grotesquely feeble horse to transport them through space an inch at a time. People do not escape from themselves by motion. They take their personalities, situations, and bodies with them wherever they go. But they do escape from their immediate surroundings. A fissure is opened between the "immobility and silence" of the walls of St. Stephen's and the cab that, after all, does move. The continuity of relations between one part of the world and another is bro-

---

33. John Hagan Jr., "The Design of Conrad's *The Secret Agent*," *ELH* 22, no. 2 (June 1955): 148–64.

ken when one of those parts is moving. This motion is the only way man has of recognizing the way time undermines what would be, in a stationary world, the changelessness of all things. Man's ability to dwell comfortably in time is one proof of the insubstantiality of his spirit, but when he turns to things it is difficult to find evidence of time and change. A moving object is not altered. It only appears to be changed to someone watching it from the outside. Inside the cab Winnie's mother's legs are as fat and swollen as ever. Nor can the movement of things be detected by the reason. Things are in one place at one time and at another in another, but motion resists logical analysis and leads the mind to contradictions, as in the paradoxes of Zeno. Whenever a man tries to fix the motion of time, it slips away, leaving him face to face with another evidence of motionlessness, so that time seems to stand still. Conrad succeeds in formulating a perfect expression for this presence and absence of time in man's experience of spatially extended things. As in similar passages in Faulkner's novels, the copresence of motion in stillness and stillness in motion is admirably expressed, and this is shown to be the fundamental quality of the ever-created, ever-destroyed now, the present moment or nick of time which, it may be, is the only reality: "Later on, in the wider space of Whitehall, all visual evidences of motion became imperceptible. The rattle and jingle of glass went on indefinitely in front of the long Treasury building—and time itself seemed to stand still" (121).

    The theme of *The Secret Agent* seems to be the disjunction between matter and spirit. Matter is solid and resists change. It never dies. Spirit, on the other hand, dwells in time. It moves across matter without being bound by it. Spirit is free. Man lives in both realms. He is incarnated in a body and is therefore part of matter which never dies. He also has a mind. The two dimensions of his existence are incompatible. He can neither incarnate spirit in matter, nor can he immaterialize matter until it takes on the quality of spirit. The gross weight of earth lies untouched behind the façade of the city, and the human mind which created that façade is as fleeting as ever. Man always dies in the end. Conrad's vision seems to culminate in the recognition of an irreconcilable dualism. Man is the meeting place of matter and spirit, and he is riven apart by their contradictions.

    Such a notion of the human situation would have at least two consolations. Though man's mind is emptiness and negation, this negation is a power. It is the basis of the changes which have produced civilization. Cities have, after all, been made with stones and bricks. Even though the brute substance of their matter may not have been altered, they have been shaped to man's uses. Society, though it may be based on a lie, still works, as long as everyone agrees to accept the lie as truth. Men have the power to create a vast system based on an "as if." This system is almost as good as if it were real, so effectively has truth been hidden away by the film which man has spread over the world. Though Conrad reveals the factitiousness of human society, he also presents it as a creation which has a pragmatic validity.

There is another comfort in a humanistic world. Though the survivors can see, in Stevie's death, the tragedy of man's participation in deathless matter, Stevie himself, so it seems, is out of this world altogether. He has escaped from what he has correctly called a "bad world for poor people" (132). In the world of atheistic humanism death is a warm blankness surrounding life on all sides. Into that dark womb all men will go at last. There all debts will be paid, and all suffering will be over. So Conrad speaks a requiem over the body of Mr. Verloc, slain by his wife: "Night, the inevitable reward of men's faithful labours on this earth, night had fallen on Mr Verloc, the tried revolutionist—'one of the old lot'—the humble guardian of society" (215).

Conrad's view of human life apparently depends on two notions of nothingness, the nothingness of consciousness, and the nothingness of death, and these support his despair and his hope. If society is based on the creative power of man's mind it is based on nothing. If death is nothingness too, it is harmless, and man is free to make of his own nothingness what he will. He can make with impunity an earthly city of man.

> Mr Verloc, getting off the sofa with ponderous reluctance, opened the door leading into the kitchen to get more air, and thus disclosed the innocent Stevie, seated very good and quiet at a deal table, drawing circles, circles, circles; innumerable circles, concentric, eccentric; a coruscating whirl of circles that by their tangled multitude of repeated curves, uniformity of form, and confusion of intersecting lines suggested a rendering of cosmic chaos, the symbolism of a mad art attempting the inconceivable. (40)

When the half-witted Stevie sits at the kitchen table his mind is not a blank. It is filled with a positive content: circles, innumerable circles, "coruscations of innumerable circles suggesting chaos and eternity" (179). These circles are the objective expression of a state which is far beyond the mind's usual absorption in a single thought. It is, as Conrad says, eternity, but this eternity is not a "damned hole" [227]. It has a definite form. It is made of circles. All parts of it have a shape which designates its constant repetition of itself. Each part goes round and round and round exactly as do all the other parts, for they are all circles. The eternal recurrence of the same perfect figure is the law of this chaos.

Though eternity is not empty, it is filled with something which denies the laws of exclusion and identity. It is the place of a horrible "uniformity of form," the incessant repetition of innumerable examples of the same unique event. In such a place everything is the same as everything else. To be in one place is the same as to be in any other place, just as to be at any one time is the same as to be at any other time. All times are simultaneous in eternity. To say that any one place or time is like any other place or time is to say that in this cosmic chaos there is no center, or, rather, that all places and times are the center. Though eternity is a circle, it is an infinite circle, and though some circles (an infinite number) may be concentric, an equal number are eccentric, and the result is not an orderly geometric diagram, but only a "confusion of intersecting lines," "a tangled multitude of repeated curves."

Stevie's "mad art" is indeed a representation of the "inconceivable," for in the realm which his pencil defines the laws of time and space and the laws of logical thought are broken. Stevie's circles represent a place of formless pullulation, a place out of place and a time out of time which is neither nothing nor something but a swarming multiplicity of identical forms which cancel one another out and yet by this mutual destruction leave the same chaos, unchanged and eternal. It is as if one were to destroy everything and were to find that this annihilation did not leave a vacuum behind but a positive presence, a presence which further acts of negation only make more oppressively active, as absolute silence becomes a murmurous sound louder than any noise.

If what lies beyond time and space is not nothingness but this contradictory presence, and if this inconceivable something is the secret ground of every man's consciousness, then the novel will have a different meaning from the one so far identified. This meaning will not so much deny the first as transcend it. Does the notion of a presence beyond ordinary consciousness occur anywhere in the novel but in the descriptions of Stevie's circles?

Of the three deaths in *The Secret Agent*, those of Stevie, Verloc, and Winnie, only one is described directly, Winnie's murder of Verloc, but in the latter case as in the others the emphasis is not on death as escape into nothingness. The focus is rather on the experience of someone who survives the death of another as if it had been his own death and remains behind as a kind of walking corpse. The survivor is transported into a horrible realm where every place is no place, and where time moves without getting anywhere. This metamorphosis is a process of depersonalization. It follows on the breakdown of the ordinary habits linking a person to the sanity of the everyday world. A man ceases to be the person he was, tied by a hundred strands to an enduring role in society, and becomes nobody, an anonymous awareness or wakefulness which cannot be called a self. The horror of this state is the way it suggests that it may be impossible to die. A man who reaches it is still alive, though everything about him is dead. Everything which had defined him as himself is gone, and yet, terrifyingly, he is still there. Only the language of exaggeration will do to describe this condition. After Winnie has killed her husband she becomes "a woman enjoying her complete irresponsibility and endless leisure, almost in the manner of a corpse" (198), and the Assistant Commissioner says of Verloc after the death of Stevie: "It sounds an extravagant way of putting it, . . . but his state of dismay suggested to me an impulsive man who, after committing suicide with the notion that it would end all his troubles, had discovered that it did nothing of the kind" (166).

To be in Verloc's state or Winnie's, is to be unable to die and yet unable to return to life. It is to persist in an interminable moment of freedom, irresponsibility, and leisure. This moment has no content. It is free of everything. Winnie does not "think at all" (198). Yet it is not nothing. It is a positive awareness of nothing. Such a state of mind is, in Conrad's precise words, "madness or despair" [228]. It is a living death whose horror is its inability to escape from itself.

The most frightful aspect of this state is the fact that chaos and eternity are not set against man as something he sees from the outside. They are inside, waiting for an opportunity to appear at the surface and engulf him. Mr. Verloc, after M. Vladimir has shattered his enclosure in the routine of his ambiguous existence, is unable to sleep. He is denied that daily oblivion which is a rehearsal of death and an expression of a man's unthinking commitment to his life. Verloc's insomnia anticipates not the forgetfulness of sweet death, but Winnie's terrifying freedom, the freedom of a living corpse. In a similar way, the Assistant Commissioner, when he disguises himself and plunges into the sinister blackness of a wet London night, becomes "unplaced" (115): "It would have been impossible for anybody to guess his occupation" (115). He is absorbed by the anonymous substance of the night:

> The Assistant Commissioner, reflecting upon his enterprise, seemed to lose some more of his identity. . . . A pleasurable feeling of independence possessed him when he heard the glass doors swing to behind his back with a sort of imperfect baffled thud. He advanced at once into an immensity of greasy slime and damp plaster interspersed with lamps, and enveloped, oppressed, penetrated, choked, and suffocated by the blackness of a wet London night, which is composed of soot and drops of water. (115, 116)

This text suggests that the substance which lies behind the coruscation of colors and the rigidity of intelligible forms is not solid matter, the stuff of which bricks and paving stones are made. It is something even more disquieting, a fluid or pulverized darkness, without form or mass, like the River Thames, which is "a sinister marvel of still shadows and flowing gleams mingling . . . in a black silence" (224). Nothing exists in this darkness except tiny particles, as of soot or drops of water. Everything seems to have come out of this fluidity, and to be in danger of returning to it on any dark, rainy night. So Conrad several times shows a London which seems to have been overwhelmed by a great flood or about to be engulfed in a new one. The fact that Winnie Verloc commits suicide by throwing herself into the stormy waters of the channel has symbolic as well as melodramatic value:

> The panes streamed with rain, and the short street . . . lay wet and empty, as if swept clear suddenly by a great flood. It was a very trying day, choked in raw fog to begin with, and now drowned in cold rain. The flickering, blurred flames of gas lamps seemed to be dissolving in a watery atmosphere. (80)

> His descent into the street was like the descent into a slimy aquarium from which the water had been run off. A murky, gloomy dampness enveloped him. (114)

> She floundered over the doorstep head forward, arms thrown out, like a person falling over the parapet of a bridge. This entrance into the open air had a foretaste of drowning; a slimy dampness enveloped her, entered her nostrils, clung to her hair. (202)

The "town's colossal forms" are "half lost in the night," in a darkness "as vast as a sea" (101, 102), and the people too are forced by a kind of deliquescence to lose their identities and melt into the fluidity of the darkness. When the Assistant Commissioner goes out in disguise he is "assimilated" by the "genius of the locality" and becomes "one more of the queer foreign fish that can be seen of an evening about there flitting round the dark corners" (114). In the same way Winnie Verloc is described as "massive and shapeless like a recumbent statue in the rough" (138), or as a "black form merged in the night, like a figure half chiselled out of a block of black stone" (209–10). The shapelessness of Winnie's body is a symbol of her secret spiritual depths. "She was mysterious," says Conrad, "with the mysteriousness of living beings" (138); "It was impossible to say what she knew" (210). These passages reveal the meaning of the motif of the interview which recurs so often in *The Secret Agent*. This motif does not express the possibility of a communication between people which might establish a luminous and honest society. It proves rather the impossibility of communication. Two people who face one another remain impenetrable mysteries. Though the clarified upper surface of another personality may be reached, the real center remains hidden. Each person merges into an impersonal darkness which is usually hidden even from the person himself.

To leave the surface levels of the mind and be merged in the night like a statue in the rough is not to lose consciousness or die. Winnie remains very much alive. She survives Stevie's death, which cuts her sole tie to the world, and lives on to drink her "cup of horrors" (223) to the last drop. The emphasis in this section of the novel is not on the death of Verloc, but on Winnie and the extraordinary state of mind she reaches. This state is described in an accumulation of details which shows her progressively approaching a state of anonymity and melting into the blackness of death. Her state is like that of a somnambulist or insomniac. She is awake. She watches with a lucid vigilance, but she does not watch anything. She looks at a blank wall:

> [Mr. Verloc] was startled by the inappropriate character of his wife's stare. It was not a wild stare, and it was not inattentive, but its attention was peculiar and not satisfactory, inasmuch that it seemed concentrated upon some point beyond Mr Verloc's person. The impression was so strong that Mr Verloc glanced over his shoulder. There was nothing behind him: there was just the whitewashed wall. . . . Mrs. Verloc gazed at the whitewashed wall. A blank wall—perfectly blank. A blankness to run at and dash your head against. (181, 184–85)

Everything Winnie sees has been turned into another expression of death. If what she sees is a symbol of death, she also contains death within herself. This inner death is a bottomless pool which reduces to its own blackness everything she looks at, even the light itself: "[Mr. Verloc] looked straight into his wife's eyes. The enlarged pupils of the woman received his stare into their unfathomable depths" (187); "A tinge of wildness in her aspect was derived . . . from the fixity of her black gaze where the light of the room was absorbed and lost without the trace of a single gleam" (195).

Winnie's depersonalization goes on through the sequence of events leading from her discovery that Verloc has caused Stevie's death to her murder of her husband, her meeting with Comrade Ossipon, their return to the shop, and his abandonment of her on the train going toward the channel boat from which she will leap at last into the dark water. The sea is another expression of the presence which lies behind or within every form and person, and Winnie's suicide is the physical fulfillment of the state she has already reached in her mind. Conrad can say of her that, even while she was alive, when she spoke "it was as if a corpse had spoken" (187), and that "she was not deadly. She was death itself—the companion of life" (217). Winnie lives on in the endless tossing of the waves and in Ossipon's awareness of how she had died, just as, when she kills Verloc, Stevie is resurrected in her, "as if the homeless soul of Stevie had flown for shelter straight to the breast of his sister, guardian and protector" (197).

Poor Comrade Ossipon, the unwilling accomplice of Winnie, is the last survivor of the chain reaction which began with M. Vladimir's shattering of Verloc's complacency. He survives to become the inheritor of the terrible knowledge which has destroyed Verloc and Winnie, and to enter a state of living death in which, walking, he does not get anywhere, and, in which he finds it impossible to sleep:

> He could walk. He walked. He crossed the bridge. . . . And again Comrade Ossipon walked. His robust form was seen that night in distant parts of the enormous town slumbering monstrously on a carpet of mud under a veil of raw mist. . . . He walked through Squares, Places, Ovals, Commons, through monotonous streets with unknown names where the dust of humanity settles inert and hopeless out of the stream of life. He walked. And suddenly turning into a strip of a front garden with a mangy grass plot, he let himself into a small grimy house with a latchkey he took out of his pocket.
>
> He threw himself down on his bed all dressed, and lay still for a whole quarter of an hour. Then he sat up suddenly, drawing up his knees, and clasping his legs. The first dawn found him open-eyed, in that same posture. This man who could walk so long, so far, so aimlessly, without showing a sign of fatigue, could also remain sitting still for hours without stirring a limb or an eyelid. (224)

The conjunction here of the motifs of walking and insomnia reveals the meaning of each. Walking does not express the freedom of spirit, its ability to skim over the surface of things and break away from the changelessness of matter. It signifies man's inability to escape from himself. Like insomnia, it corresponds to a state of mind which is contradictory or impossible, and yet real. Much earlier in the novel, Verloc's "dreary conviction that there was no sleep for him," his "mute and hopelessly inert . . . fear of darkness" (51), is expressed in the sound of footsteps in the street below his bedroom window: "Down below in the quiet, narrow street measured footsteps approached the house, then died away unhurried and firm, as if the passerby had started to pace out all eternity, from gas lamp to gas lamp in a night without end" (48–49). Insomnia is like a walking which begins nowhere and goes nowhere, but moves forever without advancing, always at the same distance from an infinitely distant starting place and an infinitely far-off goal, like the endless ticking of the Verlocs' clock on the staircase. Insomnia puts a man within a time which has not started from any remembered beginning and does not go toward any end. Time passes, but the insomniac can no longer remember when he first lay down to sleep, nor can he anticipate the morning. He seems to have left all that behind him for good. Each moment exactly repeats the others, with the same emptiness, and the same disconnection from anything before or after. The most horrible part of the insomniac's suffering is his sense that his unwinking wakefulness will persist forever in a night without end, an eternal vigilance without object. The clock's steady tick, measure of human time, melts into eternity, just as the dropping of Verloc's blood, which Winnie confounds with the sound of the clock, first accelerates and then becomes a steady flow as he dies. Walking expresses spatially what sleeplessness expresses temporally. Like insomniacs, walkers can move interminably without escaping from themselves. The city is a labyrinth of streets in which a man may go from place to place without getting anywhere, for each place is the same as all the other places. Far from proving the independence of the mind, walking shows how man, living in time and change, possesses death not as the end of his life, but as the substance of his present state.

The social fiction of laws, conventions, ideals, and personalities exists in the past and in the future, never in the present. The present reveals the substance which lies within or behind all things and persons. This secret reality is also expressed by the colors and textures of things, glimpsed evanescently in that wink of the eye between the moment of sensation and its translation into perception. Perceptions always identify an object as like something seen before, or as something which can be manipulated in the future. There is an infinitesimal time-lag which makes the perception that this is a wheel and not just a moving spot of red belong to the past or be projected toward the future. Conrad often links the momentary recognition of qualities to the motion of a thing, as in the case of the red wheels of the butcher boy's cart. The glimpse of the anonymous redness of the wheels reveals an impersonal "thereness" which is another form of the presence apprehended in insomnia and in aimless walking. All examples of the color red repeat one another as do all times in Verloc's insomnia, and as do all places in Ossipon's walking through the interminable straight perspectives of London, and through its Squares, Places, Ovals, Commons, each a monotonous repetition of the others.

Ossipon has by his unintentional complicity in Winnie's crime committed himself to that place out of place and time out of time where nothing exists but the eternal recurrence of the same. After he learns of Winnie's death he re-enacts in terrifying iteration, a repetition like Stevie's innumerable circles, Winnie's end as it was reported in the jargon of the newspaper. In the same way Winnie herself is haunted by the words which describe her anticipated death by hanging ("The drop given was fourteen feet" [201]). Ossipon's brain "pulsates wrongfully to the rhythm of journalistic phrases" (231). He repeats to himself, or some anonymous power within him repeats for him, the banal words which are slowly driving him insane: *"An impenetrable mystery seems destined to hang for ever over this act of madness or despair"* (228). Death is not the obliteration of everything. It is that which cannot end. The denouement of *The Secret Agent* sets the impasse of the Professor against the disintegration of the robust Comrade Ossipon, his inability to "think, work, sleep, . . . eat," and his absorption by the impersonal wakefulness which has claimed the other characters.

The last paragraphs of the novel juxtapose two walkers, Comrade Ossipon moving toward madness, despair, and the gutter, and the Professor, "terrible in the simplicity of his idea calling madness and despair to the regeneration of the world" [231]. This juxtaposition indicates that all the living deaths in the novel are the same death, and that the theme of *The Secret Agent* is the universal death which underlies life. As the characters get closer to death, they approach a condition in which they are equivalents of one another. There all "I's" give way to a collective "we," and communication is possible, communication not between persons, but within that which in each person is the same, the same secret agent at the heart of each.

The Professor can neither make a vacant place where spirit is able to build its own world, nor bring spirit into matter and transform the earth. The madness and despair which he calls on for the regeneration of the world are not pure emptiness of mind. They result from apprehension of the death which lies behind life. Death is a realm of madness because it is a place of contradiction, the copresence of motion and stillness, light and darkness, personality and anonymity, nothingness and substance, speech and silence, meaning and meaninglessness, servitude and freedom, time and eternity, beginning and ending held in a perpetual present. These pairs are all variations of one another, and, though the characters of *The Secret Agent* go toward death in different ways, most of them reach ultimately the same state, a state like that approached by the protagonists of Conrad's other novels, Kurtz, Marlow, Decoud, Flora de Barral, or Mrs. Travers. Conrad's novels all say the same thing, and yet are all different, as all clouds differ and yet are children of the same sky. The Professor faces a double impossibility: the impossibility of escaping from the underlying substance of madness and despair, and the impossibility of using it in any way for the regeneration of the world. He can neither make a secure place where men can create their own culture, nor can he bring the darkness of madness and despair into the world as the foundation of a viable city of man. Between these impossibilities he remains, in the sentences which end the novel, poised forever: "His thoughts caressed the images of ruin and destruction. He walked frail, insignificant, shabby, miserable—and terrible in the simplicity of his idea calling madness and despair to the regeneration of the world. Nobody looked at him. He passed on unsuspected and deadly, like a pest in the street full of men" (231).

CHAPTER 2

Lord Jim

Repetition as Subversion of Organic Form

AS A FIRST larger-scale example of the intertwining of the two modes of repetition in narrative, I choose Conrad's *Lord Jim*. This falls roughly midway in the historical span from which my seven novels come: from the early Victorian period to the eve of the Second World War.[1] *Lord Jim* provides a particularly overt case of the issues I am investigating; it invites the reader to believe that it may be comprehensible according to some mode of the first, centered form of repetition, while the actual uses of repetition in the text forbid that comprehension. And to begin after the middle of the ninety-year period from which my novels are drawn may help to forestall the assumption that I am tracing a historical development, turn, or evolution from Victorian to modern, or from simple to complex, or from realist to symbolic, or from naive acceptance of narrative conventions to sophisticated and self-conscious artistry. The telling of such a literary historical story is itself a narrative open to the same kind of challenges all seven of my novels pose to the notion of a plot with beginning, middle, and end. Each of my novels belongs to a particular moment in English

---

This essay originally appeared in *Fiction and Repetition: Seven English Novels* (Cambridge, MA: Harvard University Press, 1982), 22–41. An earlier version of this essay appeared as "The Interpretation of *Lord Jim*" in *The Interpretation of Narrative: Theory and Practice*, ed. Morton W. Bloomfield (Cambridge, MA: Harvard University Press, 1970), 211–28.

1. Conrad's *Lord Jim*, Emily Brontë's *Wuthering Heights*, William Makepeace Thackeray's *Henry Edmond*, Thomas Hardy's *Tess of the d'Urbervilles*, Hardy's *The Well-Beloved*, Virginia Woolf's *Mrs. Dalloway*, and Woolf's *Between the Acts* [Editors].

literary history, and in English social and political history too, but my claim is that these contexts do not fully determine the way repetition functions in works written in this moment or that. In each case, rather, as I shall try to show, particular materials—the historical facts of British imperialism in *Lord Jim*, for example, or social conditions in Yorkshire in the early nineteenth century in *Wuthering Heights*—become subject, when they are made into a novel, to the impossibility of telling a story which is a pure example of either of the kinds of repetitive form I have identified in my first chapter.[2] The seven novels interpreted here are variants of this situation. They do not make a historical "progression," or a "degradation" either. My chapters are attempts at readings, not attempts at the construction of a history, unless the demonstration of a movement in place or a series of nonprogressive variations is considered to be a form of history. It may be that the activity of reading, if it is carried out with rigor, tends to inhibit or even make impossible that sort of story we tell ourselves which is given the name "literary history."

Lord Jim, like most works of literature, contains self-interpretative elements. Much of it is an explication of words and signs by means of other words, as narrator follows narrator, or as narration is inserted within narration. The critic who attempts to understand *Lord Jim* becomes another in a series of interpreters. He enters into a process of interpretation in which words bring out the meaning of other words and those words refer to others in their turn. No literary text has a manifest pattern, like the design of a rug, which the eye of the critic can survey from the outside and describe as a spatial form, but the intricacies of multiple narrators and time shifts in *Lord Jim* make this particularly evident. The textuality of a text, a "yarn" spun by Conrad, is the meshing of its filaments as they are interwoven in ways hidden from an objectifying eye. The critic must enter into the text, follow its threads as they weave in and out, appearing and disappearing, crisscrossing with other threads. In doing this he adds his own thread of interpretation to the fabric, or he cuts it in one way or another, so becoming part of its texture or changing it. Only in this way can he hope to identify the evasive center or ground which is not visible as a fixed emblem around which the story is spun, but is paradoxically, as Wallace Stevens says in "A Primitive Like an Orb," a "center on the horizon,"[3] a center which is outside and around rather than within and punctual.

---

2. In the first chapter of *Fiction and Repetition*, Miller draws on Gilles Deleuze's *Logique du sens* to establish two kinds of repetition: Platonic repetition (which posits an archetypal repetition whereby every instance of repetition is a copy of the model) and Nietzschean repetition (which posits that every instance of repetition is a unique entity, different from every other instance) [Editors].

3. Wallace Stevens, *The Collected Poems* (New York: Alfred A. Knopf, 1951), 44.

Samuel Taylor Coleridge, that brilliant manipulator of the metaphors of Occidental metaphysics, presents an image of the work of art in its rounded unity corresponding to the assumption that there is such an interior center. Aesthetic wholeness in a narrative, he says, must be copied from the wholeness of a universe which circles in time around the motionless center of a God to whose eternal insight all times are co-present:

> The common end of all *narrative,* nay, of *all,* Poems is to convert a *series* into a *Whole*: to make those events, which in real or imagined History move on in a *strait* line, assume to our Understandings a *circular* motion—the snake with its Tail in its mouth. Hence indeed the almost flattering and yet appropriate Term, Poesy—i.e. poiesis-*making.* Doubtless, to his eye, which alone comprehends all Past and all Future in one eternal Present, what to our short sight appears strait is but part of the great Cycle—just as the calm Sea to us *appears* level, tho' it indeed [be] only a part of a *globe.* Now what the Globe is in Geography, *miniaturing* in order to *manifest* the Truth, such is a Poem to that Image of God, which we were created with, and which still seeks Unity or Revelation of the *One* in and by the *Many.*[4]

The concept of the organic unity of the work of art, as this passage shows, cannot be detached from its theological basis. Nor can it separate itself from mimetic theories of art. Far from asserting the autonomy of the artwork, its way of being self-sufficiently rounded in on itself, Coleridge here describes the poem as an image or a representation, even the representation of a representation. Its globular roundness miniatures not God in his relation to the creation, but the image of God created in our souls which drives us to seek the one in the many. The poem is the image of an image. Moreover, the oneness revealed in and by the many is not intrinsic but extrinsic. It is the center of a circle made up of a series of events which move in sequence but are curved back on themselves, like the fabled snake with its tail in its mouth, by the attraction of that center, just as the soul "in order to be an individual Being . . . must go forth *from* God, yet as the *receding* from *him* is to *proceed* towards Nothingness and Privation, it must still at every step turn back toward him in order to *be* at all—Now, a straight Line, continuously retracted forms of necessity a circular orbit."[5] The creation, the soul, the work of art—all three have the

---

4. Samuel Taylor Coleridge, "Letter to Joseph Cottle, 1815," in *Unpublished Letters of Samuel Taylor Coleridge, Including Certain Letters Republished from Original Sources,* ed. Earl Leslie Griggs, 2 vols. (New Haven: Yale University Press, 1933), 2:128.

5. Ibid., 2:129.

same shape, the same movement, and the same relation to a generative center. They are related in a descending series of analogical equivalences, each a copy of the one above and all able to be defined by the same geometrical or zoological metaphors.

In place of this kind of doubling, twice removed, of God's universe by the little world of the work of art, Conrad presents for both cosmos and work of literature a structure which has no beginning, no foundation outside itself, and exists only as a self-generated web:

> There is a—let us say—a machine. It evolved itself (I am severely scientific) out of a chaos of scraps of iron and behold!—it knits. I am horrified at the horrible work and stand appalled. I feel it ought to embroider—but it goes on knitting.... And the most withering thought is that the infamous thing has made itself; made itself without thought, without conscience, without foresight, without eyes, without heart. It is a tragic accident—and it has happened.... It knits us in and it knits us out. It has knitted time, space, pain, death, corruption, despair and all the illusions—and nothing matters. I'll admit however that to look at the remorseless process is sometimes amusing. (*CL* 1:425)

One way of looking at the remorseless process is by way of a novel, but a novel is not for Conrad an *image* of the horrible knitting machine and its work. It is part of the knitting, woven into its web. The infamous machine has made human beings and all their works too, including language and its power of generating or of expressing all the illusions. Works of art, like man's other works, are what they are "in virtue of that truth one and immortal which lurks in the force that made [the machine] spring into existence" (*CL* 1:425). Product of the same force which has knit the rest of the universe, a work of art has the same kind of structure. A novel by Conrad, though it invites the reader to hope that he can find a center of the sort Coleridge ascribes to the good work of art, has nothing certainly identifiable outside itself by which it might be measured or from which it might be seen. It has no visible thematic or structuring principle which will allow the reader to find out its secret, explicate it once and for all, untie all its knots and straighten all its threads. The knitting machine cannot be said to be the origin of the cloth it knits, since what the machine knits is itself, knitter and knitted forming one indistinguishable whole without start or finish, continuously self-creating. The cloth exists as the process of its knitting, the twisting of its yarns as they are looped and knotted by a pervasive "force." This force is the truth one and immortal everywhere present but nowhere visible in itself, an energy both of differentiation and of destruction. "It knits us in and it knits us out."

A familiar passage in Conrad's *Heart of Darkness* describes the indirection characteristic of works of literature like *Lord Jim*. The passage uses a variant of the image of the knitted fabric in the letter to Cunninghame Graham. "The yarns of seamen," says the narrator, "have an effective simplicity, the whole meaning of which lies within the shell of a cracked nut. But, as has been said, Marlow was not typical (if his propensity to spin yarns be excepted) and to him the meaning of an episode was not inside like a kernel but outside, enveloping the tale which brought it out only as a glow brings out a haze, in the likeness of one of these misty halos that, sometimes, are made visible by the spectral illumination of moonshine" (45). Though the meaning is outside, it may only be seen by way of the tale which brings it out. This bringing out takes place in the interaction of its different elements in their reference to one another. These the critic must track, circling from one word or image to another within the text. Only in this movement of interpretation does the meaning exist. It is not a central and originating node, like the kernel of a nut, a solid and pre-existing nub. It is a darkness, an absence, a haze invisible in itself and only made visible by the ghostlike indirection of a light which is already derived. It is not the direct light of the sun but the reflected light of the moon which brings out the haze. This visible but secondary light and the invisible haze create a halo of "moonshine" which depends for its existence on the reader's involvement in the play of light and dark which generates it. Does this invitation to believe that there is an explanatory center, without positive identification of that center or even certainty about whether or not it exists, in fact characterize *Lord Jim*? I shall investigate briefly here a series of ways the novel might be interpreted.

The theme of *Lord Jim* is stated most explicitly toward the end of chapter 5, in Marlow's attempt to explain why he concerns himself with Jim:

> Why I longed to go grubbing into the deplorable details of an occurrence which, after all, concerned me no more than as a member of an obscure body of men held together by a community of inglorious toil and by fidelity to a certain standard of conduct I can't explain. You may call it an unhealthy curiosity if you like; but I have a distinct notion I wished to find something. Perhaps unconsciously I hoped I would find that something, some profound and redeeming cause, some merciful explanation, some convincing shadow of an excuse. I see well enough now that I hoped for the impossible—for the laying of what is the most obstinate ghost of man's creation, of the uneasy doubt uprising like a mist, secret and gnawing like a worm and more chilling

than the certitude of death—the doubt of the sovereign power enthroned in a fixed standard of conduct. (43)

Jim is "one of us," an Englishman, son of a country clergyman, a "gentleman," brought up in the British traditions of duty, obedience, quiet faithfulness, and unostentatious courage. Nevertheless, he has committed the shockingly dishonorable act of deserting his ship and the helpless pilgrims it carried. Jim's desertion seems especially deplorable to Marlow because Jim looks so trustworthy, so perfect an example of the unassuming nobility of the tradition from which he has sprung. "He had no business to look so sound," says Marlow. "I thought to myself—Well if this sort can go wrong like that! . . . and I felt as though I could fling down my hat and dance on it from sheer mortification" (36); "He looked as genuine as a new sovereign, but there was some infernal alloy in his metal" (40). The discrepancy between what Jim looks like and what he is puts in question for Marlow "the sovereign power enthroned in a fixed standard of conduct." He does not doubt the existence of the standard, the seaman's code of fidelity, obedience, and obscure courage on which the British empire was built. He comes to question the power installed behind this standard and within it. This power, as its defining adjective affirms, justifies the standard as its king—its principle, its source, its law.

If there is no sovereign power enthroned in the fixed standard of conduct then the standard is without validity. It is an all-too-human fiction, an arbitrary code of behavior—"this precious notion of a convention," as Marlow says, "only one of the rules of the game, nothing more" (66). Nothing matters, and anything is possible, as in that condition of spiritual anarchy which takes over on the ship's boat after Jim and the other officers have deserted the *Patna* and left her to sink with eight hundred men, women, and children. "After the ship's lights had gone," says Jim, "anything might have happened in that boat—anything in the world—and the world no wiser. I felt this, and I was pleased. It was just dark enough too. We were like men walled up quick in a roomy grave. No concern with anything on earth. Nobody to pass an opinion. Nothing mattered. . . . No fear, no law, no sounds, no eyes—not even our own till—till sunrise, at least" (95). Marlow interprets Jim's words in a way which gives them the widest application to the derelict condition of a man who has lost faith, conviction, his customary material surroundings—whatever has given his world stability and order by seeming to support it from outside. "When your ship fails you," says Marlow, "your whole world seems to fail you; the world that made you, restrained you, taken [sic] care of you. It is as if the souls of men floating on an abyss and in touch with immensity had been set free for any excess of heroism, absurdity or abomination. Of course, as with belief, thought, love, hate, conviction or even the visual aspect of material things, there are as many shipwrecks as there are men. . . . Trust a boat on the high seas to bring out the Irrational that lurks at the bottom of every thought, sentiment, sensation, emotion" (95).

Marlow's aim (or Conrad's) seems clear: to find some explanation for Jim's action which will make it still possible to believe in the sovereign power. Many critics think that in the end Marlow (or Conrad) is satisfied, that even Jim is satisfied. The circumstances of Jim's death and his willingness to take responsibility for the death of Dain Waris ("He hath taken it upon his own head"; 312) make up for all Jim has done before. Jim's end re-enthrones the regal power justifying the fixed standard of conduct by which he condemns himself to death.

Matters are not so simple in this novel. For one thing, there is something suspect in Marlow's enterprise of interpretation. "Was it for my own sake," he asks, "that I wished to find some shadow of an excuse for that young fellow whom I had never seen before?" (44). If so much is at stake for himself, he is likely to find what he wants to find.

Marlow attempts to maintain his faith in the sovereign power in several contradictory ways. One is to discover that there are extenuating circumstances. Perhaps Jim is not all bad. Perhaps he can be excused. Perhaps he can ultimately redeem himself. At other times Marlow suggests that in spite of appearances Jim has a fatal soft spot. He cannot be safely trusted for an instant. If this is so, then he must be condemned in the name of the kingly law determining good and evil, praise and blame. At still other times Marlow's language implies that Jim is the victim of dark powers within himself, powers which also secretly govern the universe outside. If there is no benign sovereign power there may be a malign one, a principle not of light but of blackness, "a destructive fate ready for us all" (44). If this is the case, there are indeed extenuating circumstances, precisely the "shadow of an excuse." To act according to a fixed standard of conduct which is justified by no sovereign power, as perhaps Jim does in his death, is the truest heroism. It is defiance of the shadowy powers which would undermine everything man finds good. If this is so, Jim's death is nevertheless in one sense still a sham. It is a sham in the sense that it is valued by no extrahuman judge. It is only one way of acting among others.

Perhaps, to pursue this line a little further, the source of all Jim's trouble is his romanticism, that childish image of himself as a hero which has its source in fraudulent literature and sticks with him all his life: "He confronted savages on tropical shores, quelled mutinies on the high seas and in a small boat upon the ocean kept up the hearts of despairing men—always an example of devotion to duty and as unflinching as a hero in a book" (11). Perhaps it is Jim's confidence in this illusory image of himself which is the source of his inability to confront the truth about himself and about the universe. Perhaps this confidence even paradoxically explains his repeated acts of cowardice. It may be that Jim's death is no more than the last of such acts, his last failure to face the dark side of himself which is so rudely brought back before him in the person of Gentleman Brown. His death may be no more than his last attempt to act according to a fictional idea of heroic conduct. Certainly the final paragraphs of the novel show Marlow by no means "satisfied." The ending is a tissue of unanswered questions in which Marlow affirms once more not that Jim is a hero or that Jim is a coward, but that he remains an indecipherable mystery:

> And that's the end. He passes away under a cloud, inscrutable at heart, forgotten, unforgiven and excessively romantic. . . . He goes away from a living woman to celebrate his pitiless wedding with a shadowy ideal of conduct. Is he satisfied—quite, now, I wonder? We ought to know. He is one of us—and have I not stood up once, like an evoked ghost, to answer for his eternal constancy? Was I so very wrong after all? Now, he is no more, there are days when the reality of his existence comes to me with an immense, with an overwhelming force; and yet upon my honour there are moments too when he passes from my eyes like a disembodied spirit astray amongst the passions of this earth—ready to surrender himself faithfully to the claim of his own world of shades.
> Who knows? (312–13)

The ending seems to confirm Marlow's earlier statement that the heart of each thane is a dark forest to all his fellows and "loneliness" a "hard and absolute condition of existence; the envelope of flesh and blood on which our eyes are fixed melts before the outstretched hand, and there remains only the capricious, unconsolable and elusive spirit that no eye can follow, no hand can grasp" (137).

On the other hand, all that seems problematic and inconclusive about *Lord Jim* when it is approached from the point of view of explicit thematic statements and by way of Marlow's interpretation of Jim may be resolved if the reader stands back from Marlow's perspective and looks at the novel as a whole. The detached view may see the truth, according to that proverb Marlow recalls which affirms that "the onlookers see most of the game" (170). Seen from a distance, *Lord Jim* may turn out to be a pattern of recurrent motifs which reveals more about Jim than Marlow comes to understand. Jim's feeling at his trial that "only a meticulous precision of statement would bring out the true horror behind the face of things" (29) may be the clue to the aesthetic method of the book. The episodes Marlow and others relate, the language they use, may reveal to the readers of the novel a secret hidden from Marlow, from Jim, and from all the characters, a secret known only to Conrad. He may have chosen this way to show forth the truth because only as a participant in its revelation can the reader understand it.

When *Lord Jim* is approached from the perspective of its narrative structure and its design of recurrent images it reveals itself to be not less but more problematic, more inscrutable, like Jim himself. I have elsewhere argued that temporal form, interpersonal relations, and relations of fiction and reality are three structuring principles fundamental to fiction.[6] *Lord Jim* is an admirable example of the tendency of these in their interaction to weave a fabric of words which is incapable of being interpreted unambiguously, as a fixed pattern of meaning, even though the various possibilities of meaning are rigorously delimited by the text.

To begin with the structure of interpersonal relations: Victorian novels were often apparently stabilized by the presence of an omniscient narrator, spokesman for the collective wisdom of the community, though, as my Victorian examples here demonstrate, such a narrator never turns out to be unequivocally the basis of the storytelling when a given Victorian novel is interpreted in detail. Such a narrator, if he were ever to exist, would represent a trustworthy point of view and also a safe vantage point from which to watch the hearts and minds of the characters in their relations to one another. Conrad, as many critics have noted, does not employ a "reliable" narrator. In *Lord Jim* no point of view is entirely trustworthy. The novel is a complex design of interrelated minds, no one of which can be taken as a secure point of reference from which the others may be judged.

The first part of the story is told by an "omniscient" narrator who seems like the narrator of a novel by Trollope or by George Eliot. This first narrator of *Lord Jim* has the same superhuman powers of insight, including direct access to the hero's mind, that is possessed by those earlier Victorian narrators. He relinquishes that access early in the story, as though it could not provide a satisfactory avenue to the truth behind Jim's life. He then returns in chapter 36, after Marlow's narrative to his almost silent auditors is over. He returns to introduce the man who receives the letter which is Marlow's "last word" about Jim. The bulk of the novel is made up of Marlow's telling of Jim's story to the group of listeners in the darkness who are the reader's surrogates. Those listeners stand between the reader and Marlow's telling. "He existed for

---

6. J. Hillis Miller, *The Form of Victorian Fiction: Thackeray, Dickens, Trollope, George Eliot, Meredith* (Notre Dame, IN: University of Notre Dame Press, 1968).

me," says Marlow, "and after all it is only through me that he exists for you. I've led him out by the hand; I have paraded him before you" (170).

Many sections of the story are told to Marlow by Jim. In these the reader can see Jim attempting to interpret his experience by putting it into words. This self-interpretation is interpreted once more by Marlow, then by implication interpreted again by Marlow's listeners. The latter appear occasionally as intervening minds, as when one of them says: "You are so subtle, Marlow" (76). This overlapping of interpretative minds within minds is put in question in its turn, at least implicitly, by the "omniscient" narrator. He surrounds all and perhaps understands all, though he does not give the reader the sort of interpretative help provided by the narrator of *Middlemarch* or of *The Last Chronicle of Barset*. Even so, this narrator may have been brought back briefly near the end of the novel to suggest that the reader might be wise to put in question Marlow's interpretation of Jim, even though the narrator cannot or will not provide the reader with any solid alternative ground on which to stand.

Within Marlow's narrative there are many minor characters—Captain Brierly, the French lieutenant, Chester, Stein—who have their say in the story. They are irreplaceable points of view on Jim within Marlow's point of view. They are sources of parts of his story and offer alternative ways of judging it. Their own stories, moreover, are analogous to Jim's story, though whether in a positive or in a negative way is often hard to tell. Just as the crucial episodes in Jim's life echo one another, the jump from the *Patna* repeating his failure to jump in the small boat when he was in training and being repeated again by his jump over the stockade in Patusan ("Patusan" recalling *Patna*), so Captain Brierly's suicide is a jump ambiguously duplicating Jim's jumps (was it cowardly or an act of heroism following logically from a shattering insight into the truth of things?), while the French lieutenant's courage shows what Jim might have done on the *Patna*, and Stein's strange history echoes Jim's either positively or negatively. Stein appears to be either an unreliable narrator or a trustworthy commentator, depending on one's judgment of his life and personality. Is he a man who has bravely immersed himself in the destructive element to win an ultimate wisdom, or has he withdrawn passively from life to collect his butterflies and to give Marlow and the readers of the novel only misleading clues to the meaning of Jim's life?

Lord Jim is made up of episodes similar in design. In each a man confronts a crisis testing his courage, the strength of his faith in the sovereign power enthroned in a fixed standard of conduct. In each case someone, the man himself or someone else, interprets that test, or rather he interprets the words which the man's reaction to the test has already generated. There is even a parody of this pattern early in the novel, as if to call attention to it as a structuring principle or as a universal way in which men are related to one another. Just as Marlow seeks out the chief engineer of the *Patna* in the hospital "in the eccentric hope of hearing something explanatory of the famous affair from his point of view" (43), so the doctor who is tending the engineer after his brandy debauch says he "never remember[s] being so interested in a case of jim-jams before." "The head—ah! the head, of course, gone, but the curious part is there's some sort of method in his raving. I am trying to find out. Most unusual—that thread of logic in such a delirium" (46). The reader of *Lord Jim*, like the doctor, must seek the thread of logic within a bewildering complexity of words. With these words Conrad attempts to express a truth beyond direct expression in words, "for words also belong to the sheltering conception of light and order which is our refuge" (236), our refuge from the truth hidden in the darkness. In the sequence of discrete episodes which makes up the novel, no episode serves as the point of origin, the arch-example of the *mythos* of the novel, but each is, by reason of its analogy to other episodes, a repetition of them, each example being as enigmatic as all the others.

A similar complexity characterizes the temporal structure of the novel. Jim says of his memory of watching the other officers struggle to get the *Patna*'s boat in the water: "I ought to have a merry life of it, by God! for I shall see that funny sight a good many times yet before I die" (84). Of an earlier moment before the officers desert the ship he says: "It was as though I had heard it all, seen it all, gone through it all twenty times already" (73). Each enactment of a given episode echoes backward and forward indefinitely, creating a pattern of eddying repetition. If there are narrators within narrators there are also times within times—time-shifts, breaks in time, anticipations, retrogressions, retellings, and reminders that a given part of the story has often been told before. Marlow, for example, like the Ancient Mariner, has related Jim's story "many times, in distant parts of the world" (30). The novel is made up of recurrences in which each part of the story has already happened repeatedly when the reader first encounters it, either in someone's mind, or in someone's telling, or in the way it repeats other similar events in the same person's life or in the lives of others. The temporal structure of the novel is open. *Lord Jim* is a chain of repetitions, each event referring back to others which it both explains and is explained by, while at the same time it prefigures those which will occur in the future. Each exists as part of an infinite regression and progression within which the narrative moves back and forth discontinuously across time seeking unsuccessfully some motionless point in its flow.

It might be argued that the sequence of events as the reader is given them by Conrad, in a deliberately chosen order, is a linear series with a beginning, middle, and end which determines a straightforward development of gradually revealed meaning moving through time as the reader follows word after word and page after page, becoming more and more absorbed in the story and more and more emotionally involved in it. This sequence, it might be argued, generates a determinate meaning. It is true that this linear sequence is shared by any reader and that it establishes a large background of agreement about what happens and even about the meaning of what happens. That Jim jumps from the *Patna* and that this is a morally deplorable act no reader is likely to doubt. But it is also true that the linear sequence of episodes as it is presented to the reader by the various narrators is radically rearranged from the chronological order in which the events actually occurred. This could imply that Conrad, the "omniscient narrator," or Marlow has ordered the episodes in such a way that the best understanding by the reader of a total meaning possessed by one or another of these narrators will be revealed. Or it may imply, as I think it does, that the deeper explanatory meaning behind those facts open to the sunlight, about which anyone would agree, remains hidden, so that any conceivable narrator of these facts or interpreter of them is forced to move back and forth across the facts, putting them in one or another achronological order in the hope that this deeper meaning will reveal itself. The narration in many ways, not least by calling attention to the way one episode repeats another rather than being clearly a temporal advance on it, breaks down the chronological sequence and invites the reader to think of it as a simultaneous set of echoing episodes spread out spatially like villages or mountain peaks on a map. *Lord Jim* too, to borrow the splendid phrase Henry James uses in his review of Conrad's *Chance*, is "a prolonged hovering flight of the subjective over the outstretched ground of the case exposed."[7] Insofar as the novel is this and not the straightforward historical movement suggested by Aristotle's comments on beginning, middle, and end in the *Poetics*, then the sort of metaphysical certainty implicit in Aristotle, the confidence that some *logos* or underlying cause and ground supports the events, is suspended. It is replaced by the image of a consciousness attempting to grope its way to the hidden cause behind a set of enigmatic facts by moving back and forth over them. If the "facts" are determinate (more or less) the novel encourages the reader to seek the "why" behind the events, some "shadow of an excuse." It is here, I am arguing, that the text does not permit the reader to decide among alternative possibilities, even though those possibilities themselves are identified with precise determinate certainty.

The similarities between one episode and another or one character and another in *Lord Jim* no doubt appear to be deliberately designed (whether

---

7. Henry James, "The New Novel," in *Notes on Novelists* (London: J. M. Dent & Sons, 1914), 276.

by Conrad or by Marlow), like most of the cases of repetition discussed in this book. Such repetitions differ from those which are accidental or merely contingent, perhaps even insignificant, although the reader would do well not to be too sure about the existence of insignificant similarities. Moreover, the fact that Conrad probably consciously intended most of the repetitions I discuss here (though certainty about that is of course impossible) may be trivial compared to the way the novel represents human life as happening to fall into repetitive patterns, whether in the life of a single person, as Jim repeats variants of the same actions over and over, or from person to person, as Brierly's jump repeats Jim's jump. The question the novel asks and cannot unequivocally answer is "Why is this?" To say it is because Conrad designed his novel in recurring patterns is to trivialize the question and to give a misplaced answer to it.

Nor can the meaning of the novel be identified by returning to its historical sources, however helpful or even essential these are in establishing a context for our reading. The "source" of *Lord Jim*, as Conrad tells the reader in the "Author's Note," was a glimpse of the "real" Jim: "One sunny morning in the commonplace surroundings of an Eastern roadstead I saw his form pass by me—appealing—significant—under a cloud—perfectly silent. . . . It was for me, with all the sympathy of which I was capable to seek fit words for his meaning" (6). Norman Sherry, in *Conrad's Eastern World*, and Ian Watt, in *Conrad in the Nineteenth Century*, have discussed in detail the historical events which lie behind the novel.[8] *Lord Jim* can be defined as an attempt on Conrad's part to understand the real by way of a long detour through the fictive. To think of *Lord Jim* as the interpretation of history is to recognize that the historical events "behind" the novel exist now as documents, and that these documents too are enigmatic. They are as interesting for the ways in which Conrad changed them as for the ways in which he repeated them exactly. The novel is related to its sources in a pattern of similarity and difference like that of the episodes inside the novel proper. The facts brought to light by Sherry and Watt, for example the "Report of a Court of Inquiry held at Aden into the cause of the abandonment of the steamship 'Jeddah,'"[9] do not serve as a solid and unequivocal point of origin by means of which the novel may be viewed, measured, and understood. The documents are themselves mysterious, as mysterious as the Old Yellow Book on which Browning based *The Ring and the Book* or as the dry, factual account of historical events

---

8. Norman Sherry, *Conrad's Eastern World* (Cambridge: Cambridge University Press, 1966), 41–170; Ian Watt, *Conrad in the Nineteenth Century* (Berkeley: University of California Press, 1979), 259–69.

9. Sherry, *Conrad's Eastern World*, 299–309.

included at the end of Melville's *Benito Cereno*. In all these cases knowledge of the historical sources makes the story based on them not less but more inscrutable, more difficult to understand. If there are "fit words" for Jim's "meaning" they are to be found only within the novel, not in any texts outside it.

Perhaps, to turn to a last place where an unambiguous meaning may be found, the pattern of images in its recurrences somehow transcends the complexities I have discussed. It may constitute a design lying in the sunlight, ready to be seen and understood. It will be remembered that Conrad attempts above all, as he says in the preface to *The Nigger of the "Narcissus,"* to make us *see*. Matching this is the recurrent image in *Lord Jim* according to which Marlow gets glimpses of Jim through a rift in the clouds. "The views he let me have of himself," says Marlow, "were like those glimpses through the shifting rents in a thick fog—bits of vivid and vanishing detail, giving no connected idea of the general aspect of a country" (62). The metaphorical structure of the novel may reveal in such disconnected glimpses a secret which cannot be found out by exploring its narrative, temporal, or interpersonal patterns, or by extracting explicit thematic statements.

A network of light and dark imagery manifestly organizes the novel throughout. It is first established insistently near the beginning in the description of the *Patna* steaming across the calm sea: "The *Patna*, with a slight hiss, passed over that plain luminous and smooth, unrolled a black ribbon of smoke across the sky, left behind her on the water a white ribbon of foam that vanished at once, like the phantom of a track drawn upon a lifeless sea by the phantom of a steamer" (18). Black against white, light against dark—perhaps the meaning of *Lord Jim* is to be found in Conrad's manipulation of this binary pattern.

This metaphorical or "symbolic" pattern too is systematically ambiguous, as may be seen by looking at two examples, the description of Jim's visit to Marlow's room after his trial and the description of Marlow's last glimpse of Jim on the shore. The juxtaposition of light and dark offers no better standing ground from which what is equivocal about the rest of the novel may be surveyed and comprehended than any other aspect of the text. The "visual aspect of material things" and the clues it may offer to the meaning of man's life sink in the general shipwreck which puts in doubt the sovereign power enthroned in a fixed standard of conduct:

> He remained outside, faintly lighted on the background of night, as if standing on the shore of a sombre and hopeless sea.
>
> An abrupt heavy rumble made me lift my head. The noise seemed to roll away, and suddenly a searching and violent glare fell on the blind face of the

night. The sustained and dazzling flickers seemed to last for an unconscionable time. The growl of the thunder increased steadily while I looked at him, distinct and black, planted solidly upon the shores of a sea of light. At the moment of greatest brilliance the darkness leaped back with a culminating crash, and he vanished before my dazzled eyes as utterly as though he had been blown to atoms. (135–36)

He was white from head to foot, and remained persistently visible with the stronghold of the night at his back, the sea at his feet, the opportunity by his side—still veiled. What do you say? Was it still veiled? I don't know. For me that white figure in the stillness of coast and sea seemed to stand at the heart of a vast enigma. The twilight was ebbing fast from the sky above his head, the strip of sand had sunk already under his feet, he himself appeared no bigger than a child—then only a speck, a tiny white speck, that seemed to catch all the light left in a darkened world. . . . And, suddenly, I lost him. (253)

In one of these passages Jim is the light that illuminates the darkness. In the other he is the blackness that stands out against a blinding light which suddenly reveals itself from its hiding place and then disappears. Light changes place with dark; the value placed on dark and light changes place, as light is sometimes the origins of dark, dark sometimes the origin of light. Each such passage, moreover, refers to the others by way of anticipation or recollection, as the first of the texts quoted prefigures the second, but when the reader turns to the other passage it is no easier to understand and itself refers to other such passages. No one of them is the original ground, the basis on which the others may be interpreted. *Lord Jim* is like a dictionary in which the entry under one word refers the reader to another word which refers him to another and then back to the first word again, in an endless circling. Marlow sitting in his hotel room ceaselessly writing letters by the light of a single candle while Jim struggles with his conscience and the thunderstorm prepares in the darkness outside may be taken as an emblem of literature as Conrad sees it. A work of literature is for him in a paradoxical relation to a nonverbal reality it seeks both to uncover and to evade in the creation of its own exclusively verbal realm.

I claim, then, that from whatever angle it is approached *Lord Jim* reveals itself to be a work which raises questions rather than answering them. The fact that it contains its own interpretations does not make it easier to understand. The overabundance of possible explanations only inveigles the reader to share in the self-sustaining motion of a process of interpretation which cannot reach an unequivocal conclusion. This weaving movement of advance and retreat constitutes and sustains the meaning of the text, that evasive center which is everywhere and nowhere in the play of its language.

Marlow several times calls explicit attention to the unendingness of the process by which he and the readers of the novel go over and over the details of Jim's life in an ever-renewed, never-successful attempt to understand it completely and so write "Finis" to his story. "And besides," affirms Marlow apropos of his "last" words about Jim, "the last word is not said—probably shall never be said. Are not our lives too short for that full utterance which through all our stammerings is of course our only and abiding intention? . . . There is never time to say our last word—the last word of our love, or our desire, faith, remorse, submission, revolt" (171). The reader will remember here those "last words" of Kurtz ("The horror! The horror!") which Marlow in another story hears and ironically praises for their finality, their power to sum up. If this theme is repeated within *Lord Jim*, these repetitions echo in their turn passages in other novels by Conrad. If *Heart of Darkness* leads to Marlow's recognition that he cannot understand Kurtz as long as he has not followed Kurtz all the way into the abyss of death, the "ending" of *Lord Jim* is Marlow's realization that it is impossible to write "The End" to any story:

> End! *Finis!* The potent word that exorcises from the house of life the haunting shadow of Fate. This is what—notwithstanding the testimony of my eyes and his own earnest assurances—I miss when I look back upon Jim's success. While there's life there is hope, truly; but there is fear too . . . he made so much of his disgrace while it is the guilt alone that matters. He was not—if I may say so—clear to me. He was not clear. And there is a suspicion he was not clear to himself either. (135)

Nor can he, I am arguing, ever be clear to us, except with the paradoxical clarity generated by our recognition that the process of interpreting his story is a ceaseless movement toward a light which always remains hidden in the dark.

Let there be no misunderstanding here. The situation I have just described does not mean that the set of possible explanations for Jim's action is limitless, indeterminate in the sense of being indefinitely multiple and nebulous. The various meanings are not the free imposition of subjective interpretations by the reader, but are controlled by the text. In that sense they are determinate. The novel provides the textual material for identifying exactly what the possible explanations are. The reader is not permitted to go outside the text to make up other possible explanations of his own. The indeterminacy lies in the multiplicity of possible incompatible explanations given by the novel and in the lack of evidence justifying a choice of one over the others. The reader cannot logically have them all, and yet nothing he is given determines a choice among them. The possibilities, moreover, are not just given side by side as entirely separate hypotheses. They are related to one another in a system of mutual implication and mutual contradiction. Each calls up the others, but it does not make sense to have more than one of them.

Would novels from an earlier period be more open to identification of a single, unequivocal meaning? Is the ambiguity of *Lord Jim* a historical phenomenon, a feature of the time in which it was written, or of the historical and social conditions of its author, or is its presentation of specific incompatible possibilities of meaning among which it is impossible to choose characteristic in one way or another of works of literature of any period in Western culture? Only an investigation of some examples can begin to suggest tentative answers to those questions. I turn back now to several salient examples of earlier Victorian fiction to explore the workings of repetition in each.

CHAPTER 3

Heart of Darkness Revisited

I BEGIN with three questions: Is it a senseless accident, result of the crude misinterpretation or gross transformation of the mass media, that the cinematic version of *Heart of Darkness* is called *Apocalypse Now,* or is there already something apocalyptic about Conrad's novel in itself? What are the distinctive features of an apocalyptic text? How would we know when we had one in hand?

I shall approach an answer to these questions by the somewhat roundabout way of an assertion that if *Heart of Darkness* is perhaps only problematically apocalyptic, there can be no doubt that it is parabolic. The distinctive feature of a parable, whether sacred or secular, is the use of a realistic story, a story in one way or another based firmly on what Marx calls man's "real conditions of life, and his relations with his kind,"[1] to express another reality or truth not otherwise expressible. When the disciples ask Jesus why he speaks to the multitudes in parables, he answers, "Therefore speak I to them in parables: because they seeing see not; and hearing they hear not, neither do they understand" (Matthew 13:13). A little later Matthew tells the reader that "without a

---

This essay originally appeared in *Conrad Revisited: Essays for the Eighties,* ed. Ross C. Murfin (University: University of Alabama Press, 1985), 31–50.

1. Karl Marx, "Manifesto of the Communist Party," in *The Marx-Engels Reader,* ed. Robert C. Tucker, 2nd ed. (New York: W. W. Norton, 1978), 476.

parable spake he not unto them: That it might be fulfilled which was spoken by the prophet, saying, I will open my mouth in parables; I will utter things which have been kept secret from the foundation of the world" (Matthew 13:34–35). Those things which have been kept secret from the foundation of the world will not be revealed until they have been spoken in parable, that is, in terms which the multitude who lack spiritual seeing and hearing nevertheless see and hear, namely, the everyday details of their lives of fishing, farming, and domestic economy. Though the distinction cannot be held too rigorously, if allegory tends to be oriented toward the past, toward first things, and toward the repetition of first things across the gap of a temporal division, parable tends to be oriented toward the future, toward last things, toward the mysteries of the kingdom of heaven and how to get there. Parable tends to express what Paul at the end of Romans, in echo of Matthew, calls "the revelation of the mystery, which was kept secret since the world began, but now is made manifest" (Romans 16:25–26). Parable, one can see, has at least this in common with apocalypse: it too is an act of unveiling.

What might it mean to speak of *Heart of Darkness* as parabolic in form? Here it is necessary to turn again to that definition by the primary narrator of *Heart of Darkness* of the difference between Marlow's tales and the tales of ordinary seamen. This passage has often been commented on, quite recently, for example, by Ian Watt in his magisterial *Conrad in the Nineteenth Century*.[2] Watt's discussion of *Heart of Darkness* seems also the definitive placing of that novel in the historical context of the parabolic story it tells. That context is nineteenth-century world-dominating European imperialism, specifically the conquest and exploitation of western Africa and the accompanying murder of large numbers of Africans. Watt's book, along with work by Frederick Karl, Norman Sherry, and other biographers, tells us all that is likely to be learned of Conrad's actual experience in the Congo, as well as of the historical originals of Kurtz, the particolored Harlequin-garbed Russian, and other characters in the novel. If parables are characteristically grounded in representations of realistic or historical truth, *Heart of Darkness* admirably fulfills this requirement of parable.

My contention is that *Heart of Darkness* fits, in its own way, the definitions of both parable and apocalypse, and that much illumination is shed on it by interpreting it in the light of these generic classifications. As Marlow says of his experience in the heart of darkness: "It was sombre enough too—... not very clear either. No. Not very clear. And yet it seemed to throw a kind of light" (48). A narrative that sheds light, that penetrates darkness, that clarifies

---

2. Ian Watt, *Conrad in the Nineteenth Century* (Berkeley: University of California Press, 1979), 180. [Editors].

and illuminates—this is one definition of that mode of discourse called apocalyptic, but it might also serve to define the work of criticism or interpretation. All criticism claims to be enlightenment, *Aufklärung*.

Conrad's narrator distinguishes between two different ways in which a narrative may be related to its meaning:

> The yarns of seamen have an effective simplicity, the whole meaning of which lies within the shell of a cracked nut. But, as has been said, Marlow was not typical (if his propensity to spin yarns be excepted) and to him the meaning of an episode was not inside like a kernel but outside [*MS*: outside in the unseen], enveloping the tale which brought it out only as a glow brings out a haze, in the likeness of one of these misty halos that, sometimes, are made visible by the spectral illumination of moonshine. (45)

The narrator's distinction is made in terms of two figures, two versions of the relation of inside to outside, outside to inside. The hermeneutics of parable is presented here parabolically, according to a deep and unavoidable necessity. The meanings of the stories of most seamen, says the narrator, are inside the narration like the kernel of a cracked nut. I take it the narrator means the meanings of such stories are easily expressed, detachable from the stories and open to paraphrase in other terms, as when one draws an obvious moral: "Crime doesn't pay," or "Honesty is the best policy," or "The truth will out," or "Love conquers all." The figure of the cracked nut suggests that the story itself, its characters and narrative details, are the inedible shell which must be removed and discarded so the meaning of the story may be assimilated. This relation of the story to its meaning is a particular version of the relation of container to thing contained. The substitution of contained for container, in this case meaning for story, is one version of that figure called in classical rhetoric synecdoche, but this is a metonymic rather than a metaphorical synecdoche. The meaning is adjacent to the story, contained within it as nut within shell, but the meaning has no intrinsic similarity or kinship to the story. The same meaning could be expressed as well in other terms. Its relation to the story that contains it is purely extrinsic or contingent. The one happens to touch the other, as shell surrounds nut, or as shrine case its iconic image.

It is far otherwise with Marlow's stories. Their meaning is outside, not in. It envelops the tale rather than being enveloped by it. The relation of container and thing contained is reversed. The meaning now contains the tale. Moreover, perhaps because of that enveloping containment, or perhaps for more obscure reasons, the relation of the tale to its meaning is no longer that of dissimilarity and contingency. The tale is the necessary agency of the bringing into the open or revelation of that particular meaning. It is not so much that the meaning is like the tale. It is not. But the tale is in preordained correspondence to or in resonance with the meaning. The tale magically brings the "unseen" meaning out and makes it visible.

Conrad has the narrator express this subtle concept of parabolic narration according to the parabolic "likeness" of a certain atmospheric phenomenon. "Likeness": the word is a homonym of the German *Gleichnis*. Both are terms for figure or parable. The meaning of a parable does not appear as such. It appears in the "spectral" "likeness" of the story that reveals it, or rather, it appears in the likeness of an exterior light surrounding the story, just as the narrator's theory of parable appears not as such but in the "likeness" of the figure he proposes. The figure is supposed to illuminate the reader, give him insight into that of which the figure is the phantasmal likeness. The figure does double duty, both as a figure for the way Marlow's stories express their meaning and as a figure for itself, so to speak, that is, as a figure for its own mode of working. This is according to a mind-twisting torsion of the figure back on itself that is a regular feature of such figures of figuration, parables of parable, or stories about storytelling. The figure both illuminates its own workings and at the same time obscures or undermines it, since a figure of a figure is an absurdity, or, as Wallace Stevens puts it, there is no such thing as a metaphor of a metaphor. What was the figurative vehicle of the first metaphor automatically becomes the literal tenor of the second metaphor.

Let us look more closely at the exact terms of the metaphor Conrad's narrator proposes. To Marlow, the narrator says, "the meaning of an episode was not inside like a kernel but outside, enveloping the tale which brought it out only as a glow brings out a haze, in the likeness of one of these misty halos that, sometimes, are made visible by the spectral illumination of moonshine." The first simile here ("as a glow") is doubled by a second, similitude of a similitude ("in the likeness of . . ."). The "haze" is there all around on a dark night, but, like the meaning of one of Marlow's tales, it is invisible, inaudible, intangible in itself, like the darkness, or like that "something great and invincible" Marlow is aware of in the African wilderness, something "like evil or truth, waiting patiently for the passing away of this fantastic invasion" (65), or like the climactic name for that truth, the enveloping meaning of the tale, "the horror," those last words of Kurtz that seem all around in the gathering darkness when Marlow makes his visit to Kurtz's Intended and tells his lie: "The dusk was repeating them in a persistent whisper all around us, in a whisper that seemed to swell menacingly like the first whisper of a rising wind. 'The horror! The horror!'" (125).

The working of Conrad's figure is much more complex than perhaps it at first appears, both in itself and in the context of the fine grain of the texture of language in *Heart of Darkness* as a whole, as well as in the context of the traditional complex of figures, narrative motifs, and concepts to which it somewhat obscurely alludes. The atmospheric phenomenon that Conrad uses as the vehicle of his parabolic metaphor is a perfectly real one, universally experienced. It is as referential and as widely known as the facts of farming Jesus uses in the parable of the sower. If you sow your seed on stony ground it will not be likely to sprout. An otherwise invisible mist or haze at night will show up as a halo around the moon. As in the case of Jesus' parable of the sower, Conrad uses his realistic and almost universally known facts as the means of expressing indirectly another truth less visible and less widely known, just as the narrative of *Heart of Darkness* as a whole is based on the facts of history and on the facts of Conrad's life but uses these to express something transhistorical and transpersonal, the evasive and elusive "truth" underlying both historical and personal experience.

Both Jesus' parable of the sower and Conrad's parable of the moonshine in the mist, curiously enough, have to do with their own efficacy, that is, with the efficacy of parable. Both are posited on their own necessary failure. Jesus' parable of the sower will give more only to those who already have and will take away from those who have not even what they have. If you can understand the parable you do not need it. If you need it you cannot possibly understand it. You are stony ground on which the seed of the word falls unavailing. Your eyes and ears are closed, even though the function of parables is to open the eyes and ears of the multitude to the mysteries of the kingdom of heaven. In the same way, Conrad, in a famous passage in the preface to *The Nigger of the "Narcissus,"* tells his readers, "My task which I am trying to achieve is, by the power of the written word, to make you hear, to make you feel—it is, before all, to make you *see*" [*NN* xiv]. No reader of Conrad can doubt that he means to make the reader see not only the vivid facts of the story he tells but the evasive truth behind them, of which they are the obscure revelation, what Conrad calls, a bit beyond the famous phrase from the preface just quoted, "that glimpse of truth of which you have forgotten to ask" [*NN* xiv]. To see the facts, out there in the sunlight, is also to see the dark truth that lies behind them. All Conrad's work turns on this double paradox, first the paradox of the two senses of seeing, seeing as physical vision and seeing as seeing through, as penetrating to or unveiling the hidden invisible truth, and second the paradox of seeing the darkness in terms of the light. Nor can the careful reader of Conrad doubt that in Conrad's case too, as in the case of the Jesus of the parable of the sower, the goal of tearing the veil of familiarity from the world and making us *see* cannot be accomplished. If we see the darkness already we do not need *Heart of Darkness*. If we do not see it, reading *Heart of Darkness* or even hearing Marlow tell it will not help us. We shall remain among those who "seeing see not; and hearing they hear not, neither do they understand." Marlow makes this clear in an extraordinary passage in *Heart of Darkness,* one of those places in which the reader is returned to the primary scene of narration on board the *Nellie.* Marlow is explaining the first lie he told for Kurtz, his prevarication misleading the bricklayer at the Central Station into believing he (Marlow) has great power back home:

"I became in an instant as much of a pretence as the rest of the bewitched pilgrims. This simply because I had a notion it somehow would be of help to that Kurtz whom at the time I did not see—you understand. He was just a word for me. I did not see the man in the name any more than you do. Do you see him? Do you see the story? Do you see anything? It seems to me I am trying to tell you a dream—making a vain attempt—because no relation of a dream can convey the dream-sensation, that commingling of absurdity, surprise and bewilderment in a tremor of struggling revolt, that notion of being captured by the incredible which is of the very essence of dreams. . . ."

He was silent for a while.

"No, it is impossible; it is impossible to convey the life-sensation of any given epoch of one's existence—that which makes its truth, its meaning—its subtle and penetrating essence. It is impossible. We live, as we dream—alone. . . ."

He paused again as if reflecting, then added—

"Of course in this you fellows see more than I could then. You see me, whom you know."

It had become so pitch-dark that we listeners could hardly see one another. For a long time already he, sitting apart, had been no more to us than a voice. There was not a word from anybody. The others might have been asleep but I was awake, I listened, I listened on the watch for the sentence, for the word that would give me the clue to the faint uneasiness inspired by this narrative that seemed to shape itself without human lips in the heavy night-air of the river. (69–70)

The denial of the possibility of making the reader see by means of literature is made here through a series of moves, each one ironically going beyond and undermining the one before. When this passage is set against the one about the moonshine, the two together bring out into the open, like a halo in the mist, the way *Heart of Darkness* is posited on the impossibility of achieving its goal of revelation, or, to put this another way, the way it is a revelation of the impossibility of revelation.

In Conrad's parable of the moonshine, the moon shines already with reflected and secondary light. Its light is reflected from the primary light of that sun which is almost never mentioned as such in *Heart of Darkness*. The sun is only present in the glitter of its reflection from this or that object, for example, the surface of that river which, like the white place of the unexplored Congo on the map, fascinates Marlow like a snake. In one passage it is moonlight, already reflected light, which is reflected again from the river: "The moon had spread over everything a thin layer of silver—over the rank grass, over the mud, upon the wall of matted vegetation standing higher than the wall of a temple, over the great river I could see through a sombre gap glittering, glittering as it flowed broadly by without a murmur" (69). In the case of the parable of the moonshine too that halo brought out in the mist is twice-reflected light. The story, according to Conrad's analogy, the facts that may be named and seen, is the moonlight, while the halo brought out around the moon by the reflection of the moonlight from the diffused, otherwise invisible droplets of the mist, is the meaning of the tale, or rather, the meaning of the tale is the darkness which is made visible by that halo of twice-reflected light. But of course the halo does nothing of the sort. It only makes visible more light. What can be seen is only what can be seen. In the end this is always only more light, direct or reflected. The darkness is in principle invisible and remains invisible. All that can be said is that the halo gives the spectator indirect knowledge that the darkness is there. The glow brings out the haze, the story brings out its meaning, by magically generating knowledge that something is there, the haze in one case, the meaning of the story, inarticulate and impossible to be articulated, in any direct way at least, in the other. The expression of the meaning of the story is never the plain statement of that meaning but is always no more than a parabolic "likeness" of the meaning, as the haze is brought out "in the likeness of one of these misty halos that, sometimes, are made visible by the spectral illumination of moonshine."

In the passage in which Marlow makes explicit his sense of the impossibility of his enterprise he says to his auditors on the *Nellie* first that he did not see Kurtz in his name any more than they do. The auditors of any story are forced to see everything of the story "in its name," since a story is made of nothing but names and their adjacent words. There is nothing to see literally in any story except the words on the page, the movement of the lips of the teller. Unlike Marlow, his listeners never have a chance to see or experience directly the man behind the name. The reader, if he happens at this moment to think of it (and the passage is clearly an invitation to such thinking, an invocation of it), is in exactly the same situation as that of Marlow's auditors, only worse. When Marlow appeals to his auditors Conrad is by a kind of ventriloquism appealing to his readers: "Do you see him? Do you see the story? Do you see anything? It seems to me I am trying to tell you a dream—making a vain attempt—" Conrad speaks through Marlow to us. The reader too can reach the truth behind the story only through names, never through any direct perception or experience. In the reader's case it is not even names proffered by a living man before him, only names coldly and impersonally printed on the pages of the book he holds in his hand. Even if the reader goes behind the fiction to the historical reality on which it is based, as Ian Watt and others have done, he or she will only confront more words on more pages, Conrad's letters or the historical records of the conquest and exploitation of the Congo. The situation of the auditors even of a living speaker, Marlow says, is scarcely better, since what a story must convey through names and other words is not the fact but the "life-sensation" behind the fact "which makes its truth, its meaning—its subtle and penetrating essence." This is once more the halo around the moon, the meaning enveloping the tale. This meaning is as impossible to convey by way of the life-facts that may be named as the "dream-sensation" is able to be conveyed through a relation of the bare facts of the dream. Anyone knows this who has ever tried to tell another person his dream and has found how lame and flat, or how laughable, it sounds, since "no relation of a dream can convey the dream-sensation." According to Marlow's metaphor or proportional analogy: as the facts of a dream are to the "dream-sensation," so the facts of a life are to the "life-sensation." Conrad makes an absolute distinction between experience and the interpretation of written or spoken signs. The sensation may only be experienced directly and may by no means, oral or written, be communicated to another: "We live, as we dream—alone."

Nevertheless, Marlow tells his auditors, they have one direct or experimental access to the truth enveloping the story: "You fellows see more than I could then. You see me, whom you know." There is a double or even triple irony in this. To see the man who has had the experience is to have an avenue to the experience for which the man speaks, to which he bears witness. Marlow's auditors see more than he could then, that is, before his actual encounter with Kurtz. Ironically, the witness cannot bear witness for himself. He cannot see himself or cannot see through himself or by means of himself, in spite of, or in contradiction of, Conrad's (or Marlow's) assertion a few paragraphs later that work is "the chance to find yourself—your own reality—for yourself—not for others—what no other man can ever know. They can only see the mere show—and never can tell what it really means" (72). Though each man can only experience his own reality, his own truth, the paradox involved here seems to run, he can only experience it through another or by means of another as witness to a truth deeper in, behind the other. Marlow's auditors can only learn indirectly, through Marlow, whom they see. They therefore know more than he did. Marlow could only learn through Kurtz, when he finally encountered him face to face. The reader of *Heart of Darkness* learns through the relation of the primary narrator, who learned through Marlow, who learned through Kurtz. This proliferating relay of witnesses, one behind another, each revealing another truth further in which turns out to be only another witness corresponds to the narrative form of *Heart of Darkness*. The novel is a sequence of episodes, each structured according to the model of appearances, signs, which are also obstacles or veils. Each veil must be lifted to reveal a truth behind which always turns out to be another episode, another witness, another veil to be lifted in its turn. Each such episode is a "fact, dazzling, to be seen, like the foam on the depths of the sea, like a ripple on an unfathomable enigma" (86), the fact for example that though the cannibal Africans on Marlow's steamer were starving, they did not eat the white men. But behind each enigmatic fact is only another fact. The relay of witness behind witness behind witness, voice behind voice behind voice, each speaking in ventriloquism through the one next farther out, is a genre of the apocalypse. The book of Revelation, in the Bible, is the paradigmatic example in our tradition, though of course it is by no means the only example. In Revelation God speaks through Jesus, who speaks through a messenger angel, who speaks through John of Patmos, who speaks to us.

There is another reason beyond the necessities of revelation for this structure. The truth behind the last witness, behind Kurtz for example in *Heart of Darkness,* is, no one can doubt it, death, "the horror"; or, to put this another way, "death" is another name for what Kurtz names "the horror." No man can confront that truth face to face and survive. Death or the horror can only be experienced indirectly, by way of the face and voice of another. The relay of witnesses both reveals death and, luckily, hides it. As Marlow says, "the inner truth is hidden—luckily, luckily" (77). This is another regular feature of the genre of the apocalypse. The word "apocalypse" means "unveiling," "revelation," but what the apocalypse unveils is not the truth of the end of the world which it announces, but the act of unveiling. The unveiling unveils unveiling. It leaves its readers, auditors, witnesses, as far as ever from the always not quite yet of the imminent revelation—luckily. Marlow says it was not his own near-death on the way home down the river, "not my own extremity I remember best," but Kurtz's "extremity that I seem to have lived through." Then he adds, "True, he had made that last stride, had stepped over the edge while I had been permitted to draw back my hesitating foot. And perhaps in this is the whole difference; perhaps all wisdom and all truth and all sincerity are just compressed into that inappreciable moment of time in which we step over the threshold of the Invisible. Perhaps" (118). Marlow, like Orpheus returning without Eurydice from the land of the dead, comes back to civilization with nothing, nothing to witness to, nothing to reveal but the process of unveiling that makes up the whole of the narration of *Heart of Darkness*. Marlow did not go far enough into the darkness, but if he had, like Kurtz he could not have come back. All the reader gets is Marlow's report of Kurtz's last words, that and a description of the look on Kurtz's face: "It was as though a veil had been rent. I saw on that ivory visage the expression of sombre pride, of ruthless power, of craven terror—of intense and hopeless despair" (117).

I have said there is a triple irony in what Marlow says when he breaks his narration to address his auditors directly. If the first irony is the fact that the auditors see more than Marlow did because they see Marlow, whom they know, or as Conrad elsewhere puts this, "the onlookers see most of the game," the second irony is that we readers of the novel, if we happen to think at this moment of our own situation, realize that we must therefore see nothing. We see and can see no living witness, not the primary narrator, not Marlow, not Kurtz, not even Conrad himself, who is now only a voice from the dead for us. We see only the lifeless words on the page, the names Marlow, Kurtz, and so on, Conrad's name on the title page. By Marlow's own account that is not enough. Seeing only happens by direct experience, and no act of reading is direct experience. The book's claim to give the reader access to the dark truth behind appearance is withdrawn by the terms in which it is proffered.

The third irony in this relay of ironies behind ironies is that Marlow's auditors of course do not see Marlow either. It is too dark. They hear only his disembodied voice. "It had become so pitch-dark," says the narrator, "that we listeners could hardly see one another. For a long time already he, sitting apart, had been no more to us than a voice." Marlow's narrative does not seem to be spoken by a living incarnate witness, there before his auditors in the flesh. It is a "narrative that seemed to shape itself without human lips in the heavy night-air of the river" (70). This voice can be linked to no individual speaker or writer as the ultimate source of its message, not to Marlow, nor to Kurtz, nor to the first narrator, nor even to Conrad himself. The voice is spoken by no one to no one. It always comes from another, from the other of any identifiable speaker or writer. It traverses all these voices as what speaks through them. It gives them authority and at the time dispossesses them, deprives them of authority, since they only speak with the delegated authority of another. As Marlow says of the voice of Kurtz and of all the other voices, they are what remain as a dying unanimous and anonymous drone or clang that exceeds any single identifiable voice and in the end is spoken by no one: "A voice. He was very little more than a voice. And I heard—him—it—

this voice—other voices—all of them were so little more than voices—and the memory of this time itself lingers around me impalpable like a dying vibration of one immense jabber, silly, atrocious, sordid, savage or simply mean, without any kind of sense. Voices, voices—. . ." (93).

For the reader too *Heart of Darkness* lingers in the mind or memory chiefly as a cacophony of dissonant voices. It is as though the story were spoken or written not by an identifiable narrator but directly by the darkness itself, just as Kurtz's last words seem whispered by the circumambient dusky air when Marlow makes his visit to Kurtz's Intended, and just as Kurtz himself presents himself to Marlow as a voice, a voice which exceeds Kurtz and seems to speak from beyond him: "Kurtz discoursed. A voice! A voice! It rang deep to the very last. It survived his strength to hide in the magnificent folds of eloquence the barren darkness of his heart" (115). Kurtz has "the gift of expression, the bewildering, the illuminating, the most exalted and the most contemptible, the pulsating stream of light or the deceitful flow from the heart of an impenetrable darkness" (92). Kurtz has intended to use his eloquence as a means of wringing the heart of the wilderness [116]; but "the wilderness had found him out early and had taken on him a terrible vengeance for the fantastic invasion" (104). The direction of the flow of language reverses. It flows from the darkness instead of toward it. Kurtz is "hollow at the core" (104), and so the wilderness can speak through him, use him so to speak as a ventriloquist's dummy through which its terrible messages may be broadcast to the world: "Exterminate all the brutes!" "The horror!" (95, 118). The speaker too is spoken through. Kurtz's disembodied voice, or the voice behind voice behind voice of the narrators, or that "roaring chorus of articulated, rapid, breathless utterance" (114) shouted by the natives on the bank, when Kurtz is taken on board the steamer—these are in the end no more direct a testimony of the truth than the words on the page as Conrad wrote them. The absence of a visible speaker of Marlow's words and the emphasis on the way Kurtz is a disembodied voice function as indirect expressions of the fact that *Heart of Darkness* itself is words without person, words which cannot be traced back to any single personality. This is once more confirmation of my claim that *Heart of Darkness* belongs to the genre of the apocalypse. This novel is an apocalyptic parable or a parabolic apocalypse. The apocalypse is after all a written not an oral genre, and it turns on the "Come" spoken or written always by someone other than the one who seems to utter or write it.[3]

---

3. See Jacques Derrida, "D'un ton apocalyptique adopté naguère en philosophie," in *Les Fins de l'homme*, ed. Philippe Lacoue-Labarthe and Jean-Luc Nancy (Paris: Flammarion, 1981), 445–79, especially 468ff. The essay has recently been translated by John P. Learey Jr. and published in the 1982 number of *Semeia* (62–97).

A full exploration of the way *Heart of Darkness* is an apocalypse would need to be put under the multiple aegis of the converging figures of irony, antithesis, catachresis, synecdoche, aletheia, and prosopopoeia. Irony is a name for the pervasive tone of Marlow's narration, which undercuts as it affirms. Antithesis identifies the division of what is presented in the story in terms of seemingly firm oppositions which always ultimately break down. Catachresis is the proper name for a parabolic revelation of the darkness by means of visible figures that do not substitute for any possible literal expression of that darkness. Synecdoche is the name for the questionable relation of similarity between the visible sign, the skin of the surface, the foam on the sea, and what lies behind it, the pulsating heart of darkness, the black depths of the sea. Unveiling or *aletheia* labels that endless process of apocalyptic revelation which never quite comes off. The revelation is always future. We must always go on watching and waiting for it, as the primary narrator remains wakeful, on the watch for the decisive clue in Marlow's narration. Personification, finally, is a name for the consistent presentation of the darkness in terms of the trope prosopopoeia. The reader encounters the darkness always as some kind of living creature with a heart, ultimately as a woman who unmans all those male questors who try to dominate her. This pervasive personification is more dramatically embodied in the native woman, Kurtz's mistress: "the immense wilderness, the colossal body of the fecund and mysterious life seemed to look at her, pensive, as though it had been looking at the image of its own tenebrous and passionate soul" (107).

Heart of Darkness is perhaps most explicitly apocalyptic in announcing the end, the end of Western civilization, or of Western imperialism, the reversal of idealism into savagery. As is always the case with apocalypses, the end is announced as something always imminent, never quite yet. Apocalypse is never now. The novel sets women, who are out of it, against men, who can live with the facts and have a belief to protect them against the darkness. Men can breathe dead hippo and not be contaminated. Male practicality and idealism reverse, however. They turn into their opposites because they are hollow at the core. They are vulnerable to the horror. They *are* the horror. The idealistic suppression of savage customs becomes, "Exterminate all the brutes!" Male idealism is the same thing as the extermination of the brutes. The suppression of savage customs is the extermination of the brutes. This is not just wordplay but actual fact, as the history of the white man's conquest of the world has abundantly demonstrated. This conquest means the end of the brutes, but it means also, in Conrad's view of history, the end of Western civilization, with its ideals of progress, enlightenment, and reason, its goal of carrying the torch of civilization into wilderness and wringing the heart of the darkness. Or it is the imminence of that end which has never quite come as long as there is someone to speak or write of it.

I claim to have demonstrated that *Heart of Darkness* is not only parabolic but also apocalyptic. It fits that strange genre of the apocalyptic text, the sort of text that promises an ultimate revelation without giving it, and says always "Come" and "Wait." But there is an extra twist given to the paradigmatic form of the apocalypse in *Heart of Darkness.* The *Aufklärung* or enlightenment in this case is of the fact that the darkness can never be enlightened. The darkness enters into every gesture of enlightenment to enfeeble it, hollow it out, to corrupt it and thereby to turn its reason into unreason, its pretense of shedding light into more darkness. Marlow as narrator is in complicity with this reversal in the act of identifying it in others. He too claims, like the characteristic writer of an apocalypse, to know something no one else knows and to be qualified on that basis to judge and enlighten them. "I found myself back in the sepulchral city," says Marlow of his return from the Congo, "resenting the sight of people hurrying through the streets to filch a little money from each other, to devour their infamous cookery, to gulp their unwholesome beer, to dream their insignificant and silly dreams. They trespassed upon my thoughts. They were intruders whose knowledge of life was to me an irritating pretence because I felt so sure they could not possibly know the things I knew" (118–19).

The consistent tone of Marlow's narration is ironical. Irony is truth telling or a means of truth telling, of unveiling. At the same time it is a defense against the truth. This doubleness makes it, though it seems so coolly reasonable, another mode of unreason, the unreason of a fundamental undecidability. If irony is a defense, it is also inadvertently a means of participation. Though Marlow says, "I have a voice too, and for good or evil mine is the speech that cannot be silenced" (37), as though his speaking were a cloak against the darkness, he too, in speaking ironically, becomes, like Kurtz, one of those speaking tubes or relay stations through whom the darkness speaks. As theorists of irony from Friedrich Schlegel and Søren Kierkegaard to Paul de Man have argued, irony is the one trope that cannot be mastered or used as an instrument of mastery. Any ironic statement is essentially indeterminate or undecidable in meaning. The man who attempts to say one thing while clearly meaning another ends up by saying the first thing too, in spite of himself. One irony leads to another. The ironies proliferate into a great crowd of little conflicting ironies. It is impossible to know in just what tone of voice one should read one of Marlow's sardonic ironies. Each is uttered simultaneously in innumerable conflicting tones going all the way from the lightest and most comical to the darkest, most somber and tragic. It is impossible to decide exactly which quality of voice should be allowed to predominate over the others. Try reading a given passage aloud and you will see this. Marlow's description of the clamor of native voices on the shore or of the murmur of all those voices he remembers from that time in his life also functions as an appropriate displaced description of the indeterminations of tone and meaning in his own discourse. Marlow's irony makes his speech in its own way another version of that multiple cacophonous and deceitful voice flowing from the heart of darkness, "a complaining clamour, modulated in savage discords," or a "tumultuous and mournful uproar," another version of that "one immense jabber, silly, atrocious, sordid, savage or simply mean, without any kind of sense," not a voice, but "voices" (83, 93). In this inextricable tangle of voices and voices speaking within voices, Marlow's narration fulfills, no doubt without deliberate intent on Conrad's part, one of the primary laws of the genre of the apocalypse.

The final fold in this folding in of complicities in these ambiguous acts of unveiling is my own complicity as demystifying commentator. Behind or before Marlow is Conrad, and before or behind him stands the reader or critic. My commentary unveils a lack of decisive unveiling in *Heart of Darkness*. I have attempted to perform an act of generic classification, with all the covert violence and unreason of that act, since no work is wholly commensurate with the boundaries of any genre. By unveiling the lack of unveiling in *Heart of Darkness*, I have become another witness in my turn, as much guilty as any other in the line of witnesses of covering over while claiming to illuminate. My *Aufklärung* too has been of the continuing impenetrability of Conrad's *Heart of Darkness*.

CHAPTER 4

Joseph Conrad

Should We Read Heart of Darkness?

> The inaccessible incites from its place of hiding.
> —JACQUES DERRIDA

SHOULD WE READ *Heart of Darkness*? May we read it? Must we read it? Or, on the contrary, ought we not to read it or allow our students and the public in general to read it? Should every copy be taken from all the shelves and burned? What or who gives us the authority to make a decision about that? Who is this "we" in whose name I speak? What community forms that "we"? Nothing could be more problematic than the bland appeal to some homogeneous authoritative body, say professors of English literature everywhere, capable of deciding collectively whether "we" should read *Heart of Darkness*. By "read" I mean not just run the words passively through the mind's ear, but perform a reading in the strong sense, an active responsible response that renders justice to a book by generating more language in its turn, the language of attestation, even though that language may remain silent or implicit. Such a response testifies that the one who responds has been changed by the reading. Part of the problem, as you can see, is that it is impossible to decide authoritatively whether or not we should read *Heart of Darkness* without reading it in that strong sense. By then it is too late. I have already read it, been affected by it, and passed my judgment, perhaps recorded that judgment for others to read. Which of us, however, would or should want to take someone else's word for what is in a book? Each must read again in his or her turn and bear witness to that reading in his or her turn. In that aphorism about which Jacques

Derrida has had so much to say, Paul Celan says, "Niemand / zeugt für den / Zeugen (Nobody / bears witness for the / witness)."[1] This might be altered to say, "No one can do your reading for you." Each must read for himself or herself and testify anew.

This structure is inscribed in *Heart of Darkness* itself. The primary narrator bears witness through exact citation to what he heard Marlow say one night on the deck of the cruising yawl *Nellie*, as he and the other men, the Lawyer, the Accountant, the Director of Companies, representatives of advanced capitalism and imperialism, waited for the tide to turn so they could float down the Thames and out to sea, presumably on a pleasure cruise.[2] They have enough wealth and leisure to take time off to do as an aesthetic end in itself what Marlow has done for pay as a professional seaman. The profession of the primary, framing narrator is never specified. He cites with what the reader is led to believe is conscientious and meticulous accuracy just what Marlow said. What Marlow said, put within quotation marks throughout, is a story, the recounting of and accounting for what he calls an "experience" that "seemed somehow to throw a kind of light on everything about me—and into my thoughts. It was sombre enough too—and pitiful—not extraordinary in any way—not very clear either. No, not very clear. And yet it seemed to throw a kind of light" (48). That recounting and accounting centers on an attempt to "render justice," as Marlow puts it (126), to Kurtz, the man he meets at "the furthest point of navigation and the culminating point of my experience" (47–48). What Marlow says at the beginning is also an implicit promise to his

---

This essay originally appeared in *Others* (Princeton, NJ: Princeton University Press, 2001), 104–36.

1. Paul Celan, "Aschenglorie (Ashglory)," in *Breathturn*, trans. Pierre Joris, bilingual ed. (Los Angeles: Sun & Moon Press, 1995), 178–79.

2. The "original" (but what is more problematic than this concept of an original base for a fictional work?) of the framing scene was, if Ford Madox Ford is to be believed, Conrad's residence in Stanford-le-Hope in Essex from September 1896 to September 1898. There he knew various businessmen who did indeed take weekend cruises on a yawl. "He was still quivering," says Ford, "with his attempt, with the aid of the Director, the Lawyer, and the Accountant, to float a diamond mine in South Africa. For Conrad had his adventures of that sort, too—adventures ending naturally in frustration.... While waiting for that financial flotation to mature, he floated physically during week-ends in the company of those financiers on the bosom of that tranquil waterway [the Thames]." *Portraits from Life* (Boston: Houghton Mifflin, 1937), 60. "To float a diamond mine in South Africa"! Nothing is said about this in the story itself, and Marlow, the reader must always remember, must be kept strictly separate from Conrad himself, as separate as the narrator of "The Secret Sharer" must be kept from his ghostly double. Ford's testimony, however, shows that Conrad himself was complicit, or wanted to be complicit, if he could have raised the money for it, in an exploitative imperialist enterprise that is not so different from Leopold II's merciless and murderous exploitation of the Congo or from Kurtz's raiding the country for ivory. He appears momentarily to have fancied himself a miniature Cecil Rhodes.

listeners and to us as readers. He promises that he will pass on to them and to us the illumination he has received.

The observant reader will note that the language Conrad gives Marlow mixes constative and performative dimensions. On the one hand, Marlow's experience shed a kind of light on everything. It made him "see" in the double meaning Conrad habitually gives to "see," as does everyday language: see as visual seeing and see as understanding, acquiring new knowledge. On the other hand, Marlow's experience conferred an obligation that can only be fulfilled by performative language, by "rendering justice" (126) or "remaining loyal" (118). The performative and constative dimensions of any "accounting" or "recounting" are, necessarily, intertwined, as they are in any speech act. *Heart of Darkness,* however, is unusually explicit in its emphasis on the performative side of Marlow's language, the way it is a specific kind of speech act, namely, an attestation. "I have remained loyal to Kurtz," says Marlow, "to the last, and even beyond" (118). "I did not betray Mr Kurtz—it was ordered I should never betray him—it was written I should be loyal to the nightmare of my choice" (111). Who did the "ordering" or the "writing" here is not said explicitly. Presumably Marlow means it was written down in the book of his Fate, a sufficiently vague notion. It was because it was to be. Actually it was written down in the book Conrad made up about Marlow, as the reader may happen to reflect. Or rather, as Marlow confesses in his account of the last episode, his visit to Kurtz's "Intended" (after Kurtz has died on the journey back down the African river and Marlow has returned to the city that "always makes [him] think of a whited sepulcre" [50]), he has by telling his lie to the Intended failed to render full justice to Kurtz: "It seemed to me that the house would collapse before I could escape, that the heavens would fall upon my head. But nothing happened. The heavens do not fall for such a trifle. Would they have fallen I wonder, if I had rendered Kurtz that justice which was his due? Hadn't he said he wanted only justice?" (126). Kurtz had indeed said to Marlow just that: "I want no more than justice" (122).

Earlier Marlow had said, "I laid the ghost of his gifts at last with a lie" (64). Marlow's lie was to tell the Intended, with her soul as pure as a cliff of crystal, with her candid brow, that Kurtz's last words were her name, whereas his actual last words were, in "a cry that was no more than a breath," "The horror! The horror!" (117). Is Marlow's lie justified? Can we exonerate Marlow for it? Was this lie in any sense a way of rendering Kurtz justice? Marlow has told us he abhors lies, that they have a taint of mortality about them: "You know I hate, detest and can't bear a lie," he says, "not because I am straighter than the rest of us but simply because it appalls me. There is a taint of death, a flavour of mortality in lies—which is exactly what I hate and detest in the world—

what I want to forget. It makes me miserable and sick like biting something rotten would do" (62). To say a lie has a taint of death is odd. It suggests that only by telling the truth can we hold off death, though Marlow says just the reverse concerning his lie. It has laid the ghost of Kurtz's gifts, the greatest of which was the gift of speech, "the gift of expression, the bewildering, the illuminating, the most exalted and the most contemptible, the pulsating stream of light or the deceitful flow from the heart of an impenetrable darkness" (92).

A lie puts us in complicity with death, at the mercy of death. A lie lets death into the human community. This is a somewhat hyperbolic version of the repudiation of the right to lie in Immanuel Kant's opuscule, "On the Presumed Right to Lie Out of Love for Humanity." A lie is never justified, says Kant, even to save someone's life, since any lie radically threatens human society. The latter depends on strict truth-telling in every circumstance, even the most extreme. "Truth" is a key word, though an exceedingly ambiguous one, in Marlow's narration in *Heart of Darkness*. His whole story is put under the aegis of giving a true account of his experience. That obligation is passed on to the primary narrator and then on to you and me as readers. The promise to give faithful testimony is, like promises in general, always messianic. It has to do with death and the last days, with the sort of promise an Apocalypse makes. Even so routine a promise as the one made by the signatory of a mortgage note invokes death, as the etymology of "mortgage" indicates. To sign a mortgage note is to engage one's life unto death, to put one's death on the line. The great exemplary apocalypse in our tradition, the last book of the Christian Bible, *Revelations,* ends with the promise and invocation of an imminent unveiling that always remains future, never quite yet here and now: "He which testifieth these things saith, Surely I come quickly. Amen. Even so, come, Lord Jesus" (Revelation 22:20).

Marlow is in the position of someone who survives the death of another. In Kurtz's end, death and the consequent responsibilities of the survivor enter as central issues in the novel. As Marlow says, "I was to have the care of his memory" (96), just as the Intended's first words to Marlow about Kurtz are "I have survived" (122). Surely the first obligation of the survivor is to tell the truth about the dead. What is peculiar about Marlow's survival of Kurtz is that Kurtz is presented when Marlow finally encounters him as already the survivor of his own death. Kurtz is already the ghost of himself. In that sense he cannot die. This is testified to in the way he survives in Marlow's narration and in the way the dusk still whispers his last words when Marlow returns to Europe and visits Kurtz's "Intended." It is hardly the case that Marlow has laid the ghost of Kurtz's gifts with a lie, since the ghost still walks, even in the room where Marlow tells his lie to the Intended. That ghost, far from being laid, is resurrected, invoked, conjured up, each time *Heart of Darkness* is read.

Perhaps Marlow means no more than that he appeased the Intended's desire to keep Kurtz's eloquence alive by lying about what that eloquence really said and what its source was. It is not Kurtz the spectral survivor and revenant who is buried when Kurtz "dies," but his mere bodily envelope or cadaver: "But I am of course aware that next day the pilgrims buried something in a muddy hole" (117). The chain of obligation begins with Kurtz, who has passed judgment in those words "The horror! The horror!" He "had pronounced a judgment upon the adventures of his soul on this earth. . . . He had summed up—he had judged. 'The horror!' He was a remarkable man. After all, this was the expression of some sort of belief. It had candour, it had conviction, it had a vibrating note of revolt in its whisper, it had the appalling face of a glimpsed truth—the strange commingling of desire and hate" (118). The chain then goes to Marlow, who testifies as survivor for Kurtz, keeping Kurtz alive in his narration, and telling to his auditors on the *Nellie* the truth he had withheld from the Intended. The primary narrator in his turns bears witness to what Marlow said by citing it exactly and by placing it in an exegetical context that is implicitly a reading.

Exact citation, prior to any interpretation, is one of the most important ways to testify or to render justice, as in my citations from Conrad's *Heart of Darkness* here. Each quotation is accompanied by an implicit oath: "I swear to you this is what Conrad really wrote, or at least what Conrad's most authoritative editors attest he wrote."[3] The obligation to render justice is then passed from Conrad's primary narrator to any reader, each one of whom nowadays is Conrad's survivor. From each reader it is demanded once again to do justice to Conrad and to *Heart of Darkness,* to attest to what happens when the book is read—telling the truth, the whole truth, and nothing but the truth.

Bearing witness in an interpretation or reading, for example of *Heart of Darkness,* is a performative speech act, but of a peculiar and even anomalous kind. This kind is not accounted for by J. L. Austin's speech-act theory in *How to Do Things with Words.*[4] A performative interpretation transforms what it interprets. It therefore cannot be fully justified by constative, verifiable evidence, any more than can acts of bearing witness in general. No one bears witness for the witness. That the witness saw what he or she says he or she saw, or that he or she responded in a certain way in an act of reading,

---

3. The original manuscript is in the Beinecke Library at Yale University. The Norton Critical Edition cites some important manuscript passages omitted from the printed version. I shall cite from the Norton edition a few of these in my turn, trusting the Norton editor to have cited accurately.

4. J. L. Austin, *How to Do Things with Words,* ed. J. O. Urmson and Marina Sbisà, 2nd ed. (Oxford: Oxford University Press, 1980).

has to be taken on faith. That is why, in murder cases in the United States for example, the jury is asked to decide not whether the defendant is guilty but whether they believe "beyond a reasonable doubt" that the defendant is guilty. As Jacques Derrida and Werner Hamacher have in different ways affirmed, interpretation in this performative sense, an interpretation that is inaugural, that intervenes to change what is read and to initiate something new, fulfills in a paradoxical way the eleventh of Marx's Theses on Feuerbach: "The philosophers have only *interpreted* the world in various ways; the point, however, is to *change* it."[5] In this case, the interpretation does the changing. It changes the world, in however small a way, by changing once and for all an element of that world that has power to make things happen, in this case a literary text, *Heart of Darkness*.

Nor have Conrad's readers failed to respond to this demand for interpretation. A large secondary literature has sprung up around *Heart of Darkness*. These essays and books of course have a constative dimension. They often provide precious information about Conrad's life, about his experiences in Africa, about late nineteenth-century imperialism, especially about that terrible murderous devastation wrought by King Leopold II of Belgium in the Belgian Congo, as it was then called, about the supposed "originals" of characters in *Heart of Darkness*, and so on. This secondary literature, however, often also has an explicit performative dimension. Conrad's novel is brought before the bar of justice, arraigned, tried, and judged. The critic acts as witness of his or her reading, also as interrogator, prosecuting attorney, jury, and presiding judge. The critic passes judgment and renders justice.

Heart of Darkness has often received a heavy sentence from its critics. It has been condemned, often in angry terms, as racist or sexist, sometimes as both in the same essay. Examples are the influential essay of 1977 by the distinguished Nigerian novelist, Chinua Achebe ("Conrad was a bloody racist"), or an essay of 1989 by Bette London: "Dependent upon unexamined assumptions, themselves culturally suspect, the novel, in its representations of sex and gender, supports dubious cultural claims; it participates in and promotes a racial as well as gender ideology that the narrative represents as transpar-

---

5. See Werner Hamacher, "Lingua Amissa: The Messianism of Commodity-Language and Derrida's Specters of Marx," in *Ghostly Demarcations: A Symposium on Jacques Derrida's "Specters of Marx,"* ed. Michael Sprinker (London: Verso, 1998), 189–91; Jacques Derrida, *Spectres de Marx* (Paris: Galilée, 1993), 89; *Specters of Marx*, trans. Peggy Kamuf (New York: Routledge, 1994), 51. Derrida speaks here of "performative interpretation, that is, of an interpretation that transforms the very thing it interprets," and he observes that this definition of the performative does not fit Austin's definition of a speech act, any more than it fits the orthodox understanding of Marx's eleventh thesis on Feuerbach.

ent and 'self-evident.'"[6] Edward Said's judgment in *Culture and Imperialism*, though giving Conrad his due as a critic of imperialism and recognizing the complexity of doing justice to *Heart of Darkness*, is in the end equally severe in his summing up: "The cultural and ideological evidence that Conrad was wrong in his Eurocentric way is both impressive and rich."[7] These are powerful indictments. If what they say renders justice to *Heart of Darkness*, if their witness may be trusted, it might seem inevitably to follow that the novel should not be read, taught, or written about, except perhaps as an example of something detestable. Nevertheless, according to the paradox I have already mentioned, you could only be sure about this by reading the novel yourself, thereby putting yourself, if these critics are right, in danger of becoming sexist, racist, and Eurocentric yourself. Even so, no one bears witness for the witness, and no one else can do your reading for you.

To pass judgment anew, it is necessary to take the risk and read *Heart of Darkness* for yourself. I shall now try to do that. First, however, I must ask a final question. Suppose I or any other reader or community of readers were to decide that Conrad, or rather *Heart of Darkness*, is indeed racist and sexist. Would it be possible, after passing that verdict, to pardon Conrad or the novel he wrote, to exonerate *Heart of Darkness* in some way, and get him set free, so to speak? To put this another way, would truth in this case lead to reconciliation? To be reconciled is to be able to say, as the Truth and Reconciliation Commission in South Africa has hoped would happen, "I forgive you. I am reconciled with you, though I now know you tortured and murdered my father or mother, husband or wife, brother or sister, or my neighbor, my friend." Though slaves were emancipated in the United States 130 years ago and men given the vote eighty years ago, the United States is still in many ways a racist and sexist country. The sins of the fathers are visited on the children even unto the third generation. One might add that those sins are visited also on the children and the children's children of those whom the fathers have wronged. The United States, like all of Africa in different ways, will take many more generations to become reconciled to its history, to reach anything like the horizon of a more perfect democracy. This is that democracy that is always, as Jacques Derrida says, "to come." Thomas Mann, in "Death in Venice," cites a French proverb, "Tout comprendre c'est tout pardonner. [To understand everything is to forgive everything]."[8] "Death in Venice" power-

---

6. These citations are from the "Critical History" section in Joseph Conrad, *Heart of Darkness*, ed. Ross C. Murfin, 2nd ed. (Boston: Bedford Books, 1996), 107, 109.

7. Edward Said, *Culture and Imperialism* (New York: Alfred A. Knopf, 1993), 30.

8. Thomas Mann, "Death in Venice," in *Death in Venice and Seven Other Stories* (New York: Vintage, 1956), 13.

fully ironizes or puts in question that cheerful enlightenment confidence in the exonerating power of comprehension. It may be that the more knowledge we have the less able we are to pardon, or that pardoning, a speech act of the most exemplary and sovereign kind, has to occur, if it occurs, in the teeth of knowledge. On the one hand, to understand everything is, it may be, to find it almost impossible to forgive. Certainly that is the case with the critics I have mentioned. On the other hand, perhaps a true pardon is only of the unforgivable, as Derrida has been arguing in his recent seminars on "Pardon and Perjury." If it is forgivable it does not need forgiveness. Only the unforgivable requires forgiveness.

The question of forgiveness is inscribed within *Heart of Darkness* in the way Marlow's narrative is an implicit appeal to his listeners on the *Nellie*, and indirectly also to us as readers, to forgive him for his choice of nightmares, for his loyalty to Kurtz. We are also asked, paradoxically, to forgive him for his perjury, for the lie he tells the Intended, an act of disloyalty to Kurtz. Marlow's narrative is a species of confession. A confession is always a demand or prayer for forgiveness. It often reveals more that needs forgiveness than the confessor knows. In this case that might be the presumed racism and sexism of which Marlow (or Conrad) seems unaware. In his confession Marlow makes up for his lie by telling the truth, unless, in a final irony, "The horror!" and the Intended's name (just what that is the reader never learns) come to the same thing, so that Marlow uttered the truth after all, even the first time. That, however, it might be argued, is no excuse, even if for those in the know. Marlow, it could be said, tells the truth obliquely, but the result of his lie is that the Intended lives out the rest of her life within the shadowy confines of an illusion, that is, within a "horror" that she does not even know is a horror. Marlow's lie, "white lie" though it is, is performatively effective because it is believed. Kant would have condemned it for unraveling the social fabric.

Nothing is said about the response of those on board the *Nellie* to Marlow's story. We do not know whether or not they forgive him his lie. The Director of Companies, after Marlow finishes his story, says no more than "We have lost the first of the ebb" (126), meaning that Marlow's story has kept them from leaving when they ought. The primary narrator ends his account by making an observation that might seem to be evidence of the effect of Marlow's story on his way of seeing: "the tranquil waterway leading to the uttermost ends of the earth flowed sombre under an overcast sky—seemed to lead into the heart of an immense darkness" (126). Any further or more explicit passing of judgment is left to the reader. It is up to us—or rather up to me, since reading and bearing witness to what happens in reading are always solitary, lonely acts. This is the case however much such judgments may be performed within the coercive and determining context of codes, conventions, and protocols of reading. Historically and geographically determined ideologies also speak through the solitary reader when he or she sums up and passes judgment, as Kurtz did when he said "The horror! The horror!" or as Marlow did when he said of Kurtz, "He had summed up—he had judged. 'The horror!' He was a remarkable man" (118), or as Achebe did when he said "Conrad was a bloody racist." Nevertheless, each person who passes judgment must take personal responsibility for doing so. He or she must so take responsibility for whatever further consequences that act of reading may have.

The first thing to say in passing judgment on *Heart of Darkness* is that it is a literary work, not history, not a travel book, a memoir, an autobiography, or any other genre but some form of literature. It is a literary work, moreover, belonging to a particular historical time and place. It is, that is, a work of English literature written at the moment of high capitalism and imperialism. This may seem obvious enough, but much criticism forgets this fact or elides it. An example is what the editor of the Norton Critical Edition, Robert Kimbrough, says about the "Backgrounds and Sources" section of the volume. The first part of this, says Kimbrough, "sets the story within its historical context." The second "offers all that Conrad ever biographically recorded concerning his Congo experience, the artistic projection of which is *Heart of Darkness*." The third "reminds us that, autobiographical though it may be, the story was to Conrad a significant, but objective work of art."[9] Kimbrough, the reader can see, wants to have it several ways at once. *Heart of Darkness* is an objective work of art (whatever that means), but it is at the same time embedded in a historical context, the "projection" (whatever that means) of Conrad's "biographical" experience, and it is, after all, "autobiographical." These "backgrounds and sources" invite the reader to measure the novel by its referential accuracy. It is an almost irresistible temptation to do so, especially once you know these background "facts." An example of such yielding is talking about the place where the main events occur as the Congo or about the sepulchral city where Marlow gets his job as Brussels, whereas neither the Congo nor Brussels is anywhere named as such in the novel, while the Thames is named in the third sentence. At the very least such reticence needs to be recognized as a symptom. More radically, it is a signal that the only way to enter the coun-

---

9. Joseph Conrad, *Heart of Darkness*, ed. Robert Kimbrough, Norton critical ed. (New York: W. W. Norton, 1963), 84.

tries where the events of *Heart of Darkness* occur is by reading the novel, not by visiting Belgium or what is now again called the Congo.

Conrad fought a lifelong battle in his letters, prefaces, essays, and overtly autobiographical writing, such as *The Mirror of the Sea* (1906), *A Personal Record* (1912), and *Notes on Life and Letters* (1921), to get his readers and critics to accept that his work is literature, not thinly disguised autobiography or travel literature. I give two examples out of a large number. Arthur Symons, in *Notes on Joseph Conrad: With Some Unpublished Letters* (1925), cites a letter to him from Conrad in which the latter rejects Symons's identification of Conrad with his fictive character, Kurtz: "For the rest I may say that there are certain passages in your article which have surprised me. I did not know that I had 'a heart of darkness' and 'an unlawful soul.' Mr. Kurtz had—and I have not treated him with easy nonchalance."[10] A letter of July 14, 1923, to Richard Curle, responding to Curle's *Times Literary Supplement* review of the recently published Dent Uniform Edition of Conrad's works, complains bitterly of the way Curle has perpetuated the falsehood that he, Conrad, is no more than a writer of sea stories. "I was in hopes," writes Conrad,

> that on a general survey it could also be made an opportunity for me to get freed from that infernal tale of ships, and that obsession of my sea life which has about as much bearing on my literary existence, on my quality as a writer, as the enumeration of the drawing-rooms which Thackeray frequented could have had on his gift as a great novelist. After all, I may have been a seaman, but I am a writer of prose. Indeed the nature of my writing runs the risk of being obscured by the nature of my material. . . . That the connection of my ships with my writings stands, with my concurrence I admit, recorded in your book is of course a fact. But that was a biographical matter, not literary. (*CL* 8:130)

What is the difference between biography and literature? Conrad goes on in his letter to Curle to specify the difference in a striking figure. Almost all his "art," says Conrad, consists "in my unconventional grouping and perspective" (*CL* 8:131). Artistic grouping of what? Of the apparently referential or historical material of the story that is placed within the grouping and lighting. This material is necessary to the illuminating grouping and to its artistic effect in the same way that invisible radio waves require sending and receiving apparatuses to be detected, even though what is important is the invisible

---

10. Arthur Symons, *Notes on Joseph Conrad with Some Unpublished Letters* (London: Myers & Co., 1925), 15 [see *CL* 4:100; Editors].

waves, not the apparatus: "Of course the plastic matter of this grouping and of those lights has its importance, since without it the actuality of that grouping and that lighting could not be made evident any more than Marconi's electric waves could be made evident without the sending-out and receiving instruments" (*CL* 8:131). The referential, mimetic, or representational aspect of his works, Conrad is saying, is all for the sake of providing a necessary material base for bringing something invisible into visibility through an artful arrangement of that material. This figure is consonant with the often-cited passage within *Heart of Darkness* itself about the peculiar nature of Marlow's stories as opposed to the usual stories seamen tell. I shall return to that passage.

Much Conrad criticism recognizes tacitly that *Heart of Darkness* is literature but then talks about it as if it were something else. Indeed it is almost impossible to avoid making this elementary error, since every text invites a referential or what Derrida calls, following Sartre, a "transcendent" reading, that is, a reading going beyond the work's language toward the exterior world to which it presumably refers.[11] To put this another way, to call *Heart of Darkness* a literary work, as I just have, is a speech act that responds to certain possibilities in the text. I have implicitly said, "I declare *Heart of Darkness* is literature." It would be equally possible to declare that *Heart of Darkness* is history, or memoir, or autobiography. To do this would be in one way or another to label the novel a straightforwardly mimetic or referential work that deserves to be judged by its truth value, its accuracy of representation. Many critics have done just that. No distinguishing marks certainly identify a given text as literary or as nonliterary, in spite of the many conventional codes that ordinarily indicate a text is literature or not literature. This uncertainty results from the way each may present itself in the guise of the other. A page from a telephone book can be taken as literature. One can imagine a fictitious telephone book that would look exactly like a real one, though the numbers would not work if you were to try to use them to call someone.

If taking *Heart of Darkness* as literature or as not literature is a speech act, an act of belief or of bearing witness, not a constative statement, this means that whoever declares it to be one or the other must take responsibility for his or her declaration. He or she must say, "I did it. I have declared that *Heart of Darkness* is literature (or, on the contrary, is history or autobiography). I accept responsibility for the consequences of saying that." I hereby do that now for my claim that *Heart of Darkness* belongs to literature. To say *Heart of*

---

11. See Jacques Derrida, *Acts of Literature*, ed. Derek Attridge (New York: Routledge, 1992), 44: "'Transcend' here means going beyond interest for the signifier, the form, the language (note that I do not say 'text') in the direction of the meaning or referent (this is Sartre's rather simple but convenient definition of prose)."

Darkness is a literary work, I hasten to add, by no means exonerates Conrad from responsibility for what is said within it, but it does change the terms and conditions of that responsibility. Just how?

Literature as an institution in the West is of relatively recent date. It began more or less in the Renaissance. "Literature" as we Westerners know it is a radically overdetermined historical product belonging only to Western societies. Greek tragedy is not literature in the modern Western sense, nor is classical Chinese poetry, however much these may look like more or less the same thing as our literature. Greek tragedy was a species of quasi-religious ritual, and Chinese poetry had class and institutional functions, not to speak of a texture of political or historical allusions, that were not quite like anything in the West. Whether United States so-called literature or South African Anglophone so-called literature is literature in the same sense that Conrad's *Heart of Darkness* is literature is a subtle and difficult question, a question whose answer must by no means be taken for granted. I suspect the nature and social function of United States and South African literature are significantly different from those of British literature. Certainly it is difficult, for example, to apply (without distorting them) Melville, Hawthorne, or Dickinson to paradigms developed for English Victorian literature, though they are contemporary with it.

Literature in the modern Western sense is a concomitant of democracy with its precious right to free speech, of the modern nation-state, of European worldwide economic and political imperialist hegemony, of print culture, of modern notions of authorship, of copyright laws, and of post-Cartesian notions of subjectivity and of the subject/object dichotomy. Democratic freedom of speech, as guaranteed by a particular nation state, is, as Jacques Derrida has cogently argued in the prefatory interview in *Acts of Literature*, essential to literature in the modern European sense. Since it would be difficult to convict Derrida of either racism or sexism (though attempts have been made), his testimony may be valuable here in working out how to pass judgment on *Heart of Darkness*. Though of course free speech always has its limits and is never more than imperfectly achieved, always something yet to come, nevertheless in principle it makes literature possible by making it permissible to say anything and, in a certain specific sense, to disclaim responsibility for it by saying, "That is not me speaking but an imaginary character. I am exercising my right to free speech in the name of a higher responsibility."[12]

All these features I have named (democratic free speech, the nation state, European hegemony, print culture, copyright laws, Cartesian notions of the ego), make a heterogeneous system, of which literature in the modern West-

---

12. Ibid., 37–38.

ern sense is only one element. If one element is changed, the whole system is changed, including any member of it. Several of these intertwined elements are in our time being radically altered. We hear on all sides these days of the decline of the nation state. Cartesian or Hegelian notions of subjectivity are no longer taken for granted, to say the least. Print culture is being rapidly replaced by a new regime of telecommunications: television, cinema, videotapes, faxes, email, computer databases, the Internet with its unimaginable and incoherent multiplicity of data, including literature (that is being transformed by this new medium) and literary scholarship—all floating freely in global cyberspace. Among all that chaotic wealth I discovered, for example, a hypercard version of *Heart of Darkness* and downloaded it into my computer. It was prepared partly in Florida, partly in Norway, though the email address is Dartmouth College in New Hampshire. Reading *Heart of Darkness* in this version is different in many hard-to-define ways from reading it in a printed book. We live in a postcolonial world in which Europe and even the United States are less and less dominant, as, for example, East Asian economies challenge the hegemony of Western ones in size and global power. Freedom of speech on the Internet does not mean the same thing as freedom of speech in face-to-face encounters in an old-fashioned New England town meeting, or freedom of speech as exercised in a printed text. The result of these changes may be that we are coming to the end of Western-style literature as it extended from Shakespeare to Conrad and his European contemporaries. The study of this literature was institutionalized in departments of national literatures in Western-style universities all over the world. Those universities are part of the legacy of imperialism and colonialism.

Literature in the modern Western sense is, it may be, already a thing of the past. It is now an object of historical investigation and imaginative, spectral resurrection, not something that is or could be currently produced, since the enabling conditions have changed so radically. Misreadings of *Heart of Darkness* as though it were a straightforwardly historical, referential, or autobiographical document may be evidence that literature can no longer easily be understood in terms of older protocols, codes, and conventions of reading, though of course such mimetic misreadings of literature have always been current. They too are part of our legacy from the now-vanishing regime of print culture. As I have said, a fictional telephone book can always be taken as a real one. The need for the ritual disclaimer (often a manifestly lying one) saying "any resemblance to real persons, living or dead, is purely coincidental" testifies to the ubiquity of the confusion and the need to try to ward it off.

In just what way does *Heart of Darkness* invite reading as literature rather than, say, as a historical account or as an autobiography? The most obvious way is in the displacement from Conrad to two imaginary narrators, neither of whom is to be identified with Conrad, any more than Socrates, in the Platonic dialogues, is to be identified with Plato. The reader who says Conrad speaks directly for himself either in the words of the frame narrator or in Marlow's words does so at his or her peril and in defiance of the most elementary literary conventions. Whatever the frame narrator or Marlow says is ironized or suspended, presented implicitly in parabasis, by being given as the speech of an imaginary character.

Conrad's way of talking about Marlow's origin, nature, and relation, to his creator is peculiar, evasive. It is a little like the response "R.," presumably Rousseau himself, though this is not confirmed, gives, in the second preface to Rousseau's *La nouvelle Héloïse*, when he is asked by "N." whether the letters that make up the novel are real letters or fictive ones. "R." says he does not know and, when pressed by "N.," says he is afraid of lying if he answers definitely one way or the other.[13] In the "Author's Note" of 1917 to *Youth*, the volume that contains *Heart of Darkness*, as well as "Youth" (in which Marlow first appeared) and "The End of the Tether," Conrad responds to "some literary speculation" about Marlow's "origins." "One would think that I am the proper person to throw a light on the matter;" says Conrad, "but in truth I find that it isn't so easy" (5). Marlow, he goes on to say, "was supposed to be sorts of things: a clever screen, a mere device, a 'personator,' a familiar spirit, a whispering 'daemon.' I myself have been suspected of a meditated plan for his capture" (5). Conrad continues to talk ironically and ambiguously about Marlow as if he were a real not a fictive person. Or rather he speaks of Marlow as a fictive person whose existence is nevertheless inseparable from that of Conrad himself in the sense that neither would "care" to survive the other:

> That is not so. I made no plans [to "capture" him]. The man Marlow and I came together in the casual manner of those health-resort acquaintances which sometimes ripen into friendships. This one has ripened. For all his assertiveness in matters of opinion he is not an intrusive person. He haunts my hours of solitude, when, in silence, we lay our heads together in great comfort and harmony; but as we part at the end of a tale I am never sure that it may not be for the last time. Yet I don't think that either of us would care much to survive the other. In his case, at any rate, his occupation would

---

13. Jean-Jacques Rousseau, *La nouvelle Héloïse, Oeuvres completes*, ed. Bernard Gagnebin and Marcel Raymond, Pléiade ed., 4 vols. (Paris: Gallimard, 1964), 2:27–29.

be gone and he would suffer from that extinction, because I suspect him of some vanity. (5–6)

By denying that he had made premeditated plans for Marlow's capture, Conrad means to deny, I assume, that Marlow was the product of a calculated literary artifice. He just appeared, spontaneously, like a ghostly double or like that "secret sharer" who appears on the protagonist's ship in "The Secret Sharer," subject of the next chapter of this book.[14] Marlow appears to "haunt" Conrad's hours of solitude, that is, the hours he does his writing. They then "part at the end of a tale." A ghost, especially one's own specter, is both the same as oneself and yet different. This one has his own assertive opinions. These are not, Conrad implies, Conrad's own opinions, any more than Kurtz's opinions are the same as Marlow's. Just as Conrad is "haunted" by Marlow, so Marlow is haunted by Kurtz, who is spoken of repeatedly as a ghost. Marlow speaks of "the shade of Mr. Kurtz," "this initiated wraith from the back of Nowhere" (95), of Kurtz as an "apparition" (106), a "Shadow" (111), "like a vapour exhaled by the earth" (112), again as a "shade" (115), as "an eloquent phantom" (125), as a "disinterred body" (93). A ghost does not, cannot, die. It returns, as a revenant, just as Marlow hears Kurtz's voice still whispering his last words when he visits the Intended back in Europe: "The dusk was repeating them in a persistent whisper all around us" (125).

Heart of Darkness is made of a chain of these ambiguous doublings and hauntings: of Marlow by Kurtz, of the primary narrator by Marlow, of Conrad by Marlow, of the Intended by the African woman who is presumably Kurtz's mistress, and of the reader by the whole series. The reader is haunted by the tale, made to feel a "faint uneasiness" by it just as the frame narrator is by Marlow's story (70). The reader pores over and over the text trying to come to terms with it so it can be dismissed and forgotten.

A second way *Heart of Darkness* presents itself as literature is in the elaborate tissue of figures and other rhetorical devices that make up, as one might put it, the texture of the text. The simplest and most obvious of these devices is the use of similes, signaled by "like" or "as." These similes displace things that are named by one or the other of the narrators. They assert that this (whatever it is) is like something else. This something else forms through recurrence a consistent subtext. This subtext functions as a counterpoint defining everything that can be seen as a veil hiding something more truthful or essential behind.

---

14. "Conrad's Secret," in Miller, *Others* (Princeton: Princeton University Press, 2001), 137–69 (122–55 this volume [Editors]).

The first of many uses of the figure naming things veils that are lifted to reveal more veils behind comes when the frame narrator, describing the evening scene just before sunset, when the sky is "a benign immensity of unstained light" (44), as it looks from the *Nellie* at anchor in the Thames estuary, says: "the very mist on the Essex marshes was *like* [my emphasis] a gauzy and radiant fabric hung from the wooded rises inland and draping the low shores in diaphanous folds" (44). Such recurrent figures establish a structure that is apocalyptic in the etymological sense of "unveiling," as well as in the sense of having to do with death, judgment, and other last things.

These similes, as they follow in a line punctuating the text at rhythmic intervals, are not casual or fortuitous. They form a system, a powerful undertext beneath the first-level descriptive language. They invite the reader to see whatever either of the narrators sees and names on the first level of narration as a veil or screen hiding something invisible or not yet visible behind it. When each veil is lifted, however, it uncovers only another veil, according to a paradox essential to the genre of the apocalypse. "Apocalypse": the word means "unveiling" in Greek. If one had to name the genre to which *Heart of Darkness* belongs, the answer would be that it is a failed apocalypse, or, strictly speaking, since all apocalypses ultimately fail to lift the last veil, it is just that, a member of the genre apocalypse. The film modeled on *Heart of Darkness, Apocalypse Now*, was brilliantly and accurately named, except for that word "now." Apocalypse is never now. It is always to come, a thing of the future, both infinitely distant and immediately imminent.

In *Heart of Darkness* it is, to borrow Conrad's own words, as if each episode were "some sordid farce acted in front of a sinister back-cloth" (54). The novel is structured as a long series of episodes. Each appears with extreme vividness before the reader's imaginary vision, brought there by Conrad's remarkable descriptive power. It then vanishes, to be replaced by the next episode, as though a figured screen had been lifted to reveal yet another figured screen behind it. The darkness lies behind them all, like that "sinister backcloth" Marlow names. The misty Essex shore in the opening frame episode is, in the passage already cited, "like a gauzy and radiant fabric" (44). The fog that obscures the shore just before Marlow's ship is attacked is said to have "lifted as a shutter lifts" and then to have come down again, "smoothly as if sliding in greased grooves" (83). The change that comes over Kurtz's features just before he utters his judgment is "as though a veil had been rent" (117), in an explicit reference to the figure of apocalypse as unveiling, revelation, as well as to the rending of the Temple veil at the time of Christ's crucifixion.

Heart of Darkness is structured by this trope of successive revelations. These unveilings unveil not so much the truth behind as the act of unveiling itself, since no "bottom" to the series is reached, no ultimate revelation given. Each scene is in a sense just as close and just as far away from the unnamable "truth" behind it as any other. Marlow's journey in *Heart of Darkness* and that of the reader as he or she gets deeper and deeper into the book is a movement in place. The scene on the *Nellie* is replaced by the scenes in the offices of the trading company in the sepulchral city: the two old women in black at the entrance, knitting and knitting, like two Fates; the doctor who measures Marlow's head and says "the changes take place inside—you know" (52). These scenes give place to the sequence of brief episodes that makes up the central story, as Marlow makes his way deeper and deeper into the heart of darkness: the French ship firing pointlessly into the bush ("Pop, would go one of the six-inch guns; a small flame would dart and vanish, a little white smoke would disappear, a tiny projectile would give a feeble screech—and nothing happened. Nothing could happen" [55]); the dying "workers" in the grove of death; the starched and scented accountant, keeping perfect records in the midst of pointless confusion; the corpse with a bullet-hole in its forehead Marlow "absolutely stumble[s]" (62) upon during his two-hundred-mile trek to reach the beginning of inland navigation on the river, where he finds his ship has been wrecked; his encounter with the skeleton of his predecessor, who has been killed in an absurd dispute over two chickens; the storage shed at the Central Station that suddenly bursts into flames in the middle of the night; the macabre dance on the tinpot steamer's deck performed by Marlow and the chief mechanic to celebrate their expectation that rivets will come; the Eldorado Exploring Expedition, with its "absurd air of disorderly flight with the loot of innumerable outfit shops and provision stores," which vanishes "into the patient wilderness, that closed upon it as the sea closes over a diver" (73, 76); the finding of the book about seamanship, Towson's *Inquiry*, annotated in what Marlow takes to be cipher; the death of Marlow's African helmsman as the ship approaches Kurtz's station and is attacked from the shore; the encounter at the station with the Russian dressed like a harlequin; the appearance through Marlow's telescope of those "symbolic" heads on stakes; Marlow's rescue of Kurtz when the latter tries to crawl back to join the Africans he has commanded and bewitched, so that they worship him; the apparition on the shore of what the reader supposes is Kurtz's African mistress; Kurtz's death and summing up, "in a whisper at some image, at some vision . . .—'The horror! The horror!'" (117); the echo or repetition of the African woman's gesture of raising her arms in the final episode of Marlow's encounter back in Europe with Kurtz's "Intended," when he tells his lie; the return in the final brief paragraph to the deck of the *Nellie* where Marlow has been telling his story and to the concluding vision of the Thames as a "tranquil waterway leading to the uttermost ends of the earth [that] flowed sombre under an overcast sky—seemed to lead into the heart of an immense darkness" (126).

You may say that of course any narrative consists of a sequence of episodes that give place to one another. *Heart of Darkness* is nothing special in doing that. The difference, however, is in the way the materials and personages of each episode vanish, never to return again except in Marlow's memory. A novel roughly contemporary with *Heart of Darkness*, Henry James's *The Wings of the Dove*, for example, consists of a series of episodes all right, but the same characters are returned to again and again in a slow rotation of encounters that advances the action. In *Heart of Darkness* each episode is like a separate sinister farce enacted before a black backcloth. The whole is like a sequence of dream visions, each with little connection to the ones before and after. Each vanishes for good, as though a veil had been lifted to reveal yet another such scene behind it that vanishes in its turn, in a rhythm of ironic undercutting and displacement that punctuates Marlow's journey. He journeys deeper and deeper toward the fulfillment of an implicit promise, the promise to make or find a final revelation or unveiling. That promise, it hardly needs saying, is never kept. It cannot be kept. Just why that is so and just what that nonfulfillment means remain to be seen.

A third distinctively literary feature of *Heart of Darkness* has already been named in passing. The novel is ironic through and through. The reader might wish this were not the case. We may deplore Conrad's radical irony, but there it is, an indubitable fact. *Heart of Darkness* is a masterwork of irony, as when the eloquent idealism of Kurtz's pamphlet on "The Suppression of Savage Customs" is undercut by the phrase scrawled at the bottom: "Exterminate all the brutes!" (95), or as when the dying Africans in the grove of death are called "helpers" in the great "work" of civilizing the continent (58). Marlow's narrative in particular is steeped in irony throughout. The problem is that it is impossible to be certain just how to take that irony. Irony is, as Hegel and Kierkegaard said, "infinite absolute negativity," or, as Friedrich Schlegel said, a "permanent parabasis," a continuous suspension of clearly identifiable meaning. It is a principle of unintelligibility, or, in Schlegel's word, *Unverständlichkeit*.[15] Irony is a constant local feature of Marlow's narrative style. He says one thing and means another, as when the Europeans at the Central Station engaged in the terrible work of imperialist conquest, the "merry dance of death and trade" (55), are said to be, in yet another simile, like "pilgrims":

---

15. I discussed Schlegelian irony in detail in chapter 1 ["Friedrich Schlegel: Catachreses for Chaos," in Miller, *Others*, 5–42; Editors].

"They wandered, here and there with their absurd long staves in their hands like a lot of faithless pilgrims bewitched inside a rotten fence" (65).

This stylistic undercutting is mimed in that larger structure of the replacement of each episode by the next, so that each is undermined by the reader's knowledge that it is only a temporary appearance, not some ultimate goal of revelation attained. Each is certain to vanish and be replaced by the next scene to be enacted before that sinister backcloth.

A fourth ostentatious literary feature of *Heart of Darkness* is the use of recurrent prosopopoeias. The personification of the darkness (whatever *that* word means here) begins in the title, which gives the darkness a "heart." Prosopopoeia is the ascription of a name, a face, or a voice to the absent, the inanimate, or the dead. By a speech act, a performative utterance, prosopopoeia creates the fiction of a personality where in reality there is none. Or is there? Once the personifications are in place, it seems as if the personality had been there all along, waiting to be recognized by a name. All prosopopoeias are also catachreses. They move the verbal fiction of a personality over to name something unknown and unknowable. The "something" is, therefore, strictly speaking, unnamable in any literal language. It is something radically other than human personality: something absent, inanimate, or dead. It is no accident that so many traditional examples of catachresis are also personifications: "headland," "face of a mountain," "tongue of land," "table leg." The phrase "heart of darkness" is such a catachrestic prosopopoeia, to give it its barbarous-sounding Greek rhetorical name. We project our own bodies on the landscape and on surrounding artifacts. In *Heart of Darkness* the prosopopoeias are a chief means of naming by indirection what Conrad calls, in a misleading and inadequate metaphor, "the darkness," or, "the wilderness," or, most simply and perhaps most truthfully, "it."

More than a dozen explicit personifications of this "it" rhythmically punctuate *Heart of Darkness,* like a recurring leitmotif. The darkness is not really a person, but an "it," asexual or transsexual, impersonal, indifferent, though to Marlow it seems like a person. The wilderness surrounding the Central Station, says Marlow, "struck me as something great and invincible, like evil or truth, waiting patiently for the passing way of this fantastic invasion" (65). A little later Marlow says "the silence of the land went home to one's very heart—its mystery, its greatness, the amazing reality of its concealed life" (68). Of that silent, nocturnal wilderness Marlow asserts, "All this was great, expectant, mute, while the man [one of the agents at the station] jabbered about himself. I wondered whether the stillness on the face of the immensity looking at us were meant as an appeal or as a menace. . . . Could we handle that dumb thing or would it handle us? I felt how big, how confoundedly big was that thing that couldn't talk and perhaps was deaf as well" (69). "It as the stillness of an implacable force brooding over an inscrutable intention. It looked at you with a vengeful aspect. . . . I felt often its mysterious stillness watching me at my monkey-tricks, just as it watches you fellows [his listeners on the *Nellie*] performing on your respective tightropes—for—what is it? half a crown a tumble—" (77). The wilderness destroys Kurtz by a kind of diabolical seduction: "The wilderness had patted him on the head, and, behold it was like a ball—an ivory ball; it had caressed him and lo!—he had withered; it had taken him, loved him, embraced him, got into his veins, consumed his flesh and sealed his soul to its own by the inconceivable ceremonies of some devilish initiation. He was its spoiled and pampered favourite" (93). The Africans at Kurtz's Inner Station vanish "without any perceptible movement of retreat, as if the forest that had ejected these beings so suddenly had drawn them in again steadily as the breath is drawn in a long aspiration" (106).

This last citation indicates another and not unpredictable feature of the prosopopoeias in *Heart of Darkness*. The personification of the wilderness is matched by a corresponding transformation of the African people who intervene between Marlow and the "it." Just as, in Thomas Hardy's *The Return of the Native*, the extravagant personification of the nighttime heath that opens the novel leads to the assertion that Eustacia Vye, who rises from a mound on the heath to stand outlined in the darkness, is, so to speak, the personification of the personification, its exposure or visible embodiment, so, in *Heart of Darkness*, all the Africans Marlow meets are visible representatives and symbols of the "it." Though it may be racist for Marlow (who is not necessarily Conrad, the reader should remember) to see the Africans as an inscrutably "other," as simple "savages" or "primitives," when their culture is older than any European one and just as complex or sophisticated, if not more so, this otherness is stressed for the primary purpose of making the Africans visible embodiments and proofs that the "it," the darkness, is a person.

This personification of personification is an underlying feature Marlow's prosopopoeias, but it is made most explicit in the scene where the woman the reader may presume is Kurtz's African mistress appears on the shore:

> She was savage and superb, wild eyed and magnificent; there was something ominous and stately in her deliberate progress. And in the hush that had fallen suddenly upon the whole sorrowful land, the immense wilderness, the colossal body of the fecund and mysterious life seemed to look at her, pensive, as though it had been looking at the image of its own tenebrous

and passionate soul. . . . She stood looking at us without a stir and like the wilderness itself with an air of brooding over an inscrutable purpose. (107)

This passage, like the one describing the way the wilderness has seduced Kurtz, seems to indicate that this "it" is after all gendered. It is female, a colossal body of fecund and mysterious life. Since the wilderness is supposed to represent a mysterious knowledge, "like evil or truth," this personification does not jibe very well with the "sexist" assertions Marlow makes about the way women in general, for example Marlow's aunt or Kurtz's Intended, are "out of it," invincibly innocent and ignorant. At the least one would have to say that two contradictory sexist myths about women are ascribed to Marlow. One is the European male's tendency to personify the earth as a great mother, full of an immemorial, seductive wisdom. The other is the European male's tendency to condescend to women as innately incapable of seeing into things as well as men can.

Strong hints of homosexual or at least homosocial relations complicate the sexual politics of *Heart of Darkness*. Other critics have seen this in Conrad's work. Those businessmen gathered on the *Nellie* for a weekend away from any women are a splendid example of what Eve Sedgwick means by male homosociality. The pleasure yacht is suggestively, though of course also conventionally, given a familiar woman's name. Most of the doublings that organize the novel are of male by male, in that long chain I have identified. The most important of these is Marlow's infatuation with Kurtz, his extravagant fidelity to him, even beyond the grave. I have scrupulously in this chapter referred to the reader as "he or she." A moment's reflection, however, will show that men and women are unlikely to read the novel in just the same way or to feel just the same kind of obligation to account for it, to render it justice. Both genders will have that obligation, but each in a different way.

The final scene pits Marlow's intimacy with Kurtz against the Intended's. "Intimacy grows quick out there," Marlow tells the Intended. "I knew him as well as it is possible for one man to know another" (123). A strong suggestion is made that Marlow is jealous of the Intended, as a man who loves another man is jealous of that man's heterosexual loves. Marcel Proust, however, who presumably knew about this, has Marcel in *À la recherche du temps perdu* claim that the Baron de Charlus was only jealous of his lovers' other male lovers, not at all of their heterosexual partners. In any case, to the other doublings I have listed would need to be added the way Marlow doubles the particolored Russian in his fascination with Kurtz. Again hints are given that Marlow envies the Russian his intimacy with Kurtz. He wants to have Kurtz all to himself, to be Kurtz's sole survivor, so to speak, the sole keeper of his memory. The only overt reference to homosexuality occurs in an interchange between Marlow and the Russian: "'We talked of everything,' he [the Russian] said, quite transported at the recollection. 'I forgot there was such a thing as sleep. The night did not seem to last an hour. Everything! Everything! . . . Of love too.' 'Ah! he talked to you of love.' I said much amused. 'It isn't what you think,' he cried almost passionately. 'It was in general. He made me see things—things'" (101).

Conrad's invention of Marlow at once embodies, reveals, and ironically puts in question the complex system of Western imperialist and capitalist ideology. I mean "invention" here in both senses—as finding and as making up. Among the ingredients of this system are not just a certain "sexist" vision of women but also a strand of homosociality or even homosexuality. This was certainly an important feature of English society in Conrad's day. It has also been shown to be a feature of the imperialist enterprise generally, for example in the European presentation of non-European men as exotic, often even, in an obvious wish-fulfillment, as sexually perverse.

All four of the stylistic features I have identified—the use of fictional narrators, of recurrent tropes, of irony, and of personification—constitute a demand that *Heart of Darkness* be read as literature, as opposed to being taken as a straightforwardly mimetic or referential work that would allow the reader to hold Conrad himself directly responsible for what is said as though he were a journalist or a travel writer. Of course any of these features can be used in a nonliterary work, but taken all together as they are intertwined in *Heart of Darkness*, they invite the reader to declare, "This is literature."

In the name of what higher responsibility does Conrad justify all this "literary" indirection and ironic undercutting, all this suspending or redirecting of his novel's straightforwardly mimetic aspect? In the name of what higher obligation is everything that is referentially named in a pseudo-historical or mimetic way displaced by these ubiquitous rhetorical devices and made into a sign for something else? If *Heart of Darkness* is a literary work rather than history or autobiography, just what kind of literary work is it? Just what kind of apocalypse, if it is an apocalypse? What lies behind that veil? The frame narrator, in a passage often cited and commented on, gives the reader a precious clue to an answer to these questions, though it is left to the reader to make use of the clue in his or her reading:

> The yarns of seamen have an effective simplicity, the whole meaning of which lies within the shell of a cracked nut. But . . . Marlow was not typical (if his propensity to spin yarns be excepted), and to him the meaning of an episode was not inside like a kernel but outside, enveloping the tale which

brought it out only as a glow brings out a haze, in the likeness of one of these misty halos that, sometimes, are made visible by the spectral illumination of moonshine. (45)

"To spin yarns" is a cliché for narration. To tell a story is to join many threads together to make a continuous line leading from here to there. Of that yarn cloth may be woven, the whole cloth of the truth as opposed to a lie that, as the proverbial saying has it, is "made up out of whole cloth." The lie as cloth makes a web, screen, or veil covering a truth that remains hidden behind or within. This inside/outside opposition governs the narrator's distinction between two kinds of tales. On the one hand, the first kind is the sort of seaman's yarn it has been assumed by many reader's and critics Conrad was telling in his stories and novels. The meaning of such a tale lies within, like the kernel within the shell of a cracked nut. I take it this names a realistic, mimetic, referential tale with an obvious point and moral. Marlow's tales, on the other hand, and by implication this one by Conrad, since so much of it is made up of Marlow's narration, have a different way of making meaning. All the visible, representational elements, all that the tale makes you *see*, according to that famous claim by Conrad in the preface to *The Nigger of the "Narcissus,"* that his goal was "before all, to make you *see*,"[16] are there not for their own sakes, as mimetically valuable and verifiable, for example for the sake of giving the reader information about imperialism in the Belgian Congo. Those elements have as their function to make something else visible, what the manuscript calls the "unseen,"[17] perhaps even the unseeable, as the dark matter of the universe or the putative black holes at the center of galaxies can in principle never be seen, only inferred.

Conrad's figure is a different one from those black holes about which he could not have known, though his trope is still astronomical. It is an example of that peculiar sort of figure that can be called a figure of figure or a figure of figuration. Just as the mist on a dark night is invisible except when it is made visible as a circular halo around moonlight, light already secondary and reflected from the sun, and just as the mimetic elements of Marlow's tale are secondary to the putatively real things they represent at one remove, so the meaning of Marlow's yarns is invisible in itself and is never named directly. It is not inside the tale but outside. It is "brought out" indirectly by the things that *are* named and recounted, thereby made visible, just as, for example, Mar-

---

16. My task which I am trying to achieve is, by the power of the written word to make you hear, to make you feel—it is, before all, to make you *see*" (*NN* xiv).

17. Chapter 8 will show the importance of the word "unseen" in E. M. Forster's *Howards End* ["E. M. Forster: Just Reading *Howards End*," in Miller, *Others*, 183–205; Editors].

low when he visits the Intended hears Kurtz's last words breathed in a whisper by the dusk: "The dusk was repeating them in a persistent whisper all around us, in a whisper that seemed to swell menacingly like the first whisper of a rising wind. 'The horror! The horror!'" (125). The reader will note the way the whispered sound is onomatopoetically echoed here in the repetition three times of the word "whisper," with its aspirant and sibilant "whuh" and "isp" sounds. The illumination provided by the tale is "spectral," like a liminal, ghostly sound. It turns everything into a phantom, that is, into something that has come back from the dead, something that cannot die, something that will always, sooner or later, just when we least expect it, come again.

The miniature lesson in aesthetic theory the frame narrator presents here is an admirably succinct expression of the distinction between mimetic literature and apocalyptic, parabolic, or allegorical literature. In the latter, everything named, with however much verisimilitude, stands for something else that is not named directly, that cannot be named directly. It can only be inferred by those that have eyes to see and ears to hear and understand, as Jesus puts it in explaining the parable of the sower in Matthew 13. All these genres have to do with promising, with death, with the truly secret, and with last things, "things," as Jesus says, "which have been kept secret from the foundation of the world" (Matthew 13:35).

It is not so absurd as it might seem to claim that *Heart of Darkness* is a secular version of what are, originally at least, intertwined religious or sacred genres: apocalypse, parable, and allegory. Conrad himself spoke of the "piety" of his approach to writing and of his motive as quasi-religious. "One thing that I am certain of," he wrote in that letter to Symons already quoted, "is that I have approached the object of my task, things human, in a spirit of piety. The earth is a temple where there is going on a mystery play childish and poignant, ridiculous and awful enough in all conscience. Once in I've tried to behave decently. I have not degraded the quasi religious sentiment by tears and groans: and if I have been amused and indifferent, I've neither grinned nor gnashed my teeth."[18]

In the case of *Heart of Darkness*, just what is that "something else" for the revelation of which the whole story is written? The clear answer is that the something else is the "it" that Marlow's narration so persistently personifies and that Kurtz passes judgment on when he says "The horror!" All details in the story, all the mimetic and verisimilar elements, are presented for the sake of bringing out a glimpse of that "it." The revelation of this "it" is promised by the frame narrator when he defines the characteristic indirection of meaning

---

18. Symons, *Notes on Joseph Conrad*, 17 [see *CL* 4:113; Editors].

in Marlow's yarns. Many critics of *Heart of Darkness* have made the fundamental mistake of taking the story as an example of the first kind of seaman's yarn. Those critics, like F. R. Leavis,[19] who have noticed all the language about the unspeakable and "inscrutable" "it" have almost universally condemned it as so much moonshine interfering with Conrad's gift for making you *see* the material world, his gift for descriptive vividness and verisimilitude. At least such critics have taken the trouble to read carefully and have noticed there are important verbal elements in the text that must be accounted somehow and that do not fit the straightforward mimetic, descriptive paradigm.

Is the "something," the "it," ever revealed, ever brought into the open where it may be seen and judged? The clear answer is that it is not. The "it" remains to the end unnamable, inscrutable, unspeakable. The "it" is Conrad's particular version, in *Heart of Darkness* at least, of those "others" that are the subject of this book. The "it" is falsely, or at a rate unprovably, personified by Marlow's rhetoric as having consciousness and intention. It is named only indirectly and inadequately by all those similes and figures of veils being lifted. How could something be revealed that can only be encountered directly by those who have crossed over the threshold of death? The reader is told that "it" is "The horror!" but just what that means is never explained except in hints and indirections. Nothing definite can be said of the "it" except that it is not nothing, that it *is,* though even that is not certain, since it may be a projection, not a solicitation, call, or demand from something wholly other. Of the "it" one must say what Wallace Stevens says of the "primitive like an orb," "at the center on the horizon": "It is and it / Is not and, therefore, is."[20] If "it" is wholly other it is wholly other. Nothing more can be said of it except by signs that confess in their proffering to their inadequacy. Each veil lifts to reveal another veil behind.

The structure of *Heart of Darkness* is a self-perpetuating system of an endlessly deferred promise. This is the implicit promise that Marlow makes at the beginning of his tale when he says that though his meeting with Kurtz, "the furthest point of navigation and the culminating point of my experience," was "not very clear," nevertheless "it seemed to throw a kind of light" (47–48). This illumination he implicitly promises to pass on to his hearers. The primary narrator passes it on to us, the readers. The fulfillment of this promise to

---

19. F. R. Leavis, *The Great Tradition: George Eliot, Henry James, Joseph Conrad* (New York: George W. Stewart, [1948]), 174–82 [Editors].

20. Wallace Stevens, "A Primitive Like an Orb," in *The Collected Poems of Wallace Stevens* (New York: Knopf 1954), 440–43; ll. 87, 13–14.

reveal, however, remains always future, something yet to come, eschatological or messianic rather than teleological. It is an end that can never come within the series of episodes that reaches out toward it as life reaches toward death. In this *Heart of Darkness* works in a deferral analogous to the way *Revelations* promises an imminent messianic coming that always remains future, to come, beyond the last in the series, across the threshold into another realm and another regime. It is in the name of this unrevealed and unrevealable secret, out of obligation to it, in response to the demand it makes, though it still remains secret and inaccessible, that all *Heart of Darkness* is written. The presence within the novel of an inaccessible secret, a secret that nevertheless incites to narration, is what makes it appropriate to speak of *Heart of Darkness* as literature.

The place where this ultimate failure of revelation is made most explicit is Marlow's comment on the difference between Kurtz, who summed up at the moment of his death, giving words to "the appalling face of a glimpsed truth" (118), and Marlow's own illness that took him to the brink of death and then back into life again, therefore not quite far enough to see what Kurtz saw:

> And it is not my own extremity I remember best—a vision of greyness without form filled with physical pain and a careless contempt for the evanescence of all things—even of this pain itself. No. It is his extremity that I seemed to have lived through. True, he had made that last stride, had stepped over the edge while I had been permitted to draw back my hesitating foot. And perhaps in this is the whole difference; perhaps all the wisdom and all truth and all sincerity are just compressed into that inappreciable moment of time in which we step over the threshold of the Invisible. Perhaps. (118)

How would one know without crossing that bourne from which no traveler returns? You cannot "live through" another's death. The other must die his or her own death; you must die yours—both in incommunicable solitude. To "know" you must die first. If you know, you are, necessarily, no longer around to tell the tale. Even knowing this remains, necessarily, a matter of "perhaps." It is, nevertheless, in the name of this nonrevelation, this indirect glimpse, as the moon spectrally illuminates a ring of mist, that Marlow's judgment of imperialism is made. The "it" is the sinister backcloth before which all the seriocomic antics of those carrying on the merry dance of death and trade, including their racism and sexism, are ironically suspended, made to appear both horrible and futile at once. The ubiquity of the "it" allows Marlow to imply the identity between the African woman and Kurtz's Intended that is so crucial to the story. This ubiquity also allows him to assert an all-important identity between the early Roman conquerors of Britain, present-day British commerce as represented by the Director of Companies, the Lawyer, and the Accountant, and the enterprise of imperialism in Africa. Of the Eldorado Exploring Expedition, Marlow says, "Their desire was to tear treasure out of the bowels of the land with no more moral purpose at the back of it than there is in burglars breaking into a safe" (73). Something similar, however, is said about the Romans near the beginning of Marlow's narration. It is said in a way that gives it universal application: "The conquest of the earth which mostly means the taking it away from those who have a different complexion or slightly flatter noses than ourselves, is not a pretty thing when you look into it too much" (47). *Heart of Darkness* looks into it. Early readers saw the novel as an unequivocal condemnation of Leopold II and of Belgian imperialism in the Congo. I note in passing that now (2000), when a new regime has taken over in the Congo, transnational companies are fighting for the rights to exploit mineral deposits there, for example copper. This new global economy is not all that different from the imperialism of Conrad's day. Of course the novel represents, in Marlow, Eurocentric views. It was written by a European with the apparent intent of evaluating such views by embodying them in a narrator. Of course it represents sexist views. It was written to dramatize what might be said by an imaginary character, Marlow, a white male of Conrad's class and time, just as Conrad's critics today represent their times, races, sexes, and nations, however superior, more just, their judgments may be. I claim, however, that by being displaced into Marlow as narrator and by being measured against the "it," these Eurocentric views are radically criticized and shown as what they are, that is, as elements in a deadly and unjust ideology.

What of Kurtz, however? Is he not different from the other agents of imperialism? The latter are possessed by "a flabby, pretending, weak-eyed devil of a rapacious and pitiless folly" (57). They have no insight into the way they are victims of the imperialist ideology as well as victimizers of those it exploits. Kurtz, on the other hand, "was a remarkable man," as Marlow himself repeatedly asserts, in a phrase he picks up from one of the agents. Kurtz was a kind of universal genius: a painter, a musician, a poet (he recites his own poetry to the Russian), spectacularly successful in getting ivory, an extremely gifted journalist, a brilliantly powerful speaker, a forceful writer, the author of a stirring pamphlet, his report to "the International Society for the Suppression of Savage Customs": "'By the simple exercise of our will we can exert a power for good practically unbounded,' etc. etc. From that point he soared—and took me with him. The peroration was magnificent; though difficult to remember, you know. It gave me the notion of an exotic Immensity ruled by an august Benevolence. It made me tingle with enthusiasm. This was the unbounded power of eloquence—of words—of burning noble words" (95). Kurtz was potentially a great politician, as the journalist Marlow meets back in Europe after Kurtz's death assures him: "'but heavens! how that man could talk! He electrified large meetings. He had the faith—don't you see—he had the faith. He could get himself to believe anything—anything. He would have been a splendid leader of an extreme party.' 'What party?' I asked. 'Any party,' answered the other. 'He was an—an—extremist'" (120). The famous scrawled note at the end of the pamphlet's manuscript, "Exterminate all the brutes!" (95), says with brutal candor the truth, that the suppression of savage customs culminates in the suppression of the "savages" themselves. That footnote scrawled "in an unsteady hand" testifies to Kurtz's remarkable understanding of the imperialist, philanthropic, and missionary enterprise.

Just what goes wrong with Kurtz? His case is obviously of greater interest than that of any of the others Marlow meets or even than that of Marlow himself. The latter has survived and speaks as a sane man, "one of us," in the voice of ironic, European, enlightened rationality. Or rather he could be said to speak in that voice except for his fascination with Kurtz and with that "it" that solicits him to speech. What he says of the Russian's infatuation with Kurtz could be said of his own fascination: "He had not meditated over it. It came to him, and he accepted it with a sort of eager fatalism. I must say that to me it appeared about the most dangerous thing in every way he had come upon so far" (101). Marlow gives the reader his diagnosis of Kurtz's "madness." Speaking of those heads on stakes, Marlow says:

> There was nothing exactly profitable in these heads being there. They only showed that Mr Kurtz lacked restraint in the gratification of his various lusts, that there was something wanting in him—some small matter which when the pressing need arose, could not be found under his magnificent eloquence. Whether he knew of this deficiency himself I can't say. I think the knowledge came to him at last—only at the very last. [The ms originally added here: If so, then justice was done.] But the wilderness had found him out early and had taken on him a terrible vengeance for the fantastic invasion. I think it whispered to him things about himself which he did not know, things of which he had no conception till he took counsel with this great solitude—and the whisper had proved irresistibly fascinating. It echoed loudly within him because he was hollow at the core. (104)

On the one hand, the story of Kurtz's degradation is an example of the familiar narrative cliché of the European who "goes native." Kurtz, like Lingard in *The Rescue*, like Lord Jim in *Lord Jim*, and like Charles Gould in *Nostromo*, crosses over a border and ceases to be wholly European. Kurtz sets himself up as a sort of king in the alien land, thereby anticipating the destiny of most colonies to become ultimately independent nations. In doing so, they thereby betray in one way or another the ideals, the ethos, the laws and conventions of the colonizing country. The United States did that in 1776. The somewhat hysterical fear that this will happen, or that it will necessarily be a disaster if it does happen, has haunted the colonial enterprise from the beginning. On the other hand, Kurtz never completely makes that break. After all, he allows Marlow to rescue him when he has crawled back ashore in his attempt to join the Africans who have become his subjects. He dies oriented toward Europe and toward the desire that he will "have kings meet him at railway stations on his return from some ghastly Nowhere where he intended to accomplish great things" (116).

What goes wrong with Kurtz? How might he, or another person, Marlow for example, protect himself from the corrupting whisper of the wilderness? Just here Marlow's rhetoric, or Conrad's rhetoric as ascribed to Marlow, is contradictory. It is contradictory in an interesting and symptomatic way. Marlow names several different ways to protect oneself from the threat of counterinvasion by the "it" that has entered Kurtz because he is "hollow at the core" (104).

One way is blind insensitivity: "Of course, a fool, what with sheer fright and fine sentiments, is always safe" (80). That includes most of the "pilgrims," the agents of imperialism.

Another way to protect oneself from the darkness is through devotion to hard but routine physical or mental work, what Conrad calls "the devotion to efficiency" (47). This he identifies as a fundamental feature of the capitalist and imperialist ethos. Indeed it still is a feature of our ideology in the United States. The stated mission of the University of California, for example, is to "help make California competitive in the global economy." University "downsizing" for efficiency's sake matches corporate downsizing for profit's sake. The starched and scented accountant in *Heart of Darkness* is protected by his fanatical devotion to keeping his books accurate and neat. Marlow, so he tells the reader, is saved from succumbing to the darkness through his focus on getting his wrecked steamer back in working order and then getting it safely up the river: "Fine sentiments, be hanged! I had no time. I had to mess about with whitelead and strips of woollen blanket helping to put bandages on those leaky steam-pipes—I tell you. I had to watch the steering, and circumvent those snags, and get the tin-pot along by hook or by crook. There was surface-truth enough in these things to save a wiser man" (80).

The third way to protect oneself seems clear enough. It turns out, however, to be the most equivocal. This is indicated by changes and omissions in the manuscript. Just after saying "the conquest of the earth . . . is not a pretty thing when you look into it too much," Marlow goes on to add: "What redeems it is the idea only. An idea at the back of it; not a sentimental [*MS*: mouthing] pretence but an idea; and an unselfish belief in the idea—something you can set up, and bow down before, and offer a sacrifice to" (47). The ironic religious language at the end here sounds a little ominous. More or less the same thing, however, with much less evident irony is asserted much later in the story when Marlow is talking about the appeal made to him by the dancing, shouting Africans on the shore: "Let the fool gape and shudder—the man knows, and can look on without a wink. . . . But he must meet that truth [the truth of the "prehistoric" men's dancing that is closer to the origin of mankind: certainly a familiar racist cliché there, since modern African cultures are no closer to the origins of mankind than modern European ones are] with his own true stuff—with his own inborn strength. Principles? Principles won't do. Acquisitions, clothes, pretty rags—rags that would fly off at the first good shake. No, you want a deliberate belief. An appeal to me in this fiendish row—is there? Very well; I hear; I admit, but I have a voice too, and for good or evil mine is the speech that cannot be silenced" (80).

The contradiction here is a double one. In an excised passage from the early place where, apropos of the Roman invasion of Britain, Marlow says the idea redeems it, he says that he admires the Roman conquerors because they did not have any redeeming idea but were just robbers and murderers on a grand scale: "The best of them is they didn't get up pretty fictions about it. Was there, I wonder, an association on a philanthropic basis to develop Britain, with some third rate king for a president and solemn old senators discoursing about it approvingly and philosophers with uncombed beards praising it, and men in market places crying it up. Not much! And that's what I like!"[21] No doubt this was cut in part because it was too overt an attack on King Leopold II, but it is also in direct contradiction to Marlow's claim a moment later in the published version, just after where the cut passage would have gone, that "what redeems it [imperialism whether Roman or modern] is the idea only. An idea at the back of it; . . . and an unselfish belief in the idea" (47).

The other contradiction, however, lies in that phrase "deliberate belief" and in the way Kurtz is defined as an adept at deliberate belief: "He could get himself to believe anything—anything" (120). A deliberate belief is a contradiction in terms, an oxymoron. You either believe or do not believe. A deliberate belief is a pretense to believe even though you know the belief is a

---

21. From the ms, quoted in Armstrong's Norton Critical Edition, 94. (In the latest Norton Critical Edition of *Heart of Darkness*, edited by Paul B. Armstrong [New York: Norton, 2017], this excised passage is quoted on page 94 [Editors].)

fictional confidence in something that does not exist or that you do not really believe exists, in this case a solid base for the philanthropic ideals that justify imperialism. To say "I declare I believe so and so" or "I will myself deliberately to believe so and so" is a paradigmatic speech act of a kind not envisioned by Austin. It is an anomalous performative, in the strong sense of anomalous: outside the law. This sort of performative creates its own ground out of whole cloth. It lifts itself by its own bootstraps. A deliberate belief, praised so unreservedly here by Marlow, is, however, what makes Kurtz hollow at the core and so vulnerable to invasion by the "wilderness." You must believe and not believe. Such a belief undoes itself in the act of affirming itself. It is hollow at the core. Belief in what? In the capitalist idea, but in that idea as promise, as the promise of an ultimate messianic revelation and an ultimate millennial reign of peace and prosperity for the whole world. This is that "exotic Immensity ruled by an august Benevolence" that Kurtz's pamphlet promises is to come. This promise is still being made today on behalf of the new global economy and the new universal regime of scientifico-bio-techno-tele-mediatic communications.

The reader will perhaps have foreseen the conclusion toward which my evidence is drawing me. The complex contradictory system of Kurtz's imperialist ideology matches exactly the ideology that proposes a literary work as the apocalyptic promise of a never-quite-yet-occurring revelation. It would not be a promise if it were not possible that the promise might not be kept. The literary promise of an always postponed revelation is strikingly exemplified not only by Marlow's narration but also by *Heart of Darkness* as a whole. Conrad's novel, not just Marlow's fictive account, fits this paradigm. The novel is made up of a chain of spectral duplications that is reinforced by formal and figural features I have described.

Just how does Kurtz's ideology repeat that of Marlow and of Conrad? The literary work, for example *Heart of Darkness* or Marlow's narration within it, is governed by what Derrida calls "the exemplary secret of literature."[22] This secret makes it possible for the work to be the endlessly deferred promise of a definitive revelation that never occurs. This pattern is not only literary but also linguistic. It depends on the way a work of literature is made of language and not of any other material or substance. Marlow stresses over and over that though Kurtz was a universal genius, an artist, musician, journalist, politician, and so on, his chief characteristic was his gift of language: "A voice! a

---

22. Jacques Derrida, "Passions," trans. David Wood, in *On the Name*, ed. Thomas Dutoit (Stanford: Stanford University Press, 1995), 29.

voice! It was grave, profound, vibrating, while the man did not seem capable of a whisper.... Kurtz discoursed. A voice! A voice! It rang deep to the very last. It survived his strength to hide in the magnificent folds of eloquence the barren darkness of his heart" (107, 115). Kurtz, in short (a pun there on Kurtz's name, which means "short" in German; Marlow makes a similar joke [106]), has a magnificent mastery of language that is similar to Marlow's own, or to Conrad's. "An appeal to me in this fiendish row—is there? Very well; I hear; I admit, but I have a voice too, and for good or evil mine is the speech that cannot be silenced" (80).

What does Kurtz talk or write about? The reader is told of the lofty idealism of the pamphlet on the Suppression of Savage Customs. Kurtz has bewitched the particolored Russian, as Marlow ironically attests, by "splendid monologues on, what was it? on love, justice, conduct of life and what not" (104). Most of all, however, Kurtz's discourse is dominated by unfulfilled and perhaps unfulfillable promises made to the whole world on behalf of Eurocentric imperialist capitalism and in support of his role own as its embodiment: "All Europe contributed to the making of Kurtz" (95). Kurtz is like a John the Baptist announcing the new capitalist messiah, or perhaps is himself that self-proclaimed messiah. That his betrothed is called "the Intended" is the emblem of this future-oriented, proleptic feature of Kurtz's eloquence. "I had immense plans," he "mutters," when Marlow is trying to persuade him come back to the boat. "I was on the threshold of great things" (113). Later, as he lies dying on the ship that is taking him back toward Europe, his "discourse" is all future-oriented, all promises of great things to come: "The wastes of his weary brain were haunted by shadowy images now—images of wealth and fame revolving obsequiously round his unextinguishable gift of noble and lofty expression. My Intended, my ivory, my station, my career, my ideas—these were subjects for the occasional utterances of elevated sentiments" (115).

The fulfillment of these promises is cut short by a death that seals a secret or "mystery" that Kurtz carries with him to the grave. This secret is the necessary accompaniment of his grandiose promises. In being inhabited by this mystery, Kurtz is the embodiment not just of European capitalist imperialism's ideology but also of its dark shadow, a ghost that cannot be laid, the "it" that is the inevitable accompaniment of imperialism. Marlow identifies this "it," in figure, both with Kurtz and with the "wilderness" that has invaded his soul. Since Kurtz embodies the darkness, when it has invaded his hollowness, it is logical that he himself should become the "god" that the Africans worship and crawl before. This strikingly anticipates the fascist or violent authoritarian possibilities within capitalist imperialism. Kurtz's soul, like the "it," is an "inconceivable mystery" (114). He has "a smile of indefinable meaning" (114). "His was an impenetrable darkness" (116). Marlow's allegiance to Kurtz and through Kurtz to the wilderness makes him feel as if he too were "buried in a vast grave full of unspeakable secrets" (109), just as the African woman matches the wilderness in having "an air of brooding over an inscrutable purpose" (107). The forest has an "air of hidden knowledge, of patient expectation, of unapproachable silence" (103). It was "the stillness of an implacable force brooding over an inscrutable intention" (77). These words—"unspeakable," "inscrutable," "unapproachable"—must be taken literally. Kurtz in his actions and words is no more able to remove the last veil in an ultimate revelation than Marlow or Conrad can in their narrations. In all three cases a promise is made whose fulfillment or definitive nonfulfillment always remains yet to come.

What can one say to explain this contradiction: that Kurtz's magnificent idealistic eloquence is at the same time inhabited by an impenetrable darkness? Both Marlow's narration and Kurtz's eloquence, since both are based on that special speech act called a promise, are subject to two ineluctable features of any promise: (1) A promise would not be a promise but rather a constative statement of foreknowledge if it were not possible that the promise will not be kept. A possible nonfulfillment is an inalienable structural feature of any promise, whether made in literature or in politics. (2) Any promise is an invocation of an unknown and unknowable future, of a secret other that remains secret and is invited to come into the hollow uncertainty of the promise.

In the case of Marlow's narration, which I claim is an exemplary literary work, what enters the narration is all that talk of the inscrutable, the impenetrable mystery, the unspeakable secret, and so on, that has so offended some of Conrad's readers. In Kurtz's case the millennial promise made by imperialist capitalism, since it is hollow at the core, cannot be separated from the possibility, or perhaps even the necessity, of invasion by the "it," what Conrad calls the "heart of darkness." Kurtz's case is exemplary of that. It is a parable or allegory of this necessity. No imperialist capitalism without the darkness. They go together. Nor has that spectral accompaniment of capitalism's millennial promise of worldwide peace, prosperity, and universal democracy by any means disappeared today. Today the imperialist exploitation of Conrad's day and its accompanying philanthropic idealism have been replaced, as I have said, by the utopian promises made for the new global economy and the new regime of telecommunications, but injustice, inequality, poverty, and bloody ethnic conflicts continue all over the world.

As Jacques Derrida and Werner Hamacher have recognized, the political left and the political right are consonant in the promises they make. The promise of universal prosperity made for the new economy dominated by science and transformative communications techniques echoes the messianic promise, a messianism without messiah, of classical Marxism. It also echoes the promises made by right-wing ideologies, even the most unspeakably brutal, for example the Nazi promise of a thousand-year Reich. We are inundated, swamped, and engulfed every day by the present form of those promises—in newspapers and magazines, on television, in advertising, on the Internet, in political and policy pronouncements. All these promise that everything will get bigger, faster, better, more "user-friendly," and lead to worldwide prosperity. These promises are all made by language or other signs, "the gift of expression, the bewildering, the illuminating, the most exalted and the most contemptible, the pulsating stream of light or the deceitful flow from the heart of an impenetrable darkness" (92).

I return to my beginning. Should we, ought we to, read *Heart of Darkness*? Each reader must decide that for himself or herself. There are certainly ways to read *Heart of Darkness* that might do harm. If it is read, however, as I believe it should be read, that is, as a powerful exemplary revelation of the ideology of capitalist imperialism, including its racism and sexism, as that ideology is consonant with a certain definition of literature that is its concomitant, including the presence in both capitalism and literature of a nonrevelatory revelation or the invocation of a nonrevealable secret, then, I declare, *Heart of Darkness* should be read. It ought to be read. There is an obligation to do so.

CHAPTER 5

Conrad's Secret

> The moment of decision is a madness.
> —KIERKEGAARD

IN A STATEMENT already quoted in chapter 5,[1] Conrad said, "My task which I am trying to achieve is, by the power of the written word, to make you hear, to make you feel—it is, before all, to make you *see*" (*NN* xiv). What most immediately strikes the reader of "The Secret Sharer" is Conrad's extraordinary descriptive power. Conrad excels in what might be called a force not so much of representation as of presentation. He can use words to make things present. From the opening depiction of the Gulf of Siam as seen from a ship anchored at sunset off the mouth of the Meinam River all the way through to the climactic account of the ship's agonizingly slow reversal of direction just before it goes aground on Koh-ring Island, the reader is almost made to feel that he or she has been there and has had these experiences. The fact that the topographical names are of real places reinforces this verisimilitude.

This representational vividness is not limited to the outward appearances of sea, sky, and the details of seafaring. Conrad succeeds also in making the reader feel as if he or she had been, so to speak, inside the narrator's skin and had experienced all his subjective feelings as well as seen what he saw. The reader becomes the sharer of the narrator's secret feelings, just as the narrator

---

This essay originally appeared in *Others* (Princeton: Princeton University Press, 2001), 137–69.

1. "Joseph Conrad: Should We Read *Heart of Darkness?*" in *Others* (Princeton: Princeton University Press, 2001), 124; 110 in this volume [Editors].

says he was able to put himself inside Leggatt's feelings and thoughts when he told how he killed an insolent seaman: "I did not think of asking him for details when he told me the story roughly in brusque, disconnected sentences. I needed no more. I saw it all going on as though I were myself inside the other sleeping suit."[2]

"To make you *see*," as you can see, has a double meaning. It can refer to physical seeing or to seeing in the sense of having an intimate understanding, as when someone says, "Now I see." Seeing names not just detached, external vision. It also names a penetrating vision that gets inside what might be thought of as impenetrably hidden within the other person. Narration as the sharing of secrets—that might be an alternative way to express what Conrad means by saying he wants "to make you see." If Leggatt shares his secret with the narrator, the narrator shares the secret again, along with his own secrets, at least some of them, with the reader. This happens, in the case of the narrator's understanding of Leggatt, to a considerable degree by a wordless telepathy that has its uncanny side. The reader in turn is asked to understand things that, as in most works of fiction, are only implied, not fully spelled out. We are invited to have the kind of telepathic understanding of the narrator that the narrator has of Leggatt.

Just what it might mean to share a secret or what kind of secret it is that can be shared remains to be seen. It would seem that to keep a secret secret it would need to be kept jealously secret. An "open secret" is not really a secret, as the ironic oxymoron of the phrase implies. Nevertheless, "The Secret Sharer" depends on the assumption that some secrets can be shared without ceasing to be secret.

The story suggests, moreover, that such sharing is more than the imparting of knowledge. It also lays on the one who receives the secret an obligation, a responsibility to judge, to decide, to act. The narrator of "The Secret Sharer," for example, must decide whether to hide the fugitive Leggatt or to turn him over to the law as embodied in the captain of the *Sephora*, Leggatt's ship.[3] Moreover, he must do this instantaneously, precipitously, as is often the case

---

2. Joseph Conrad, "The Secret Sharer," in *'Twixt Land and Sea*, ed. J. A. Berthoud, Laura L. Davis, and S. W. Reid (Cambridge: Cambridge University Press, 2008), 89; hereafter cited parenthetically.

3. In *Under Western Eyes* (1911), the composition of which Conrad interrupted in order to write "The Secret Sharer," the same situation is presented with a reverse outcome. Whereas the narrator of "The Secret Sharer" hides and protects Leggatt, in *Under Western Eyes* the hardworking, ambitious student, Razumov, turns a revolutionary activist, Victor Haldin, over to the police when the latter comes to his room seeking asylum after having assassinated an official of the repressive czarist regime. It seems as if Conrad were compelled to write the same story twice with opposite choices by the person on whom another person makes a demand.

with ethical decisions. He does not have time to think it all out and weigh the pros and cons. Once he has decided and has hidden Leggatt in his cabin, he cannot go back on his decision, since to do so would be to admit his own guilt, his complicity in Leggatt's crime.[4] Even if he had infinite leisure to think over what he should do, his final decision would be precipitate, an interruption, irruptive, since a just ethical decision can never be clearly made on the basis of preexisting rules or laws. It is a leap in the dark, always at least implicitly violent, like Leggatt's murderous attack on the mutinous seaman, or like his spontaneous decision to leap into the water off the deck of the *Sephora*: "Then a sudden temptation came over me. I kicked off my slippers and was in the water before I had made up my mind fairly" (93).[5] Or it is like the narrator's decision to hide Leggatt. We must, therefore, pass judgment not only on Leggatt but also on the narrator. Did he do right or wrong in hiding the fugitive murderer Leggatt? On what basis did he make that decision? On what basis should we judge him?

What should *we* do, if anything, when we have read "The Secret Sharer"? Reading the story is a little like having our privacy intruded on in the same way as Leggatt suddenly and unexpectedly enters the narrator's life. It puts on us an obligation to act in some way, but act how? What should we do? Or, rather, what should *I* do, since the act of reading is a personal, individual, and secret event. Others can see that I hold the book in my hands and am running my eyes from line to line, but what is going on inside my mind and feelings is hidden, unless I choose to make it public, to bring it out into the open. Even then I am unlikely to be able to communicate my feelings clearly. In the same way, the episode in the narrator's life recounted in "The Secret Sharer" would have remained secret if he had not chosen to write it down and publish

---

4. The alert reader will note the doubling of two letters that turns "legate" (meaning emissary, as in "papal legate"; it comes from the Latin *legare*, to depute, commission, charge) into a proper name, Leggatt. The pronunciation would perhaps be the same. The doubling of letters is not only another example of the doubling that is ubiquitous in the story, but by way of the pun on "legate" also defines Leggatt as an emissary of some sort and the narrator as the recipient or legatee of a charge transmitted to him by Leggatt. This legacy from Leggatt the narrator passes on to the readers of the story, or rather to me as a solitary reader who must take sole responsibility for what I make of the story. "Legate," "legacy," and so on are related etymologically to words like "legal" and "legislate" (from Latin *lex*) that have to do with law-making, law-giving. In some obscure way, Leggatt comes to the narrator bearing a legacy that has the force of law.

5. Readers of Conrad's *Lord Jim* will juxtapose Leggatt's jump to Jim's quite different jump from the *Patna*. Jim abandons the ship with all its passengers, the one thing a ship's officer is not supposed to do. "I had jumped. . . . It seems," says Jim, as if it were an event that was not the result of conscious decision and that he cannot now remember doing (88). Nevertheless, he is held accountable for it by the law and disgraced for life as punishment for his act. Should we not hold Leggatt accountable for the determining acts of *his* life?

it so all the world might read it. Conrad's idea for this story would also have remained secret if he had not written the story. In this it would have been like all that host of unwritten novels we are told swarmed in Dostoevsky's mind. My reading of "The Secret Sharer" would also remain secret unless I were to decide to talk about my reading, to teach the story, or to write an essay about it, such as this one. I have then told my own secret and have submitted my judgment of the story to the judgment of others. Literature, particularly storytelling in literature, as well as teaching and writing about literature, seems to have something essentially to do with the sharing of secrets.

To apply that to this specific case, however, raises some puzzling questions. To whom is the narrator of "The Secret Sharer" speaking, or to whom or for whom is he writing? In other works by Conrad, for example *Lord Jim* or *Heart of Darkness*, an elaborate fiction gives the narrator a name (Marlow) and a distinct individuality. These novels also put the narrator in a described situation. They show him telling the story to specified auditors, motivated to do so by a particular demand for narration. All that specificity is missing in "The Secret Sharer." The story just begins. It starts with an abrupt sentence in the first person, past tense. This sentence transports the reader to a place and to an event that took place at some unidentified time in the past, though we are told later in the story that it was years earlier: "On my right hand there were lines of fishing-stakes resembling a mysterious system of half-submerged bamboo fences" (81). To whom is the narrator addressing these words? Are we to imagine him as speaking or as writing? Where? When?

Since no time, no situation of narration, no specific auditors are given, it might even be possible to imagine that the narrator is talking to himself. The verbs are in the past tense. The speaker or writer may be remembering these events in an inward musing reminiscence that we as readers have magically been given the power to overhear. It might be said that "The Secret Sharer," in its lack of a circumstantial accounting for its coming into existence, exposes by negation the dependence of any confession on some external, technological device, some means of recording or inscription. A confession I make to myself is not a confession, though in the tradition of religious confession the confession might be made inwardly to God. St. Augustine's *Confessions*, for example, purport to be addressed to a God who knows it all already. We as readers are just overhearing a confession that is addressed to a divine other. Unless "The Secret Sharer" had been written down and published by a relay of handwriting or typewriting, typesetting, and printing, it would have remained secret. It needs also to be remembered that *The Secret Sharer* is a fictive confession, a story that Conrad has made up. The only access to the secrets the story tells is by way of the story itself. If all copies of the story were to vanish, so too would vanish any means of reaching the secret it tells, or perhaps does not tell. That remains to be seen.

The narrator's confession, moreover, is curiously incomplete. Neither the narrator nor the ship he commands is given a name. Those names are kept secret, whereas the name of the man the narrator hides in his cabin, "Leggatt," is given, along with the name of his ship, the *Sephora*, and a possible name for its captain, "Archbold." The name is ironically inappropriate, since Archbold is anything but bold. He is certainly not an original or "arch" model of boldness. The carefully guarded namelessness of the narrator and of his ship means that the narrator has confessed without confessing. We can hardly hold him publicly responsible or hail him before the law if we do not even know his name, not to speak of the exact date of the events, the name of his ship, and so on. Such details would have been obtained first of all from a witness testifying in a court of law.

Nor will it do to assume that the story is straightforwardly autobiographical. We cannot take it for granted that the name of the narrator is the same as the name of the author on the title page: Joseph Conrad. We know from external biographical evidence that the events narrated in "The Secret Sharer" did not, so far as anyone knows, happen to Conrad, though they were based in part on real events that happened to other people.[6] But Conrad has apparently made up the central episode, the hiding of the fugitive. To put this another way, absolutely no verification of this one way or the other exists. It is an impenetrable secret. Who knows? Maybe something of the sort did happen to Conrad back in the 1880s and he had kept it secret all those years, until he wrote the story in 1910. The story itself is the only evidence we have, and that is no evidence one way or the other, since a work of fiction proves nothing about the historical existence of the things it names.

It may be, however, that the best self-portrait is the portrait of another. An author is always revealing secrets about himself, even when he tells the stories of people most unlike himself. This would parallel the way the narrator of "The Secret Sharer," in spite of strongly identifying himself with Leggatt as his secret self, his double, his alter ego, nevertheless insists that "he was not a bit like me really" (91). In any case, the narrator of "The Secret Sharer" jealously preserves the situation of isolation from human judgment he describes at the beginning of the tale: "In this breathless pause at the threshold of a long passage we [he and his ship] seemed to be measuring our fitness for a long and arduous enterprise, the appointed task of both our existences to be carried on,

---

6. The best account of the factual background of "The Secret Sharer" is in Norman Sherry, "'The Secret Sharer': The Basic Fact of the Tale" in *Conrad's Eastern World* (Cambridge: Cambridge University Press, 1966), 253–69.

day after day, far from all human eyes, with only sky and sea for spectators and for judges" (82). The narrator will be judged only by the sky and sea, or he wants only to be judged by them. In the same way, Leggatt refuses to be judged by the appointed civil authorities. "But you don't see me coming back to explain such things to an old fellow in a wig and twelve respectable tradesmen, do you?" he scornfully asks. "What can they know whether I am guilty or not—or of *what* I am guilty, either?" (111). The narrator at no point asks for an exonerating judgment from the reader. He says he wants only sky and sea for spectators and judges. Even so, by telling the story, he breaks that isolation, "far from all human eyes," though he does not tell us his name or the name of his ship. Even if the reader is only by accident, so to speak, overhearing the narrator musing to himself, that means we have been made stand-ins for the sea and sky, which are the real spectators and judges. The narrator, like Leggatt, has sidestepped the officially empowered legal authorities. He has gone over their heads to appeal first to the sky and sea and then indirectly, perhaps even inadvertently, to us the readers, or rather to me as reader, since my reading and judgment are, at least initially, solitary and remain solitary unless I choose to reveal it to others.

"The Secret Sharer," you can see, is a curious form of testimony, witness, or deposition. The reader is implicitly put in the position of judge or jury. The phrase saying only the sea and sky are spectators and judges invites the reader to think of his or her duty as going beyond spectatorship to judgment. We must pass judgment on Leggatt. Was he justified in strangling the mutinous crewman or was it unjustified manslaughter, voluntary or involuntary? What should his punishment be? We must also pass judgment on the narrator. Did he do right or wrong in harboring the fugitive murderer, Leggatt? Did he pass the test qualifying him as fit for the command of a ship on a long and arduous voyage? An anxiety about that is a primary motif in the story, as in other stories and novels by Conrad, for example *The Shadow-Line*, *Typhoon*, and *The Nigger of the "Narcissus."* The narrator tells us that he was "untried as yet by a position of the fullest responsibility," and he says, "I wondered how far I should turn out faithful to that ideal conception of one's own personality every man sets up for himself secretly" (83).[7] Here is another form of doubling, not that of the narrator by Leggatt, but an internal doubling whereby the narrator is doubled by his ideal image of himself. That other self presides over his evaluation of himself, not any external code. It may be that Leggatt is, for the narrator, no more than a fortuitous external representation of that hidden secret self, that ideal conception of himself to which he must be faithful.

---

7. See Byron James Caminero-Santangelo, "Failing the Test: Narration and Legitimation in the Work of Joseph Conrad" (PhD diss., University of California, Irvine, 1992).

The narrator keeps emphasizing the solitude of a ship captain's situation. The captain represents the law on board ship. He must make the ultimate decisions and take the final responsibility, as in the last episode of "The Secret Sharer," when the narrator brings the ship dangerously close to the shore before bringing the ship about. In doing this he is guided only by what he calls his "conscience" (98), though just what he means by that is not wholly clear. I shall return to this question. Just as the crew cannot challenge his commands, though they think he is irresponsible, drunk, or mad, so no other member of the ship's crew would have the legal right to judge him for secretly harboring a murderer in his cabin. As he says, "Of course theoretically I could do what I liked with no one to say me nay within the whole circle of the horizon" (97). In practice, he is constrained by an immense set of rules and conventions for a captain's behavior. He transgresses these rules and conventions at his peril, as when, against all custom, he takes an anchor watch himself or when he takes the ship too close to shore.[8] The first of these transgressions brings Leggatt, as if by magic, before him as a demand for an immediate, isolated, decision.

All that I have said so far presupposes that "The Secret Sharer" is a challenge to any reader's tact and perception as a reader. Like all good works of literature, it puts the reader on trial, so to speak. If the primary aim of "The Secret Sharer" is to make the reader *see*, hardly any reader can avoid feeling that at the same time it must have another meaning besides the manifest one of telling a good story, making us see it. Certainly the story has traditionally been read as having some further purport. "The Secret Sharer," almost all its readers have assumed, must have a more esoteric or secret significance in which "this" (some realistic detail in the story) stands for "that" (some symbolic or allegorical meaning). Like many other works by Conrad, "The Secret Sharer" seems as if it must be some kind of parable, allegory, or fable. It must have some deeper meaning. This the reader ought by appropriate decoding to be able to identify, just as the parables of Jesus in the New Testament, though they are stories about everyday life in ancient Judea, stories about farming, fishing, and household life, nevertheless have parabolic meanings about the kingdom of heaven and how to get there. We know this because Jesus tells the disciples just what those meanings are, in so many words, for example in the parable of the sower in the Gospel of Matthew: "But he that received the seed into stony places, the same is he that heareth the word, and anon with joy receiveth it; Yet hath he not root in himself, but dureth for a while: for when tribulation

---

8. As Norman Sherry tells us Conrad himself did when he had his first command ("'The Secret Sharer,'" 267).

or persecution ariseth because of the word, by and by he is offended" (Matthew 13:20–21), and so on. More generally the Gospel of Matthew affirms that Jesus spoke to the multitude in parables "that it might be fulfilled which was spoken by the prophet, saying, I will open my mouth in parables; I will utter things which have been kept secret from the foundation of the world" (Matthew 13:35). The parables of Jesus are a way of revealing secrets, sharing them with all the world, while at the same time keeping them secret, since, as Jesus says, most of his auditors will not understand them.

The problem of course is that "The Secret Sharer," if it is a parable, is a secular one. It does not have the large context of centuries of biblical interpretation and of institutionalized Christianity that helps with the parables of Jesus, even though Conrad's other work, modernist fiction, English literature as a whole, and an enormous contradictory tradition of modern literary theory and criticism form a context establishing a horizon of expectations about what sort of allegorical meanings might be plausible in a story like this. Nevertheless, "The Secret Sharer" itself nowhere in so many words tells the reader just what the second level of meaning is. In spite of that, readers have not failed to rise to the bait, so to speak. No careful reader can doubt that any good reading of the story would need to take account of the way it has to do with the narrator's relation to himself, with his relation to other persons, especially Leggatt, and with important social questions of law, justice, and authority.

Many different interpretations have been proposed on the assumption that "The Secret Sharer" must have some further meaning beyond the manifest one of telling a good story. It would be a long business to recapitulate these in their diversity. "The Secret Sharer" has been interpreted as a disguised autobiography, by way of its relation to the events of Conrad's life as a seaman. It has been interpreted as a story about homosexuality, as a version of the widespread motif of the *Doppelgänger,* as a story about the role of the test in establishing the fitness of males to be members of the elite group of leaders during the period of British imperialism, and so on, in somewhat incoherent profusion. One could imagine plausible interpretations in terms of Freud's "uncanny" or of Lacan's notion that the unconscious is the discourse of the other. All these explanations take the form of explicitly or implicitly saying: "All the others have got it wrong, but I can tell you what 'The Secret Sharer' is *really* about." They claim to have found out the story's secret meaning.

A distinction may be made at this point between all such interpretations, which may be called "hermeneutic," and another way of approaching the story that may be called "rhetorical reading." This distinction corresponds to one made by the primary narrator in Conrad's *Heart of Darkness.* That narrator, you will remember from the previous chapter, distinguishes between two kinds of stories: those whose meaning is separate and identifiable, like a nut in a nutshell, and those whose meaning the story brings out through its own verbal activity, as the moon makes visible an otherwise invisible haze in the night air. The distinction I am making parallels this one. It sets "interpretation" against "reading." The former interprets the story by way of its relation to something distinct from the words. The latter interrogates the words themselves in their interplay. A hermeneutic interpretation is guaranteed by the reference of the words to something distinct from them, as the kernel of the nut is distinct from the nutshell. The "something distinct" may be the life of the author, or historical facts, either general or specific, or some external code of interpretation—religious, Freudian, Lacanian, feminist, new historicist, postcolonial, or whatever—some interpretative procedure that knows what it is going to find and can therefore always find what it seeks. Such a procedure knows how to crack the nut and find the kernel, or, to vary the metaphor, it knows how to crack the code and decipher anything written in that code. A Freudian version of such an interpretation, for example, might read the narrator's exclamation when he first sees Leggatt's naked body in the water beside the ship ("A headless corpse!" [86]) and say, "Ah ha! Decapitation. That means castration."

Freud himself, of course, was usually not so mechanical in his readings, conspicuously not so in the essay called "Das 'Unheimliche'" ("The 'Uncanny'"). Freud's "Das 'Unheimliche'" is itself an uncanny text in its repetitions, contradictions, revisions, apologies, and doublings. It is uncanny also in being the site of a battle between hermeneutic and rhetorical procedures. As such, it is not a dictionary of symbolic equivalences that can be used to translate details in a "this for that" (e.g., "headless corpse = castration"), but a text that must itself be rhetorically read in a way similar to the way we read a literary work. I am not saying that Freud's essay is a work of literature, only that it has to be read as carefully as if it were a work of literature and to some degree by the same procedures.

What I am calling a rhetorical reading of "The Secret Sharer" might even ultimately come to the same conclusion about that headless corpse (that it has something to do with castration), but only on the basis of a more or less elaborate internal reading. A rhetorical reading starts with the words and stays with them, paying close attention to subtle nuances of suggestion in figures of speech, in recurrences of words and nuances of wordplay. It presumes that the meaning of the tale is generated or constituted by the words of the tale, or brought out into the open out of the "unseen" by them and by them alone, like the mist by the moon, rather than being something that preexists them, something to which they refer. In the case of "The Secret Sharer," as with literary works in general, every detail, every figure of speech, every word or phrase and variation on those when they recur, counts. This means that a full reading of the story would require a virtually interminable accounting, something impossible to give in reasonable compass. What can be given here is the outline of a full reading and some exemplary readings of details.

Take, for example, the hat the narrator gives to Leggatt that then appears in the water just in the nick of time to help the narrator bring the ship about before it goes aground. Few readers will have failed to notice that hat and to see that it comes at a turning point in the story, in more ways than one. It must have some "symbolic" meaning. If beheading means castration, a hat, as a covering for the head, must be a phallic symbol. A hat fetishist displaces his anxiety about a part of his body, the phallus, to a fascination with an article of clothing that protects a different part of the body, a part that is a displaced representative of the phallus. Does the hat in "The Secret Sharer" work this way? Is it a symbol of the bond between the narrator and Leggatt, the manhood the narrator shares with Leggatt? He gives Leggatt his hat at the last minute before Leggatt prepares to dive into the water and swim ashore to confront whatever strange destiny awaits him there. He is motivated by his sense of identity with Leggatt, by a foresuffering of what Leggatt is likely to have to endure in his wanderings. He gives Leggatt his own hat in a silent, semicomic pantomime: "A sudden thought struck me. I saw myself wandering barefooted, bareheaded, the sun beating on my dark poll. I snatched off my floppy hat and tried hurriedly in the dark to ram it on my other self. He dodged and fended off silently. I wonder what he thought had come to me before he understood and suddenly desisted" (115). The giving of the hat is presented as a curiously violent, quasi-sexual event, almost like a kind of rape. Their groping, lingering handshake, the most overt sign of homosexual affection between them, follows. To give another person your own hat is certainly a mark of intimacy and affection. For Leggatt to wear the narrator's hat is a sign of their doubling identity. To say all this would be an example of hermeneutic interpretation, relating the signs to an external code that gives you meanings, in this case Freud's system of phallic or genital symbols. A shoe usually means the female genitals, in whatever dream it is encountered. A hat usually means the phallus. Loss of hat equals loss of head equals loss of penis. To take off your hat to someone is symbolically to disarm and unman yourself momentarily. The king's subjects usually may not wear their hats in the presence of the king. As a special privilege, those who hold doctorates from the University of Zaragosa are allowed to wear their academic hats in the presence of the king of Spain. They (the male ones, that is) are allowed to retain the symbols of their manhood even before the king.

This all seems plausible enough, and clearly applicable to an interpretation of "The Secret Sharer," but the hat does not quite work that way in the story. Leggatt leaves the hat behind in the water. He thereby repudiates whatever identity with the narrator wearing the narrator's hat would symbolize. This leaving behind of the hat is the moment of definitive division of Leggatt and the narrator. They go their separate ways. The narrator is freed of the burden of responsibility for his double and can take up his command of his ship and the men on her, as well as his affectionate intimacy with the ship, consistently seen as feminine throughout the story. When Leggatt swims away and the ship turns, the narrator turns from a homosexual to a heterosexual orientation. But this turning is made possible by a new meaning given by the narrator to the hat. This new meaning is an example of a rhetorical reading by the captain, not a hermeneutic interpretation:

> Was she moving? What I needed was something easily seen, a piece of paper which I could throw overboard and watch. I had nothing on me. To run down for it I didn't dare. There was no time. All at once my strained, yearning stare distinguished a white object floating within a yard of the ship's side. White on the black water. . . . I recognized my own floppy hat. It must have fallen off his head and he didn't bother. Now I had what I wanted—the saving mark for my eyes. . . . It had been meant to save his homeless head from the dangers of the sun! And now—behold—it was saving the ship, by serving me for a mark to help out the ignorance of my strangeness. Ha! It was drifting forward warning me just in time that the ship had gathered sternway. (118)

The hat has now become just a hat, white on the black water. Anything discernible would have done as well, as the narrator says, a piece of blank paper, for example, the paper in that case playing the role of the sign rather than the matrix for receiving signs, white on black rather than black on white. Whatever meaning the hat may have had as something shared between Leggatt and the captain is now forgotten, erased. The hat now becomes a neutral marker, in itself indifferent, like a blank bit of paper on which anything can be inscribed. You can write anything you like on it. It is up to you. You have to read it, but the reading is an active intervention. Reading now becomes a kind of writing or positing. The captain reads the hat as evidence that the ship is moving backward, so he can come about, shift the sails, and save the ship from going aground. The hat gives him the cue for the command: "Shift the helm" (118). The hat passes from the captain to Leggatt and back again, or back again to the neutral space between them, the space that now divides them.

The hat now becomes the marker of the narrator's turning away from Leggatt to sail off alone, a proud sailor confronting his new destiny, just as the narrator defines Leggatt, in the last sentence of the story, as "a free man, a proud swimmer striking out for a new destiny" (119). Leggatt is free of the tie to the narrator that keeping the latter's hat would have signified.

A rhetorical reading may begin with tropes, for example the sexual meanings attributed to the hat, but it ends with performative positing. Such positing characteristically involves some element of irony as the undermining of clear knowledge. The irony here lies in the difference between the narrator's understanding of the story and Conrad's or the reader's, as well as in the lingering doubt the reader may have about the way we should judge the narrator's action and the grounds for that judgment. That white hat stands out against the unfathomable darkness of the sea as a catachrestic name covers over the unknowability of what it names. I shall return to this perhaps obscure formulation.

What I am calling rhetorical reading and have exemplified in the meaning the captain gives to the hat does not deny the referential force of words. The Gulf of Siam, the River Meinam, and the pagoda really exist and are named by the story. Conrad accurately reports the details of seafaring and shiphandling. The story does have the immense and overdetermined context of Conrad's life, modern European history, and the history of Western imperialism. These must be presumed in any reading. The more we know about them the better. A rhetorical reading shows, however, that the story appropriates and reworks the referential force of the words for its own performative purposes. The meaning of the story is not exhausted by its historical references. In the case of the hermeneutic interpretation, the meaning, as the word "hermeneutic"[9] suggests, is a preexisting secret outside the words of the story, to which those words refer, and that proper procedures of interrogation may discover. It is a secret, but it may be made manifest. It may be known. A rhetorical reading hypothesizes that the story appropriates those referential meanings and makes of them a new meaning generated performatively by the words. The secret, if there is one, is all in the words, not behind them or in some other ascertainable realm, even though the words seem to be a response to another kind of secret, a secret not reachable at any sort of hermeneutic depth but rather absolutely unpresentable by any direct means. The unseen is unseen.

A complication in my distinction between interpretation and reading must, however, at this point be noted. This further twist is already present

---

9. It comes from a Greek word, *hermeneuein*, to interpret. "Hermeneutics" is "the science and methodology of interpretation, especially of Scriptural text" (*The American Heritage Dictionary*).

in Conrad's distinction between two kinds of stories. Both sorts of meaning, after all, are outside the words of the story, even though the distinction is clear between a seaman's story that can be summarized "in a nutshell," as we say, and a story like one of Marlow's whose meaning is insubstantial, a ghostly implication, "a misty halo," as Conrad puts it, "made visible by the spectral illumination of moonshine" (*HD* 45). In both cases, nevertheless, the meaning is distinct from the story, though in a quite different way for each. A story whose meaning is like the nut in the nutshell is controlled by its reference to something that preexists it and that could be reached by other means. We do not need "The Secret Sharer" to tell us that beheading stands for castration. Freud already told us that. The historical and biographical facts to which "The Secret Sharer" refers can be known in other ways, by reading history books about British imperialism or by reading Conrad's biography. That misty halo, however, though it is outside the story, can only be made visible by just this story, by just these words in just this order. The words of the story bring the meaning into the open, though it seems, after that exposure, to have been there all along waiting to be revealed. The story seems to be a response to a demand by that meaning to get itself told, narrated, revealed, just as the invisible mist is there waiting to be made visible by the illumination of moonshine. The story is a speech act, a performative. It is constitutive, inaugural. It makes something happen. It is a way of doing things with words. Nevertheless, the meaning it reveals always seems to have been there already, waiting to be revealed, like that invisible mist. Jacques Derrida expresses succinctly the way a work of literature as a singular speech act is both the inauguration of the new and at the same time a strange act of memory: "Reading as much as it writes, deciphering or citing as much as it inscribes, this act is also an act of memory (the other is already there, irreducibly), this act enacts [*cet acte prend acte*]."[10]

These two ways of deciphering, and some variants, are, it happens, embodied more or less covertly in "The Secret Sharer" itself. The chief mate, with his "terrible growth of whisker" and his habitual ejaculation, "Bless my soul sir! You don't say so!" (82) is a comic embodiment of the hermeneutic approach. As the narrator tells us, "He was of a painstaking turn of mind. As he used to say, he 'liked to account to himself for' practically everything that came in his way" (83). He says, "Bless my soul" to protect himself from the possibly malign or devilish influence of a scandalous piece of information, just as we say "God bless you" when someone sneezes, to prevent the devil from rushing in during the brief moment when the sneezer has expelled his soul by sneezing and

---

10. Jacques Derrida, "Fourmis," in *Lectures de la différence sexuelle*, ed. Mara Negron (Paris: Des femmes, 1994), 89; my translation.

the place where the soul was is empty.[11] If the devil got in, it might be a case of possession by one's diabolical double or devilish other. Until the first mate has found a rational, lawful explanation or "accounting" for everything that seems anomalous, unaccountable, he fears not so much for his sanity as for his salvation, his soul's health.

The comic example the narrator gives of this has an emblematic, allegorical force. The first mate, says the narrator, wanted painstakingly to explain everything, "down to a miserable scorpion he had found in his cabin a week before. The why and the wherefore of that scorpion—how it got on board and came to select his room rather than the pantry (which was a dark place and more what a scorpion would be partial to), and how on earth it managed to drown itself in the inkwell of his writing desk—had exercised him infinitely" (83). This is a good example of the way small, apparently insignificant details or locutions in "The Secret Sharer" count, must be scrutinized, and may have a covert meaning beyond the obvious literal one. That miserable scorpion surely corresponds to Leggatt who, like the scorpion, has mysteriously come aboard the ship. As an outlaw Leggatt is a scorpion-like danger to all the crew and their orderly life. Later in the story, after the captain of the *Sephora* has visited the narrator's ship looking for Leggatt, the chief mate quotes the crew's scandalized rejection of the idea that he might be on board: "As if we would harbor a thing like that" (104). It is not, moreover, without significance that the scorpion has drowned itself in an inkwell, in a manner of speaking contaminating or poisoning the ink, just as the ink with which the narrator (or Conrad himself) writes down the story accounting for Leggatt has been adulterated by the presence of that particular scorpion, though Leggatt does not in the end drown himself[12] but plunges into the sea to swim away toward shore and vanish, a free man ready to begin his new life.

The chief mate applies his hermeneutic technique of accounting to explain with careful reasoning and to his own satisfaction just what it means that another ship is anchored behind an island nearby: "She was, he doubted not, a ship from home lately arrived. Probably she drew too much water to cross the bar except at the top of spring tides. Therefore she went into that natural harbour to wait for a few days in preference to remaining in an open roadstead" (83). The second mate confirms that the chief mate has interpreted the

---

11. In a way something like this appearance of the devil when you sneeze, it could be argued, it is not without significance that Leggatt appears just after the narrator-captain has broken the normal rules of good seamanship and sent all the crew to bed so he can take a solitary five-hour anchor watch himself. His law-breaking or rule-breaking has made him vulnerable to the apparition of Leggatt.

12. He did initially intend to swim on in the open sea until he sank from exhaustion, as no doubt the scorpion in the inkwell did, if scorpions can swim.

signs correctly and drawn the correct logical conclusions, that he is a good hermeneut: "That's so.... She draws over twenty feet. She's the Liverpool ship *Sephora* with a cargo of coal. Hundred and twenty-three days from Cardiff" (83). How does the second mate come by these facts? The tugboat skipper has told him. If the chief mate represents the hermeneutic method as a deductive accounting by way of a rational interpretation of signs, the second mate represents the confirmation of such an interpretation by external historical facts. The latter would parallel an interpretation of "The Secret Sharer" such as Norman Sherry presents in *Conrad's Eastern World* by giving us the results of his historical research into the background facts on which Conrad based the tale. It would also be confirmed by what Conrad himself says about "The Secret Sharer."[13] In the "Author's Note" of 1920, Conrad says, "The basic fact of the tale I had in my possession for a good many years. It was in truth the common possession of the whole fleet of merchant ships trading to India, China and Australia." He goes on to say he had learned of the episode even before it got into the newspapers: "I had heard of it before, as it were privately, among the officers of the great wool fleet in which my first years in deep water were served" [6]. The episode happened on a ship called the *Cutty Sark,* belonging to a certain Mr. Willis, "a notable ship-owner in his day" (*SL* 32–33). What Conrad calls the "basic fact," however, is apparently not the central motif of his story, the hiding by the narrator of the fugitive murderer, but the murder itself, if it is a murder. That is up to us to decide.

The problem with a hermeneutic interpretation of "The Secret Sharer" is that the events presented in the story lend themselves neither to the logical and deductive accounting represented by the chief mate nor to the historical confirmation represented by the second mate. The narrator of "The Secret Sharer" represents the alternative of a rhetorical reading of those events as they are manifested by signs. His procedures of reading involve (1) a respect for what is mysterious and perhaps ultimately unaccountable in those signs; (2) an exacting attention to those signs in all their detail, in their materiality; (3) a procedure of displacement whereby the signs are in the act of narration displaced sideways in one way or another into other figurative signs; (4) an implicit recognition that reading, like the tropological change that says "this is like that," in one way or another is a performative speech act that reads signs by proffering new signs that can never be rationally authorized by the text but have another kind of authorizing. Such an act of reading is never a mere impersonal "accounting for." Reading is an active, transformative inter-

---

13. In the "Author's Note" of the 1920 reprint of the volume *'Twixt Land and Sea* of 1912. The latter contained the original book publication of "The Secret Sharer." Its first publication was in serialized form in *Harper's Magazine* in August to September 1910.

vention, not a passive reception. The narrator's procedures of reading also involve (5) an acceptance of the fact that the one who performs such a speech act must take responsibility for it and for its effects on others, in a shifting from rational accounting to performative engagement and obligation; and, finally, (6) recognition that such a retelling is a response to a demand made by some "other" that leads to a new form of understanding, understanding not as rational accounting but as an inaugural repetition or doubling, as what the narrator does obscurely doubles what Leggatt has done and must do so if he is to be able to say "I understand" in response to Leggatt's "I understand."[14] The reader, in turn, is called upon not just to understand rationally but to take his or her place in a chain of inheritance imposing a legacy of responsibility. Just how this might happen remains to be shown.

It is not certain beforehand what is the best way to read "The Secret Sharer." Only an actual reading will tell, one that starts, as always should be the case, with questions.

Let me begin at the beginning, with the title. It seems transparent enough, but just what does it mean? To whom or to what in the story does it refer? Like all titles, it functions as a clue. It is, the reader assumes, a synecdochic summing up whereby the part stands for the whole and is presumably like the whole. A reader asks himself or herself, "Why did he call it this?" A title is both outside what it names, an alien or stranger to the text that may conceivably be related to it only ironically, and at the same time part of the text, a member of the family of terms we use to understand it. A title is outside and inside at once. In the case of "The Secret Sharer," though not of course with all titles, the title is actually repeated inside the story, not just something outside it that gives it a name. The phrase is used more than once to define Leggatt when the narrator of the story is hiding him in his cabin. He calls Leggatt early in the story "the secret sharer of my life" (98), then, soon after, "the secret sharer of my cabin" (101), and in the story's last sentence, "the secret sharer of my cabin and of my thoughts" (119).

What is a secret sharer? A secret *sharer*? A *secret* sharer? A different meaning arises depending on which word is stressed. If "sharer" is stressed, "secret" is an adjective modifying "sharer." Leggatt secretly shares the narrator's cabin, lives there with him, shares his thoughts, though no one else knows. If "secret"

---

14. "He kept silent for a while, then whispered: 'I understand.'
    'I won't be there to see you go,' I began with an effort. 'The rest . . . I only hope I have understood too.'
    'You have. From first to last'" (114).

is stressed, "secret" is a noun and "sharer" is another noun. Leggatt is someone who shares a secret or secrets. But does the title name only Leggatt? Its use as a title that sums up the whole story invites the reader to look for a wider reference. Does the narrator not, as I have already suggested, share Leggatt's secret when Leggatt tells his story, and then share it again with the reader in telling his story? Just what is a secret, if there is such a thing? If there is such a thing, can it be shared? Does it remain a secret when it has been shared? Is there such a thing as a shared secret? Does it not cease to be secret when it is shared? What does it mean to speak of a secret as "shared"? Divided, cut in two? As when we speak of a shared meal? All these questions are raised by an attempt to decide the exact force of the title. "Shared" is related in meaning and etymology to "sheared," as a ploughshare cuts the furrow, dividing the earth. To share something usually means to cut it into at least two pieces, though it can also mean "to have in common," as when we say "They shared a bed." A secret, it would seem, cannot be cut in two in this way. It is an indivisible whole, is it not, like a single person? It is incapable of being doubled. When a secret becomes an open secret, shared promiscuously, it is hardly a secret any longer. Anyone with some small experience of life knows that when you say "I'll tell you a secret, if you promise to keep it," you might as well be shouting it from the housetops or printing it on the front page of *The New York Times*.

As Jacques Derrida has demonstrated (in *Donner le temps: 1. La fausse monnaie*,[15] in *Passions*,[16] and in a series of admirable seminars given some years ago now, prior to those books), a true secret, if there is such a thing, cannot be revealed. If it can be revealed it is not really a secret, or, to put this another way, one must distinguish between those quasi-secrets that can be revealed, such as state secrets or secret recipes, and another kind of more secret secret that cannot by any means be revealed. Does "The Secret Sharer" hide a secret of that sort? What would the traces or marks of such a secret be? Even if it is an unpresentable and unrevealable secret, we would not know of its existence unless it manifested itself in indirect signs of some sort announcing its hidden existence. Something must say, "There is a secret there." That would give another reading of the title. To share a secret might not mean to share it with another person, but to participate in the secret, to be subject to its force, even though the secret as such cannot be revealed. What would then

---

15. Jacques Derrida, *Donner le temps: 1. La fausse monnaie* (Paris: Galilée, 1991); Derrida, *Given Time, I: Counterfeit Money*, trans. Peggy Kamuf (Chicago: University of Chicago Press, 1992).

16. Jacques Derrida, *Passions* (Paris: Galilée, 1993); Derrida, "Passions," trans. David Wood, in *On the Name*, ed. Thomas Dutoit (Stanford: Stanford University Press, 1995), 2–31.

be passed on from Leggatt to the narrator is not some identifiable secret that might be revealed, but subjection to the irresistible force of a secret that cannot be revealed as such but that nevertheless imposes a pitiless obligation on those who come to be subject to it, to share in it.[17] That may be, but, after all, there seems little we would like to know about "The Secret Sharer" that we cannot know. It seems as if the narrator tells all. He shares all the secrets with the reader. What remains still secret at the end of the story?

Jacques Derrida has, in the various works just referred to, seen an essential relation between literature and the secret. Literature keeps its secret. A work of literature is all on the surface, all there in the words on the page, imprinted on a surface that cannot be gone behind. This means that there are certain secrets or enigmas in a work of literature that cannot by any means be penetrated, though answers to the questions they pose may be essential to a reading of the work. We cannot know, for example, whether Leggatt is telling the truth in his version of the murder. He is in this like a witness in the witness box. We have only his word for it. Nor can we know how the narrator came to be captain of this ship. He refrains openly from telling us: "In consequence of certain events of no particular significance, except to myself, I had been appointed to the command only a fortnight before" (82). When someone talks like that, it is reasonable to think he may be hiding something. What that something may be we shall never know. Nor is the reader told what was the name of the captain of the *Sephora*. Archbold? Maybe, but the narrator cannot remember, or says he cannot remember: "It was something like Archbold—but at this distance of years I hardly am sure" (99). Archbold would, as I said earlier, certainly be an ironically inappropriate name for him, since the narrator says he was a shy man whose "main characteristic" was "a spiritless tenacity." He gives his ship's name and other particulars "in the manner of an unpentinent criminal making a reluctant and doleful confession" (99). This makes him an ironic double of Leggatt and the narrator, both of whom make confessions. Conrad's figure puts in the readers' minds the topic of confession. It reminds us that we are reading a confession about a confession, neither of which is either reluctant or doleful.

Or are they? The narrator's testimony is incomplete. He seems reluctant to tell us everything. If I were a lawyer for the prosecution I would have a few questions to ask him, beyond asking him to tell me his name, the name of his ship, and a few more particulars in the way of dates and facts. For example, the reader can never know just what was the version of the murder given by the captain of the *Sephora*, since the narrator explicitly refuses to give that other

---

17. I owe this reading of "secret sharer" to Kevin Yee.

version: "he had to raise his voice to give me his tale. It is not worth while to record that version" (100). Why not? One would have thought the captain would have been a valuable additional witness. Certainly he would have been called upon in a court of law to tell his story. The narrator seems so certain that Leggatt told the truth that he discounts any other version. In doing so, he does keep a secret from the reader, a secret the reader therefore has no way of ever knowing.

As a matter of fact, the narrator gives the reader the essence of the *Sephora*'s captain's interpretation of what happened. Captain Archbold, if that is really his name, sees the events as evidence of God's providence, not, as Leggatt sees them, as evidence of his (Leggatt's) bravery in setting the reefed foresail in the midst of a terrible storm. "God's own hand in it," says the captain of the *Sephora*. "Nothing less could have done it. I don't mind telling you that I hardly dared give the order" (101). Leggatt insists that the captain gave no such order, that he, Leggatt, acted on his own and saved the ship, just as he (according to him) justifiably took the law into his own hands when he killed the mutinous crewman. The latter was an "ill-conditioned snarling cur" (88). It might be noted that a few lines later Leggatt himself becomes in retrospect doglike when he tells how he took the crewman by the neck and "[shook] him like a rat" (89). This doubling is redoubled much later when the narrator shakes the chief mate to get him to go forward to tend to the head-sheets when they are about to go aground: "You go forward—shake—and stop there—shake—and hold your noise—shake—and see these head-sheets properly overhauled—shake, shake—shake" (117). Leggatt obscurely doubles the rebellious crewman, as the narrator doubles Leggatt. Like the crewman, both Leggatt and the narrator transgress against convention or law. The covert similarity is hidden by the narrator's strong endorsement of Leggatt's judgment that the crewman was one of those "miserable devils that have no business to live at all. He wouldn't do his duty and wouldn't let anybody else do theirs" (88). The narrator agrees. He tells the reader, "I knew well enough the pestiferous danger of such a character where there are no means of legal repression" (89). Readers of *The Nigger of the "Narcissus"* (1897) will remember in that novel the sullen, resentful, and mean-spirited character Donkin as another Conradian character who malingers, complains, and refuses to do his duty.

What the narrator says of the crewman Leggatt kills in "The Secret Sharer" would seem to give support to a reading of Conrad as an arch-conservative spokesperson for British ideas of hierarchy, duty, fidelity, imperial responsibility, the white man's burden, and so on, with the overtones of sexism and racism that are associated with such allegiances. Conrad's narrator asserts that on board ship "there are no means of legal repression" (89). To preserve the laws of duty, obedience, and so on, someone must act against the law, outside the law, in a strange kind of unlawful law-preserving or law-establishing violence.[18] "The Secret Sharer," in its confrontation of this disquieting aspect of the law, in particular law on board ship, is analogous to Herman Melville's *Billy Budd*. To read them side by side would be instructive.

It is not exactly the case, however, that on board ship "there are no means of legal repression," as the captain of the *Sephora* indicates when he says to Leggatt, "I represent the law here" (93). A ship captain is not the law, but he represents the law. This, however, is also the case on shore. The law is never present in person, but only in its representatives: the police, a lawyer, a judge, a jury. The whole apparatus of the law is not the law but a representation of the absent law. The way the captain represents the law makes the narrator's claim that there are no means of legal repression of an insubordinate crewman seem strangely problematic. The captain of the *Sephora*, for example, does not hesitate to "arrest" Leggatt and keep him locked in his cabin.

Captain Archbold, as against the narrator's judgment and as against Leggatt's self-evaluation, sees Leggatt as without question a murderer. He must be turned over "to the law" (101) as soon as he can be got ashore. In fact the captain is morbidly concerned with his responsibility for doing that: "His obscure tenacity on that point had in it something incomprehensible and a little awful; something as it were, mystical. . . . Seven-and-thirty virtuous years at sea . . . seemed to have laid him under some pitiless obligation" (101). Why is this sense of obligation "incomprehensible," "awful," "mystical"? Perhaps because it is a sense of justice that leads beyond itself to injustice. It uses an appeal to law to justify the unjustified and unjustifiable. In any case, neither Leggatt nor the narrator feels that pitiless obligation. Their obligation is rather to another force of law, to one that may be equally incomprehensible, awful, even mystical, whatever Conrad may mean by such portentous terms. Which obligation should we credit? Which behavior should we approve of and imitate? Moral life is full of situations not entirely unlike Leggatt's situation or the narrator's. What would I have done in Leggatt's situation or in

---

18. See Walter Benjamin's "Critique of Violence" ("*Zur Kritik der Gewalt*" [1921]) as the most troubling and searching investigation of this problem. See also Jacques Derrida's discussion of Benjamin's essay and related questions of the grounds of justice in *Force de loi* (Paris: Galilée, 1994); Derrida, "Force of Law: The 'Mystical Foundation of Authority,'" trans. Mary Quaintance, in *Deconstruction and the Possibility of Justice*, ed. Drucilla Cornell, Michel Rosenfeld, and David Gray Carlson (New York: Routledge, 1992), 3–67.

the narrator's? What *should* I have done, and on the basis of what moral and public law, or secret and private one?

It might seem that by the end all that is of importance in "The Secret Sharer" has been laid open, all secrets revealed, so that they are not secret any more. The fact of the murder was known to everyone in the whole merchant fleet in that area. The narrator tells us the whole story, at least his version of it. Nothing of importance seems to remain hidden. Nevertheless, nagging questions remain as to the grounds for Leggatt's act and its doubling in what the narrator does. The narrator speaks of Leggatt as "the secret sharer of my life." That seems to limit the title to naming Leggatt as the secret presence hidden from all the others on board the ship, but who nevertheless shares the narrator's life, eats his food, sleeps in his bed in his sleeping suit, uses his bathroom, sees him in the most intimate acts, for example taking a bath. We cannot even be sure that they may not share the captain's bed, after that first night, when the narrator tells us that he spent the night on his couch. On the question of whether or not they slept together in the same bed the narrator gives no information. It is an impenetrable secret, though the reader would like to know. A good bit of affection exists between them, in any case, as well as a strong sense of identity, most overtly in their farewell handshake as they crawl on hands and knees in the dark sail locker: "Our hands met gropingly, lingered united in a steady, motionless clasp for a second. . . . No word was breathed by either of us when they separated" (115).

Leggatt, as the story tells the reader again and again, is the narrator's hidden double, his other self, as intimately known and understood as his own self. The narrator lies for Leggatt, for example by persuading the captain of the *Sephora* that Leggatt is not there. How can we be sure he is not lying to us or withholding some important secret in the guise of telling all? Apparently complete openness, as Poe's "The Purloined Letter" notoriously shows, is the best way to hide something. The narrator is also a secret sharer in another way. He shares his secret with us, or with me as reader. Even if I think of him as talking to himself, reminiscing, his secret thoughts have in some miraculous way been exposed, so that I can read his mind, just as the narrator says he can read Leggatt's mind. The reader, I as reader, become the secret sharer of a secret. My sharing is secret because reading is secret. What it does to me, as I have said, is silent, leaves no mark. "The Secret Sharer," as one can see, is made of a whole series of secret sharers, in both senses, *secret* sharers and secret *sharers* who are also doubles of one another: Leggatt, the narrator, the reader, even Captain "Archbold," anyone who writes an essay about the story and so passes the secret and the responsibility for the secret on to another person, anyone who reads that essay, this one for example, and thereby becomes a secret sharer, a sharer of the secret.

To try to formulate more exactly just what that secret might be, I turn now to the first paragraph of the story. This paragraph is a striking example of the way the narrator's tale is not just objective description but at every turn a figurative transformation and an active intervention, as what I would call "rhetorical reading" must always be. The narrator's way with language gives the reader a model for his or her own activity.

Along with the wonderfully vivid scene-setting that the opening paragraph has as its apparent main goal, it also unostentatiously sets up several other horizons of expectation that are crucial to the meaning of the narration that begins after the scene has been set. (1) The first paragraph introduces the motif of doubling and redoubling. (2) It initiates the reader into a process whereby one thing stands for another or is like another. In this it is a primer or introductory handbook about how to read parabolically. (3) It gives the reader the first example of something that is mysterious, incomprehensible, something not open to rational knowing.

The very first sentence does all three of these things at once, besides being effective at making us *see*: "On my right hand there were lines of fishing stakes resembling a mysterious system of half submerged bamboo fences, incomprehensible in its division of the domain of tropical fishes, and crazy of aspect as if abandoned for ever by some nomad tribe of brown fishermen now removed to the other end of the earth, for there was no sign of human habitation as far as the eye could reach" (81). This is an accurate description of a real place in the real world. It tells the reader that the water is quite shallow off the mouth of the River Meinam at the head of what used to be called the Gulf of Siam. It tells us, moreover, that there were bamboo fish weirs there, that is, fenced enclosures with a narrow opening that traps schools of small fish when they swim in the opening and cannot find their way out again. Such fish weirs, though not of bamboo, are still used in the shallow waters around Deer Isle, Maine, where I spend my summers. I have (in December 1994) seen such weirs, probably in this case of bamboo, in the shallow water on the western side of Taiwan, south of the city of Kaohsiung, much closer geographically to the ones Conrad describes than Deer Isle, Maine.

Though Conrad knew they were fish weirs, since he calls them "fishing stakes," nevertheless he chose to describe them, in a way that is characteristic of his art of description throughout his work, as if he did not quite understand them, as if they were "mysterious," "incomprehensible." They look like "half-submerged bamboo fences" whose purpose is inscrutable. Just as words can become strange, uncanny, when they are repeated over and over, so, looked at in a certain way, even ordinary things can seem to harbor some unfathomable secret, as the life of the fishermen who made these "crazy" (in the sense of "dilapidated," but also with a hint of "insane") fish weirs is unknown. In a similar way, much later in the story, the narrator stresses what is mysterious about the human life on the islands where Leggatt is put ashore: "Unknown to trade, to travel, almost to geography, the manner of life they harbour is an unsolved secret" (112).[19]

The first sentence also unostentatiously introduces the theme of division, sharing, or doubling. The system of bamboo fences is incomprehensible in its *division* of the domain of tropical fishes. A little later in the paragraph, "two small clumps of trees, one on each side" (81) of the river mouth, are a small-scale doubling like that introduced later when the narrator tells us that in the cuddy (that is, the room on the ship used as the officers' dining room), "Two bunches of bananas hung from the beam symmetrically, one on each side of the rudder casing" (90). The next sentence makes explicit the parallel between the bananas and the doubling of the narrator by Leggatt: "two of [the] captain's sleeping suits were simultaneously in use" (90). The name Leggatt, though it may be modeled on "legate" and pronounced the same, contains, as I have noted, two sets of doubled consonants. These are a material inscription of Leggatt's connection with doubling.

Later in the first paragraph, to return to that, the entire scene is divided and then subdivided in a mirroring that anticipates and universalizes that of the two main characters. The narrator sees "the straight line of the flat shore joined to the stable sea edge to edge with a perfect and unmarked closeness" (81). The doubling of shore and sea in its unmarked intimacy is like the intimate doubling of the narrator and Leggatt. What happens to the one seems almost to happen to the other. The narrator often feels he is outside himself and dwelling inside the skin or inside the sleeping suit of the other man: "I was constantly watching myself, my secret self, as dependent on my action as my own personality" (97); "That mental feeling of being in two places at once affected me physically as if the mood of secrecy had penetrated my very soul" (106). The doubling of sea and shore, however, that so distinctly anticipates the relation between the narrator and Leggatt, preparing the reader unawares for it, is doubled once more in the description of the whole expanse of the

---

19. Since Conrad wrote this story, partly through colonization of the political or of the economic sort, partly through the work of many busy Western anthropologists, fewer and fewer places on the globe are unsolved secrets to the West in this way.

earth, sea and sky together. The great dome of the evening sky, an elemental and sublime[20] spectacle, doubles the sea and shore: "one levelled floor, half brown, half blue, under the enormous dome of the sky" (81).

Conrad's phrasing in this last quotation, however, exemplifies one more of the chief stylistic features of this opening paragraph. It is a feature also present in Kant's celebrated example in *The Critique of Judgment* of the arching sky over the sea as in its inhuman materiality a correlate of sublime feelings. In Conrad, as in Kant, the sea and shore together become a "levelled floor" and the sky becomes a "dome." The whole scene becomes one gigantic architectural construction. It is as though it is not possible to confront directly a scene representing sublime feelings and then name it without turning its alien otherness into something more familiar and human, in this case a man-made dwelling. "Floor" and "dome" are examples of those original catachreses whereby we give names to what has no proper name and cover over what is wholly other by giving it familiar labels that make it seem something within which we can be at home.

This transformation of inhuman nature into a humanized architectural construction is already present earlier in the paragraph when the narrator sees the "group of barren islets" as something "suggesting ruins of stone walls, towers and blockhouses" (81). The paragraph is a tissue of such comparisons. The fish weirs look "as if abandoned for ever by some nomad tribe of brown fishermen" (81). The curving river inland is intermittently visible in "gleams as of a few scattered pieces of silver," and the tug winding up that river eventually disappears "as though the impassive earth had swallowed her up without an effort, without a tremor" (81). All these "as ifs," the reader can see, are humanizations of the inhuman nature they serve to name. The sky is like a dome, the sea and shore a floor. The islets are ruined buildings, the river is like silver coins, the earth is a huge beast that can swallow whole tugboats at a gulp. An

---

20. I mean the word "sublime" in the strong, traditional sense of the word, as it is used from Longinus through Kant and Burke up to present-day theorists of the sublime such as Thomas Weiskel, Jean-François Lyotard, or Paul de Man. For all of these philosopher-critics the sublime, in one way or another, is a subjective feeling mingling fear and inordinate pleasure. Strictly speaking, no object is sublime, but the feeling of the sublime may be aroused or represented by some aspect of nature that exceeds human comprehension, something that is terrifying because it is unknown and unknowable. The sublime can only be named in figures that are illegitimate in the sense that they are not proper names and are not commensurate with the frightening unknowability they seek to make apparently namable. An empty sea under the empty sky is one example Kant gives of the sublime, though, like Conrad, he sees this in architectural terms. It cannot be seen in its sheer materiality. See Paul de Man, "Phenomenality and Materiality in Kant," in *Aesthetic Ideology*, ed. Andrzej Warminski (Minneapolis: University of Minnesota Press, 1996), 70–90.

imaginary narrative about nomad fishermen is invented to account for the crazy aspect of those fish weirs.

These figures show that the first paragraph, far from being, as I began by saying, just wonderfully vivid description that makes the reader feel he or she had been there, is the site of a strong verbal will to power on Conrad's part (or the narrator's part). This will to mastery describes things by transforming them into something they are not. What might at first appear to be neutral description is a series of performative speech acts. These do not just describe. They posit. They do this on their own independent, unauthorized say-so. In this they fulfill Aristotle's remark in the *Poetics* that a gift for metaphor is a mark of genius in a poet, the one thing the poet cannot learn from another.[21] It is as if the narrator were saying, "let these barren islets be seen as ruined towers, walls, and blockhouses," and so on. If "The Secret Sharer" is obliquely the story of how the narrator grew up to the point where he was worthy of the solitude and independent responsibility of command, the verbal mastery of the first paragraph is evidence that he has long since achieved that right to command. He has command over words. He can use words performatively to change what is there before him into something else—the sky into a dome, rocky islets into ruined cities, the sea and shore into a floor, the fish weirs into abandoned fences, the whole natural inhuman landscape into a humanized architectural scene of abandonment and desolation. What it might mean to say that these speech-act transformations are unauthorized or only secretly authorized and how that might correspond to other unauthorized acts in the story remains to be seen.

One way to investigate this further is to recognize that the story throughout turns on a series of key words and word clusters that gain a peculiar meaning and force through their repetition. Objections have been made, by Marvin Mudrick[22] and other critics, to these repetitions as a notable characteristic

---

21. Aristotle, *Poetics*, 22:9, 1459a. William Wordsworth, in the "Preface" of 1815, is true to Aristotle when he sees such metaphorical transformations as prime evidence of the poetic imagination. See William Wordsworth, *Poetical Works*, ed. Thomas Hutchinson and Ernest de Selincourt (London: Oxford University Press, 1966), 754. This passage is cited and discussed in chapter 1 ["Friedrich Schlegel: Catachreses for Chaos," in Miller, *Others* (Princeton: Princeton University Press, 2001), 25–26; (Editors)]. For Wordsworth, as for Conrad, the primary evidence of word power is the ability to use words in personifications of the inanimate and depersonifications of the animate.

22. Marvin Mudrick, "Conrad and the Terms of Modern Criticism," *Hudson Review* 7, no. 3 (Autumn 1954): 419–26 [Editors].

of Conrad's style. They are said to be tedious and obvious. Such critics have missed the point. "Double," "stranger," "secret," "ghostly," "mysterious," "conscience," "understand"—the repetition of these words, and their variants, calls attention to them, singles them out by using them over and over in somewhat different surrounding verbal contexts. They thereby become strange and even progressively emptied of meaning, as any word does when it is repeated many times. A word's materiality, what gives it force, begins to show through its immaterial meaning if it is repeated often enough. It becomes senseless sound or marks on the page.

The most salient examples of this are the manifold repetitions of the word "double," though the same thing could be demonstrated with all the other words I listed above: "In a moment he had concealed his damp body in a sleeping suit of the same grey-stripe pattern as the one I was wearing and followed me like my double" (87); "murmured my double distinctly" (88); "My double gave me an inkling of his thoughts" (88); "my double there was no homicidal ruffian" (89); "he would think he was seeing his captain double" (90); "My double followed my movements" (90); "anybody bold enough to open [the door] stealthily would have been treated to the uncanny sight of a double captain busy talking in whispers to his other self" (91); "My double breathed into my very ear anxiously" (94); "I took a peep at my double" (97), and so on and on, double and after double, through many more doublings.

The careful reader will note that the word "double" appears first as an explicit trope, a simile. Dressed in a striped sleeping suit like the one the narrator is wearing, Leggatt follows the narrator *"like* [his] double" (my italics). The first-time reader cannot tell at this point whether this is important or only a passing figure inserted for vividness. From then on, however, the simile, weakest of tropes, becomes a literal assertion. Leggatt is "my double," just that, and said over and over to be so, as if the verbal similitude had had the power to materialize itself. It is as though a simile could be a speech act, a way of doing things with words. It makes happen as literal fact what it initially names as an "as if." The insistent repetition matches the opening tropological transformations. It is another curious version of the performative will to power over words or the will to make use of words in acts of power.

The will in question is not that of a subjective ego in full possession of its free power of volition. The words seem rather to act on their own, or they promise to do so. Such word use is a process creating the self. The narrator of "The Secret Sharer" ceases to be a stranger to himself and becomes worthy of command through his response to the demand made on him by Leggatt. That response operates through the narrative transformations that make up the verbal texture of "The Secret Sharer." The story does what it talks about.

Words repeated insistently, as Conrad does in this story, become detached, enigmatic. They seem to harbor a secret. The repetition of the key words makes them somehow uncanny. They become intruders into the sentences in which they are used so that they stand out rather than being fully assimilated into a local meaning.[23] In this they are like Leggatt himself, the ghostly guest who invades the narrator's ship as an alien presence. Such words in their repetition work as repetitive speech acts: "secret"; "secret"; "secret"; "secret"; "double"; "double"; "double"; "double," etc., in a mad and maddening refrain that has annoyed some readers. They have not seen how the repetition mimes the story's central theme. The narrator himself more than once says that his sense of being double and living within two minds and bodies was almost a form of insanity: "all the time the dual working of my mind distracted me almost to the point of insanity" (97); "I think I had come creeping quietly as near insanity as any man who has not actually gone over the border" (109–10). To be of two minds, to be subject to a doubling repetition, is to be on the brink of insanity.

The collective force of this cluster of words as they are repeated again and again in different combinations is to make of the story as a whole a large-scale version of the kind of transformation effected by the performative tropes of the first paragraph. In the latter, the scene of sea, sky, islets, and shore is turned into a sublimely desolate architectural construction. In the former, the literal story of the harboring by the narrator of a fugitive murderer is changed by the narrator's language into an uncanny story of doubling and repetition. The narrator's performative positings turn objective description into a testimony or confession addressed to me as reader. The episode becomes what it was not in itself, without the narrator's intervention, namely, a narrative of the invasion of a safe domicile by a ghostly stranger who upsets the familiar economy of that home and puts a terrible burden of responsibility on its inhabitant. This is the traditional mission of such ghostly invaders in older similar narratives, for example "Sir Gawain and the Green Knight."

---

23. William Carlos Williams long ago formulated this strange effect of certain word uses apropos of Marianne Moore's poetry, though with emphasis on the making material of words rather than on the uncanny draining away of meaning I am stressing. "Miss Moore," wrote Williams, "gets great pleasure from wiping soiled words or cutting them clean out, removing the aureoles that have been pasted about them or taking them bodily from greasy contexts. For the compositions which Miss Moore intends, each word should first stand crystal clear with no attachments; not even an aroma." *Selected Essays* (New York: Random House, 1954), 128.

The usual pattern of the *Doppelgänger* story, however, is given a significant variation in Conrad's telling of it. Or perhaps it would be better to say that "The Secret Sharer" makes explicit an implicit feature of the *Doppelgänger* story. Here the one who is haunted by a strange double is already, as he tells us, a stranger on the ship. The rest of the crew have all been together for a year and a half, while the captain has quite recently joined the ship as its new and untried captain. Moreover, he is also, as he tells us, a stranger to himself. By this he appears to mean that he does not yet know whether he will be able to measure up to the demands of command or whether he will measure up to his own secret conception of himself: "All these people had been together for eighteen months or so and my position was that of the only stranger on board. . . . But what I felt most was my being a stranger to the ship; and if all the truth must be told, I was somewhat of a stranger to myself" (82–83). The invasion of the captain's life by an even stranger stranger, Leggatt, the double of the captain's strangeness, is explicitly said to be brought about by the captain's own strangeness. It is the captain's decision to transgress the "established routine of duties" (85) on the ship that with seemingly magic promptness brings Leggatt into his life as the objective embodiment of his own strangeness: "I felt painfully that I—a stranger—was doing something unusual when I directed [the mate] to let all hands turn in without setting an anchor watch" (84).

Sigmund Freud, citing Schelling, defines "uncanny" (*unheimlich*) as "the name for everything that ought to have remained . . . hidden and secret and has become visible."[24] As I said earlier, Freud's essay is inexhaustibly rich and complex, not least in its contradictions. This is not the place to try to read it in detail. Conrad's story in one place, already cited, uses the word "uncanny": anyone coming into the captain's cabin "would have been treated to the uncanny sight of a double captain busy talking in whispers with his other self" [91]. In many ways, moreover, the story corresponds to key aspects of Freud's examples of the uncanny. Not only is doubling in itself uncanny, according to Freud, as are other forms of repetition, but Freud also stresses the gruesome aspects of the uncanny and their relation to sexual mutilation, as well as to ghost effects and to the invasion of the home by a spooky personage who represents something familiar that ought to be kept secret.

Leggatt appears first, in a passage I have quoted, as a headless corpse [86]. In the water he is "ghastly, silvery, fishlike" (86). Once he is hidden in the narrator's cabin he becomes a phantom presence there, attired "in the ghostly grey

---

24. Sigmund Freud, "The Uncanny," in *Studies in Parapsychology*, ed. Philip Rieff (New York: Collier, 1963), 27.

of [his] sleeping suit" (88). That doubling presence makes "a scene of weird witchcraft: the strange captain having a quiet confabulation by the wheel with his own grey ghost" (90). At one point, the narrator says, "an irresistible doubt of his bodily existence flitted through my mind: Can it be, I asked myself, that he is not visible to other eyes than mine? It was like being haunted" (109). The narrator's success in keeping Leggatt hidden raises the question of whether others can see him at all, whether he is not the narrator's personal ghost.

The English word "uncanny" does not of course fully translate the German word *unheimlich*. Both, however, are double or antithetical words. "Uncanny" comes from "can," to know how, be able. "Canny" means not only shrewd but "susceptible of human understanding; explicable; natural," while uncanny is the opposite: "exciting wonder and fear: inexplicable; strange, as in 'an uncanny laugh.'" The second meaning of "uncanny," however, shows that it is not so much the opposite of "canny" as it is canny knowledge and insight carried to that hyperbolic point where it reverses itself and becomes uncanny: "so keen and perceptive as to seem preternatural, as in 'uncanny insight.'"[25] In the same way, as any reader of Freud's essay knows, what is uncanny about the word *unheimlich* is that it too reverses itself and comes to mean not something alien to the home, unhomey, but precisely something familiar to the home, a home secret that ought to have been kept hidden, but has come out of the closet, so to speak. "Thus 'heimlich,'" says Freud, "is a word the meaning of which develops towards an ambivalence, until it finally coincides with its opposite, 'unheimlich.' 'Unheimlich' is in some way or other a sub-species of 'heimlich.'"[26]

Understanding the uncanny, the reader can see, means comprehending the incomprehensible, since the uncanny is by definition strange, inexplicable. If the reader has "The Secret Sharer" in mind, he or she will remember both the emphasis on what is mysterious and indescribable about Leggatt for the narrator and the counterstress on the total understanding that the narrator and Leggatt have of one another. Of Leggatt's telling of his story the narrator says: "There was something that made comment impossible in his narrative, or perhaps in himself; a sort of feeling, a quality, which I can't find a name for" (94). Naming is here opposed to feeling and wordless understanding. Though he cannot name it, he can understand it, as their ultimate exchange of affirmations asserts: "I understand"; "I only hope I have understood too"; "You have. From first to last" (114).

---

25. These definitions are drawn from *The American Heritage Dictionary*.
26. Freud, "The Uncanny," 30.

The "individual instances" of the *unheimlich* Freud examines in large part depend on a resource of the German word not present in the English one. "Heim" means "home" in German. The group of "heim" words, including *unheimlich*, is associated with family relationships and with the domestic economy of the house and its grounds—its division into separate rooms devoted to different uses; its doors, windows, closets, walls, and gates. The English word "uncanny" does not so overtly have such associations. Freud's discussion of E. T. A. Hoffmann's "The Sandman" is the most extended of his investigations of uncanny literary works. Hoffmann's story involves the invasion of a home and family enclosure. Conrad's story is also an admirable exploitation of the relation of the uncanny to the home and to the opposition between belonging to the home, being a familiar there, and being a stranger. A ship is like a large home with many rooms. The crew is in a manner of speaking one big family. The narrator stresses how they all know one another. He is the only stranger. He is an alien guest who nevertheless dwells within the heart of the home, the captain's quarters, and has a right to be there. Leggatt enters the captain's quarters as the double of the narrator's strangeness, an inner strangeness within what is already strange.

Much of the meaning of "The Secret Sharer" is carried unostentatiously by the careful attention to the exact layout of the captain's quarters and to the way the narrator lives there and manages to keep Leggatt hidden. If the captain's quarters are deep within the ship, in a protected place near the stern, those quarters are themselves further divided and subdivided within, so that there are insides of the insides, outside insides and inside insides. The cabin itself is L-shaped, the narrator tells us, with the door opening into a public inside, so to speak, where the captain's desk and couch can be seen from the door. Around the corner, invisible from the door, an inside of the inside, is the long leg of the L, where the captain's "bed place," as he somewhat curiously calls it, is located. This bed place is a raised bunk with drawers beneath and curtains that may be drawn to protect its privacy, making it an inside of the inside of the inside. Beyond that, at the end of the L, are coats hung on hooks, behind which Leggatt part of the time hides crouching on a camp stool. In that L is also the door to the captain's bathroom, another inside of the inside of the inside, where Leggatt spends most of his time, since it is the most hidden and private place of all. Nevertheless, just as there are portholes in the bedplace giving the farthest inside direct access to what is outside the whole ship, exterior to its labyrinthine or *mise en abyme* domestic structure, so there is another door in the bathroom leading back into the saloon (the name for a common sitting area on board ship). That door is never used, except by the steward when he enters to clean the bathroom, but it is another example of the way the most inside and private nevertheless leads to the public and outside.

This whole configuration is an admirable materialization of the narrator's relation to Leggatt and to the ship's crew. The trick is to make the whole area appear public, for example to give normal access to it for the steward who cleans the rooms, keeps them in order, and brings the captain his morning coffee, as well as for the chief mate and for the captain of the *Sephora* when the latter comes aboard looking for Leggatt, while at the same time keeping Leggatt invisibly hidden there, giving him a bed to sleep in, feeding him, and so on. This part of the story is a wonderfully concrete externalization of the fear of having one's most secret and even shameful privacies invaded and exposed to public view.

Just what is the uncanny secret that is as familiar as one's own private part of the house? It must be a secret that is in danger of being exposed, or rather that *is* apparently exposed by the captain's narration though it ought to remain hidden, or perhaps still does remain hidden after all the narrator's confessional openness. The secret can hardly be Leggatt's act of murder, since that is known by all on board the *Sephora*. It will ultimately be known to sailors all over that part of the world. The secret must be the narrator's complicity in that murder, his doubling of Leggatt's act by harboring him, and, most hidden secret, the secret behind the secret, the occult ground or obligation that justifies that act in its doubling and makes it the right thing to do.

Conrad repeatedly emphasizes the similarity between the narrator and Leggatt in their propensity to lawless transgression and consequent guilt. This similarity is most overt when the narrator's sense of identity with Leggatt makes him feel guilty too when the captain of the *Sephora* comes seeking Leggatt: "I felt as if I personally were being given to understand that I too was not the sort of man that would have done for the chief mate of a ship like the *Sephora*. I had no doubt of it in my mind" (101); "I believe that he [the captain of the *Sephora*] was not a little disconcerted by the reverse side of that weird situation, by something in me that reminded him of the man he was seeking—suggested a mysterious similitude to the young fellow he had distrusted and disliked from the first" (102).

That "mysterious similitude" can be identified, at least in part. Both Leggatt and the narrator have the same social and class background. Both have been trained in the same naval school in preparation for assuming the loneliness of command and the responsibility of independent decision. Such training was an essential part of the formation of those Englishmen who dominated so much of the world during the time of the British Empire. Both have taken the law into their own hands. Both have made an instantaneous decision or a series of decisions that reaffirms the law by transgressing the law. Leggatt has killed an insubordinate crewman in order to save his ship in the storm and in order to maintain the hierarchy of command that is essential on board ship. He has preserved law and order where, according to the narrator, "no means of legal repression" were available. The narrator has, in a spontaneous decision, taken Leggatt on board his ship and has repeated the murderer's crime by hiding him. In doing so he becomes an accessory after the fact, liable to the same punishment as Leggatt himself might receive from the law. Already the narrator has transgressed the ship's normal rules by taking the night-time anchor watch himself. He doubles both of those transgressions again at the end of the story when he shaves the shore dangerously close, risking his ship and horrifying the crew, in order, on his "conscience," to bring Leggatt just as close to shore as he can. These transgressions, the whole force of the story implies, are absolutely necessary to make the narrator worthy of command. Only through those acts can he, at the end of the story, leave Leggatt "to take his punishment—a free man, a proud swimmer striking out for a new destiny" (119). This separation allows the narrator to replace the homosocial relation to Leggatt with the heterosexual relation to his ship that means he is no longer a stranger aboard: "Already the ship was drawing ahead. And I was alone with her. Nothing, no one in the world should stand now between us, throwing a shadow on the way of silent knowledge and mute affection; the perfect communion of a seaman with his first command" (119).

"The Secret Sharer" shows that law and order, the justice that validates command and hierarchy, cannot be maintained by the simple reaffirmation of rules and conventions that are already in place and remain in place. That justice must be periodically interrupted by some decisive act that reaffirms the law by breaking the law. Such an irruptive or disruptive act always has something violent, dangerous, or illicit about it. Its emblems in "The Secret Sharer" are Leggatt's act of murder and the narrator's secret hiding of Leggatt. The ground for such acts remains secret. It is felt only by those on whom it imposes a "pitiless obligation," though that ground is absolutely compelling in the responsibility it lays on the one who receives its commands.

Conrad's name for this command is a traditional one, "conscience," twice repeated as the name for what drives him to go so close to the shore: "It was now a matter of conscience to shave the land as close as possible" (116); hidden in the sail locker Leggatt "was able to hear everything—and perhaps he was able to understand why, on my conscience, it had to be thus close—no less" (117). In a brilliant recent book on Shakespeare, *Daemonic Figures,* Ned Lukacher has shown how the word "conscience" is at the confluence of the two great lines of the Western tradition, the Socratic and Hellenic tradition of the daemon who commands me to act in a certain way and the Judeo-Christian tradition of the still small voice of conscience, the voice of God within the soul that imposes an implacable obligation to act in a certain way in witness of the truth, even if it is against the law. An example of the latter is the appeal to conscience by English protestants under Catholic rule during the reign of Mary Tudor. They refused in the name of conscience to recant, even when that refusal meant they would be burned at the stake. In their case, as in the case of the narrator's risking of his ship and all aboard, the call of conscience is stronger even than the wish to live, stronger than the appeal of any established law.[27]

The law can be preserved and reaffirmed only by acts that are apparently against the law. The ground for these acts remains private, hidden, secret, apparent only to those who are sensitive to it, who hear its call. It is apparent even then only in not being apparent. It is something that I cannot show to others, something that is, strictly speaking, unpresentable, unrepresentable, just as the narrator cannot find a word for that "sort of feeling, a quality," he senses in Leggatt.

If, however, this secret ground of law-preserving and law-affirming transgression cannot be presented, nevertheless it can be passed on to those who are fit to "understand," as the narrator understands Leggatt. It can be transmitted in a narration like "The Secret Sharer" that makes its demand on the reader for a similar understanding. The ultimate secret of "The Secret Sharer" remains a secret, but that by no means deprives it of power.

Near the beginning of this essay I asked: "Did the narrator do right or wrong in hiding the fugitive murderer Leggatt? On what basis did he make that decision? On what basis should we judge him?" Now I am in a position to answer those questions, after a fashion. Yes, he did right, he acted justly, but we cannot know the ground of that rightness and justice. We can only feel or "understand" its effect in another doubling—or perhaps, on the contrary, not feel it. That cannot be known beforehand or safely predicted for a given reader. The story itself gives the reader a model of an inaugural act that

---

27. See Ned Lukacher, *Daemonic Figures: Shakespeare and the Question of Conscience* (Ithaca: Cornell University Press, 1994). I owe the example of the protestants' appeal to conscience in sixteenth-century England to an admirable lecture by Steven Mullaney: "Reforming Resistance: Class, Gender, and Legitimacy in Foxe's *Book of Martyrs*."

responds to a secret demand. The story is a violent tropological transformation turning "the basic fact of the tale" into a story of testing and testimony. What led Conrad to make this transformation cannot be known. It remains secret. The basis of ethical decision and act, including the act of writing or reading, is the ultimate secret, the most secret secret. This secret cannot be revealed. It is not the object of a possible clear knowledge. Nevertheless, it is a secret I can share, though it remains secret. This secret can only be passed on to me as an obscure but commanding force that comes from something absolutely other. If it cannot be named, it can be made into a story and so transferred to me when I read it. That reading imparts another strong demand for response and taking of responsibility. An example of such a response would be teaching "The Secret Sharer" or writing an essay about it, such as this one.

CHAPTER 6

Revisiting "Heart of Darkness Revisited"

(in the company of Philippe Lacoue-Labarthe)

THE CONTRIBUTORS to this volume have been asked to say something about Philippe Lacoue-Labarthe's superb essay on *Heart of Darkness*, "L'horreur occidentale," translated now as "The Horror of the West." I hope the phrase in my title, "in the company of," does not seem disrespectful of Lacoue-Labarthe's memory. I mean to call attention by that phrase to the strong presence in his essay of the author's voice speaking to his auditors, as when he says, "This evening, in front of you, I would like to try to justify myself, [*essayer de me justifier*].... This type of exercise, as we know, is dangerous. I therefore ask you, in advance, to forgive me [*Je vous demande à l'avance de bien vouloir m'en excuser*] if my remarks will be a little experimental."¹ When I read his essay, Lacoue-Labarthe seems to be speaking to me too, as well as to his original auditors. He exhorts me to see his reading of *Heart of Darkness* as a bearing witness that may need excusing or that may be an act of self-justification.

This essay originally appeared as the prologue for *Conrad's Heart of Darkness and Contemporary Thought: Revisiting the Horror with Lacoue-Labarthe*, ed. Nidesh Lawtoo (London: Bloomsbury, 2012), 17–35.

1. Philippe Lacoue-Labarthe, "The Horror of the West," in *Conrad's Heart of Darkness and Contemporary Thought: Revisiting the Horror with Lacoue-Labarthe*, ed. Nidesh Lawtoo (London: Bloomsbury, 2012), 111–12. Hereafter, quotations from this essay will be cited parenthetically.

Excusing and self-justifying, we know, are speech acts. They are performative, not constative, utterances, as is the act of bearing witness through speech, through a voice. Both Lacoue-Labarthe and I have a lot to say in our essays about voice as testimony in *Heart of Darkness*. Conrad's novel, we both say, is made of a relay of testifying voices, one nested inside the next like Russian dolls, each bearing witness for the one before, back (or forward) to the most inside voice, Kurtz's. His voice speaks the ultimate testifying words. Of these words Marlow says, "He had summed up—he had judged. 'The horror!'" (118). A critical essay too, Lacoue-Labarthe's or mine, is a bearing witness, a speech act. It does not so much say, "This is the truth about this work," as "I swear to you that I believe this is the truth about this work, though you may need to excuse me for what I say."

It is an important event to have Lacoue-Labarthe's essay now available in English. "L'horreur occidentale" is a major essay on Conrad's novel, one of the best ever written. About it one can say what Lacoue-Labarthe says about *Heart of Darkness* itself that it is an "event of thought" [*événement de pensée*] (112) or, in his even more striking phrase, something that "prompts an emotion of thought" [*provoque une émotion de la pensée*] (111). I shall return to this latter phrase. "The Horror of the West" should be in the top group of any list of essential essays on *Heart of Darkness*.

Philippe Lacoue-Labarthe was an extremely learned, original, and distinguished philosopher. He had a special interest in the philosophy of art, as in his two essential books, *Typographie* and *L'imitation des modernes*.[2] He might not have been expected, nevertheless, ever to turn his attention to *Heart of Darkness*, even in its French translation, which has such an odd sound to English-speaking ears: *Au coeur des ténèbres*. We are fortunate that he did so. One important feature of his reading is the way he makes a strongly persuasive case for seeing Kurtz as a hyperbolic example of the West's idea of the artist, from Plato through Diderot down to Nietzsche and Rimbaud. The Western artist, he argues, is, like Kurtz, nothing because able to be everything. The Western artist is totally *disponible*. Therefore, he or she is "hollow at the core" (*HD* 104). As a consequence, the artist is vulnerable to invasion by the darkness, the horror. That is a strikingly original and provocative perspective. It is an issue on which my own essay does not touch. Was Joseph Conrad also hollow at the core and so vulnerable to the darkness? I think not. He defended himself by various strategies, especially by irony.

---

2. Philippe Lacoue-Labarthe, *Typographies 1: Le sujet de la philosophic* (Paris: Galilée, 1979); Lacoue-Labarthe, *Typography: Mimesis, Philosophy, Politics*, ed. Christopher Fynsk and Linda M. Brooks (Cambridge: Harvard University Press, 1989); Lacoue-Labarthe, *L'imitation des modernes (Typograhies 2)* (Paris: Galilée, 1986).

Reading "The Horror of the West" has given me occasion to reread my old essay of 1983 and to juxtapose Lacoue-Labarthe's essay with mine. For the most part, I agree whole-heartedly with Lacoue-Labarthe's reading. I have learnt much from it. We agree, for example, as I have said, in stressing the importance of *voice* in Conrad's story. We agree that voices are used in the story as a series of transmissions that bear witness to Kurtz's experience and to a truth that can only be expressed indirectly. We agree in seeing *Heart of Darkness* as one of the most important indictments of Western imperialism, and even in seeing it as "one of the greatest texts of Western literature" (111). Everyone seriously interested in Conrad should read Lacoue-Labarthe's essay.

Now I shall bear witness, mildly and hesitantly, hoping you will excuse me for my temerity, to some small points of difference. It would not be worth doing this if questions of general importance were not at stake.

First difference: I would not assert, as Lacoue-Labarthe does, that the story fundamentally says: "the West *is* the horror." I would rather say that *Heart of Darkness* says Western imperialism is one aspect of a more ubiquitous and pervasive underlying horror. Lacoue-Labarthe's discussion of the horror and of its embodiment in the Western will to power is subtle and persuasive. Nevertheless, the phrase "Horror of the West" invites the reader to think of Conrad's horror as specifically political and as peculiar to the West and to its destructive "technics of death" [*technique de la mort*] (119).

The words of *Heart of Darkness*, however, especially its figures of speech, indicate rather that what is named by Kurtz as "the horror" is a universal quasi-metaphysical entity, not a limited political one. The horror is something present deep within every man and woman, everywhere, at all times. It is also present at all times behind every aspect of nature everywhere. Lacoue-Labarthe says the first of these by way of his reference to Lacan's *la Chose*, to Heidegger's *das Ding*, the Thing, and to Augustine's *extime*, his *interior intimo meo* (117), something inside me but unattainably beyond me. Lacan, Heidegger, and Augustine provide three other names for the horror. After all, Lacoue-Labarthe's essay was given as a lecture before an on-going seminar of 1995–96 called *Psychiatre, Psychothérapie et Culture(s)*. Some reference to the psychiatric aspects of Conrad's presentation of Kurtz was in order, though Lacoue-Labarthe does not follow-up on Conrad's assertion that Kurtz, to speak plainly, has been driven mad by the wilderness. If so, he is deeply in need of psychotherapy. At one moment Marlow says, "I wasn't arguing with a lunatic either" (*HD* 113), but the next moment he says, "but his soul was mad—being alone in the wilderness it had looked within itself and by Heavens! I tell you, it had gone mad" (113–14).

It would be a mistake, however, to identify the horror exclusively with something in the depths of every human psyche. Many passages in the novel affirm that the horror is also within or behind non-human nature, as for example when Marlow says, in a striking extended prosopopoeia, that the superb native Woman who comes down to the shore is the image of the personified wilderness: "And in the hush that had fallen suddenly upon the whole sorrowful land, the immense wilderness, the colossal body of the fecund and mysterious life seemed to look at her, pensive, as though it had been looking at the image of its own tenebrous and passionate soul" (107). I agree with Lacoue-Labarthe, however, that what the West has done in its centuries-long world-conquering imperialisms is perhaps a major embodiment of this ubiquitous horror as it secretly motivates apparently idealistic action for example in causing in the name of enlightenment the deaths of so many Africans in the Congo during the Belgian occupation and exploitation at the end of the nineteenth century ("bringing the torch of civilization to darkest Africa," as we used to say). Another example is the way the United States has, much more recently, brought about so many deaths during the invasion of Iraq—perhaps as many as a million civilians by some counts and the displacement of many millions more. I would differ from Lacoue-Labarthe's emphasis on Western imperialism; however, by claiming that Conrad's horror is perhaps best identified, as I say in my essay, with death as universal, that is, with a heart of darkness that beats everywhere, absolutely everywhere, not just in the West. This is the horror that Kurtz glimpses and then passes over into at the climax of the story:

> Since I had peeped over the edge myself [says Marlow, speaking of his near-fatal illness during his return from meeting Kurtz] I understand better the meaning of his stare that could not see the flame of the candle but was wide enough to embrace the whole universe, piercing enough to penetrate all the hearts that beat in the darkness. He had summed up—he had judged. "The horror!" . . . It is his extremity that I seem to have lived through. True, he had made that last stride, had stepped over the edge while I had been permitted to draw back my hesitating foot. And perhaps in this is the whole difference; perhaps all the wisdom and all truth and all sincerity are just compressed into that inappreciable moment of time in which we step over the threshold of the Invisible. Perhaps. (*HD* 118)

This climactic passage equates the horror with death. Death, however, is no more than another name, like "horror," for something that remains invisible and unnameable, though underlying everything. The word "death" is a catachresis, that is, it is a displaced name for something that has no proper name, but can be named only in tropes. That is what Paul de Man meant when he said "death is a displaced name for a linguistic predicament,"[3] and what Conrad means when he says that you can only know death when you die. Dead men, as we know, tell no tales, though survivors can in a way speak for them, as Marlow speaks for Kurtz. His speaking, however, is indirect, not based on his own experience. In this, it is subject to Paul Celan's interdict against secondary bearing witness, for example, to the Holocaust: "No one bears witness for the witness."[4] What Giorgio Agamben calls "Levi's paradox" applies to Kurtz's knowledge in *Heart of Darkness* too.[5] The only direct witness to the horrors of the gas chambers would be by someone who had experienced them first hand. But no one survived that experience. Similarly, Kurtz witnessed the horror directly, but only at the moment he stepped over the threshold into death. Other catachrestic figures for what Conrad names by the word "horror" pervade *Heart of Darkness,* figures of the jungle wilderness, or of London, or of England when the Romans invaded it, or of African "savagery," or of those heads on stakes Marlow glimpses through his "glasses" (97), or, in the famous passage that Lacoue-Labarthe comments on, as I do at length in my essay, of the halo around the moon on a foggy night. This multiplicity of images indicates that none is adequate. Conrad has to keep trying, unsuccessfully, to get it right to find just the right figure, just the right form of words for what Kurtz calls "the horror."

The final scene of *Heart of Darkness* confirms the horror's ubiquity. When Marlow visits Kurtz's "Intended" back in Europe and lies to her about Kurtz's last words (he says they were her name rather than "The horror! The horror!"), he wonders why she cannot hear Kurtz's true words spoken everywhere in the dusk, even back home in Europe: "I was on the point of crying at her, 'Don't you hear them?' The dusk was repeating them in a persistent whisper all around us, in a whisper that seemed to swell menacingly like the first whisper of a rising wind. 'The horror! The horror!'" (125).

∿

3. Paul de Man, "Autobiography as De-Facement," in *The Rhetoric of Romanticism* (New York: Columbia University Press, 1984), 81.

4. Paul Celan, *"Niemand/zeugt für den/Zeugen* Paul Celan, Aschenglorie," in *Breathturn,* bilingual ed., trans. Pierre Joris (Los Angeles: Sun & Moon Press, 1995), 179.

5. Giorgio Agamben, "The Muselman," in *Remnants of Auschwitz: The Witness and the Archive,* trans. Daniel Heller-Roazen (New York: Zone Books, 2002), 41–86; Primo Levi, *The Drowned and the Saved,* trans. Raymond Rosenthal (New York: Vintage, 1989), 83–84.

A second mild demurrer has to do with the way Lacoue-Labarthe accepts perhaps a little too easily the explanatory power of an autobiographical reading of *Heart of Darkness*. He says in so many words, "This narrative is, in large part, autobiographical (written in 1899, it narrates a voyage Conrad undertook between spring and winter 1890)" (112). Lacoue-Labarthe assumes that the first speaker in the tale, the one who reports Marlow's storytelling on the deck of the yacht named the *Nellie*, is straightforwardly Conrad himself. This is already a little confusing, as it is Marlow who is delegated to tell in the first person the "autobiographical" story of Conrad's voyage. I do not deny that *Heart of Darkness* has an autobiographical basis, the details of Conrad's voyage of 1890, what the Congo was like at that time and so on.[6] Nevertheless, seeing the text as so straightforwardly referential allows a reader a little too easily to say, "I see. It's just a disguised autobiography. The sources are wholly explanatory, and we need think no more about it."

Lacoue-Labarthe does, of course, a lot more thinking about it, but his reading is still basically a referential, representational, or realistic one. His reading is validated by its truth of correspondence to things outside the text, for example, Belgium's perfidy in the Congo or Conrad's trip there in 1890. Even Lacoue-Labarthe's use of Plato, about which I shall say more below, supports this referentiality. I should prefer to put the autobiographical facts in brackets and to see *Heart of Darkness* as a radically fictional transposition of historical and biographical facts that can by no means be fully explained by them, formally, thematically, or rhetorically. We must read the text with close attention, for itself, for example, by seeing that first narrator as a fictional invention like all the other "voices" that speak in this story. The story would be perfectly readable by someone who had no knowledge of its autobiographical basis, no matter how interesting these autobiographical details are.

This leads me to my third observation about the difference between our two essays. This is perhaps the most important difference, though it is not so much a disagreement as a recognition that our essays exemplify two substantially different methodologies of reading. These yield, not surprisingly, rather different results. These differences can be identified in two different ways, ways that nevertheless converge or that come to more or less the same thing. One way is to say that Lacoue-Labarthe's methodology is to a large degree what many

---

6. For a summary, see Ross Murfin, "Introduction: Biographical and Historical Contexts," in Joseph Conrad, *Heart of Darkness: Complete, Authoritative Text with Biography and Historical Contexts*, ed. Ross C. Murfin 2nd ed. (Boston: Bedford Books, 1996), 3–16.

people today would call narratological, whereas mine is more what would be called "rhetorical." Rhetorical refers, in this case, not to persuasion so much as to the deployment of tropes, as in what I have already said in this prologue about catachresis. The other way to specify the methodological difference between us is to say that Lacoue-Labarthe's approach is more Greek or Hellenic, whereas mine is more Biblical, with some overlapping, of course.

Let me explain what these methodological differences mean. Plato is the great grandfather of narratology, as Lacoue-Labarthe affirms when he says "if you allow me to use Plato's categories (in reality, they are the only ones we have)" (113). Though Lacoue-Labarthe does not refer to the complex narratological terms and distinctions that were, being developed by Gérard Genette, Wayne Booth, James Phelan, and many others (implied author as against real author, reliable as against unreliable narrators, use of prolepsis, analepsis, multiple forms of diegesis and so on, in inexhaustible proliferation),[7] he is right to say that Plato in Book 3 of the *Republic* had already made the distinctions that are essential to narratological thinking. *Diegesis,* in Plato's usage, is a narrative that tells a tale in the voice of the author. *Mimesis* is a tale told by someone who assumes the voice of another, as Homer pretends to speak as Ulysses in the *Odyssey.* Conrad, according to Lacoue-Labarthe, speaks as himself, in *diegesis,* in the opening pages of the story (though Conrad, as Lacoue-Labarthe observes, usually says "we," meaning all those on the deck of the *Nellie* hearing Marlow tell his story). Marlow's story is a *mimesis,* Conrad pretending to speak as Marlow. The whole story is a myth (*muthos*), meaning any story, not necessarily one about the gods, though Lacoue-Labarthe gives myth, in a splendid formulation, a specific (and still Platonic) definition, "Myth means here," he says,

> a spoken word [*parole*] which offers itself, by means of some *testimony,* as a bearer of truth. An unverifiable truth, prior to any demonstration or any logical protocol. [There speaks the professional philosopher! A philosophical truth ought to be demonstrable and follow an accepted logical protocol.

---

7. Gérard Genette, "Discours du récit," in *Figures III* (Paris: Seuil, 1972), 65–282; Genette, *Narrative Discourse: An Essay in Method,* trans. Jane E. Lewin (Ithaca, NY: Cornell University Press, 1980); Wayne C. Booth, *The Rhetoric of Fiction* (Chicago: University of Chicago Press, 1961); James Phelan, *Living to Tell about It: A Rhetoric and Ethics of Character Narration* (Ithaca, NY: Cornell University Press, 2005). These books are only the tip of a huge iceberg. Other distinguished narratologists would include Gerald Prince, Seymour Chatman, Shlomith Rimmon-Kenan, Shen Dan, Dorrit Cohn, Mieke Bal, Robert Scholes, Robert Kellogg, Wallace Martin, Jakob Lothe, and many others. An attempt to do for *Heart of Darkness* what Genette did for *A la recherche du temps perdu* might repay the effort, since the narrative structure of Conrad's novel is extremely complex. I say "might" because narratology may become merely descriptive rather than revelatory of meaning. One says, "Yes, I see that is an analepsis, but so what?"

(JHM)] A truth too difficult to enunciate directly, too heavy or too painful, above all, too obscure. (113)

A Greek example would be the Oedipus myth that says human beings, especially those in high places, are cursed by the gods, who never forget a slight, and that all men want to kill their fathers and sleep with their mothers. Marlow's story and its indirect testimony to the truth of the horror are put by Lacoue-Labarthe under the aegis of the Greek or Platonic concept of myth: "Conrad's entire undertaking consists in trying to find a witness for that which he wants to bear witness to. The Ancients invoked the gods; Conrad invents Marlow. But they do so in order to convey the same truth, a truth of the same order" (114). I suppose, to make the formulations strictly parallel, he might have to say, "The Ancients invented Oedipus; Conrad invents Marlow."

Lacoue-Labarthe, you can see, stresses narrative complexities in his reading, and as for Plato, these complexities of *mimesis* are grounded in a realistic or referential *diegesis*. Homer was a real person who at times in the *Odyssey* pretended to speak as Ulysses. Conrad was a real person, the basic "I" of the story, who pretends to speak as Marlow. The authenticating ground of the story is "realistic"—referential or representational, autobiographical in Conrad's case. This means that figures of speech used in the telling are ornamental or illustrative as in Lacoue-Labarthe's way of reading the tropes of the cracked nut and the halo around the moon as more or less transparent figures for two different kinds of stories.

It is not surprising, therefore, that Lacoue-Labarthe follows Heidegger (though without mentioning this specific link) in having relatively little interest in the rhetoric of tropes, nor surprising that he sees Conrad's story as modeled on the Greek descent into the underworld (with those knitting women at the beginning as the Fates). He even sees the savage clamor that Marlow hears on the shore as he approaches Kurtz as a species of chorus, such as that used in Greek tragedy. The only non-Greek narratological context Lacoue-Labarthe gives is an odd claim that *Heart of Darkness* can be seen as an oratorio, with the savage clamor as chorus and the characters' speeches as arias. Lacoue-Labarthe's citation of Schelling at the end of his essay to deny that *Heart of Darkness* is an allegory is in harmony with his Hellenizing, literalizing, and representational approach. For him, *Heart of Darkness* just means what it says, literally:

> Schelling says that "myths" are not "allegorical." They say nothing other than what they say; they do not have a different meaning from the meaning they enunciate. They are *tautegorical* (a category Schelling borrows from Coleridge). *Heart of Darkness* is no exception to this rule. It is not an alle-

gory—say, a metaphysico-political allegory—at all. It is the tautegory of the West—that is, of art (of *techne*). (120)

If Lacoue-Labarthe's presuppositions for reading are narratological and Greek, mine follow the other stem of the West's divided lineage. My reading is Biblical and tropological. It is therefore not surprising that we come to somewhat different conclusions, though I hereby testify that I think my approach gets closer to the truth at the heart of darkness. The key terms in my reading are Biblical ones: parable, apocalypse, and allegory. All of these words are Greek in origin, of course, but they were appropriated by the Christian Bible and by Biblical exegesis for non-Greek purposes. The Gospels transmit the parables of Jesus. The *Book of Revelation,* the last book of the New Testament, is the greatest and most influential example of the apocalypse genre.[8] The English word derives from a Greek word meaning "unveiling" or "revelation." Though "allegory" is a word in Greek rhetoric and its descendants, meaning, literally, "saying something otherwise in the town square," the word was appropriated in Biblical exegesis, as in Dante's notorious distinction, in his *Letter to Can Grande,* between "allegory of the poets" and "allegory of the theologians," or in Walter Benjamin's use of the term "allegory" in his book on German seventeenth-century *Trauerspiele,* mourning plays. Paul de Man in his influential distinction between allegory and symbol later picked up on Benjamin's use of the term.[9] I claim in *"Heart of Darkness* Revisited," contra Lacoue-Labarthe, that *Heart of Darkness* is parabolic, that it is an allegory, and following Der-

---

8. Nidesh Lawtoo has helpfully informed me that Lacoue-Labarthe uses the word "apocalypse" apropos of the Holocaust in an essay on Heidegger and Nazism: "In the apocalypse at Auschwitz, it is no more or less than the essence of the West that is revealed." Philippe Lacoue-Labarthe, "Neither an Accident nor a Mistake," trans. Paul Wissing, *Critical Inquiry* 15, no. 2 (Winter 1989): 484. The word "apocalypse" is used a little figuratively here, as it is in the title of the film modeled on *Heart of Darkness, Apocalypse Now*. The word "apocalypse," strictly speaking, names the unveiling of what is going to be revealed at the end of the world, not the uncovering of anything that can be revealed in any "now" during the course of history. Saint John of Patmos, the putative author of *The Book of Revelation,* thought the end of the world was at hand, as writers of apocalypses generally do. Saying the Holocaust reveals the essence of the West is, of course, analogous to saying "the West is the horror." "Essence" and "is" are totalizing words. They are even metaphysical, logocentric, or essentialist words when used in the way Lacoue-Labarthe uses them. Indeed, it is hard to use them otherwise.

9. Dante Alighieri, "Letter to Can Grande," accessed April 23, 2011, http://www.english.udel.edu/dean/cangrand.html. This gives Dante's Latin, with an English translation by James Marchand. Walter Benjamin, *Ursprung des deutschen Trauerspiels* (Berlin: 1928; reissued in Frankfurt: Suhrkamp, 1963); Benjamin, *The Origin of German Tragic Drama,* trans. John Osborne (London: New Left Books, 1977); Paul de Man, "Allegory and Symbol," in "The Rhetoric of Temporality," in *Blindness and Insight* (Minneapolis: University of Minnesota Press, 1983), 187–208.

rida's essay on apocalypses,[10] that it is a quasi-apocalypse or a parodic apocalypse, an apocalypse that unveils the impossibility of an ultimate unveiling.

Though the difference between our two essays is a matter of nuance, my Biblical orientation means that I pay more attention than Lacoue-Labarthe does to small-scale tropes that work as catachresis, such as that halo around the moon bringing the fog into view by the spectral illumination of moonshine. For me the word "horror" is a catachresis, not a literal naming. Though Lacoue-Labarthe, like me, speaks of indirect knowledge, he also follows Schelling's concept of "tautegory" when he says "the horror" *is* "the truth of the West," as though the word "horror" were a literal name. As opposed to that, I see the narrative of *Heart of Darkness* as a way of indirectly speaking about, and bearing witness to, something that cannot be spoken of literally or directly but only in parable or allegory and that can be borne witness to only in a sequence of voices, each speaking for the one before. As Marlow says, you can only confront what the word "horror" indirectly names by stepping over the last threshold to enter that "undiscovered country, from whose bourn / No traveller returns," as Shakespeare's Hamlet puts it [3.1.79–80].

Now a word or two about affect, to conclude. I begin by saying that I have been a little suspicious of the turn to affect in recent theory, in cultural studies and in literary studies, in spite of my respect for the strong affective commitment of those who have made this turn. Like the recent vogue of "the body," the turn to affect may be a way to avoid looking directly at language and other sign systems used by literature and cultural artifacts generally in order to ask just what this language or this collection of signs means or does. Body and its emotions seem so solid and tangible, as opposed to the abstractions of language and of language-based theory! Just as I agree with Jean-Luc Nancy, however, that "there is no such thing as *the* body,"[11] so that body is a deep and vexing philosophical problem, not something that can be taken for granted as an entity everyone knows and understands, *a priori,* so I have problems with the empirical study of emotions, though the problems are different in the case of affects. Though I have no doubt that reading *Heart of Darkness* generates affects in readers, me included, and though I am much struck by

---

10. Jacques Derrida, *D'un ton apocalyptique adopté naguère en philosophie* (Paris: Galilée, 1983); Derrida, "Of an Apocalyptic Tone Recently Adopted in Philosophy," trans. John P. Leavey Jr., *The Oxford Literary Review* 6, no. 2 (December 1984): 3–37.

11. Jean-Luc Nancy, *Corpus,* trans. Richard A. Rand (New York: Fordham University Press, 2008), 119; Nancy, *Corpus* (Paris: Metailie, 2006), 104.

Lacoue-Labarthe's phrase asserting that reading *Heart of Darkness* or hearing it performed by a gifted reader, "provokes an emotion of thought" (111), my problems begin when I try to think how one could be precise about just what those emotions are.

English, for example, has a great many affect words: "anger," "joy," "happiness," "love," "affection," "fear," "anxiety," "exaltation," "exultation," "enthusiasm," "grief," "melancholy," "mourning," "dismay," "uneasiness," "terror," "horror," and the like. The list could be extended indefinitely. We have, no doubt, many more different affect words even more than the names Inuits have for different kinds of snow. They are all feelings, but feelings differ from one another. It is all snow, but there are many different kinds of snow. Even a single one of these affect words names many different feelings. As George Eliot says in *Middlemarch*, "there are many wonderful mixtures in the world which are all alike called love, and claim the privileges of a sublime rage which is an apology for everything (in literature and the drama)."[12] The difficulty is that though our affect words discriminate among different subjective feelings, and though we all know more or less what these discriminations are, such words nevertheless remain rather coarse sieves. Though we know how anger differs from joy, "anger" still names an indefinitely wide range of feelings. Just how do I know that my friend means the same thing I would mean when he or she says, "I am angry" or "I am afraid." As Edmund Husserl long ago recognized, to his lifelong chagrin, we do not have direct phenomenological access to other people's minds, including their feelings but only an indirect "analogical apperception" of them, an "appresentation."[13] We must assume that what other people call anger is analogous to what I call anger, but we have no way to prove that assumption.

Nor, I am sorry to say, do recent brain studies help all that much. We can show what part of the brain lights up when a person seems to be angry, joyful, or afraid, but those brain scans do not tell us what that person feels like when he or she says, "I am really angry now." Surely, affect is a matter of subjective feeling, not of activity in a certain part of the brain. Or is it? One might say, "Anger *is* an increased activity in a certain part of the brain. That is its essence, its being." We could then have people read *Heart of Darkness* and see what parts of their brains light up. Many people, however, me included, would not

---

12. George Eliot, *Middlemarch* (Oxford: Oxford University Press, 1999), 333–34.
13. Edmund Husserl, "Fifth Meditation: Uncovering the Sphere of Transcendental Being as Monadological Intersubjectivity," in *Cartesian Meditations: An Introduction to Phenomenology*, trans. Dorion Cairns (The Hague: Martinus Nijhoff, 1960), 89–151. See especially paragraph 50, "The mediate intentionality of experiencing someone else, as 'appresentation' (analogical apperception)" (108–11).

be entirely enthusiastic about this sort of empirical approach, though much interest exists these days in cognitive science as a basis for literary study. Some literary scholars see it as the solution to all our problems. I, however, cannot quite be satisfied by the vision of literary studies happily reduced to the study of brain scans.

I have mentioned anger as one of my affect words because I have had in mind two brilliant essays by J. L. Austin, "Other Minds" and "Pretending." In both these essays, the question of how I can know that another person is angry comes up as an example of the general problem of "other minds."[14] Discussing these essays would be a long business, but I cite one passage from "Pretending" as exemplary of the problem with "affect" I find most perplexing, as does Austin. The passage is also wonderfully ironic and funny, as Austin often is. Austin is discussing a paper by Errol Bedford. The question is, "How can we know a person is *really* angry and not just pretending?"

> Our man [*sic*], then, is "behaving as if he were angry." He scowls, let us say, and stamps his foot on the carpet. So far we may (or perhaps must?) still say "He is not really angry: he is (only) pretending to be angry." But now he goes further, let us say he bites the carpet: and we will picture the scene with sympathy—the carpet innocent, the bite untentative and vicious, the damage grave. Now he has gone too far, overstepped the limit between pretence and reality, and we cannot any longer say "He is pretending to be angry" but must say "He is really angry."[15]

You see the problem. Perhaps the man is still pretending and only trying to convince us that he is really angry by the theatrical gesture of viciously biting the innocent carpet. Or perhaps, anger is best defined as angry behavior, without any attempt to get at what the angry person is feeling. The problem with this out, as Austin goes on to say, is that being angry, in ordinary language, means feeling angry. In criticism of Bedford, Austin says, "we are still not told what really being angry, for which this [biting the carpet] is only the *evidence, is*, not therefore shown that it does not involve, or even reside in, the feeling of a feeling—the evidence *might* be evidence that he is feeling a certain feeling."[16] This problematic of "the feeling of a feeling" might be followed interminably and tautegorically, but I do not think we would ever get beyond the limitations of not having direct access to the feelings of another person, even the feelings

---

14. J. L. Austin, "Other Minds" and "Pretending," in *Philosophical Papers*, ed. J. O. Urmson and G. J. Warnock (Oxford: Oxford University Press, 1979), 76–116 and 253–71.
15. Austin, "Pretending," 254.
16. Ibid., 255.

of imaginary persons in works of fiction, and of not having a clear and precise definition of just what anger, or any other affect, "really *is*." Echoing Nancy, I would say, "There is no 'the' anger, no 'the' horror," in spite of Kurtz's use of the latter locution. "The" horror is a diffuse and multitudinous terror.

I conclude with a word or two more about "horror." Horror is certainly an affect. The word "horror" is at the center of the complex verbal integument that is woven in *Heart of Darkness*. Lacoue-Labarthe and I agree about that, though in somewhat different ways. Why did Conrad choose just the word "horror"? It has a good many valences, including many trivializing ones. "I encountered a huge lion in the bush. I was horrified." "Belgian genocide in the Congo is horrifying to learn about." "'*Horreurs!*,' she said, when she found the tea was already cold." "Her dress and makeup were, as usual, horrors." I suppose the literary pretexts for *Heart of Darkness* are so-called horror stories, but *Heart of Darkness* is certainly an odd or anomalous example of the genre. This is the case not least because the object of horror is never specified as such, only given in endless figurative substitutions for something that cannot be literally named, whereas horror stories usually embody the horror. You might argue that this makes *Heart of Darkness* the ideal or paradigmatic horror story. Horror stories are often tales about zombies, werewolves, vampires, and other uncanny apparitions. These give the reader something concrete to be horrified by. It is easy to find such stories laughable, as Jane Austen did in *Northanger Abbey*, or as do college students when they laugh delightedly at horror movies they have seen dozens of times. The vogue of horror stories precedes *Heart of Darkness*. It goes back at least to late eighteenth century Gothic tales. *Horror Stories* was the name of a pulp magazine of the 1930s. I googled "horror stories" and got 4,690,000 results in 0.09 seconds.[17] That rapidity makes me more than a little uneasy. Conrad appropriates the word to name something invisible and intangible that only Kurtz sees. Marlow's evidence that the horror exists is that he hears Kurtz utter the word as a name for something he sees at his moment of death. Marlow also hears the word whispered in the dusk when he goes to visit Kurtz's Intended back in Europe. What is odd about Conrad's usage is that he hypostatizes an affect word and uses it as the name for something external and universal, "*the* horror," not as the name of an internal affect, as when one might say, "I am horrified by this," or "I feel horror."

Does reading *Heart of Darkness* generate horror in me, I mean horror at "'the' horror"? Not really, I must admit, though that may make me seem cold-hearted. Reading *Heart of Darkness* does generate in me anger (I dare

---

17. Accessed April 21, 2011, http://www.google.com/search?client=safari&rls=en&q=horror+stories&ie=UTF-8&oe=UTF-8.

to use that word) and grief (more inconsolable melancholy than appeaseable mourning, to remember Freud's distinction) about what the Belgians did in the Congo and, by displacement, about all the other genocides down to those the present day. I would even say that I am horrified at the thought of them. How could human beings be so inhuman? I can testify to feeling those affects.

Conrad's masterwork, however, generates in me, in addition to anger and grief, what Marlow says the manager of the Central Station generated in him: "He inspired uneasiness—that was it. Uneasiness. Not definite mistrust—just uneasiness—nothing more. You have no idea how effective such a . . . a . . . faculty can be" (*HD* 63). That's it! Reading *Heart of Darkness* inspires in me the affect we call "uneasiness." Conrad's story has that faculty. One uneasiness is my uncertainty about whether *Heart of Darkness* proves that Conrad was, as Chinua Achebe famously asserts, "a thoroughgoing racist."[18] I want to believe, as many other critics do believe, that Conrad was not a racist and that he was in *Heart of Darkness* attacking the racist side of imperialism, partly by embodying it ironically in Marlow. Nevertheless, the novel employs many racist stereotypes as well as racist clichés from journalism and popular literature of the time: the idea of "darkest Africa" implicit in the title; the "savage clamour" on the shore; native dances ("They howled and leaped and spun and made horrid faces; but what thrilled you was just the thought of their humanity—like yours—the thought of your remote kinship with this wild and passionate uproar" [79]); distant tom-toms in the jungle (drums *were* used for communication at the time, but it is still a cliché); notions about African primitivism ("Going up that river was like travelling back to the earliest beginnings of the world" [77]); and so on. These require some explaining.

My affective response to reading *Heart of Darkness* is an "emotion of thought" in the sense that my feeling of uneasiness prompts me to read the novel again and again in an attempt to think out just what it means and just how I should pass judgment on it. I want to understand just what it means that the entire novel's episodes echo one another, one behind the other, each like a curtain opened to expose another curtain. Emotion and thought are to some degree opposing movements of the mind. An "emotion of thought" is an oxymoron, as Lacoue-Labarthe was doubtless aware. All my thinking about *Heart of Darkness* may be unconsciously apotropaic. It may be a not wholly successful attempt, like Conrad's (or Marlow's) pervasive irony, to ward off a feeling of horror. This might be a horror of thought, in another sense, objective genitive rather than subjective genitive, in which case it would name a

---

18. Chinua Achebe, "An Image of Africa: Racism in Conrad's *Heart of Darkness*," in Joseph Conrad, *Heart of Darkness*, 4th ed., ed. Paul B. Armstrong (New York: W. W. Norton, 2006), 336–49. Also available at, accessed April 22, 2011, http://kirbyk.net/hod/image.of.africa.html.

resistance to emotive thinking. This horror at the thought of thinking about *Heart of Darkness* might render me speechless with terror at where my feeling-thoughts are taking me.

The essays that make up this volume are distinguished in their originality, learning, and insight as well as in the diversity of their responses to *Heart of Darkness* and to Lacoue-Labarthe's essay. One might have thought that everything of importance that *could* be said about *Heart of Darkness has* been said, but these essays show that this is by no means the case. These admirable essays show that a great masterpiece like *Heart of Darkness* is always inexhaustibly open to further illuminating commentary. Why is this? I think the source of this inexhaustibility is the extreme complexity of rhetorical, narratological, conceptual, and figurative language in a work like *Heart of Darkness,* though no other work has just this specific complexity. The specificity of each work means that as a reader of literary texts you are always pretty much on your own. Generalizations about "literary language" plus tons of narratological or tropological sophistication are not of much help in a given case. Blanchot eloquently expressed in *The Writing of the Disaster* this excess of literature over literary theory: "all theories, however different they may be, constantly change places with one another, distinct each from the next only because of the writing which supports them and which thus escapes the very theories purporting to judge it."[19] The authors of the essays in this volume have responded aggressively to this impasse by returning to the text of *Heart of Darkness* itself as it is illuminated by the new radiance shed on it by Lacoue-Labarthe's distinguished essay. This happens just as the glow of moonlight brings out a haze, to borrow Conrad's own figure.

What strikes me most about these essays is not only their high quality and originality but also their diversity. Who would have thought that Lacoue-Labarthe's instigation would produce so many new ways of reading *Heart of Darkness,* sometimes indeed in opposition to what Lacoue-Labarthe says. From Michael Bell's placement of *Heart of Darkness* in the context of modernist thinking about myth and ideological *Weltanschauungen* from Nietzsche through Heidegger down to Lacoue-Labarthe himself; to Nidesh Lawtoo's reading of *Heart of Darkness* in the context of Lacoue-Labarthe's theories about mimetic contamination or "enthusiasm"; to Martine Hennard Dutheil de la Rochère's demonstration that Conrad was influenced in his presentation

---

19. Maurice Blanchot, *The Writing of the Disaster,* trans. Ann Smock (Lincoln: University of Nebraska Press, 1995), 80; Blanchot, *L'Écriture du désastre* (Paris: Gallimard, 1980), 128.

of Kurtz and other characters in *Heart of Darkness* by the then new technique of X-rays, a technique that turns bodies into visible skeletons, as if they were dead already; to Henry Staten's focus on the complex ideas about masculinity in Conrad's novel, including its assumptions about what emotions manly men can legitimately feel and acknowledge (as opposed to a more common focus on Marlow's deplorable ideas about women)—but I pause here.[20] I could go on through a complete inventory of these remarkable essays. These examples, however, will make my point about their diversity and originality. I have learnt much from them. I shall never read *Heart of Darkness* again in the same way. That is meant as high praise.

---

20. "Modernism, Myth and *Heart of Darkness*" (55–66); "A Frame for 'The Horror of the West'" (89–108); "Sounding the Hollow Heart of the West: X-rays and the *technique de la mort*" (221–38); "Conrad's Dionysian Elegy" (201–20), respectively, all in *Conrad's Heart of Darkness and Contemporary Thought: Revisiting the Horror with Lacoue-Labarthe*, ed. Nidesh Lawtoo (London: Bloomsbury, 2012) [Editors].

CHAPTER 7

Conrad's Colonial (Non)Community

Nostromo

In memory of Edward W. Said

When you do hermeneutics, you are concerned with the meaning of the work; when you do poetics, you are concerned with the stylistics or with the description of the way in which a work means. The question is whether these two are complementary, whether you can cover the full work by doing hermeneutics and poetics at the same time. The experience of trying to do this shows that it is not the case. When one tries to achieve this complementarity, the poetics always drops out, and what one always does is hermeneutics. One is so attracted by problems of meaning that it is impossible to do hermeneutics and poetics at the same time. From the moment you start to get involved with problems of meaning, as I unfortunately tend to do, forget about the poetics. The two are not complementary, the two may be mutually exclusive in a certain way, and that is part of the problem which Benjamin states, a purely linguistic problem.[1]

This essay originally appeared in *Communities in Fiction* (New York: Fordham University Press, 2015), 139–231. This essay revises and expands upon Miller's "'Material Interests': Conrad's *Nostromo* as a Critique of Global Capitalism," from *Joseph Conrad: Voice, Sequence, History, Genre*, ed. Jakob Lothe, Jeremy Hawthorn, and James Phelan (Columbus: Ohio State University Press, 2008), 160–77, and his essay "Text, Action, Space: Emotion in Conrad's *Nostromo*," from *Exploring Text and Emotions*, ed. Lars Sætre, Patrizia Lombardo, and Julien Zanetta (Aarhus, Denmark: Aarhus University Press, 2014), 91–117, as well as a section from his foreword to *Conrad in the Twenty-First Century: Contemporary Approaches and Perspectives*, ed. Carola M. Kaplan, Peter Lancelot Mallios, and Andrea White (New York: Routledge, 2005), 11–13 [Editors].

PRELUDE

Henry James, in a review of Conrad's *Chance*, says Conrad is "absolutely alone as a votary of the way to do a thing that shall make it undergo most doing."[2] What James says would be even truer of *Nostromo*. That means anything like a complete accounting for *Nostromo* in a critical essay like this one also requires an exorbitant doing. "*Pour la commodité du récit*," as Proust puts it, for ease of my narration, to make it perspicuous, I have divided this chapter into four sections, with many labeled subsections in each section: The Origins of *Nostromo*; Material Vision in *Nostromo*: As Conrad Does It, "Material Interests"; *Nostromo* as Critique of Capitalist Imperialism; and Ideologies of Love and War: Psychodramas of Intertwined Isolatoes in *Nostromo*.

THE ORIGINS OF *NOSTROMO*

Conrad opens the "Author's Note" to *Nostromo* (1904) of October 1917 by saying that "*Nostromo* is the most anxiously meditated of the longer novels which belong to the period following upon the publication of the *Typhoon* volume of short stories."[3] This "Author's Note" (or "Note," as the Modern Library edition calls it) is an exceedingly peculiar document in a number of ways. What does that mean: "most anxiously meditated"? I suppose what it means seems obvious enough. *Nostromo* is a big novel, Conrad's biggest, with the largest number of characters whose stories are more or less completely told. It is natural that such a novel would take a lot of planning, a lot of meditative figuring out beforehand and even in the course of writing. Why that meditating should be "anxious" is not quite clear, however. I suppose it is plausible to assume that Conrad was worried about whether he could get such an ambitious novel to come out right. Writing is always a matter of anxiety.

It is not at first clear, nevertheless, whether Conrad means by "anxiously meditated" no more than what Heidegger calls *Sorge*, "care" for some task ready at hand, or whether he means something like what Heidegger calls

---

1. Paul de Man, "Conclusions: Walter Benjamin's 'The Task of the Translator,'" in *The Resistance to Theory* (Minneapolis: University of Minnesota Press, 1986), 88.

2. Henry James, "The New Novel," in *Literary Criticism: Essays on Literature; American Writers; English Writers*, ed. Leon Edel (New York: The Library of America, 1984), 147.

3. Joseph Conrad, "Note," in *Nostromo* by Joseph Conrad (New York: The Modern Library, 1951), 1. All references to *Nostromo* are by page numbers to this edition, with "Note" added for citations from that. The "Note" is paginated in Arabic numbers and then the pagination begins again for the novel proper. I have used this edition because it reprints the first book version and has some passages Conrad later cut.

genuine existential angst. Angst is an anxiety that goes all the way down to the depths of one's being. It exceeds any particular "care." What follows in the "Author's Note" makes it clear that Conrad suffered angst, all right, over *Nostromo*. The note is precious evidence of the way Conrad's imagination worked, at least according to his testimony. He may, of course, be making it up, romanticizing a prosaic process or ironically inflating it. Conrad was an ironist through and through.

After he finished the *Typhoon* volume, says Conrad, he went into a peculiar and disquieting state, at least for a professional writer, as he was. He was someone who needed to write in order to earn his daily bread. Conrad says there was a "change"

> in that mysterious, extraneous thing which has nothing to do with the theories of art; a subtle change in the nature of the inspiration, a phenomenon for which I cannot in any way be held responsible. What, however, did cause me some concern was that after finishing the last story of the *Typhoon* volume ("To-morrow") it seemed somehow that there was nothing more in the world to write about. ("Note" 1)

That is pretty terrifying. At one time the writing is going along swimmingly. "Inspiration," as Gerard Manley Hopkins puts it, "comes unbidden."[4] Conrad writes story after story as though the vein of inspiration could never dry up. Then suddenly, involuntarily, through what Conrad calls not a drying up of inspiration, but "a subtle change in the nature of the inspiration," it seems somehow that there is nothing more in the world to write about. Conrad's ability to write remains in undiminished strength. That is, I suppose, one definition of "inspiration." Now, however, through a "subtle change," nothing seems left as an object on which to exercise that power of writing. Conrad stresses that it is not his fault. It just happened. It was a "phenomenon for which I cannot in any way be held responsible." Nor is this change caused by some change in "the theories of art," Conrad's or anyone else's. Conrad could mean by this, I suppose, either that a change in theories of art could lead to new exigencies that might make writing something like *Typhoon* no longer possible, or that certain theories of art, perhaps theories of art's sources, might explain his sudden change of inspiration. No, it was a change in what Conrad calls the "mysterious, extraneous thing" that governs the nature of his inspi-

---

4. Hopkins, in a September 1, 1885, letter to Robert Bridges; see *The Letters of Gerard Manley Hopkins to Robert Bridges*, ed. Claude Colleer Abbott (London: Oxford University Press, 1959), 221 [Editors].

ration, something wholly outside himself and wholly outside his control. The change just happens, mysteriously. That causes anxiety, concern, angst.

The rest of the "Author's Note" details the steps by which Conrad escaped what might be called, in a Kierkegaardian phrase, this "sickness unto death" and came to write *Nostromo*. It is important to note at the outset that Conrad does not say anything like what critics say about the "sources" of *Nostromo*. For whatever reason, Conrad does not say,

> I had been reading Edward B. Eastwick's *Venezuela*, G. F. Masterman's *Seven Eventful Years in Paraguay*, S. Perez Triana's *Down the Orinoco*, and writings on South America by my friend R. B. Cunninghame Graham. These gave me the idea of writing a novel about an imaginary South American country that would amalgamate material from these various books, including South American history, its landscapes, as well as characters' names and personalities drawn from real people as described in these books.[5]

Why does Conrad not say that? Why does he hide his "sources"? Was it a somewhat guilty cover-up, or an honest forgetting, or is it evidence that Conrad disagreed by anticipation with modern "art theories" about the genesis of literary works? In any case, the story Conrad tells in 1917 of the origin of *Nostromo* is quite different from those of modern Conrad critics.

Just what does Conrad actually say about the genesis of *Nostromo*? His account parallels many of Henry James's accounts in the prefaces to the New York Edition of his novels and stories, where he tells the reader how a small germ or *donnée*, for example a vagrant anecdote told at the dinner table, produced a big novel when James's imagination began developing it. In Conrad's case, according to his testimony, he once heard, back in 1875 or 1876, on the only sea voyage he made to South America, or rather to the Gulf of Mex-

---

5. See Cedric T. Watts's succinct account of Conrad's sources in "A Note on the Background to *Nostromo*,'" in *Joseph Conrad's Letters to Cunninghame Graham*, ed. C. T. Watts (Cambridge: Cambridge University Press, 1969), 37–42. A fuller account is given in his *Joseph Conrad: Nostromo* (London: Penguin, 1990), 19–51. For other accounts of Conrad's sources and his uses of them, as well as for a few of the multitudinous readings of *Nostromo* as well as of Conrad and imperialism, see, for example, Eloise Knapp Hay, *The Political Novels of Joseph Conrad: A Critical Study* (Chicago: University of Chicago Press, 1963); Avrom Fleishman, *Conrad's Politics: Community and Anarchy in the Fiction of Joseph Conrad* (Baltimore: Johns Hopkins Press, 1967); Jacques Berthoud, *Joseph Conrad: The Major Phase* (Cambridge: Cambridge University Press, 1978); Robert Hampson, *Joseph Conrad: Betrayal and Identity* (New York: St. Martin's Press, 1992); Ian Watt, *Joseph Conrad: Nostromo* (Cambridge: Cambridge University Press, 1988); Peter Lancelot Mallios, "Untimely Nostromo," *Conradiana* 40, no. 3 (2008): 213–32; Benita Parry, *Conrad and Imperialism* (London: Macmillan, 1983); Stephen Ross, *Conrad and Empire* (Columbia: University of Missouri Press, 2004).

ico, of a man who had stolen a lighter full of silver during the turmoil of a South American revolution. A "lighter" is a barge used for transporting goods short distances, for example from the shore out to an anchored ship. A sail or sails move the lighter in *Nostromo,* not an engine. Years later, Conrad says, quite by accident he "came upon the very thing in a shabby volume picked up outside a second-hand-book shop" ("Note" 2). This book contained a circumstantial account of that extraordinary theft and of the brazenly villainous man who did it. Sure enough, scholars (Halverson and Watt) have identified the shabby volume as *On Many Seas: The Life and Exploits of a Yankee Sailor,* by H. E. Hamblen writing under the pseudonym of "Frederick Benton Williams."[6] Though, as Conrad says, he had spent only a few hours ashore in Venezuela, when he was "very young" ("Note" 1), nevertheless, according to him, the account in the shabby volume vividly reminded him of "that distant time when everything was so fresh, so surprising, so venturesome, so interesting: bits of strange coasts under the stars, shadows of hills in the sunshine, men's passions in the dusk, gossip half-forgotten, faces grown dim" ("Note" 3). The result of this flood of half-forgotten memories from Conrad's youth was a sudden reversal of his inspiration's suspension: "Perhaps, perhaps, there was still in the world something to write about" ("Note" 3). To "invent a circumstantial account of the robbery" seemed to Conrad uninteresting: "I did not think the game was worth the candle" ("Note" 3). It was only when it came to him that the thief need not be villainous that the possibility of making a Conradian novel out of this anecdote came to him. Here at last would be something worth writing about.

Conrad's expression of this transition is odd in two ways. He says that the notion that the thief might be a "man of character," just that quite narrow shift, gave him suddenly his first glimpse of the whole province of Sulaco. "Man of character," by the way, may be an allusion to Thomas Hardy's *The Mayor of Casterbridge.* The subtitle of Hardy's novel is "A Story of a Man of Character." The tiny germ transformed in Conrad's imagination, that thief turned from villainous to good, or at least into a "man of character," gave him the entire novel, or a glimpse of it, like a "little bang" expanding into an entire fictive cosmos. Conrad's image is of a dawning. He did not think it out rationally. It just dawned on him, out of nowhere, all of a sudden. That what dawned was a separate cosmos or imaginary world Conrad's insistence on Sulaco's isolation and totalizing self-enclosure confirms. Nevertheless, what is outside Sulaco

---

6. See Cedric Watts, *Joseph Conrad: Nostromo,* 21, and his footnote there to John Halverson and Ian Watt, "The Original Nostromo: Conrad's Source," *Review of English Studies* n.s. no. 37 (1959): 45–52.

intervenes decisively, as I shall show. That destructive intervention is a central theme of *Nostromo*.

The other oddness is that Conrad, however ironically, speaks of Sulaco not as something he invented but as something he discovered. It was already in existence waiting to be found and described, not something he made up out of the materials of his reading. Here are Conrad's exact words:

> It was only when it dawned upon me that the purloiner of the treasure need not necessarily be a confirmed rogue, that he could be even a man of character, an actor, and possibly a victim in the changing scenes of a revolution, it was only then that I had the first vision of a twilight country which was to become the province of Sulaco, with its high, shadowy sierra and its misty campo for mute witnesses of events flowing from the passions of men shortsighted in good and evil.
>
> Such are in very truth the obscure origins of *Nostromo*—the book. ("Note" 3–4)

In the remainder of the "Author's Note," Conrad goes on consistently speaking of Sulaco as something that was there already waiting to be discovered and then revealed through Conrad's written and ultimately printed account. It is as though he were the first explorer of a hitherto unknown country. Sulaco is like one of those blank places on the world map that so fascinated the Marlow of Conrad's *Heart of Darkness* when he was a child, just as Conrad himself was fascinated. Few, if any, blank places still exist for us today anywhere on the globe, or even on the surface of the moon, Mars, Venus, Jupiter, or the sun. We have mapped them all. No doubt Conrad is speaking figuratively when he speaks of Sulaco as a real place only he had discovered, but the figure is solemnly, if ironically, with a straight face, kept up through the whole of the "Author's Note." Conrad speaks of his fear that he might, as he says, "lose myself in the ever-enlarging vistas opening before me as I progressed deeper in my knowledge of the country" ("Note" 4).

A moment later, the trope defining the writing of the novel as the record of a discovery, not an invention, is given an extravagant and ostentatious expression. It is compared to what everyone knows is a hyperbolically fantastic work of fiction, a parody of early travel books, that is, *Gulliver's Travels*. Conrad speaks, no doubt ironically, half-jokingly, and, as he says, "figuratively" ("Note" 4), of his two years' absorption in writing *Nostromo* as his absence in that imaginary country: "my sojourn on the Continent of Latin America, famed for its hospitality, lasted for about two years. On my return I found (speaking somewhat in the style of Captain Gulliver) my family all well, my wife heartily glad to learn that the fuss was all over, and our small boy considerably grown during my absence" ("Note" 4). What is odd about this and other similar passages in the "Author's Note" is not only that Conrad speaks of the people and places of Costaguana as having a real existence, independent of his language, not as something he has invented through language, but also the way he asserts that only he has access to this strange place and to its people. He says, for example:

> My principal authority for the history of Costaguana is, of course, my venerated friend, the late Don José Avellanos, Minister to the Courts of England and Spain, etc., etc., in his impartial and eloquent "History of Fifty Years of Misrule." That work was never published—the reader will discover why [the manuscript gets destroyed by the revolutionary mob]—and I am, in fact, the only person in the world possessed of its contents. ("Note" 4)

Conrad, of course, invented Don José and all the rest of the characters, or, perhaps it might be better to say, he "discovered" them by an effort of the imagination. We can encounter Don José and his "History of Fifty Years of Misrule" only by reading Conrad's book.

Robert Penn Warren expresses this succinctly, in his introduction to the Modern Library Edition of 1951, based on the first Doubleday edition of 1904.[7] The latter has, by the way, some important variant readings here and there, differences from the standard Heinemann and Dent editions of the 1920s. C. T. Watts gives an account of these and also an account of differences between the edition of 1904 and the serial version.[8] "Long before, in 1875 and 1876," says Warren, "when on the *Saint-Antoine* (running guns for a revolution), Conrad had been ashore for a few hours at ports on the Gulf of Mexico, but of the coast that might have given him a model for his Occidental Province and its people he knew nothing. There were books and hearsay to help, the odds and ends of information. But in the end, the land, its people, and its history had to be dreamed up, evoked out of the primal fecund darkness that always lies below our imagination."[9] I'm dubious about that "primal fecund darkness," which sounds like something borrowed from the Marlow of *Heart of Darkness*, but I'll buy "dreamed up." That's right on. *Nostromo*

---

7. Harper & Brothers published the first edition of *Nostromo* in England and America in 1904. Doubleday later bought the rights to the novel from Harper & Brothers and in 1916 reprinted the original 1904 edition [Editors].

8. Watts, *Joseph Conrad: Nostromo*, 52–58 [Editors].

9. Robert Penn Warren, introduction to *Nostromo*, by Joseph Conrad (New York: Modern Library, 1951), ix.

was "dreamed up." The "Author's Note" specifies just how that happened. The "dreaming up," however, as we know now, was based not just on the sources Conrad acknowledges in the "Note," but on those books about South American landscape and history Conrad had read. He had never been to the west coast of Central America in his life, though he says he landed for brief visits on the east coast, in Colombia and Venezuela, whereas his novels and tales about Malaysia were based on extensive first-hand experience.

This difference can be taken as a striking testimony to the performative power of reading. Conrad read Cunninghame Graham, Masterman, Eastwick, Páez, et al. Out of this he created in his mind, or discovered there as a spontaneous vision, an imaginary Central American country made of the transformation and amalgamation of bits and pieces from all those books that stuck in his memory, or below the level of his conscious memory, undergoing many sea-changes there, into something "rich and strange." When you or I read *Nostromo*, something analogous happens. Each reader creates in his or her mind, on the basis of the words on the page, in response to their performative power, a mental image, or what I call a virtual reality, unique in each case, or perhaps even different in each reading by the same person, of the landscape of Sulaco, the town, its inhabitants, and all the events of the novel: the re-establishment of the mine, the murder of Hirsch, the suicide of Decoud, the accidental shooting of Nostromo, and so on. The words on the page become the instigators of a mental cinema or magic show, just as Conrad's reading of those source books was another such instigator.

My discourse about *Nostromo* here adds itself to the almost innumerable other essays about the novel. Almost one hundred new essays a year on Conrad get listed in the MLA bibliography. That boggles the mind. You could spend a lifetime just reading the old ones and keeping up with the new. Though it is good to learn all you can from these "secondary works," it is probably best to read Conrad for oneself. It is best to trust one's own imagination and to allow it to create a new, unique, and private mental cinema on the basis of the words Conrad wrote. I said "secondary works." It might be better to say "tertiary," since my words are a response to Conrad's words which were a response to those "source books" he read.

In the remainder of the "Author's Note" Conrad goes on to express, in the same mock-solemn, half-ironic way, in a parody of acknowledgments in a book preface, his obligation to the hospitality of the people of Sulaco, especially Mrs. Gould and Charles Gould, whom he speaks of as if they were real people whom he had visited for two years: "I confess that, for me, that time is the time of firm friendships and unforgotten hospitalities. And in my gratitude I must mention here Mrs. Gould, 'the first lady of Sulaco,' . . . and Charles Gould . . ." ("Note" 5).

Conrad then goes on at some length, in blatant contradiction to the trope of invention as discovery, as opposed to mimetic copying, he has been sustaining, to explain that Nostromo (the character) is modeled in part on a Mediterranean sailor he had known in his early days, "Dominic, the Padrone of the *Tremolino*" ("Note" 6). Antonia Avellanos, the political radical loved by the radical skeptic Decoud, is modeled, Conrad says, in part on an early schoolboy love of Conrad's, with Conrad himself playing the role played by Decoud in the novel: "I was not the only one in love with her; but it was I who had to hear oftenest her scathing criticism of my levities—very much like poor Decoud—or stand the brunt of her austere, her scathing invective" ("Note" 8).

Once more, however, what Conrad here says reveals the degree to which Nostromo, Antonia, Decoud, and the rest are not so much "modeled" on their "sources" as radical transformations of these in the alembic of Conrad's imagination. In a similar way, the politics of the novel are "modeled," in part, on Polish revolutionary politics as Conrad knew them in his youth. Antonia's invectives against Decoud's skepticism about politics are a transformation of Conrad's boyhood beloved's invectives against Conrad's waverings. The "Author's Note" ends with an image of the "beautiful Antonia" as she is today in Sulaco, "awaiting impatiently the dawns of other New Eras, the coming of more revolutions" ("Note" 9). Conrad asks, in parentheses, "(or can it be the Other)" ("Note" 8). He means, I suppose, "Can it be that youthful love of mine whom I abandoned forever when I left Poland to go to sea, and whom I imagine, by way of my imagination of the fictitious Antonia, as she may be today."

In *A Personal Record,* Conrad takes a somewhat different way of defining the way Costaguana is a virtual reality:

> I had, like the prophet of old, "wrestled with the Lord" for my creation, for the headlands of the coast, for the darkness of the Placid Gulf, the light on the snows, the clouds on the sky and for the breath of life that had to be blown into the shapes of men and women, of Latin and Saxon, of Jew and Gentile. These are, perhaps, strong words, but it is difficult to characterise otherwise the intimacy and strain of a creative effort in which mind and will and conscience are engaged to the full, hour after hour, day after day, away from the world, and to the exclusion of all that makes life really lovable and gentle . . . (91)

Conrad's creation of the world of Costaguana is spoken of in this passage as a counter-creation, as something that he had to wrestle with the Lord to obtain, since it is in opposition to His creation. Conrad's writing of *Nostromo* is something like Jehovah's breathing of life into Adam and Eve. This creation of an alternative world, complete with its own landscape and geography, takes place "away from the world," that is, away from God's creation, in a solitary creative struggle that, Conrad says, is like nothing so much as "the everlasting sombre stress of the westward winter passage round Cape Horn" (*PR* 91).

Just as God's creation, in the thought of certain seventeenth-century French theologians, depends absolutely on what they called "continuous creation," that is, on God's willing from moment to moment to keep the world and all the people in it in existence, since otherwise they would vanish, so Costaguana depends for its existence on the continuous exercise of Conrad's will and creative imagination. This must be kept up from minute to minute, day after day, and month after month. If Conrad's effort flags, the whole shebang disappears in an instant, like a snuffed candle. This happens when a neighbor, a general's daughter, walks in on him unawares while he is writing and says, "How do you do?" (*PR* 91). Conrad stresses the quasi-material nature of *Nostromo*'s virtual world, a "materiality without matter," as it existed in his imagination and nowhere else. It is a matter of mountains, sea, and clouds, even of grains of sand, as well as of imaginary people. In this passage, Conrad also stresses the way Costaguana is a spatio-temporal whole. It exists as a "whole world," all at once, present all together in his mind. All novels create a counterworld, separate from the real one, with its own laws, geography, weather, and other characteristics, but I know of no other novel that makes this so explicit as *Nostromo* does, for example in the initial description of its topography in the opening chapters. The visit of the general's daughter destroys it all:

> The whole world of Costaguana (the country, you may remember, of my seaboard tale), men, women, headlands, houses, mountains, town, *campo* (there was not a single brick, stone, or grain of sand of its soil I had not placed in position with my own hands); all the history, geography, politics, finance; the wealth of Charles Gould's silver-mine, and the splendour of the magnificent Capataz de Cargadores, whose name, cried out in the night (Dr. Monygham heard it pass over his head—in Linda Viola's voice), dominated even after death the dark gulf containing his conquests of treasure and love—all that had come down crashing about my ears. I felt I could never pick up the pieces— (*PR* 92)

We can have access to Costaguana only because Conrad wrote down his vision, whereas Conrad apparently lived there before he wrote it down. Or perhaps the act of imagining Costaguana coincided with the act of writing it down. This might be called a performative "act of literature," a special mode of speech act. Edward Said, with his usual clairvoyance as a reader, even when what he sees goes to some degree against what he might wish to find, notices in his own way, employing the musical analogy that recurs in the interview now printed in *Conrad in the Twenty-First Century*, how *Nostromo* detaches itself from its sources:

> What Conrad is attempting in *Nostromo* is a structure of such monumental solidity that it has an integrity of its own quite without reference to the outside world. Though this is only a speculation, I think that halfway through the book it's as if Conrad loses interest in the real world of human beings and becomes fascinated with the workings of his own method and his own writing. *It* has an integrity quite of its own—the way, for example, Bach might construct a fugue around a very uninteresting subject, and by the middle of the piece you are so involved in keeping the five, or four, voices going, and understanding the relationships between them, that this becomes the most interesting thing about it. I think there is a similar impulse at work in *Nostromo*.[10]

Said is right on the mark. Having assembled his Costaguana from the imaginative transformation of various miscellaneous materials, he then became more and more absorbed in working out the intertwined destinies of the characters with which he had peopled his heterotopia.

I conclude from all I have said so far that, like *The Return of the Native*, though with some differences, *Nostromo* is a work of literature, not a work of history, autobiography, political theory, ethnography, psychoanalysis, ecology, or travel. I mean by this that *Nostromo* was conceived, written, published, read, and reviewed as a work within the established genre of literature as it has been defined in the West since the seventeenth century. This has been the print epoch. It has coincided with the development of Western-style democracies with their putative right to free speech. That means, in the case of literature, the right to invent anything whatsoever and not be held responsible for its referential or constative value, its value as truth of correspondence.

The era of printed literature is now coming to an end, in what promises to be a long, drawn-out agony, as new media replace the printed book: cinema, television, popular music downloaded from the Internet, video games,

---

10. "An Interview with Edward Said," in *Conrad in the Twenty-First Century: Contemporary Approaches and Perspectives*, ed. Carola M. Kaplan, Peter Lancelot Mallios, and Andrea White (New York: Routledge, 2005), 293.

Facebook, Twitter, and so on. It will not do to be condescending to these new media. They have immense power to influence the way people think, believe, and behave, while literature's power, once paramount, is fading. The presentation of the war in Iraq on network news, for example the film clips that were chosen and that are shown repeatedly, are obviously influenced by the conventions of war films and video games. An example is a clip, shown over and over in different contexts on NBC Nightly News during the Iraq War, of American soldiers in battle dress and armed to the teeth breaking into a supposed Iraqi terrorist house. This scene of breaking in is a common motif in video games. For every few people who have read *Heart of Darkness*, thousands of people, I am sure, have seen the film *Apocalypse Now*.

A lot of literary creativity as well as amazing technical know-how goes into video games. If Conrad were around today, he would probably be writing movie or television scripts, or programming video games. I can imagine a game called "Costaguana," in which the players try to bring off or thwart a revolution in an imaginary South American republic, just as there is a video game as well as a film for *The Lord of the Rings*. The goal of "Costaguana" would be to establish a new nation state, with a constitution, laws, institutions, industries, corporations, and so on, as we tried to do in Afghanistan and Iraq. The fading of literature's power may be one reason why such strenuous efforts have to be made by university professors to justify the study of literature. They love literature, but they are sometimes perhaps a little embarrassed to be caught reading a work of literature "for pleasure," "for its own sake." By "for its own sake" I mean for the sake of the entry into a purely imaginary realm, unique and different in each case, that each literary work allows. The social and personal function of reading literature is no longer so easily taken for granted. As a consequence, humanities professors disguise their love of literature, if they still have it, in the masquerade of hard-headed, empirical, politically progressive cultural studies; or feminist studies; or studies in gender, class, and race; or investigations into the material bases of culture; or studies based on the recent vogue in the humanities of cognitive science.

One difference between *Nostromo* and *The Return of the Native* is that the former is even more obviously a dreamland rather than an imaginative picture of an actual place, as Hardy's novel is. Another difference is that Conrad is much more self-conscious and articulate about the formation of *Nostromo* as a counter-creation than Hardy is. Hardy is more matter-of-fact. He takes literature more or less for granted as a public institution. He is writing a novel, and everybody knows what novels are. Literature is already for Conrad something problematic in itself. It was also increasingly problematic for Conrad's "modernist" contemporaries, whether in France with Mallarmé, Valéry, and Proust, or in the German-speaking part of Europe, with Mann, Kafka, or Musil, or in England and Ireland, with Joyce, Woolf, and Conrad's friend and collaborator, Ford Madox Ford.

MATERIAL VISION IN *NOSTROMO*: AS CONRAD DOES IT

Conrad had long discussions with Ford about literary technique. Together they developed a self-conscious theory of literary "impressionism." This was somewhat analogous to impressionism in painting and was to some degree modeled on Steven Crane's narrative technique in *The Red Badge of Courage*. As Eloise Knapp Hay has shown in an authoritative essay, Conrad's relation to impressionism was complex. It went, according to her, through three phases. Conrad initially deplored and detested impressionism in painting. In 1890, he called it "the school of Charenton" after the name of a madhouse.[11] Later, however, in separate essays on Stephen Crane and Alphonse Daudet, Conrad praised an impressionist method in fictional narration, though with reservations about its failure to get to the bottom of things. Impressionist writers, in this case Daudet, have a gift for seeing "only the surface of things . . . for the reason that most things have nothing but a surface."[12] Most people who know anything about Conrad remember that in the Paterian preface to *The Nigger of the "Narcissus*," he said that "art may be defined as a single-minded attempt to render the highest kind of justice to the visible universe" (xi), and "My task which I am trying to achieve is, by the power of the written word to make you hear, to make you feel—it is, before all, to make you *see*" (xiv). The irony of these high-minded statements, when set against *Nostromo*, is, of course, that Sulaco is precisely invisible, or visible only to Conrad's inner eye. It does not exist as a place one could visit to check the accuracy of Conrad's act of "rendering justice." His goal in *Nostromo* is to make the reader *see* an imaginary, never-never land.

The third stage of Conrad's relation to impressionism was a late change to less equivocal admiration for Stephen Crane and to a self-conscious attempt to remain on the surface of things in his own writing: "I am only a story-teller. . . . I do not want to go to the bottom of things. I want to consider reality as something rough and crude over which I let my fingers play. Nothing more."[13]

---

11. Eloise Knapp Hay, "Joseph Conrad and Impressionism," *The Journal of Aesthetics and Art Criticism* 34, no. 2 (Winter 1975): 139.

12. Quoted in ibid., 138.

13. Quoted in ibid., 143.

WELL, SO WHAT?

What difference does it make that *Nostromo* is a virtual reality, like a Bach fugue, as Said says, in which complex internal relationships are all-important, and in which the straightforward referential function of language is suspended? This does not mean we should not learn all we can about Conrad's "sources," or "contexts," or about what Benita Parry calls the "historical, political, and ideological materials" of *Nostromo*.[14] Robert Hampson's recent discussion of *Nostromo* is exemplary in doing this.[15] Nor does it mean that we should not concern ourselves with Conrad's relevance to our globalized political and economic situation today. It is hard to read *Nostromo* and not think of the long sad history, before and after Conrad wrote that novel, of United States intervention in South America, or even of our recent intervention, governed as it has been by "material interests," in Iraq and Afghanistan. I shall have more to say about these analogies. Dick Cheney, the erstwhile CEO of the global transnational corporation Halliburton, is a twenty-first-century version of the American capitalist Holroyd in *Nostromo*. It could be argued that Cheney to some degree lowered himself by becoming a mere Vice President of the United States, though as Vice President he remained to some degree still the agent of Halliburton and other such "material interests." His business "expertise" also meant that he and the rest of the George W. Bush administration ran the United States government as much as they could in the same way that Fastow and Kenneth Lay ran Enron. Running the United States as if it were a corporation was a wonderful opportunity for plunder, trillions of dollars taken from American citizens rather than the mere billions Enron purloined from stockholders. Conrad's Holroyd prophetically anticipates those more recent devotees of "material interests" and imperial power.

The relation of *Nostromo* to history, politics, and ideology dramatizes one specific form such a relation can have. In one direction, towards its origin, *Nostromo* is a transformation, in what I have called the alembic of Conrad's creative imagination, of the materials that went into it. It is a magical translation or transmogrification of those materials into something rich and strange. The sum total of the "sources" cannot predict this result, nor can they fully account for it. The real person Dominic does not explain the character Nostromo. The small anecdote Conrad had encountered about the "original" of

---

14. Benita Parry, "The Moment and Afterlife of *Heart of Darkness*," in *Conrad in the Twenty-First Century: Contemporary Approaches and Perspectives*, ed. Carola M. Kaplan, Peter Lancelot Mallios, and Andrea White (New York: Routledge, 2005), 39.

15. Robert Hampson, "Conrad's Heterotopic Fiction: Composite Maps, Superimposed Sites, and Impossible Spaces," in *Conrad in the Twenty-First Century: Contemporary Approaches and Perspectives*, ed. Carola M. Kaplan, Peter Lancelot Mallios, and Andrea White (New York: Routledge, 2005), 121–35.

Nostromo (the villain who stole the lighter full of silver) is completely transcended by the complex personality and story Conrad has invented for his fictional Capataz de Cargadores. One has to read the novel to find out about Nostromo. The same thing can be said for the novel's relation to all its other "sources," including the facts of South American history, its revolutions, and its acts of nation-building.

In the other direction, toward the future, *Nostromo* enters back into history not by giving us constative facts about South American history. History books are the place to find out about that. *Nostromo* re-enters history, rather, by way of the unpredictable performative effects it may have on its readers. It may do its work by getting its readers to see history differently by way of a fiction, rather than by a direct representation of history. A work of fiction "works" performatively not by way of discursive statements but, as Aristotle knew, by its action, its plot, the stories it tells. Its essential dimension is temporal sequence. A novel may possibly work to get its readers to see their own histories differently, and to behave differently as a result. They might vote differently in the next election, for example, though I would not count on that. Conrad's characteristic ironic method of narration, which is by no means absent from *Nostromo,* paradoxically aids in bringing about this performative effect. Irony, as Paul de Man surprisingly affirms in "The Concept of Irony," excuses, and promises, and consoles.[16] It may also work as an effective exhortation to political action. Marx's *Das Kapital* and *The German Ideology* are, among other things, wonderful works of sustained ironic invective, often in the admirably devastating discussions in footnotes of Marx's adversaries. This use of irony does not mean that *Das Kapital* and *The German Ideology* are any the less world-changing works.

Reading *Nostromo*

In order to understand how *Nostromo* might be performatively effective as opposed to mimetically accurate or constatively informing, it will be necessary to read the novel with attentive care. This is no easy task with such a big work. Moreover, *Nostromo* seems to me an exceedingly peculiar use of modernist conventions of narration. No other novel I know of is at all like it, even among Conrad's other works. By "reading" *Nostromo,* I mean scrupulous attention to matters of technique and to rhetorical features, to the puzzling materiality of those words and letters on the page as they give birth in the reader's mind to

---

16. Paul de Man, "The Concept of Irony," in *Aesthetic Ideology,* ed. Andrzej Warminski (Minneapolis: University of Minnesota Press, 1996), 165.

the whole province of Sulaco: mountains, plains, town, harbor, islands, sea, and the people there. The performative force of a literary work lies not in thematic generalities that can be distilled from it, nor in a description of the characters, nor in a summary of the plot. That force lies in local details as they accumulate. A reading, if such a thing is possible, must try to take account of these in their enigmatic power to change the world of the reader, in however small a way.

Determining whether or not Sulaco is a community and, if so, just what kind of a community it is, is my chosen focus in this chapter. The question of communities in fiction is also my central concern in the other chapters of this book. As a means of getting to that, however, I must say something about the setting and about the mode of presentation, that is, about the specific qualities of Costaguana and about the narrator or, it might be better to say, the "narrative voice."

Nostromo, after all, begins not with the people and their stories, but with the landscape. It is the landscape that seems to have formed itself in visionary fashion within Conrad's mind when he first glimpsed the possibility that something to write about might still exist after all. That is one similarity with *The Return of the Native*. The latter begins not with the people but with the long personifying description of Egdon Heath as night falls. I have elsewhere written in detail about Hardy's prosopopoeia of the heath and its function in *The Return of the Native*.[17] Conrad's topographical rhetoric is, however, quite different from Hardy's, as I shall show. First, however, it is worth reflecting on what is odd about beginning with landscape rather than plunging into some scene involving the main characters of the novel. Henry James's late masterpieces all begin with such a plunge. It is a hallmark of the New Historicism, one of its conventions or presentational reflexes, to begin with some specific detail or scene. Doing so is a way of saying, "You are reading a work in the mode of the New Historicism. I do not begin with generalities or with statistics. I begin with an odd historical fact, in all its apparently absurd circumstantiality. You will understand later what I am up to."

Henry James's *The Ambassadors*, for example, begins *in medias res*, with Strether's arrival at the hotel in Chester after his transatlantic voyage from America: "Strether's first question, when he reached the hotel, was about his friend; yet on his learning that Waymarsh was apparently not to arrive until evening he was not wholly disconcerted."[18] "Not wholly disconcerted"—who but James could have concocted such a self-cancelling phrase, with its double

---

17. See my "Philosophy, Literature, Topography: Heidegger and Hardy," in *Topographies* (Stanford, CA: Stanford University Press, 1995), 9–56, especially 26–29.

18. Henry James, *The Ambassadors* (New York: Charles Scribner's Sons, 1909), 3.

negative, turning on "not" and "dis-," after an earlier "not": "was apparently not to arrive"? "Apparently"? "Not wholly"? All Strether's fastidious doubleness is presented in these locutions. The double negative programs all his behavior to its culmination in his refusal of Maria Gostrey's offer of herself to him. He refuses, he says, so he will not have gotten anything out of it for himself. *The Wings of the Dove* begins no less abruptly: "She waited, Kate Croy, for her father to come in, but he kept her unconscionably, and there were moments at which she showed herself, in the glass over the mantel, a face positively pale with the irritation that had brought her to the point of going away without sight of him."[19] *The Golden Bowl*'s first words are, "The Prince had always liked his London, when it had come to him. . . ."[20] Such openings leave the reader wondering just who Strether, Waymarsh, Kate Croy, and the Prince are and just what in the world they are doing at those moments.

Nor does Conrad never open a novel is this way. His first novel, *Almayer's Folly*, started in 1889, begins with enigmatic words, called out by some unknown person: "Kaspar! Makan!" and then plunges the reader immediately into Almayer's consciousness: "The well-known shrill voice startled Almayer from his dream of a splendid future into the unpleasant realities of the present hour." Those peremptory words, "Kaspar! Makan!" were the first words of Conrad's writing career. They were a sort of dawning or wakeup call to his vocation. "Rise and shine, Joseph Conrad!"

The Opening of *Nostromo*

The first words of *Nostromo*, written fourteen years later, in 1903, are quite different: "In the time of Spanish rule, and for many years afterwards, the town of Sulaco—the luxuriant beauty of the orange gardens bears witness to its antiquity—had never been commercially anything more important than a coasting port with a fairly large local trade in ox-hides and indigo" (3). In Henry James's beginnings, setting is almost incidental. The reader only gradually learns just where the characters are. The immediate focus is on the consciousness of one of the protagonists, as it is presented intimately and yet ironically in the discourse of the narrator. In *Nostromo*, Conrad gives the empty setting without the people—as yet. The whole of the first chapter is too long, alas, to cite *in toto* here, though it takes up only six pages. Those pages are completely devoted to creating in the mind of the reader the entire panorama of Conrad's

---

19. Henry James, *The Wings of the Dove* (New York: Charles Scribner's Sons, 1909), 3.
20. Henry James, *The Golden Bowl* (New York: Charles Scribner's Sons, 1909), 3.

imaginary province of Sulaco as it existed already in Conrad's mind or, perhaps, as he discovered it in the act of writing about it.

Several salient features of this performative topographical act ("Let there be Sulaco!") may be identified. As in the "Author's Note" of 1917, so in the novel itself, Conrad stresses the more or less complete hermetic self-enclosure of Sulaco. Speaking of his departure from Poland and from his youthful ladylove there, Conrad in the "Author's Note" says he "was really going away for good, going very far—even as far as Sulaco, lying unknown, hidden from all eyes in the darkness of the Placid Gulf" ("Note" 8). Sulaco was unknown and hidden from all eyes because it did not exist, or rather it came into existence only when Conrad discovered it in the depths of his imagination as an invented place on the west coast of South America, and wrote it down so we can visit the place by reading the book. Conrad had, as I have said, never been to the west coast of South America in his life.

That Sulaco is secret, hidden, and unknown, is re-enforced by the topography Conrad ascribes to it. In *The Mirror of the Sea* Conrad says that a seaman's life in relation to the shore is made up of "the rhythmical swing" of "Landfall and Departure." He goes on to specify that "Landfall" means the first glimpse of a shore as your ship approaches it from the open sea, not the actual arrival on shore: "Your Landfall, be it a peculiarly shaped mountain, a rocky headland, or a stretch of sand-dunes, you meet at first with a single glance."[21] Anyone who is even a small boat sailor, as I am, will know how strange, how magical, how inviting, and yet how somehow ominous, a shore, even one you know well, appears from the sea. Conrad presents Sulaco as though the reader were approaching it from the sea. This perspective is even reinforced by the subtitle of the novel: "A Tale of the Seaboard." It is neither a story of land nor a story of the sea, but, precisely, a story of the edge or boundary between them, the seaboard.

As is so often the case with Conrad's topographical descriptions, the mode of the description almost seems as if it were intended as directions for a movie-camera crew. This scenario tells the camera-man to move from a distant view closer and closer in by stages until focusing finally on the jetty in the inner harbor of the Oceanic Steam Navigation Company. The reader sees this as it appears from the beach of the Great Isabel, the largest of the three islands not far out in the Golfo Placido. The reader might not notice at first that the cinematic nature of the initial description is enhanced by the way it is all in the present tense. The narration slips almost unnoticeably into the usual past tense somewhere in the second paragraph of the second chapter.

---

21. Joseph Conrad, *The Mirror of the Sea* (Garden City, NY: Doubleday, Page & Co., 1926), 3.

This opening in the present tense is what might be called visionary. It is the exposure by way of a figurative ship making landfall of the whole inner topography of *Nostromo* as a virtual reality Conrad had "discovered." The shift to the past tense throws all the events of the novel back into the past, as objects of a mnemonics. These events become accessible to the total recall of the quite impersonal narrative voice as it moves back and forth over the past in the sometimes bewildering time shifts, flashbacks, flashforwards, encapsulated episodes, accounts of iterated actions, that make up the novel. If the space of the novel is a panoramic whole, the past, too, is panoramic, spread out as a unit before the narrator's total recall. That leaves the narrative voice free to choose any piece to narrate. The narrative is not bound by sequential or causal chronology, or by some single teleological goal, though the death of Nostromo more or less brings the need for narration to an end. As Conrad says at the end of the "Author's Note": "the moment the breath left the body of the Magnificent Capataz, the Man of the People freed at last from the toils of love and wealth, there was nothing more for me to do in Sulaco" ("Note" 9). He means, I suppose, that there was nothing more to narrate, no more story to tell. The endpoint of narratability in *Nostromo* is not marriage, as in Jane Austen's novels or in so many novels by Anthony Trollope, but death, the death of the principle protagonist, as, for example, in *Hamlet*.

One implicit target of Conrad's complex narrative sequencing in *Nostromo* is the ordinary assumption about how history should be written. It takes the reader quite a while to realize that the center of the novel is an account of the revolution that leads indirectly to the founding of the separate Republic of Sulaco, to the saving of the silver mine, and to Nostromo's theft of the lighter full of silver. All of these take place in a relatively short space of time, but much moving backwards and forwards is necessary to account for these events fully and adequately.

The present tense of the opening chapter works unostentatiously to suggest that the whole scene is timeless, always the same from day to day, month to month, and year to year. Sulaco is close enough to the equator not even to have much in the way of seasons. It is always sunshiny by day and cloudy by night. The entire landscape was there before mankind came, and it will still be there when mankind has vanished. The narrator's Landfall vision stresses the unapproachability of the Placid Gulf. "Never a strong wind had been known to blow upon its waters" (*N* 6). (This is an unlikelihood, by the way. Any open water will get strong wind some of the time.) Sailing ships routinely get becalmed for days in the Golfo Placido within sight of the harbor. That is a little spooky, if you think of it. There you are, almost there, but you are magically suspended just short of the goal by something so seemingly trivial as a chronic lack of wind at that spot on the seaboard. This predictable windlessness, along with the great range of mountains on the inland side, beyond the plain, has for generations, before steam navigation, safely sequestered Sulaco from the outside world. It is almost like an enchanted island or like a sleeping beauty princess. "Some harbors of the earth," says the narrator, "are made difficult of access by the treachery of sunken rocks and the tempests of their shores" (3). Sulaco is protected, on the contrary, "by the prevailing calms of its vast gulf" (3): "Sulaco had found an inviolable sanctuary from the temptations of a trading world in the solemn hush of the deep Golfo Placido as if within an enormous semicircular and unroofed temple open to the ocean, with its walls of lofty mountains hung with the mourning draperies of clouds" (3). I shall return to the significance of this elaborate architectural metaphor, or rather simile. Conrad says "as if."

After this initial Landfall view, the narrative perspective moves gradually inward, first with a minute description on one side of the Punta Mala, "an insignificant cape," "the last spur of the coast range" (4). Conrad does not say whether left or right, but it is probably on the right or starboard side of the gulf as you approach from the sea. I shall return to the question of mapping Sulaco. On the other side of the semicircle is the much more impressive "peninsula of Azuera." It is called that presumably because it looks from a distant sea approach like "an isolated patch of blue mist float[ing] lightly on the glare of the horizon" (4). Azuera is rocky and full of ravines. It is absolutely dry and barren, except for the thorny thickets at its entrance. The narrator tells a folk story, believed to be true by all the poor people of Sulaco, about two gringo sailors and a "good-for-nothing mozo" (4) (Native American) who tried to hack their way by machete onto the peninsula to get the buried treasure in gold reputed to be there. After the smoke from their first night's campfire, they were never seen or heard from again: "The sailors, the Indian, and the stolen burro were never seen again" (5). Their ghosts, everyone believes, now rich but everlastingly hungry and thirsty, still haunt the ravines and rocks of Azuera. This fable anticipates the fate of all those in the main story whose desires and fantasies are captured by the San Tomé silver mine. *Nostromo* is on one level a somewhat wry and ironically twisted version of a parable or cautionary tale as old, at least, as Chaucer's "Pardoner's Tale," with its stern moral: *Radix malorum est cupiditas*. You see, I told you that *Nostromo* is a fantasy invented by Conrad, with some help from tradition.

The narrator's account then moves through a spectacular view of the distant mountains, the Cordillera, crowned with the snow-covered Higuerota, to a description of the everlasting diurnal sequence, as experienced by a ship becalmed on the gulf, with clouds rising over the mountains but never quite making it out over the water, except at night, when it becomes pitch black and the sailors can hear but not see showers beginning and ceasing here and there on the gulf, though there is still no wind. The narration then moves to a circumstantial description of the three uninhabited islets, the Great Isabel, the Little Isabel, and Hermosa ("Beautiful"), the smallest. These islets stand opposite the entrance to the harbor of Sulaco. The chapter ends with a sentence about the town of Sulaco itself, out of direct line of sight from the sea, but visible at a little distance from within the harbor itself, with its "tops of wall, a great cupola, gleams of white miradors [towers] in a vast grove of orange-trees" (8).

This first chapter is a wonderful opening for the novel. It confirms that Conrad had a clear and detailed vision of Sulaco's topography in his mind, whatever critics like Berthoud and Hampson may have said about its being a de Certeauvian heterotopia, that is, not always quite making non-contradictory rational sense as something you could put down on a map. Conrad, it happens, did sketch a topographical relief map of Sulaco on page 345 of the manuscript. It is reproduced in Eloise Knapp Hays's *The Political Novels of Joseph Conrad*.[22] I must say the map is a little difficult to interpret. It is hard to decide just which is the Punta Mala, which the Azuera, just where is the harbor, where the town of Sulaco is, as they are described in the opening pages of the novel. I think that large projection in the middle of the coastline must be the Azuera and that tiny black rectangle to its right must be the harbor dock. Presumably Conrad knew, but he has not put any place names on his map. Cedric Watts, in his admirable small book on *Nostromo*, provides detailed maps of the region and of the town of Sulaco.[23] He is an expert, so he must know where all these items are located, just how high Higuerota is, and so on.[24]

Material Vision in the Opening

Two fundamental and related features of this scene-setting opening may be identified.

First: The topographical features are presented in what might be called a materialist mode. They are just the physical elements that happen to be there

---

22. Hay, *Political Novels of Joseph Conrad*, 173.
23. Watts, *Joseph Conrad: Nostromo*, 64–65.
24. Watts's map of the geography of the Occidental Province includes the islands, bodies of water, and mountains, along with such features as the Custom House and the O.S.N. offices. Watts also includes distances between places mentioned in the novel. His map of part of Sulaco situates the Amarilla Club, the Intendencia, and other prominent places noted in the novel [Editors].

and that make an impression on the senses of the imaginary narrating spectator. They are barely identified as shapes, as colors, as sounds, with minimal names: clouds, mountains, rocks, sea surface, and so on. They are given, one might say, almost at the level of pure phenomenal sensation rather than of perception. They are named, in Kant's words, "as the poets do it," that is, with almost complete literality.[25] They are wholly indifferent to mankind, without prescribed or projected meaning for men and women. They are presented as a materialist vision.

Second: This materialism goes along with another related feature. Almost completely lacking in *Nostromo* is the sort of landscape personification that permeates Hardy's description of Egdon Heath at the beginning of *The Return of the Native*, or Conrad's own description of the African jungle in *Heart of Darkness*. Nor is there any projection of some metaphysical "darkness" behind appearances, as happens throughout the stylistic texture of landscape description in *Heart of Darkness*. The topography of *Nostromo* is almost completely depthless. It is like a superficial stage set, with nothing behind it.

These topographical appearances are not symbolic. They are not allegorical, at least not in the everyday sense of that word. They do not stand for anything beyond themselves. There is apparently nothing hidden behind them, no portentous "other," nothing like "the stillness of an implacable force brooding over an inscrutable intention" that is invoked by Marlow in *Heart of Darkness* (77). The topographical appearances in *Nostromo* are all surface. They have no sympathy for the human actions that are performed with them as backdrop, nor are they antagonistic. They are just implacably indifferent, though even to say that is to humanize them too much. They are just what happens to be there, what the eye can see, the ear can hear. The scene is not teleological. It does not lead to anything, nor is it good for anything. It just goes on repeating

---

25. Andrzej Warminski has written a brilliant and already classic essay on this phrase in its context. See Andrzej Warminski, "'As the Poets Do It': On the Material Sublime," in his *Ideology, Rhetoric, Aesthetics: For De Man* (Edinburgh: Edinburgh University Press, 2013), 38–64. Warminski's essay on Kant is inspired by Paul de Man's "Phenomenality and Materiality in Kant," *Aesthetic Ideology*, ed. Andrzej Warminski (Minneapolis: University of Minnesota Press, 1996), 70–90. More recently, Claire Colebrook has returned once more to Kant as read by de Man in order to argue that the proper attitude in these days of catastrophic climate change is a material sublime that sees nature as fragmented, mechanical, and indifferent, as against personifications of Mother Nature. See "The Geological Sublime," section 4 of Claire Colebrook's superb extended essay, "What is the Anthropo-Political" [81–125], her part of Tom Cohen, Claire Colebrook, and J. Hillis Miller, *Twilight of the Anthropocene Idols* (London: Open Humanities Press, 2016). "Such a sublime," says Colebrook, "would be aesthetic in de Man's sense *not* because it has to do with art and composition, but because it would propose a mode of seeing *without sense or teleology*.... What if we could look at all forces with the eye that is not detached *from 'the world'* but is confronted with decomposition, fragmentation and detachment *tout court*," 120.

itself endlessly as the sun rises and sets, day after day. This radical difference from *Heart of Darkness* has important consequences for the lives of the people in *Nostromo*, as I shall show.

Conrad and Kant

The attentive reader, however, will have noted my qualifications in the words "almost" and "apparently" in the previous paragraph. Such a reader will probably also have noticed that Conrad's description of the Golfo Placido is not quite so straightforwardly literal as I have so far claimed. Let me look again at the passage I have cited: "Sulaco had found an inviolable sanctuary from the temptations of a trading world in the solemn hush of the deep Golfo Placido as if within an enormous semicircular temple open to the ocean, with its walls of lofty mountains hung with the mourning draperies of cloud" (3). As you can see, the whole landscape of Sulaco is figured architectonically as like an enormous "temple," with its walls the encircling mountains and its roof the sky. It is as if the relatively neutral word "sanctuary" had called up the temple trope, by way of the tradition that evil-doers and those subject to temptation can find inviolable sanctuary in a church. Conrad's temple image looks to me more like a Catholic cathedral whose walls are hung with black mourning draperies in honor of some funeral than like a Greek temple. Conrad would have known such churches in his youth in Poland. The figure of the church is superimposed spectrally on the literal scene. What can we, or what should we, make of that? I have already alluded to Kant, an extremely unlikely presence in *Nostromo*. Though I do not imagine Conrad sitting down one evening to read *The Critique of Judgment*, he just happens to have invented a trope that is remarkably like the well-known one Kant employs in a climactic passage on the dynamic sublime:

> If, then, we call the sight of the starry heaven *sublime*, we must not place at the basis of our judgment concepts of worlds inhabited by rational beings and regard the bright points, with which we see the space above us filled, as their suns moving in circles purposively fixed with reference to them; but we must regard it, just as we see it [*wie man ihn sieht*], as a distant, all-embracing vault [*ein weites Gewölbe*]. Only under such a representation can we range that sublimity that a pure aesthetical judgment ascribes to this object [*müssen wir die Erhabenheit setzen, die ein reines ästhetisches Urteil diesem Gegenstande beilegt*]. And in the same way, if we are to call the sight of the ocean sublime, we must not *think* of it as we [ordinarily] do, as implying all kinds of knowledge (that are not contained in immediate intuition

[*in der unmittelbaren Anschauung*]). For example, we sometimes think of the ocean as a vast kingdom of aquatic creatures, or as the great source of those vapors that fill the air with clouds for the benefit of the land, or again as an element which, though dividing continents from each other, yet promotes the greatest communication between them; but these furnish merely teleological judgments. To find the ocean nevertheless sublime we must regard it as poets do [*wie die Dichter es tun*], merely by what the eye reveals [*was der Augenschein zeigt*]—if it is at rest, as a clear mirror of water [*als einem klaren Wasserspiegel*] bounded by the heavens; if it is stormy, as an abyss [*Abgrund*] threatening to overwhelm everything.[26]

The same elements are here as in the passage from Conrad: sky, sea, clouds, stars, though not the shore as such. Stars are mentioned by Conrad in a passage about nighttime on the Golfo Placido that I have not so far cited: "The few stars left below the seaward frown of the vault shine feebly as into the mouth of a black cavern. In its vastness your ship floats unseen under your feet, her sails flutter invisible above your head" (7). Note the evanescent personification in "frown" and "mouth." These are catachreses. In order to name these natural appearances at all, since they have no literal names, words must be brought in from another realm, most commonly, as here, from the human body, which is projected on nature in a self-canceling trope. Though the dark vault of the shoreward sky at night is not really a face, we say it has a "mouth" and that it "frowns," in order to be able to say anything about it at all. In a similar way both Kant and Conrad speak of the sky as a "vault," *Gewölbe* in German, as though it were a cathedral ceiling.

The crucial passage from Kant distinguishes two different ways of looking at such a scene. One is teleological. It sees the sea as a reservoir of fish, the clouds as making rain that irrigates the arable land. Against that kind of looking Kant puts the non-telelogical, purely material vision that sees things as the eye sees them, as pure *Augenschein*, "eye shine," prior to any interpretation of their usefulness. This, Kant claims, is to see the way poets do. He has a remarkable confidence that poets are free of ideological distortions or teleological orientations. This seems an extraordinary claim, the more extraordinary the more you think of it. Andrzej Warminski, following Paul de Man, observes that Wordsworth's poetry does not fit Kant's description.[27] Poets, in a long tradition going back to Sydney and before him to Plato, are, as everybody knows, proverbially described as natural-born liars, prevaricators, myth-

---

26. Immanuel Kant, *Kritik der Urteilskraft, Werkausgabe*, ed. Wilhelm Weischedel (Frankfurt am Main: Suhrkamp Taschenbuch, 1979), 196; Kant, *The Critique of Judgment*, trans. J. H. Bernard (New York: Hafner, 1950), 110–11, translation slightly altered.

27. Warminski, "'As the Poets Do It,'" 40–41.

makers, fashioners of magical and deceiving shows, though Sydney claims that the poet does not really lie, since he "nothing affirmeth."[28] The poet does not pretend to be telling the truth, only to be proffering fictions.

Kant, however, sees true poets as telling the truth in a quite specific way, that is, by not deviating from naming what their eyes see, the uninterpreted *Augenschein*, eye appearance. A poet like Wordsworth, with all his talk of "something far more deeply interfused,"[29] does not at all fit Kant's blithe assumption about how poets see and what they do with what they see in naming it. Only Friedrich Hölderlin, among German poets, comes to my mind as possibly doing it right, but his major poetry was written, of course, after Kant's *Critique of Judgment*. Only this kind of seeing and poetical naming deserves the name of "that sublimity that a pure aesthetic judgment ascribes to this object." "Aesthetic judgment [*ästhetisches Urteil*]" here does not mean "artistic," but according to pure uninterpreted sensation, as opposed to perception that this is, for example, a salty ocean full of edible fish. Conrad's narrator's initial vision of the Golfo Placido is, I claim, a sublime seeing and naming of this sort. It is against this background of a sublime materialist vision of the scene as a whole that the human stories of *Nostromo* are told.

Warminski on de Man on Kant

The most authoritative readings of the passage from Kant are those already identified in a footnote: Warminski's admirable essay, "As the Poets Do It"; one of Paul de Man's most remarkably original, penetrating, and rigorous essays, "Phenomenality and Materiality in Kant"; and Colebrook's "The Geological Sublime." Warminski's essay is a reading and subtle modification of de Man's reading. The modification, never acknowledged as such, occurs, as it should, by way of a return to Kant. Just as de Man asserts that "the critical power of a transcendental philosophy," in Kant, "undoes the very project of such a philosophy leaving us, certainly not with an ideology—for the transcendental and ideological (metaphysical) principles are part of the same system—but with a materialism that Kant's posterity has not yet begun to face up to,"[30] so it can be

---

28. "Now for the *Poet*, he nothing affirmeth, and therefore never lyeth," Sir Philip Sydney, *The Defense of Poesy* (Glasgow: R. Urie, 1752), 64–65 [Editors].

29. "Lines Written a Few Miles above Tintern Abbey" (line 97) [Editors].

30. Paul de Man, "Phenomenality and Materiality in Kant," *Hermeneutics: Questions and Prospects*, ed. Gary Shapiro and Alan Sica (Amherst: University of Massachusetts Press, 1984), 89.

said that, with a few exceptions,[31] de Man's posterity has not yet begun to face up to the implications for literary study and for cultural studies of "Phenomenality and Materiality in Kant," not to speak of de Man's other essays. Probably I am not facing up to those implications either.

Just what does de Man mean by Kant's materialism, the kind of materialism that I have dared to ascribe to *Nostromo*? One must read de Man's essay for oneself to find out, no easy task, but here are the essential assertions. "The predominant perception," in the Kant passage, de Man begins by asserting, "is that of the heavens and the ocean as an architectonic construct. The heavens are a vault that covers the totality of earthy space as a roof covers a house."[32] Similarly, I might note, the heavens are a dark "vault" in Conrad's description, or in another figure Conrad uses, a poncho: "Sky, land, and sea disappear together out of the world when the Placido—as the saying is—goes to sleep under its black poncho" (7). De Man goes on to find in Kant a figure that is even closer to Conrad's figure of the great semi-circular "temple" of the Placid Gulf:

> Space, in Kant as in Aristotle, is a house in which we dwell more or less safely, or more or less poetically, on this earth. [The allusion is to Hölderlin's phrase "Poetically man dwells," and to Heidegger's commentary on that aphorism.] This is also how the sea is perceived or how, according to Kant, poets perceive it: Its horizontal expanse is like a floor bounded by the horizon, by the walls of heaven as they close off and delimit the building.[33]

De Man goes on, in passages later in the essay, to specify just what he means by Kant's materialist vision:

> The poet who sees the heavens as a vault is clearly like the savage [or, one might add, like Frankenstein in one scene in Mary Shelley's novel, or like "a wild man who, from a distance, sees a house of which he does not know the use"[34]], and unlike Wordsworth. He does not see prior to dwelling, but merely sees. He does not see in order to shelter himself, for there is no

---

31. Tom Cohen has written powerfully in analysis and defense of de Man's "materialism" in "Toxic Assets: de Man's Remains and the Ecocatastrophic Imaginary (an American Fable)," in Tom Cohen, Claire Colebrook, and J. Hillis Miller, *Theory and the Disappearing Future: On de Man, On Benjamin* (London: Routledge, 2012), 89–129.
32. "Phenomenality and Materiality in Kant," 81.
33. Ibid.
34. Cited by de Man from Kant, *Logic, Werkausgabe*, ed. Wilhelm Weischedel (Frankfurt am Main: Suhrkamp, 1978), 6:457. This is the edition of which I have used the paperback version of 1979, referred to in footnote 26.

suggestion made that he could in any way be threatened, not even by the storm—since it is pointed out that he remains safely on the shore. The link between seeing and dwelling, *sehen* and *wohnen,* is teleological and therefore absent in pure aesthetic vision. . . . No mind is involved in the Kantian vision of ocean and heaven. To the extent that any mind, that any judgment, intervenes, it is in error—for it is not the case that heaven is a vault or that the horizon bounds the ocean like the walls of a building. That is how things are to the eye, in the redundancy of their appearance to the eye and not to the mind, as in the redundant word *Augenschein,* to be understood in opposition to Hegel's *Ideenschein,* or sensory appearance of the idea; *Augenschein,* in which the eye, tautologically, is named twice, as the eye itself and as what appears to the eye. . . . Kant's vision can therefore hardly be called literal, which would imply its possible figuralization or symbolization by an act of judgment. The only word that comes to mind is that of a *material* vision, but how this materiality is then to be understood in linguistic terms is not, as yet, clearly intelligible. . . . The sea is called a mirror, not because it is supposed to reflect anything, but to stress a flatness devoid of any suggestion of depth. In the same way and to the same extent that this vision is purely material, devoid of any reflexive or intellectual complication, it is also purely formal, devoid of any semantic depth and reducible to the formal mathematization or geometrization of pure optics. The critique of the aesthetic ends up, in Kant, in a formal materialism that runs counter to all values and characteristics associated with aesthetic experience, including the aesthetic experience of the beautiful and of the sublime as described by Kant and Hegel themselves. The tradition of their interpretation, as it appears from near contemporaries such as Schiller on, has seen only this one, figural, and, if you will, "romantic" aspect of their theories of the imagination, and has entirely overlooked what we call [he means, "what I, Paul de Man, call"] the material aspect. Neither has it understood the place and the function of formalization in this intricate process.[35]

The Mirror of the Sea is the name of one of Conrad's two autobiographical books. Perhaps Conrad did read Kant after all, or by prophetic insight had read de Man's commentary on Kant! It almost seems one or the other must have been the case. Conrad's impressionism in *Nostromo,* his attempt to use the power of words to make the reader *see* the surface of non-human things, however much he may have gone behind, gone into the depths, of the characters' souls, is, I claim, a modernist version of Kant's materialism as understood

---

35. "Phenomenality and Materiality in Kant," 81–83.

by Paul de Man. Conrad's narrative voice reports on an act of "merely seeing." He sees as, according to Kant, the poets do.

The Materiality of the Letter in Conrad

De Man's essay ends, notoriously, with a claim that the endpoint of Kant's materialism is a "prosaic materiality of the letter"[36] that disjoins words and parts of words from one another and leaves the reader staring at meaningless marks on the page. This turn at the end fulfills de Man's implicit promise earlier to explain how we can understand Kant's materiality "in linguistic terms": "To the dismemberment of the body corresponds a dismemberment of language, as meaning-producing tropes are replaced by the fragmentation of sentences and propositions into discrete words, or the fragmentation of words into syllables or finally letters."[37] De Man's example from Kant is the play between closely related words, echoes that are indigenous to German and impossible to translate, *Verwunderung* (surprise) as it is echoed by *Bewunderung* (admiration), or, in a specific passage, "a constant, and finally bewildering alternation of the two terms, *Angemessen(heit)* ['adequacy'] and *Unangemessen(heit)* ['inadequacy'], to the point where one can no longer tell them apart."[38] At that point, the words are drained of meaning and opposites merge, as when any word is repeated aloud over and over until it finally becomes just senseless sound, the sheer materiality of vibrating air, or as Kant's words, for someone ignorant of German, are just ink marks on a page.

Warminski often uses the motif of a stuttering repetition that drains words of meaning as the powerful culmination of one or another of his essays:

> One must (only) as the poets must (nevertheless be able to find sublime) as one must as the poets must. (I've tried out the German: "Man muß bloß, wie die Dichter es tun, müssen"; "Man muß müssen"; "One, we, *must must.*") ... The event of this repetition is what gets disseminated all along the narrative line and thus renders the text an allegory of its inability to account for its own production (an allegory of unreadability, to coin a phrase)—with Rousseau's autobiographer doomed to mindlessly, mechanically, repeating "Marion" over and over again, and Kant's critical philosopher "I *must* be able to bridge pure reason and practical reason," "I *must* exhibit the ideas of

---

36. Ibid., 90.
37. Ibid., 89.
38. Ibid., 89–90.

reason," "I *must* be able to find sublime," "I *must must*," "Ich muß müssen, muß miissen, muß müssen [...]"[39]

Is there anything of that sort in Conrad, any "materiality of the letter"? It would seem not. Conrad is a master of the English language. His English is eloquent and correct. He is little given to puns and wordplay, in spite of the joke in the place-name "Costaguana": guano is hardened bird-dung, used in fertilizer and explosives. Conrad is, however, much given to irony, as in his description of himself as Gulliver when he was writing *Nostromo*. Irony always introduces a dangerous shimmering in discourse, a wavering in the meaning that may lead to meaninglessness. Nevertheless, Conrad's words, for the most part, all seem powerfully to retain their literal meaning and force as a way of getting the reader to see his imaginary realm by way of the words. Studies have been made of the effect of Polish, Russian, and French (languages Conrad knew before he learned English) on Conrad's syntax, semantics, and grammar, but I must say that it sounds, for the most part, like pretty idiomatic English to me, though it is often a little florid and oratorical.

Once in a great while, however, something strange happens to Conrad's masterful command of English. He makes a definite mistake in English. The two examples I have noticed in *Nostromo*, strangely enough, involve, in one case, writing and reading, and in the other case, dumb materiality as illusory or erroneous meanings are projected into it.

In the first example, the narrator reports the effect on Charles Gould, then a schoolboy in England, of reading his father's letters: "In about a year he had evolved from the lecture of the letters a definite conviction that there was a silver-mine in the Sulaco province of the republic of Costaguana, where poor Uncle Harry had been shot by soldiers a great many years before" (63). "Lecture of the letters" for "reading the letters" is a Gallicism, not proper English.

The other mistake I noticed comes in an account of the way Emilia Gould projected all sorts of ideal meanings into the first bar of silver produced by the newly re-opened San Tomé mine: "She had laid her unmercenary hands, with an eagerness that made them tremble, upon the first silver ingot turned out still warm from the mould; and by her imaginative estimate of its power she endowed that lump of metal with a justificative conception, as though it were not a mere fact, but something far-reaching and impalpable, like the true expression of an emotion or the emergency of a principle" (118). By "emergency of a principle," I suppose Conrad meant the emerging or coming into the open of a principle. That's not the way you say it in English!

---

39. Warminski, "'As the Poets Do It,'" 55, 61.

The effect of these mistakes in locution is odd. It is as though the façade of Englishness, Conrad as master mariner in the British merchant marine, Conrad as a great British writer, was momentarily pulled away, revealing, like the shabby reality behind the wonderful Wizard of Oz, Józef Teodor Konrad Nałęcz Korzeniowski, the Pole for whom English was an acquired language, known less well even than French. The polyglot cosmopolitan Korzeniowski almost decided to write in French, rather than in English. He frequently lapses into French in his letters to Cunninghame Graham, especially in the gloomiest and most skeptical parts. The materiality of the letter shows through, as the reader puzzles over "lecture" and "emergency," if she happens to have noticed the mistakes. They cannot have their normal semantic meaning. What was Conrad trying to say?

The first passage has to do with the meaning Charles Gould ascribes to the letters he receives from his father, a meaning that is ludicrously and ironically reductive of the endless laments from his father that the authorities in Costaguana are impoverishing him by demanding payment for the mine Concession that he is not even using. If letters are readable, a reader will project some meaning into them, but if that projection is incomplete or erroneous, the discrepancy between the materiality of the letter as a mark on the page and any meaning ascribed to it becomes momentarily glimpsed in an act of *lecture,* which is the French word for "reading."

In the second passage, a discrepancy between letter and meaning is even more apparent. In itself a lump of silver is a "mere fact," like those surface facts of Sulaco topography the narrative voice objectively and dispassionately names with a kind of ironic reserve that is characteristic of that voice. Mrs. Gould projects into that lump of silver all her hopes for bringing law and order into Sulaco by way of what an often-repeated leitmotif of the novel calls "material interests." A typographical error is in French called a *coquille,* a shell, as though one had bitten down on a bit of eggshell in one's omelet or perhaps as a name displaced from what a broken piece of type in book-printing is called. "Emergency" is a coquille. It is a bit of shell that interferes with the powerful expression of meaning in the sentence, just as a glimpse of the silver as "mere fact" suspends the grandiose meanings that Emilia Gould, holding it with trembling fingers, imposes on it. The phrase "material interests" contains in itself this contradiction. Matter has no "interest" in itself. It becomes interesting; it is worth investing time, effort, and money in; it bears interest; it becomes money in itself, only when it is stamped with signs. Doing that assimilates sheer matter into human making and doing, buying and selling, all the circuits of exchange and substitution, in this case those of global imperialist capitalism already in full swing in *Nostromo.* Silver ingots must be stamped into coin to emerge into meaning, but that meaning is fictive. It parodies a tropological system of exchange and substitution whose value rests on nothing but blind faith. That is indeed the case with the global financial system. Returning to the gold standard would not help matters one bit because gold (or silver) has only the meaning and value that is ascribed to it. The wild fluctuations in 2013 in the monetary value of gold are a good proof of that.

Conrad's *coquilles*, I claim, are examples of the prosaic materiality of the letter in his discourse. They call attention to the meaningless material base of language.

I have set Conrad and Kant side by side and have found striking similarities. Does this mean that Conrad is "saying the same thing" as Kant? Is Conrad Kantian through and through? Can I just transfer de Man's and Warminski's readings of Kant to my reading of a passage in Conrad's *Nostromo*? By no means. Side-by-side comparisons in critical readings are for the sake of differentiation, not for making identical. Well, what's the difference?

Kant's goal in *The Critique of Judgment*, especially in the sections on the mathematical and dynamic sublimes, is to erect a trustworthy bridge between *The Critique of Pure Reason* and *The Critique of Practical Reason*, transcendental knowledge and ethics. De Man and Warminski persuade me that this attempt fails: "In Kant's 'Analytic of the Sublime,'" writes Warminski, "the attempt to ground the critical discourse, to found the very subject of the critical philosophy and transcendental method, instead *un*grounds, *un*founds, itself in the disarticulation of tropological and performative linguistic models by, ultimately, the 'last' linguistic 'model': the prosaic materiality of the letter, material inscription."[40]

Conrad, of course, has no such goal. His aim is to show by way of an elaborate imaginary set of events how human history occurs if its background is the total impersonality and "indifference" of nature, its total lack of transcendent ground, even of a negative one like that in Heart of Darkness.

"MATERIAL INTERESTS":
NOSTROMO AS CRITIQUE OF CAPITALIST IMPERIALISM

I turn now to investigating whether or not Conrad succeeds in reaching his goal. I begin by asking what sort of human community, if it is a community, does Conrad's narrator describe as having imposed itself through the centuries on the mute, indifferent Sulaco landscape? This happens analogously to

---

40. "Phenomenality and Materiality in Kant," 61.

the way a bit of silver may be turned into a silver dollar by being stamped with certain words and signs. "Communities in fiction," after all, is the topic of this book. All I have said so far about *Nostromo* is preliminary to identifying what sort of community Sulaco is, if it is a community.

The objective, laconic descriptions of the Sulaco landscape and of other "phenomenal" appearances do not stop with the first chapter. *Nostromo* is punctuated with reminders that the mute, impersonal land and what one might call mechanical physical occurrences go on happening behind, beside, or adjacent to the human events with which the novel is most concerned. One example is a description of the early morning in Sulaco at a particularly tense moment two-thirds through the novel. Pedrito Montero is about to arrive. Sotillo has already entered Sulaco and has taken over the port. He is maddened by his search for the silver he knows must be hidden somewhere. The passage is like a late impressionist painting in the way it reduces everything visible to shapes of light and shadow:

> The sun, which looks late upon Sulaco, issuing in all the fullness of its power high up on the sky from behind the dazzling snow-edge of Higuerota, had precipitated the delicate, smooth, pearly grayness of light, in which the town lies steeped during the early hours, into sharp-cut masses of black shade and spaces of hot, blinding glare. Three long rectangles of sunshine fell through the windows of the sala, while just across the street the front of the Avellanos house appeared very somber in its own shadow seen through the flood of light. (419)

The effect of this passage in its context is peculiar. It does not suggest, as Heidegger might have done, that the characters and their affairs are embedded in the landscape, at home there, building, dwelling, and thinking (to borrow the title of an essay by Heidegger) in a way that is circumscribed by the material features of just that landscape. Quite the reverse. The implication is that the sun goes on rising day after day, producing, day after day, the same senseless assemblage of visible blocks of blinding light and contrasting shadow, in complete indifference to the human dramas enacted there and in complete separation from them. Except for the almost effaced tropes (for example, "The sun, which looks late upon Sulaco"), the Alain Robbe-Grillet of *Jalousie* (1957) might almost have written the passage. Conrad's personages are not shown to be at all aware of the visible scene, so preoccupied are they with their own sorrows, anxieties, and concerns. It is only the anonymous narrative voice that notices the scene and records it, like a camera eye, or like an impressionist painter trying to suspend our normal inattention in order to paint and make us see not what perception interprets but what impersonal sensation records, what the eye sees.

One more chilling example of this, out of many that could be cited, is the account of the blue smoke that arises after a couple of the tyrant Guzman Bento's aristocratic prisoners are taken behind some bushes and summarily shot: "The irregular report of the firing-squad would be heard, followed sometimes by a single finishing shot; a little bluish cloud of smoke would float up above the green bushes, and the Army of Pacification would move on over the savannas, through the forests" (N 152–53). The careful notation of the color-sensations that would have struck the eye of a dispassionate spectator (the blue smoke above the green bushes) is a characteristic example of Conrad's "impressionism." The sentence just quoted is also an example of an iterative narrative technique in the early part of the novel. Conrad writes that "a little bluish cloud of smoke *would* float up," not "*did* float up." The narrative voice does not here record a single event, but an event that occurred again and again, like the endless substitution of one work-shift for another in the newly reopened San Tomé silver mine. The passage is, moreover, part of a flashback or analepsis breaking the account of Charles Gould's success in getting the silver mine going again with an account of Don José Avellanos's sufferings as one of Guzman Bento's captives. These took place long before the novel begins, if it can be said to have a starting point in the ordinary sense. Those sinister puffs of blue smoke are something that happened over and over in that distant time. Analepsis, prolepsis, iterative narration, time shifts, hiatuses, sudden changes in perspective, tense shifts—Conrad employs all these sophisticated devices to break up straightforward chronological narration long before Gérard Genette identified them and appropriated or concocted barbarous-sounding names for them from Greek rhetorical terms.[41]

Narrative Complexities in *Nostromo*

Nostromo is extremely complicated in its narrative organization. It offers narratologists great opportunities to demonstrate in detail the various kinds of narrative complexity employed by modernist authors such as Faulkner, Woolf, James, or Conrad himself. Just about every narrative device that specialists in narrative form have identified is employed in one way or another: time shifts;

---

41. See Gérard Genette, "Discours du récit," in *Figures III* (Paris: Seuil, 1972), 65–278; Genette, *Narrative Discourse*, trans. Jane E. Lewin (Ithaca, NY: Cornell University Press, 1980). The best interpretation of Conrad's work from a narratological perspective is Jakob Lothe, *Conrad's Narrative Method* (Oxford: Clarendon Press, 1989).

analepsis; prolepsis; breaks in the narration; shifts in "focalization" from one character's mind to another by way of the "omniscient" (or, as I should prefer to say, following Nicholas Royle, "telepathic"[42]) narrator's use of free indirect discourse, or by way of interpolated first person narration or spoken discourse; shifts by the narrator from distant, panoramic vision to extreme close-ups; retellings of the same event from different subjective perspectives; citations of documents, and so on.[43] The chronological trajectory of Sulaco history can be pieced together from these indirections. The story begins in the middle and then shifts backward and forward in a way that the reader may find bewildering, as he or she wonders just where on a time scale a given episode is in relation to some other episode. It is as though all these episodes were going on happening over and over, continually, in the capacious and atemporal mind of the narrator, like the endless succession of similar days and nights over the Golfo Placido that is the setting of *Nostromo*. The story is presented in an almost cubist rendering of abruptly juxtaposed episodes, rather than by way of the impressionist technique Conrad is often said to have employed.

If the goal of *Nostromo* is to reconstruct the history of an imaginary Central American country, the formal complexity of the novel does more than implicitly claim that form is meaning—that is, that the complexity was necessary if Conrad was to tell at all the story he wanted to tell. *Nostromo*'s narrative complications also oppose what it suggests is false linear historical narration to another much more complex way to recover through narration "things as they really were." I shall turn later to the question of the social, political, and ethical "usefulness" of modernist narration of this sort.

Identifying the complexities of Conrad's non-linear narrative, however, is not enough, nor, of course, does Lothe limit himself to that. The most important question is: Why did Conrad do it this way? One answer is that he saw such a to and fro mode of storytelling a more truthful way to render history. Another, perhaps even more important, answer is that such jagged narration establishes the narrator, or rather the narrative voice, as being ubiquitous within Sulaco over all the time of its modern history. The narrative voice has a total simultaneous possession of all the events down to the tiniest detail, spread out before it like a spatial panorama. The narrative voice can move at will back and forth across this spatio-temporal continuum, zooming in or

---

42. See Nicholas Royle, "The 'Telepathy Effect': Notes toward a Reconsideration of Narrative Fiction," in *The Uncanny* (Manchester: Manchester University Press, 2003), 256–76; also available in *Acts of Narrative*, ed. Carol Jacobs and Henry Sussman (Stanford: Stanford University Press, 2003), 93–109.

43. See Lothe, *Conrad's Narrative Method*.

zooming out as may seem necessary, entering and leaving the secret thoughts and feelings of the characters at any time or place. The narrative voice can break up chronological order in order to get the story told in what seems the best way to convey an understanding of it to the reader.

One might say that each zoomed-in episode forms a self-enclosed bubble within the circumambient much larger self-enclosed bubble that is all that the narrative voice knows. The narrative voice recounts what happens within each small bubble in moment-to-moment detail, often as the confrontation of two of the characters in conversation with one another. A given episode is often separated by time shifts, hiatuses, breaks in the narrative sequence, from what comes before and after. Not all the narrative voice presumably knows is revealed. The reader is led to believe that the narrative voice could recount a great many more conversations and episodes if it chose to do so. No novel could be long enough to hold them all. What it does not tell remains permanently a secret, known only to Joseph Conrad, just as only he had read the *History of Fifty Years of Misrule*. All that additional information, known only to Conrad, he carried to the grave on August 3, 1924, though the reader may feel with such a big novel that he or she has been told enough, all that it is necessary to know.

Henry James identified brilliantly this back and forth hovering aspect of Conrad's narrative technique when he praised Conrad in a review of *Chance*. Conrad, said James, was "absolutely alone as a votary of the way to do a thing that shall make it undergo most doing."[44] *Chance* exemplifies this, James claimed, in Marlow's "prolonged hovering flight of the subjective over the outstretched ground of the case exposed."[45] I would change James's formulation, however, to say, awkwardly enough, it is more the prolonged hovering flight over the outstretched ground of the case exposed by an anonymous, ubiquitous linguistic power of turning imaginary events into words that have performative power to make the reader *see*. I must add that this power is quite "unrealistic," in the sense that it cannot be operated on real historical events and persons. The text records the fantasy of a magic clairvoyance that is matched by a magic power of presentation through a species of linguistic prestidigitation. This sleight of hand makes Nostromo, Emilia Gould, Dr. Monygham, and the rest seem like real people whom we know by a quite extraordinary telepathic power. The narrator's uncanny omnipresence could not exist in the real world. It can only exist in verbal virtual realities of the type called "literary works." This is true however much it may be the case that

---

44. James, "The New Novel," 147.
45. Ibid., 149.

Conrad is implicitly arguing that such an accounting is the only means of actually knowing history "as it really happens." Anything other than such a prolonged hovering flight, the narration implies, is a falsification.

Nostromo as Community History

Fredric Jameson's slogan, "Always Historicize," means that we should read modernist English literature, or any other literary work of any time, in its immediate historical context. He is no doubt right about that. Nevertheless, certain works of English literature from the beginning of the twentieth century have an uncanny resonance with the global situation today. Examples would be the exploitation of Africa by the Wilcox family in E. M. Forster's *Howards End*, or the presentation of the effects of combat on Septimus Smith in Virginia Woolf's *Mrs. Dalloway*. Charles Gould and the American financier Holroyd, in *Nostromo*, are even better examples. Their collaboration is remarkably prophetic of the current course of American global economic aspirations as well as of the effects of these on local cultures and peoples around the world. I shall indicate some of those disquieting consonances later.

If *Nostromo* is a novel not so much about history as about alternative ways to narrate history, this means its goal is not to recover a single life story (as, say, *Lord Jim* does), but to recover the story of the ways a whole group of individuals were related, each in a different way, to their surrounding community as it evolved through time. *Nostromo* is a novel about an imagined community, a fictitious community based on Conrad's reading about South American history.

A spectrum or continuum of different ways the individual may be related to others can be identified, going from smaller groups to larger. At the small end is my face-to-face encounter with my neighbor, with my beloved, or with a stranger, in love, friendship, hospitality, indifference, or hostility. A family, especially an extended family or a clan, is a larger group, in this case bound by ties of blood or marriage. A community is somewhat larger. A community is a group of people living in the same place who all know one another and who share the same cultural assumptions. They are not, however, necessarily related by blood or marriage. A nation is larger still. Most commonly a nation is made of a large number of overlapping but to some degree dissonant communities. Largest of all is the worldwide conglomeration of all human beings living on the planet Earth and all more and more subject to the same global economic and cultural hegemonies. At each of these levels, the individual has a relation to others, different in each case and subject to different constraints and conventions. It is, of course, often difficult, in a given case, if not impossible, to maintain a sharp boundary between the different-sized groups.

Each form of living together, or of what Heidegger called *Mitsein*, "being with," has been the object of vigorous theoretical investigation in recent years, for example Lévinas's focus on the face-to-face encounter of two persons, or Jacques Derrida's similar focus in *The Politics of Friendship*, or work by Bataille, Blanchot, Nancy, Lingis, and others on the concept of community. These have been identified in the first chapter of this book.[46] In what I say about (non)community in Conrad's *Nostromo* I shall interrogate primarily the relation of the individual to the community, or lack of it, in this novel, in the context of an intervention by global capitalism.

It can certainly be said that the citizens of Sulaco form a community, at least in one sense of the word "community." They all live together in the same place. All share, more or less, the same moral and religious assumptions. Whether rich or poor, white, black, or Native American, they have been subjected to the same ideological interpellations, the same propaganda, the same political speeches, proclamations, and arbitrary laws. Most of all, they share the same history. Don José Avellanos calls this, in the title of his never-to-be-published manuscript, "Fifty Years of Misrule." The narrator, magically and quite improbably, has nevertheless read it and can cite from it (157). Though Sulaco is a community of suffering, as one revolution after another brings only more injustice and senseless bloodshed, nevertheless, it can be argued, it is a true community. It is small enough so that most people know one another. Don Pépé, who runs the mine, knows all the workers by name. Almost all belong to a single religious faith, Catholic Christianity.

If the reader reconstructs the story from a distance, putting the broken pieces of narration back in chronological order, *Nostromo* appears as a tale of nation-building, the creation of one of those "imagined communities" Benedict Anderson describes in his book of that name.[47] After fifty years of misrule by the central government of Costaguana in Santa Marta, Sulaco, through a series of serio-comic events and accidents, becomes what looks like a prosperous, modern, peaceful, independent state, the Occidental Republic of Sulaco. An example of the fortuitous "causes" of this historical change is the cynical plan for secession devised by the skeptic Decoud shortly before his death. His plan is not motivated by political zeal or belief, but by his love for Antonia Avellanos. I shall return to this later. Nevertheless, Captain Mitchell, in

---

46. "Theories of Community: Williams, Heidegger, and Others," in *Communities of Fiction* (New York: Fordham University Press, 2015), 1–17 [Editors].

47. Benedict Anderson, *Imagined Communities: Reflections on the Origin and Spread of Nationalism* (New York: Random House, 1983).

his fatuous incomprehension, recounts the creation of the Republic of Sulaco as a connected story whose destined endpoint is the present-day prosperous nation. He recounts the sequence, in tedious detail, "in the more or less stereotyped relation of the 'historical events' which for the next few years was at the service of distinguished strangers visiting Sulaco" (529).

The pages following the previous quote give an example of Captain Mitchell's version of Sulaco history. Captain Mitchell is the spokesperson for an exemplary "official history." Such a history has a naïve conception of "historical events" as following one another in a comprehensible linear, causal, and progressive sequence. Conrad quite evidently disdains such history-writing. That false kind of history is represented, in one degree or another, by those source books on South American history by Masterman, Eastwick, Cunninghame Graham, and so on that Conrad had read.[48] Though *Nostromo* is about the nation-building of an imaginary South American republic, not a real one, nevertheless it is, among other things, a paradigmatic example of an alternative mode of history-writing, difficult to bring off. Conrad implicitly claims that this counter-history is much nearer to the truth of human history and much more able to convey to readers the way history "really happens."

SULACO AS A NON-COMMUNITY

If the reader looks a little more closely at what the narrative voice says about Sulaco society, however, it begins to look less and less like a community of the traditional kind—that is, less and less like a community of those who have a lot in common. Sulaco is not much like those egalitarian rural English villages on the Welsh border Raymond Williams, in *The Country and the City*, so much admires, even though he to some degree resists idealizing them.[49]

For one thing, Sulaco "society" is made up of an extraordinary racial and ethnic mixture. This mixture is the product of its sanguinary history, as the narrator emphasizes from the beginning. The Spanish conquistadores enslaved the indigenes, the Native Americans. Wars of liberation from Spain led to wave after wave of military revolutions, one tyranny after another, with incredible bloodshed, cruelty, and injustice. Nevertheless, a large class of aristocratic hacienda-owning, cattle-ranching, pure-blooded Spanish people, "creoles," remain. They are the core of the "Blanco" party. Black slaves were imported. Then a series of migrations from Europe, people coming either as

---

48. See footnote 5, p. 176.
49. See chapter 1 [of Miller's *Communities of Fiction*, cited above] for a discussion of Williams on community [see footnote 46, p. 208; Editors].

workmen, political exiles, or as imperialist exploiters, brought English, French, Italians, even a few Germans and Jews. Sailors, like Nostromo, deserted from merchant ships to add to the mix. Much intermarriage of course occurred.

Bits of three languages other than English exist in the novel: Spanish, French, and Italian. The narrator often uses Spanish names for occupations and ethnic identifications, as well as for place names such as Cordillera, the name of the overshadowing mountain range. A good bit of the conversation in the novel must be imagined to be carried on not in the English the narrator gives, but in Spanish. Decoud and Antonia are native-born Costaguanans, but they have been educated in France. They talk to one another in French. Giorgio Viola, the old Garibaldino, and his family are Italian, as is Nostromo. They speak Italian to one another. This is signaled even in this English-language book by the way Nostromo addresses Viola as "Vecchio," Italian for "old man." Conrad does not specify what language the descendants of black slaves and the indigenes speak, but presumably some bits of their original languages persist beneath their Spanish. Charles Gould and all his family are English, though Gould was born in Costaguana and educated in England, as is the custom in that family. His wife is English, though her aunt has married an Italian aristocrat, and Charles Gould meets his future wife in Italy. The railroad workers are partly locals, Indios, but engineers from England run the operation, and some workmen are European.

Sulaco, I conclude, is a complex mixture of races, languages, and ethnic allegiances. Sulaco is not all that different in this from the United States, by the way, though we have had, so far, only one, successful, "democratic revolution." The so-called American Revolution (as if the United States were the whole continent) ushered in government of the people, by the people, and for the people, with liberty and justice for all. I say those words with only a mild trace of irony, though the liberty, justice, and equality did not of course in 1776 extend to black slaves, or to Native Americans, or to women, or even to men who were not above a certain level of wealth. My houses in Maine are on land taken from the Native Americans who had lived in the Penobscot Bay region for at least seven thousand years before the white man came and destroyed their culture in a few generations. "Liberty and justice for all" still has a hollow ring for many Americans—for example, for the African-American men and women who populate our prisons in such disproportionate numbers, or who swell the ranks of the unemployed.

The Sulaco (non)community exists, moreover, like the United States one, as a complex layering of differing degrees of power, privilege, wealth, with the African-Americans and Indios at the bottom, extending up through European working-class people, to the Creoles and the dominating quasi-foreigners like

Charles Gould. Though the Gould family has been in Sulaco for generations, they are still considered Anglos, Inglesi. They are English in appearance, sensibility, mores, and language. The chief form of social mobility in Sulaco is through bribery, chicanery, or outright thievery, such as Nostromo's theft of the silver, or by way of becoming the leader of a military coup and ruling the country through force, as the indigene Montero momentarily does in *Nostromo*. It is not much of a community!

Martin Decoud at one point sums up succinctly the nature of the Sulaco (non)community in a bitter speech to his idealistic patriotic beloved, Antonia Avellanos. He quotes the great "liberator" of South America, Simón Bolívar, something for which the "Author's Note," oddly enough, apologizes. I suppose that is because the citation of Bolívar is a parabasis suspending momentarily the dramatization of a purely imaginary Central American state with an intrusion from actual history. In the "Note" Conrad has been defending, ironically, the "accuracy" of his report of Sulaco history, based as it is on his reading of Avellanos's "History of Fifty Years of Misrule." The joke (almost a "postmodern" rather than "modernist" joke) is of course that Avellanos's "History" is fictitious, along with the whole country of which it tells the story. No way exists to check the accuracy of Conrad's account against any external referent, nor any way to check what the narrator says against what Avellanos says. Conrad can make it up any way he likes. The quotation of Bolívar reminds Conrad that some actual historical references do exist in the novel, and that these are a discordance:

> I have mastered them [the pages of Avellanos's "History"] in not a few hours of earnest meditation, and I hope that my accuracy will be trusted. In justice to myself, and to allay the fears of prospective readers, I beg to point out that the few historical allusions are never dragged in for the sake of parading my unique erudition, but that each of them is closely related to actuality—either throwing a light on the nature of current events or affecting directly the fortunes of the people of whom I speak. ("Note" 4–5)

"Actuality"? "Current events?" The words must refer here to the pseudo-actuality of Costaguana history.

One such parabasis-like intrusion is Decoud's citation of Bolívar: "After one Montero there would be another," the narrator reports, in free indirect discourse, Decoud as having said:

> The lawlessness of a populace of all colors and races, barbarism, irremediable tyranny. As the great Liberator Bolívar had said in the bitterness of his

spirit, "America is ungovernable. Those who worked for her independence have ploughed the sea." He did not care, he declared boldly; he seized every opportunity to tell her [Antonia] that though she had managed to make a Blanco journalist of him, he was no patriot. First of all, the word had no sense for cultured minds, to whom the narrowness of every belief is odious; and secondly, in connection with the everlasting troubles of this unhappy country it was hopelessly besmirched; it had been the cry of dark barbarism, the cloak of lawlessness, of crimes, of rapacity, of simple thieving. (206)

It should be remembered that although what the narrative voice reports Decoud as having said agrees more or less with what the narrative voice itself says, speaking on its own, nevertheless Decoud is explicitly presented as an "idle boulevardier." He only thinks, falsely, that he is truly Gallicized. His corrosive skepticism leads ultimately to suicide. One might say that Decoud is a side of Conrad that he wants to condemn and separate off from himself, leaving himself someone who is at least earnestly committed to the endless hard work of the professional writer who earns his daily bread by putting words on paper. Conrad's letters to Cunninghame Graham often express, it must be said, a skeptical pessimism that is close to Decoud's, as in one famous passage about the universe as a self-generated, self-generating machine: "It knits us in and it knits us out. It has knitted time space, pain, death, corruption, despair, and all the illusions—and nothing matters" (*CL* 1:425). In any case, what Decoud says matches closely what the narrative voice says about Sulaco's deplorable history.

How did Sulaco come to be such a non-community, or, to give Jean-Luc Nancy's term a somewhat different meaning from his own, how did Sulaco come to be an inoperative or "unworked" community, a *communauté désoeuvrée*? Nancy's book begins with the unqualified statement that "The gravest and most painful testimony of the modern world, the one that possibly gathers together all other testimonies that this epoch finds itself charged with assuming [*chargée d'assumer*], by virtue of who knows what decree or necessity (for we bear witness also to the exhaustion of thinking by way of history [*l'épuisement de la pensée de l'Histoire*]), is the testimony of the dissolution, the dislocation, or the conflagration of community."[50] *Nostromo*, it might be said, is a parabolic fable or allegory, a paradigmatic fiction, of the dissolution, the dislocation, or the conflagration of community.

---

50. Jean-Luc Nancy, *La communauté désoeuvrée* (Paris: Christian Bourgois, 1986), 11; Nancy, *The Inoperative Community*, ed. Peter Connor, trans. Peter Connor, Lisa Garbus, Michael Holland, and Simona Sawhney (Minneapolis: University of Minnesota Press, 1991), 1, translation modified.

Just how does this disaster come about, according to Conrad? Who are the villains in this sad event? It is an event that can no longer even be understood historically. Nancy's view of *"la pensée de l'Histoire,"* the reader will note, is quite different from Jameson's "always historicize." The dislocation of community must be borne witness to as something that we, or rather I, have experienced even if we (I) cannot explain it: "I have witnessed the conflagration of community. I testify that this is what has happened. I give you my personal word for it, even though I cannot explain it through conventional historicizing." The magically telepathic narrative voice in *Nostromo* is such a witness.

No doubt, Conrad, quite plausibly, ascribes a lot of stupidity, knavery, limitless greed, thievery, and wanton cruelty to his Costaguanans. Someone had to obey orders and torture Dr. Monygham or Don José Avellanos. Someone had to do as they were told and string Señor Hirsch up to a rafter by his hands tied behind his back, just as someone has had to commit Saddam Hussein's tortures in Iraq, and someone had to push the buttons and pull the triggers to kill all those Iraqi soldiers and civilians when we took over Iraq and during our occupation, and some particular people did that torturing of the detainees in the Iraqi jail, Abu Ghraib, even if they acted on orders from higher up. Someone has done all the torturing of detainees we have been guilty of since the Afghanistan and Iraq invasions started. Someone pulled the triggers or devised the bombs to kill all the teachers, physicians, government officials, and other "intellectuals" in Iraq who were assassinated after "the end of hostilities," not to speak of all the Iraqi civilians and police who have been killed and are still in 2014 being killed. Someone had to wield all those machetes that butchered men women and children, whole villages of them, in Rwanda not all that many years ago. A human decision and act was necessary to drop all those bombs on Kosovo, or to murder all those Chechnyans, or to retaliate with human suicide bombs in Moscow. Human beings are boundlessly capable of lethal cruelty to one another. It will not do to blame the "authorities" for this or to say, "I was just carrying out orders." We have seen a lot of examples of this human propensity for murder, rape, and sadistic cruelty all over the world in recent years. A recent example is the Boston Marathon bombing that left three dead and an estimated 264 injured, some grievously.

Nostromo's Representation of Capitalist Imperialism

Nostromo provides a parabolic representation of the violent and unjust side of human history. These traits of human nature, organized in civil wars, revolutions, and "acts of terror," have certainly stood in the way of Sulaco becoming a community, to put it mildly. Nevertheless, one needs to ask just what has made these deplorable aspects of so-called "human nature" especially active in Sulaco. These aspects always stand in the way of law, order, justice, democracy, and civil society. The answer is twofold. First there was the murderous invasion of South America by the Spanish that killed many of the indigenous population and enslaved the rest, driving them to forced labor and destroying their cultures. Mrs. Gould has a sharp eye for the present condition of the indigenous population. She sees them during her travels all over the country with her husband to get support for the new opening of the mine and to persuade the *Indios* to come as workmen for the mine:

> Having acquired in southern Europe a knowledge of true peasantry, she was able to appreciate the great worth of the people. She saw the man under the silent, sad-eyed beast of burden. She saw them on the road carrying loads, lonely figures upon the plain, toiling under great straw hats, with their white clothing flapping about their limbs in the wind; she remembered the villages by some group of Indian women at the fountain impressed upon her memory, by the face of some young Indian girl with a melancholy and sensual profile, raising an earthenware vessel of cool water at the door of a dark hut with a wooden porch cumbered with great brown jars. (98)

This passage is a good example of that shift from a panoramic view to the specificities of an extreme close-up, in this case in a report of Mrs. Gould's memory, as it diminishes from her general knowledge of "the great worth of the people" to that "earthenware vessel of cool water at the door of a dark hut with a wooden porch cumbered with great brown jars." Conrad's narrator observes that many bridges and roads still remain in Sulaco as evidence of what slave labor by the *Indios* accomplished (99). Whole tribes, the narrative voice says, died in the effort to establish and work the silver mine. At several places the narrator describes the Native American survivors in their sullen reserve.

As the Bible says, "For whatsoever a man soweth, that shall he also reap" (Galatians 6:7). The consequences of the Spanish conquest still remain as the inaugural events in the whole region. The effect of these events cannot be healed or atoned for even after hundreds of years. They still stand in the way of the formation of any genuine community, Christian or secular, in the usual sense of the word "community." This "origin" was not a unified and unifying originating event, like the big bang that initiated our cosmos, from which Costaguanan history might have followed in a linear and teleological fashion toward some "far off divine event" of peace and justice for all. It was rather a moment of what Jean-Luc Nancy calls, in a play on the word, "exposition." The indigenous community, whatever it was like (and it will not do to idealize it too much; pre-Columbian history in South America was extremely bloody, too), was disposed of by being displaced, posed or placed beside itself, unseated, dis-posed. This happened through the violent occupying presence of an alien culture bent on converting the "savage heathens" to Christianity and on enslaving them as workers in the Europeanizing of Sulaco.

This divisive violence at the origin—or origin as *polemos,* division, exposition—also helps account for the way South American history, as represented by what Conrad in *A Personal Record* calls events on this "imaginary (but true) seaboard" (98), is a long story of civil wars, tyrannies, and revolutions. Nor has the history that is Conrad's "background" for *Nostromo* come to an end. Twentieth-century events in Brazil, Argentina, Panama, Uruguay, Chile, or Haiti bear witness to this. (A bloody rebellion against the Haitian government of Aristide, led by armed paramilitary forces and parts of the army, was taking place at the moment I first drafted this essay, back in February 10, 2004. The George W. Bush government, in typical United States interventionist fashion, put its support behind Aristide's ouster. Never mind that he was the democratically elected President.) These sad "but true" histories are the background, the assumed subsoil, of the "imaginary" story Conrad tells.

The next phase of Sulacan society was the subsequent invasion of Europeans, in a second wave, after South American republics achieved independence. This was the invasion of global capitalism. It was already in full swing in Conrad's day. Of course that invasion is still going on today. It is now more often, but not always, transnational corporations, centered in the United States, rather than in Europe, that are doing the exploiting. *Nostromo*'s main action is a fable-like exemplum of the effects of Western imperialist economic exploitation. The novel can be read with benefit even today as an analysis of capitalist globalization.

Nostromo circles around one decisive event in such a history, the moment when foreign capital, what Conrad calls "material interests," makes it possible to resist a threatened new local tyranny. This happens by way of a successful counter-revolution, and the subsequent establishment of a new regime. The new Occidental Republic of Sulaco will allow foreign exploitation, in this case the working of the San Tomé silver mine, to continue operating peacefully in a stable situation, a nation with law and order. The silver will flow steadily north to San Francisco to make rich investors constantly richer. This prosperity leaves the men who work the mine still earning peasants' wages, though they now have a hospital, schools, better housing, relative security, and all the benefits that the Catholic Church can confer. Nevertheless, references to labor unrest, strikes and the like, are made toward the end of the novel. Charles Gould was quite wrong to believe permanent law and order would be established by the triumph of "material interests." Conrad's narrator gives a haunting picture of the mine workers at shift-changing time:

> The heads of gangs, distinguished by brass medals hanging on their bare breasts, marshalled their squads; and at last the mountain would swallow one-half of the silent crowd, while the other half would move off in long files down the zigzag paths leading to the bottom of the gorge. It was deep; and, far below a thread of vegetation winding between the blazing rock faces, resembled a slender green cord, in which three lumpy knots of banana patches, palm-leaf roofs,[51] and shady trees marked the Village One, Village Two, Village Three, housing the miners of the Gould Concession. (111)

What is most terrifying about this process of exploitation is Conrad's suggestion of its inevitability, at least in the eyes of the capitalist exploiters. It does not matter what are the motives of the agents of global capitalism, how idealistic, honest, or high-minded they are. They are co-opted in spite of themselves by forces larger than themselves. Charles Gould has inherited the Gould Concession from his father, who was destroyed by it, since, though he was not working the mine, constant levies were made on him by the central government in Santa Marta, until he was ruined financially and spiritually. "It has killed him," says Charles Gould, when the news of his father's death reaches him in England (67). He resolves to atone for that death by returning to Sulaco, raising capital on the way, and working the mine, just as, it might be argued, George W. Bush's actions as president were in part retaliation for the failed assassination attempt against his father. Moreover, as he said in a press conference during his presidency, he thought he had a divine calling to invade Iraq and bring democracy to the world. What went on and still goes on in the mind of George W. Bush is inscrutable, probably extremely strange, frighteningly strange, an imminent threat. Nevertheless, one may guess that one of Bush's motives for the invasion of Iraq was a desire to make up for his father's failure to "take out Saddam Hussein" and secure Iraqi oil for Western use. His closest advisors (Cheney, Rumsfeld, and others) certainly encouraged him in that.

Charles Gould was, as I have said, born in Sulaco. His sentimental and idealistic belief is that what he calls "material interests" will eventually bring

---

51. The text has "roots," as does the Dent edition, but surely that is a misprint for "roofs." "Palm-leaf roots" doesn't make sense.

law and order to his unhappy homeland because these will be necessary to the working of the mine. "What is wanted here," he tells his wife,

> is law, good faith, order, security. Anyone may declaim about these things, but I pin my faith to material interests. Only let the material interests once get a firm footing, and they are bound to impose the conditions on which alone they can continue to exist. That's how your money-making is justified here in the face of lawlessness and disorder. It is justified because the security which it demands must be shared with an oppressed people. A better justice will come afterwards. That's your ray of hope. (92–93)

That noble but naïve confidence found its echoes in American neo-conservative arguments for bringing democracy to Iraq in order to secure the smooth working of the oil industry there. That is our present-day form of "material interests." The latter (oil exploitation) is bound to bring the former (Western-style capitalist democracy)—in good time—since oil exploitation requires law and order. This is a version of the "trickle down" theory, or, in George W. Bush's words, "it's our calling to bring democracy to the world," "to change the world." Of course this has not worked. Both Iraq and Afghanistan, after we finally "pulled out," have been even more violent and unstable. Western-style democracies they are not.

Charles Gould, in spite of his English sentimental idealism and practical efficiency, is no more than a tool of global capitalism. The latter is represented, as every reader of the novel will remember, by the sinister American businessman and entrepreneur from San Francisco, Holroyd. Holroyd funds the re-opening of the San Tomé mine as a kind of personal hobby. It is one small feature of his global enterprise. That enterprise includes, as a significant detail, a commitment to building protestant churches everywhere the influence of his company reaches. Or, rather, Holroyd funds not the mine, but Charles Gould. It is Gould he has bought, not the mine, out of his confidence in Gould's integrity, courage, practicality, mine-engineering know-how, and fanatical devotion to making the mine successful at all costs. Holroyd's recompense is the steady flow of large amounts of silver north by steamer to San Francisco from the port of Sulaco.

Holroyd has a canny sense of the precariousness of the San Tomé enterprise. He is ready at a moment's notice to withdraw funding if things go badly, for example through a new revolution installing another tyrannical dictator who will take over the mine for his own enrichment. Nevertheless, Holroyd sees global capitalism as destined to conquer the world. He states this certainty in a chilling speech to Charles Gould. Gould does not care what Holroyd believes as long as he (Gould) obtains the money necessary to get the mine working. Holroyd's speech is chilling because it is so prescient. A CEO of ADM, "Supermarket to the World," or Enron, or Bechtel, or Fluor, or Monsanto, or Texaco, or Halliburton, Dick Cheney, for example, when he ran Halliburton, might make such a speech in our own time, at least in private, to confidantes or confederates. It is not insignificant that Holroyd's big office building of steel and glass is located in San Francisco, since so many transnational corporations even today are located in California, if not in Texas. Conrad foresaw the movement of global capitalism's center westward from Paris and London first to New York and then to Texas and California. What Conrad did not foresee is that it would be oil and gas rather than silver or other metals that would be the center of global capitalism. Nor did he foresee that the development and use of oil and gas would cause environmental destruction and global warming that would sooner or later bring the whole process of economic imperialism to a halt and inundate our coastal cities, if nuclear war does not finish us all off before that.

Western-style industrialized and now digitized civilization, as it spreads all over the world, requires oil and gas not just for automobiles and heating, but for military might and explosives; for the airplanes that span the globe; for plastics, metal, and paper manufacture; for producing fertilizers and pesticides that grow the corn and soybeans that feed the cattle that make the beef that feeds people; and now for the production of personal computers, television sets, satellites, fiber optic cables, and all the rest of the paraphernalia of global telecommunications and the mass media. Surprisingly, it takes two thirds as much oil or coal-based CO_2-emitting energy to produce a PC as to produce an automobile, a large amount in both cases. When the oil and gas are gone, in a hundred years or less, we are going to be in big trouble, up the proverbial creek without a paddle, and with rising waters to boot.

Holroyd, by the way, is a perfect United Statesian, that is, a mixture of many races. He is also a splendid exemplar of religion's connection to the rise of capitalism. He is a "millionaire endower of churches on a scale befitting the greatness of his native land" (84). "His hair was iron gray," says the narrator, "his eyebrows were still black, and his massive profile was the profile of a Caesar's head on an old Roman coin. But his parentage was German and Scotch and English, with remote strains of Danish and French blood, giving him the temperament of a Puritan, and an insatiable imagination of conquest" (84). Here is this insatiable capitalist's prophetic account of the way United States-based global capitalism is bound to take over the world:

> Now what is Costaguana? It is the bottomless pit of ten per cent. loans and other fool investments. European capital had been flung into it with both

hands for years. Not ours, though. We in this country know just about enough to keep in-doors when it rains. We can sit and watch. Of course, some day we shall step in. We are bound to. But there's no hurry. Time itself has got to wait on the greatest country in the whole of God's universe. We shall be giving the word for everything—industry, trade, law, journalism, art, politics, and religion, from Cape Horn clear over to Smith's Sound, and beyond, too, if anything worth taking hold of turns up at the North Pole. And then we shall have the leisure to take in hand the outlying islands and continents of the earth. We shall run the world's business whether the world likes it or not. The world can't help it—and neither can we, I guess. (84–85)

Holroyd makes this remarkable statement to Charles Gould, during the latter's visit to Holroyd's office in San Francisco to raise venture capital for the mine. The reader will remember the huge losses the Bank of America and other banks incurred some years ago from bad South American loans. This was long before the recent global financial melt-down. These American banks in their boundless greed seem to have forgotten the lesson that Conrad's Holroyd already knew. Holroyd was right in the short run, but now, in 2013, the United States's global economic hegemony is coming to an end through the folly of our banks, financial institutions, and politicians. The "great Holroyd building" is described as "an enormous pile of iron, glass, and blocks of stone at the corner of two streets, cobwebbed aloft by the radiation of telegraph wires" (89). That sounds pretty familiar, except that today such a building, for example the old Enron building in Houston before they went broke through fraud and greed, would have more glass and less visible iron and stone. The cobweb of telegraph wires would be replaced by invisible underground optic cables or by discreet satellite dishes. Nevertheless, Conrad's circumstantial account of the determining role of the telegraph and of trans-oceanic cables in Sulaco's affairs anticipates the role of global telecommunications today.

Gould's reaction to Holroyd's speech about the way the United States will take over the world is a slight disagreeable uneasiness caused by a sudden insight into the smallness, in a global perspective, of the silver mine that fills his whole life. Holroyd's "intelligence was nourished on facts," says the narrator, and, oddly, says his words were "meant to express his faith in destiny in words suitable to his intelligence, which was unskilled in the presentation of general ideas" (85). This commentary is odd because Holroyd's speech, it seems to me, expresses with great eloquence the "general idea" or ideological presuppositions of United States's "exceptionalism." I mean our presumption that it is our destiny to achieve imperialist economic conquest of the world, with military help when necessary. Holroyd's grandiose conceptions are not all that solidly nourished on facts. Charles Gould, on the other hand, "whose imagination had been permanently affected by the one great fact of a silver-mine, had no objection to this theory [Holroyd's] of the world's future. If it had seemed distasteful for a moment it was because the sudden statement of such vast eventualities dwarfed almost to nothingness the actual matter in hand. He and his plans and all the mineral wealth of the Occidental province appeared suddenly robbed of every vestige of magnitude" (85).

My own reaction to Holroyd's speech is that chill or frisson I have mentioned as a reaction to Conrad's prescience. It is also the reflection that United States global economic imperialism may already be coming to an end, like all imperialisms, as China will soon become the world's largest economy, as Indian software displaces Silicon Valley, as United States jobs flee by the hundreds of thousands to worldwide "outsourcing" and manufacturing (millions of jobs lost to China alone in the last few years), and as non-Americans, such as the Australian Rupert Murdoch, are coming to dominate the worldwide cable and satellite media. The triumph of global capitalism means the eventual end of nation-state imperialist hegemony. That includes the United States. We should make no mistake about that. Dick Cheney, as I said earlier in this chapter, had more power when he was CEO of Halliburton than he had as Vice President of the United States, in spite of all the mischief he did in the latter capacity. The American people could have refused to re-elect him if they had chosen to do so, whereas as a CEO of a multinational corporation he was not subject to such inconvenient restraints.

Somewhat paradoxically, one of the best ways to understand what is happening now in our time of globalization is to read this old novel by Conrad, written just a hundred years ago. That is one answer to the question of literature's "usefulness" these days. The way military intervention by the United States is necessary to secure and support its worldwide economic imperialism is indicated in one small detail in *Nostromo*. The narrator notes that the climax of the successful secession and establishment of the new Occidental Republic of Sulaco, a United States warship, the *Powhatan* [a real American Navy ship, by the way, ironically named for a Native American chief], stood by in the offing to make sure that the founding of the new republic did not go amiss [N 544]. This parallels the historical fact that when Panama through United States conniving, split off from Colombia after Colombia refused to approve the Panama Canal, American naval vessels stood by to make sure the split really happened and the Colombians did not try to take Panama back.

It would be too long a tale to tell the whole story here of United States military and economic intervention, not to speak of covert action, in South America. Conrad's *Nostromo* gives an admirable emblematic fictional example of it. Whether or not Conrad himself agreed unequivocally with Holroyd's economic determinism is another question, just as it is questionable whether Conrad expresses without qualification his own radical skepticism in the Parisian dandy Decoud, "the man with no faith in anything except the truth of his own sensations" (*N* 254), as though he were a perfect "impressionist." I think the answer is no in both cases.

The biographical evidence, for example that provided succinctly by Cedric Watts,[52] indicates that though Conrad learned a lot about South American history and topography from Eastwick, Masterman, et al., it was especially through his friendship and conversations with the Scottish socialist aristocrat R. B. Cunninghame Graham, descendant of the famous King of the Scots, Robert the Bruce (1274–1329), and through reading Graham's writings, that Conrad achieved his understanding of the bad things Western imperialism had done over the centuries in South America. He more or less adopted Graham's attitude toward these historical facts.

As many distinguished critics, such as Edward Said and Fredric Jameson, have noted before, I conclude that *Nostromo* is, among other things an eloquent and persuasive indictment of the evils of military and economic imperialism exercised by first-world countries, especially by the United States, against so-called third-world countries everywhere. The reader needs to be on guard, however, against confusing analogy with identity. I have used words like "allegory," "parable," "fable," "consonance," and "uncanny resonance" to indicate that *Nostromo* is a commodious *emblem* of economic imperialism. It is not a direct representation of actual historical events. *Nostromo* is a fictional work. Historical events analogous to those it recounts have recurred from time to time in post-Renaissance world history. They always happen, however, in significantly different ways at different moments in history. Oil and gas, for example, have replaced silver as the preferred loot from third-world countries. New telecommunications—email, iPhones, and the Internet—have replaced the telegraph lines and undersea cables of Conrad's day. That is a huge difference. The recent global financial meltdown depended absolutely on the use of computers and digitized trading programs, for example credit default swaps, derivatives, and micro-second execution of stock trades. The differences, we must always remember, are as important as the similarities. A parable is not a work of history. It is a realistic story that stands for something else in an indirect mode of reference. One might call each such a literary work a reading of history. Literature, to express this in Conrad's own terms, is a way of using language in a mode that is "imaginary (but true)."

---

52. Watts, *Joseph Conrad: Nostromo*, 23–39 [Editors].

The claim I am making is complex and problematic. I am sticking my neck out in making this claim in the way I do. It is impossible to do justice to the complexity in question in a single essay. A parable is not the same mode of discourse as an allegory, nor is it the same as an emblem, a paradigm, or a reading. Careful discriminations would need to be made to decide which is the best term for Conrad's procedure in *Nostromo* of making an imaginary story "stand for" history. That little word "for" in "stand for" is crucial here, as is the word "of" in the phrases "parable of," "emblem of," "allegory of," "paradigmatic expression of," and "reading of." What displacement is involved in that "for"? What is the force of "of" in these different locutions? What different ligature or separation is affirmed in each case? The differences among these "of"s might generate a virtually endless analysis of *Nostromo* in their light.

I have used a series of traditional words for Conrad's displacement of "realist" narration to say something else. The multiplicity is meant to indicate the inadequacy of all of them. *Nostromo* is not exactly a parable, nor an emblem (though I just used that word), nor an allegory, nor a paradigm, nor a reading. Each of these words is in one way or another inadequate or inappropriate. A parable, for example, is a short, realistic story of everyday life that stands for some otherwise inexpressible spiritual truth. An example is Jesus's parable of the sower, in Matthew 13:3–9. *Nostromo* is hardly like that. All the other words I have used can be disqualified in similar ways. Nevertheless, it is of great importance not to read *Nostromo* as a straightforward "historical fiction." Historical realities as Conrad knew them, primarily from reading, but also through conversations with Cunninghame Graham, not from direct experience, are used as the "raw material" for the creation of a fictive "world" that is "imaginary (but true)."

Conrad's own phrase is perhaps, after all, the best way to express the use of realist narrative techniques to create a place swarming with people and events that never existed anywhere on land or sea except within the covers of copies of *Nostromo,* and before that in Conrad's imagination. The magnificent opening description of the sequestered province of Sulaco, cut off from the outside world by the Golfo Placido and by the surrounding mountains, is one way this isolation of Sulaco's imagined (non)community is expressed in *Nostromo*. The second part of Conrad's phrase, "but true," argues that the fictive events that take place in *Nostromo* correspond to the way things really happened in Central America at that stage of its history, that is, the moment of United States imperialist and global capitalist interventions. The novel is "true to life."

The words "but true" suggest a claim by Conrad that this transformation of historical fact into a complex modernist narrative form is better than any history book at indicating the way history actually happens. History happens, that is, in ways that are distressingly contingent. History is "caused" by peripheral factors such as Decoud's love for Antonia Avellanos or Nostromo's vanity. Conrad's phrase, "imaginary (but true)," is, after all, echoing, with his own modernist twist, what Aristotle said in the *Poetics* about the way poetry is more philosophical than history because "[history] relates what has happened, [poetry] what may happen."[53] The "modernist twist" is the implicit claim that the narrative complexities and indirections I have been identifying get closer to "what has happened" than "official" histories. Aristotle would probably not have approved of those complexities, any more than Plato, in *The Republic*, approved of Homer's "double diegesis" in pretending to narrate as Odysseus.

In spite of its narrative complexities, *Nostromo*'s indirect way of "standing for" the real South American history Conrad knew from books and hearsay also means that, *mutatis mutandis*, it is also an indirect way of helping to understand what is going on in the United States and in the world today, in 2014.[54] That understanding would then make possible, it might be, responsible action (for example by voting) as a way of responding to what is going on. This, I am aware, is an extravagant claim for the social, ethical, and political usefulness of literature.

I conclude also that *Nostromo* demonstrates, to my satisfaction at least, that all its notorious narrative complexities of fractured sequence, reversed temporality, and multiple viewpoints are not goods in themselves. Not telling a story by way of a single point of view and in straightforward chronological order can be justified only if, as is the case with *Nostromo*, such extravagant displacements or "dis-positions" are necessary to get the meaning across more successfully to the reader's comprehensive understanding.

The final twist in an account of *Nostromo*'s problematic genre is that my account of Conrad's representation of how historical events actually take place must be modified further by recognizing that *Nostromo* is performative as well

---

53. Aristotle, *Poetics*, 1451b, in *Aristotle's Theory of Poetry and Fine Arts*, ed. and trans. S. H. Butcher (New York: Dover, 1950), 35.

54. F. R. Leavis, in *The Great Tradition*, first published in 1948, makes a strikingly similar claim for the relevance of *Nostromo* to understanding the history of Leavis's own time. Speaking of "Charles Gould's quiet unyieldingness in the face of Pedrito's threats and blandishments," Leavis says this episode "reinforce[s] dramatically that pattern of political significance which has a major part in *Nostromo*—a book that was written, we remind ourselves in some wonder, noting the topicality of its themes, analysis, and illustrations, in the reign of Edward VII [1901–1910]." *The Great Tradition: George Eliot, Henry James, Joseph Conrad* (Harmondsworth: Penguin, 1962), 218. I owe this reference to Jeremy Hawthorn. I am no Leavisite, but am, nevertheless, happy to find myself in agreement with Leavis about *Nostromo*'s perennial relevance, though I do not agree with Leavis's implied admiration for Gould's political ideology. Leavis, moreover, would no doubt have had little sympathy with my insistence on the way *Nostromo* is "parabolic," that is, "imaginary (but true)."

as constative. *Nostromo* is a speech act. Conrad claimed that *Nostromo* was a truer representation of history as it actually happens than any history book he had ever seen. "The historical part," wrote Conrad in a letter, "is an achievement in mosaic too, though, personally, it seems to me much more true than any history I ever learned" (*CL* 6:231). *Nostromo* is, after all, a work of fiction, a virtual reality, as I have emphasized. The words on the pages are the material basis of an internal theatrical or cinematic show, not a treatise on politics or on the economics of global capitalism. As is appropriate for its genre, *Nostromo* embodies imaginary historical events by way of what may be seen by the narrative eye and by way of the presentation of its imaginary protagonists' beliefs and actions.

Whatever effect the novel may have on its readers will be the result not only of a constative conveying of information about imperialism but also of a performative intervention generated by the imaginary narrative. This may even lead the reader to choose and act differently today in his or her present situation, for example by voting differently. That performative effect, which is the true social function of literature, is unpredictable in a given case. No determinable straight line exists between the novel taken as a speech act and the result of that speech act. Some readers may have their eyes opened by *Nostromo* to the evils of United States imperialism now as then. Others may see Conrad's message as essentially a conservative one. They may even conclude (wrongly) that Conrad believes that lawless and unstable places like Sulaco need a little intervention by the United States to set up a democracy like our own and to install law and order, so enterprises like the San Tomé mine (read Iraqi oil reserves) can be peacefully exploited for the good of the world (read the good of multinational oil companies and American consumers).

IDEOLOGIES OF LOVE AND WAR: PSYCHODRAMAS OF INTERTWINED ISOLATOES IN *NOSTROMO*

The previous section focused on Conrad's extremely complex to-and-fro "mosaic-like" presentation of the events of history as a way of exposing capitalist imperialism in an imaginary example. The ideologies of imperialism, however, are of course embodied in the personages of the novel. Moreover, love both romantic and erotic is, for Conrad, also a crucial cause of the way history happens. This final section of this chapter investigates the novel's psychodramas.

Conrad's Cinematic Vision

My chief topic, the reader may remember, is the relation of individual to community, or lack of it, in *Nostromo*. I have already established that Sulaco is not a community at all in the ordinary sense of that word. It is at best a grotesque parody of a community, a non-community or an "unworked" community. The European invasions have seen to that. Historical events, I have said, are partly represented in *Nostromo* in terms of highly circumstantial visual images. An example, one chosen out of a great many, is the description of the changing of shifts at the San Tomé mine, cited earlier. These visions, as they might almost be called, are remarkably cinematic. They make the reader *see*, almost as vividly as if a camera eye had recorded the scene. Many of Conrad's fictions have, it happens, been made into films. This has occurred twice already for *Nostromo*, once back in the 1920s as a film and then again quite recently for television. Conrad's novels and stories seem to invite such translation into the predominantly visual medium of cinema. Sometimes the text, with its careful notation of colors and shapes, almost reads like detailed directions for its filming, as in the following small example, one of a great many: "From the middle of the gulf the point of the land itself [of the Punta Mala] is not visible at all; but the shoulder of a steep hill at the back can be made out faintly like a shadow on the sky" (4).

The camera eye is by no means entirely impersonal. The camera itself is an apparatus that receives light in certain ways. The cinematic image is framed and organized by all sorts of ideological, technological assumptions and manipulations by the director and the cameraman. The viewer has, moreover, been elaborately trained to interpret filmic visual images in certain ways. This happens partly by the way a given scene appears to an adept viewer as an allusion to some scene in an earlier film that has now become a recognizable stereotype. Even so, and in spite of that, the actual film through which the projector light shines to put the image on the screen is, by however complicated a series of relays and manipulations, the record of light falling on the sensitive film or, nowadays, on the digital apparatus. Beneath everything cinema is the indifferent and impersonal register by the camera eye of what Conrad and his contemporaries called "impressions." Conrad's text, though of course it is no more perfectly impersonal than a camera eye, nevertheless often attempts to come as close as possible, in what now can be seen as a period style. It is a historically dated mannerism, inaugurated by Stephen Crane and imitated later by Faulkner. The attempt is to give the impersonal record of just what was there to be seen, with minimal interpretation.

Part of the function of this mode of presentation is to challenge traditional, monumental, or teleological versions of history. These are represented in parody form in *Nostromo* by Captain Mitchell's retrospective account of the founding of the Occidental Republic of Sulaco and by recurrent notations of the way he sees things that he has been in the thick of as momentous historical "events." However, as the narrative voice observes apropos of his presence in Mrs. Gould's salons, he hasn't a clue as to what is going on:

> And there was also to be seen Captain Mitchell, a little apart, near one of the long windows, with an air of old-fashioned neat old bachelorhood about him, slightly pompous, in a white waistcoat, a little disregarded and unconscious of it, utterly in the dark, and imagining himself to be in the thick of things. The good man, having spent a clear thirty years of his life on the high seas before getting what he called a "shore billet," was astonished at the importance of transactions (other than relating to shipping) which takes place on dry land. Almost every event out of the usual daily course "marked an epoch" for him or else was "history"; unless with his pomposity struggling with a discomfited droop of his rubicund, rather handsome face, set off by snow-white close hair and short whiskers, he would mutter:
> "Ah, that! That, sir, was a mistake." (124–25)

This passage is a good example of Conrad's cinematic vision. He clearly had a vivid mental image of just what Captain Mitchell looked like, hair, whiskers, red face, white waistcoat and all, and wants to reconstitute that vision in the mind of the reader, along with Mitchell's pompous incomprehension of history. The cinematic presentation suggests that "historical events" are not something abstractly political, but are always materially embodied in ways that can be registered on the senses, heard or touched or smelled, but especially seen. An example is the "flat, joyless faces" of the mine workers changing shifts. They look all the same to Mrs. Gould, "as if run into the same ancestral mould of suffering and patience." Actually, the narrative voice tells the reader, they have skins of many different colors, "infinitely graduated shades of reddish-brown, of blackish-brown, of coppery-brown backs" that indicate their racial mixtures and that a cameraman should try to register (110–11).

Conrad also gives by way of his cinematic specificities a good bit of support to his conviction that history is often made by sheer senseless accident. It just happens that the deposed dictator Ribiera rides into Sulaco on a dying donkey at the moment the rioting crowd is in the street at that spot. It just happens that the commandeered steamship from Esmeralda bearing the revolutionist Sotillo collides in the pitch dark with the lighter manned by Nostromo and Decoud and carrying the silver from the mine. It just happens that the stowaway on the lighter grabs hold of the steamship's anchor as it slips by the lighter in the collision and is carried away with the steamship and so to his torture and death. It just happens that old Giorgio Viola mistakes Nostromo for an unwanted suitor of his daughter and shoots him dead.

UNIQUE SUBJECTIVITIES IN *NOSTROMO*

History is always materially embodied, often in grotesque accidents that may have unforeseen consequences. What happens, as a result, resists abstract generalization about what constitutes a "historical event." Nevertheless, that embodiment is also materially determined, though also in ironic and disquieting ways, by the thoughts, ideals, imaginations, fantasies, and intentions, in short the "ideologies," of the people who make history happen.

Much of the "mosaic" text of *Nostromo* is taken up by investigations of the inner worlds of the various protagonists. The narrative voice has uncanny and telepathic access to these, as it centers on now one interiority and now another. It might be argued that because Conrad's main goal in *Nostromo* is to show how history really happens, taking as his example an imaginary case of nation-founding and nation-building, he would naturally make his protagonists exemplary of the races, classes, and genders in Sulaco. Nostromo is a typical working-class Italian immigrant, a "man of the people"; old Giorgio is a typical Garibaldino; Charles Gould is a typical third generation English imperialist; and so on. No doubt some stereotyping of this sort happens, as in the anti-Semitism in the presentation of Hirsch as a cowardly, cringing Jew, or in a remark about Sotillo: "There is always something childish in the rapacity of the passionate, clear-minded southern races, wanting in the misty idealism of the northerners, who at the smallest encouragement dream of nothing less than the conquest of the earth. Sotillo was fond of jewels, gold trinkets, of personal adornment" (370–71). Sotillo is typical of the southern races, but his childishness takes the specific form of a fondness for trinkets. This kind of specificity or singularity is even truer of the chief protagonists. In essence each main character is atypical, singular.

SUBJECTIVE ISOLATION IN *NOSTROMO*

Edward Said was right. The whole long ending of the novel is like a working out of the interwoven themes of a Bach four-part composition.[55] In this case, however, even more parts are woven in, one at least for each of the main char-

---

55. Kaplan, Mallios, and White, "An Interview with Edward Said," 293.

acters and even for some of the lesser actors in this drama: Charles Gould, Emilia Gould, Nostromo, Decoud, Antonia, Giorgio Viola, Dr. Monygham, even Captain Mitchell, the villainous Sotillo, and the hapless Hirsch. The destiny of each main character is followed to its end in death or in some kind of stasis. Each life is presented in a complex interweaving of alternating motifs. Each one of these goes on and on. Each follows its own logic indefatigably and without apparent worry about the reader's patience, again like a Bach invention.

Conrad, for example, extended considerably from the magazine version in *T. P.'s Weekly* to the first book version of the final episode of Nostromo's courtship of the Viola daughters and his death at the hands of their father. In this final extended episode, the investigation of history in an imaginary example seems left far behind and almost forgotten. W. B. Yeats, speaking of his own experience as a poet and playwright, has, in "The Circus Animals' Desertion," succinctly named what has happened in this case with Conrad too:

> and yet when all is said
> It was the dream itself enchanted me:
> Character isolated by a deed
> To engross the present and dominate memory.
> Players and painted stage took all my love,
> And not those things that they were emblems of.[56]

It is a basic rule or law of *Nostromo* that the characters do not have direct access to one another's minds. Each is isolated within himself or herself. Sometimes the characters guess right about one another on the basis of the evidence, but they cannot enter directly the mind of the other. The narrator has the sovereign power to do that. We readers therefore also do so by way of that strange species of imaginary telepathy I have already identified, something "unrealistic" and yet a fundamental a part of the conventions of realist fiction in the West. Each character, though impinged upon no doubt by the surrounding characters, is nevertheless a self-enclosed bubble or monad within the larger bubble that is the encompassing mind of the narrative voice.

Conrad's consistent characterization of each of the protagonists is that each is dominated by a secret obsession only partially glimpsed by the other characters. The word "secret" echoes through the "Author's Note" as the best word to describe the way the characters are imprisoned within a single solitary incommunicable preoccupation that makes them what they are. What

---

56. W. B. Yeats, "The Circus Animals' Desertion," *The Variorum Edition of the Poems*, ed. Peter Allt and Russell K. Alspach (New York: Macmillan, 1957), 630, lines 27–32.

they are is separate singularities who have nothing in common but their singularity, their impenetrable difference from one another. In the "Note," Conrad speaks of "the secret purposes of their hearts revealed amongst the bitter necessities of the time" ("Note" 5), of "the secret devotion of Dr. Monygham" ("Note" 5), and of Nostromo's secret: "In his secret love and scorn of life and in the bewildered conviction of having been betrayed, of dying betrayed he hardly knows by what or by whom, he still is of Them [the People], their very own Great Man—with a private history of his own" ("Note" 7). "Nostromo," of course, means "our man" in Italian. Each protagonist has "a private history of his or her own." These secret obsessions differ from what is usually understood by the term "ideology." An ideology, though no less fallacious, is more public, more a matter of avowed beliefs, as in the willingness of many United States citizens today to affirm publicly that they believe the poor are just lazy and pampered by welfare handouts

Charles Gould's power over others lies in part in his English taciturnity. No one can ever be sure what he is thinking. What he is thinking, with single-minded concentration, night and day, is how to secure safely the working of the San Tomé mine. In order to do this, he is willing to bribe everyone in sight, to organize a law-suspending revolution putting Ribiera in power as a dictator governing on the basis of what a passage in the serial version that was later cut calls "the Five-Year Mandate, which suspended the fundamental laws of the estate [*sic*], but at the same time aimed at keeping private ambitions from interfering in the work of economic reconstruction. Peace at home and credit abroad!"[57] Gould is also willing to be more or less "owned" and manipulated by the great American financier, Holroyd, to help fulfill the latter's own aims of world conquest and the conversion of all South Americans to Protestant Christianity. Gould, you will remember, tells his wife that he pins his faith in material interests and in the power those interests have to establish law and order. In supporting the Ribierist revolution, in order to establish law he suspends law.

We have had some experience of that lately, in the suspension of whatever law there was in Iraq before the invasion by the United States, or the so-called coalition. We promised the eventual establishment, sometime in the future, of Western-style law, after free elections, so our "material interests" in Iraq could be protected. Meanwhile Iraq was for many years after the invasion under martial law. Iraq was subject to the sovereign power of a foreign occupying country. In a similar way, the "terrorist attack" of 9/11 has justified the suspension, through the strangely named "Patriot Act," of civil liberties and of

---

57. Cited in Watts, *Joseph Conrad: Nostromo*, 53.

the rights guaranteed under the constitution in the name of the War on Terror and in the name of Homeland Security. This has, alas, continued under Barack Obama's presidency, with immensely enhanced electronic surveillance and data-gathering of United States citizens' phone calls, emails, and "snail mail" by the NSA, or National Security Agency, as well as increased killing of foreign citizens by drone strikes intended to kill suspected terrorists. Almost every day during the summer of 2013 brought new information about the extent of surveillance of United States Citizens. As President Bush repeatedly said during his Presidency, the United States is at war. This war, we were told, was going to last a long time. It was still going on in August 2013, just as had lasted the incommunicado detention, without access to lawyers, of our "war prisoners" at Guantanamo Bay, or as had lasted the treatment of those subject to "extraordinary rendition." The latter phrase is a shorthand euphemism for detainees' transportation to secret prisons in some foreign country where they can be subjected to interrogation by torture, or to just plain torture. These situations have been, to some degree, mitigated as this book goes to press.

The War on Terror, logically, will last in perpetuity, as long as a single "terrorist" still exists, thereby putting the United States at war forever because there will always be more terrorists. We are in a permanent state of what Carl Schmitt called "exception." This exceptional state is used to justify the suspension of law, of habeas corpus; of the right to a prompt, free, and open trial; of the right to free speech; of the right to read and write what we like; of the right to take any book out of the library or to open any website without knowledge by the police of what we are reading. To change this disastrous state of affairs would constitute nothing less than a revolution against our elected representatives, even if that revolution were to be carried out through the elective process. The powers given by the Patriot Act to the Department of Homeland Security have, paradoxically, made all United States citizens homeless. We are all treated as potential alien terrorists, under constant surveillance, without a homeland, without the security of the constitutional rights we once enjoyed, under law.

Charles Gould's Secret Obsession

Charles Gould's fanatical devotion to his mine leads him to be willing to blow up himself and the mine in order to keep it from falling into the hands of the Monterist revolutionaries. It also estranges him from his wife, whom he has inspired to love him and to follow him to Costaguana out of her deep admiration for his courageous idealism. The mine becomes like a great barrier of silver between them. He loves it more than he does his wife. Moreover, far from bringing unequivocal peace and prosperity to the new Occidental Republic of Sulaco, after the Monterists have been defeated and a new state with a new stable government established, the mine becomes the agent of a new economic tyranny.

Both Dr. Monygham and Emilia Gould recognize this toward the end of the novel. They pass harsh judgment, presumably, though of course not certainly, with the concurrence of the discreet narrative voice. Dr. Monygham says, near the end of the novel:

> There is no peace and rest in the development of material interests. They have their law and their justice. But it is founded on expediency, and it is inhuman; it is without rectitude, without the continuity and force that can be found only in a moral principle. Mrs. Gould, the time approaches when all that the Gould Concession stands for shall weigh as heavily upon the people as the barbarism, cruelty, and misrule of a few years back. (571)

Emilia Gould later comes to agree with what Dr. Monygham says in a passage cited later in this section. Neither Dr. Monygham, nor Emilia Gould, nor the narrative voice, by the way, ever says anything about the environmental degradation and poisoning of earth and water caused by mining. Global warming was at that point an unknown thing of the future.

Cedric Watts cites as commentary on the damning appraisals by Monygham and Emilia a passage from *The Communist Manifesto*: "The bourgeoisie, wherever it has got the upper hand, has put an end to all feudal, patriarchal, idyllic relations. It has pitilessly torn asunder the motley feudal ties that bound man to his 'natural superiors,' and has left remaining no other nexus between man and man than naked self-interest, than callous 'cash payment.'"[58] Marx and Engels are arguing in this passage, with surprising conservatism only slightly touched by irony, that feudalism, however unjust and cruelly hierarchical, made possible communities of a sort. The rise of bourgeois capitalism has replaced all community ties with the cash nexus. Conrad's presentation of the social situation in Sulaco is quite different. Marx and Engels are not, in this citation at least, speaking about global imperialist capitalism nor about the social structure of a colony like the imaginary Sulaco. Holroyd is not a member of the bourgeoisie, but an elite member of what we would call today the top 1 percent. Conrad shows that nothing like idyllic feudalism ever existed in Sulaco.

---

58. Karl Marx and Friedrich Engels, *Manifesto of the Communist Party* (Moscow: Foreign Languages Publishing House, 1957), 78. Cited in Watts, *Joseph Conrad: Nostromo*, 71.

For Conrad, it is not so much the cash nexus that cuts people off from one another as the impenetrable enclosure of each person in his or her secret subjectivity. Each person is focused on a hidden obsession. The non-community of Sulaco presupposes the destruction by imperialist capitalism, military invasions, and ethnic mixing of any indigenous, homogeneous community. That unworking of community, however, is compounded by the secret life each person lives within the non-community. This isolation would apparently occur under any circumstances that the narrative voice can imagine. It is a given in Conrad's fictions. A hidden private life cuts each person off from all the others and imprisons each in his or her singularity. This results in a non-community, a "*communauté désoeuvrée*," of those who have nothing in common but the fact that each harbors a secret that each will carry to the grave. Historical events, for Conrad, are brought about by actions that are determined by the secret obsessions of individual persons. These actions, however, do not bring about what the actors intend. Their actions are wrested from them by the irresistible force of material interests and bring about disastrous unintended consequences.

Conrad's most eloquent expression of the way material interests appropriate the idealistic motives of those who think to use them for social good comes almost at the end of the novel by way of a passage giving in free indirect discourse Emilia Gould's understanding of the way her husband's devotion to the mine has destroyed their marriage:

> Incorrigible in his devotion to the great silver mine was the Señor Administrador! Incorrigible in his hard, determined service of the material interests to which he had pinned his faith in the triumph of order and justice. Poor boy! She had a clear vision of the gray hairs on his temples. He was perfect—perfect. . . . There was something inherent in the necessities of successful action which carried with it the moral degradation of the idea. She saw the San Tomé mountain hanging over the Campo, over the whole land, feared, hated, wealthy, more soulless than any tyrant, more pitiless and autocratic than the worst government, ready to crush innumerable lives in the expansion of its greatness. He did not see it. He could not see it. It was not his fault. He was perfect, perfect; but she would never have him to herself. Never; not for one short hour altogether to herself in this old Spanish house she loved so well! (581–82)

Charles Gould is a major, but by no means the only, example of the sad law in *Nostromo* that successful action morally degrades the idea. Gould's secret obsession is to atone for his father's miserable death by putting the mine back in working order and thereby installing the law and order that are necessary for the safety of material interests. The result is, by the implacable logic of material interests, a new tyranny in Sulaco, as Dr. Monygham and Emilia Gould both come to understand.

It is not quite the case, however, that Conrad buys a Marxist notion of economic and materialist determinism. The founding of a new state in Sulaco is an inaugural performative if there ever was one, but it depends on a whole series of acts that are undertaken with quite other motives. The new state would not have come into being without those individual and secretly motivated acts that enter the material world and change it. The main characters are driven either to despairing, empty lives or to that universal end that awaits us all, death, not by the implacable working of global capitalism or by the impersonal working of material interests, but by the intersection of those with the secret obsessions that dominate the life of each. Of Charles Gould, for example, Conrad says in the "Author's Note" that he is "the Idealist-creator of Material Interests, whom we must leave to his mine—from which there is no escape in this world" ("Note" 5). In a similar way, those gringo ghosts, probably *Americanos*, in the desolate Azuera are chained, even after death, to the treasure that is perhaps hidden there, so the local folk who have created this fable believe (*N* 4–6). This inaugural fable echoes the way the characters in Chaucer's "Pardoner's Tale" are destroyed by that root of all evil, cupidity, and also the way the "incorruptible Capataz," Nostromo, is ultimately corrupted by the silver he steals.

The value of silver lies primarily in its incorruptibility, in its resistance to rust, and in its inability to combine easily with other elements, though of course it may easily be amalgamated, with mercury for instance in old-fashioned tooth fillings. Incorruptible silver can be given value when minted into coins or when, in this novel, made into those silver buttons on his costume that Nostromo fancies and that are a sign of his boundless vanity. He cuts them off his coat in a public scene and gives them with lighthearted generosity to his current mistress. Charles Gould too is ultimately corrupted by the silver, as he recognizes in a rare moment in the novel when his silence is penetrated by the narrative voice and his thoughts are represented in a combination of free indirect discourse and direct report. His habitual British reticence and silence is his greatest political weapon. It makes him inscrutable to all those officials and rich people he must manipulate in order to get the mine going again. Nobody, except the narrator, knows what he is thinking at a given moment, not even his wife, and the narrator rarely penetrates his silence. Gould's imperious and imperial silence, along with his ruthless efficiency in running the Gould Concession, make him known everywhere in

Costaguana as "*el Rey de Sulaco,*" the king of the "*imperium in imperio,*" which is the mine and therefore king of Sulaco, too. Gould just maintains an imperturbable silence, whatever happens. The failure of the Ribierist government, which he has stooped to establish, breaking his rule against political intervention, leads him to recognize that he has made a mistake in judgment and to condemn himself for that failure. The sight of a dying cargadore lying outside the entrance to his big house as he returns to it brings home to him his folly and the "irremediable folly" of his countrymen, as one absurd and bloody revolution follows another:

> Unlike Decoud, Charles Gould could not play lightly a part in a tragic farce. It was tragic enough for him, in all conscience, but he could see no farcical element. He suffered too much under a conviction of irremediable folly. He was too severely practical and too idealistic to look upon its terrible humors with amusement, as Martin Decoud, the imaginative materialist, was able to do with the dry light of his skepticism. To him, as to all of us, the compromises with his conscience appeared uglier than ever in the light of failure. His taciturnity, assumed with a purpose, had prevented him from tampering openly with his thoughts, but the Gould Concession had insidiously corrupted his judgment. He might have known, he said to himself, leaning over the balustrade of the corridor, that Ribierism could never come to anything. The mine had corrupted his judgment by making him sick of bribing and intriguing merely to have his work left alone from day to day. Like his father, he did not like to be robbed. (405–6)

The reader will remember that Marx's *Eighteenth Brumaire,* possibly echoed here, asserts that the tragedies of history are condemned to repeat themselves as farce, for example in the repetition by Louis Napoleon of Napoleon Bonaparte.

Secrets Intertwined: The Irony of Iterated Epithets

The narrator shows the reader how similar secret obsessions dominate each of the other main characters, and minor ones too, almost always in an ultimately destructive way. Each personage's hidden life follows its own course like a given part in one of Bach's inventions, more or less on its own and in counterpointed detachment from the others, just as another Gould, Glenn Gould, seems to have hands whose fingers act independently of one another, as each finger follows its own line of notes when he plays Bach's *Well-Tempered Clavier* or *The Goldberg Variations*.

One evidence of this relative detachment of the characters from one another is the difficulty in deciding in what order to arrange a demonstration that each has a single hidden obsession. The order does not really matter, or at least I cannot see that it matters. So I shall put them down pell-mell, as they come to my mind, in the apparent disorder in which Conrad himself alternates in presenting the interiorities of the characters one after another in unpredictable order, and with a good bit of iteration, again like the return of different parts, motifs, melodies, figures, or themes in a Bach invention: Gould, Monygham, Decoud, Emilia, Nostromo, then Nostromo, Decoud, Antonia, Gould, Emilia, Monygham, and so on, until the death of each or the attainment of a fixed immobility of solitude and secret despair. It is as true in *Nostromo* as it is in *Heart of Darkness* that "We live, as we dream—alone" (70).

The themes of course, as with Bach, undergo modulation, development, changes in tempo, and variation as they return again and again and as they are intertwined with other themes. It is as though Conrad were exhausting bit by bit different ways of saying the same things about each of his characters. This repetition, again as in a Bach fugue or invention, takes place at the micro-level of phrases or epithets. Some of these are repeated many times. They become something like leitmotifs. Nostromo, for example, is called the "magnificent capataz de cargadores" again and again. The perpetual white cloud over the Golfo Placido is more than once said to shine like a bar of silver, ironically referring to the real silver from the mine.

The last sentence of the novel is like a final chord or recapitulating sequence of notes. Linda Viola cries out into the night that she will never forget the dead Nostromo: "Never! Gian' Battista," in a repetition of the name her mother had used so often for Nostromo, for example in her last words just before she dies. The narrative voice, in an ultimate echo, says: "In that true cry of love and grief that seemed to ring aloud from Punta Mala to Azuera and away to the bright line of the horizon, overhung by a big white cloud shining like a mass of solid silver, the genius of the magnificent capataz de cargadores dominated the dark gulf containing his conquests of treasure and love" (631). Almost every phrase of this sentence repeats words or phrases the reader has heard before.

The effect of this iteration is triply odd. It tends to freeze the characters and the scene in a permanent tableau. Nostromo is always, whatever he is doing, even after he becomes a thief and is no longer head of the longshoremen of Sulaco, the magnificent capataz de cargadores. He is always someone who is successful in conquests of treasure and love, just as the sunset over the Placid Gulf is the same day after day, with its emblematic white cloud, like a solid bar of silver.

The second oddness is that this constant iteration moves the stylistic texture of the novel away from what we normally expect in a "realist" novel toward something closer to the echoing repetitions of poetry, as in the epithets of Homeric epic or the leitmotifs in a Wagner opera. Homer's epithets, too, remain ironically attached to the persons they define even when they no longer literally apply, as Matthew Arnold and John Ruskin long ago recognized. Hector, in *The Iliad*, in a fine irony, remains "Tamer of Horses" even after he is dead ("Thus made they funeral for Hector, Tamer of Horses"), just as Nostromo is already dead when he is called "the magnificent capataz de cargadores" for the last time. The example used by both Arnold and Ruskin is what Helen says to Priam, in *The Iliad*, when she is pointing out the various Greek heroes. She says she cannot see her brothers, Castor and Pollux. They too were born, as she and Clytemnestra were, from Leda's eggs. She wonders if her brothers are too cowardly to show themselves, not knowing that, in the translation Ruskin gives, "them, already, the life-giving earth possessed, there in Lacedæmon, in the dear fatherland."[59] Arnold cites the same passage, with a different translation, as one of his characteristically ironic and pathetic "touchstones" in "The Study of Poetry."[60] The earth is still called "life-giving," even though it has swallowed up the dead bodies of Castor and Pollux, in an act that is present in the word "sarcophagus," which means "body-eating," in Greek. "The poet," says Ruskin, "has to speak of the earth in sadness, but he will not let that sadness affect or change his thoughts of it. No; though Castor and Pollux be dead, yet the earth is our mother still, fruitful, life-giving."[61]

The third odd effect of Conrad's iterated phrases is the way they gradually call attention to themselves as language, reminding the reader that the whole world of Sulaco and all the people in it are performative effects of language. This language has no literal referent. It creates the imaginary world to which it refers, in an act of autopoeisis. The iteration, furthermore, once the reader begins to notice its frequency, gradually empties the words of meaning until they become more and more like those senseless sounds that echo in Martin Decoud's mind before he kills himself, or like mere material marks on the page, *coquilles*, or like those mistakes in English that Conrad makes, which I discussed earlier.

---

59. John Ruskin, "The Pathetic Fallacy," in *Modern Painters III, The Works of John Ruskin*, ed. E. T. Cook and Alexander Wedderburn, 39 vols. (London: George Allen, 1904), 5:213.

60. Matthew Arnold, "The Study of Poetry," in *Essays in Criticism Second Series* (London: Macmillan, 1888), 16, 17 [Editors].

61. Ruskin, "The Pathetic Fallacy," 5:213.

Conrad's "poetic" iterations are, it happens, one of the chief instruments of the irony that pervades his narrative style. As Laurence Davies has recently argued in a fine essay, Conrad, for better or for worse, is an ironic writer through and through.[62] Adeptness in reading him requires a skill in reading irony, no easy accomplishment. The word "irony" recurs frequently in Conrad's self-characterizations. An example is his description of *The Secret Agent*, in the "Author's Note" of 1920, as based on the attempt to apply "an ironic method to a subject of that kind," "in the earnest belief that ironic treatment alone would enable me to say all that I felt I would have to say in scorn as well as in pity" (7). The "Author's Note" is itself ironic through and through, as, surely, is the subtitle of *The Secret Agent: "A Simple Tale."* Ha!

I would differ from Davies, however, in taking Friedrich Schlegel and Paul de Man as better cues for understanding irony, Conrad's or that of any other writer, than Kierkegaard and D. C. Muecke, who are Davies's authorities. Schlegel, and de Man after him, make it clear that the distinction between the *alazon* and the *eiron*, the dumb guy victim of irony and the smart guy master-ironist, is extremely tricky. They change places all the time, rather than being stable positions. No one is more the victim of irony, Schlegel said, than the person who thinks he or she has mastered it and is the smart guy. Another fundamental feature of irony is that it is a performative use of language. As de Man, somewhat surprisingly, puts it in "The Concept of Irony": "Irony also very clearly has a performative dimension. Irony consoles and it promises and it excuses. It allows us to perform all kinds of performative linguistic functions. . . ."[63] Conrad's pervasive irony in *Nostromo* has the performative effect of bringing the narrator's posture closer to Decoud's.

Davies's essay ends by saying that Conrad's irony is "fortifying," rather than "decadent" or "paralyzing." "Fortifying" would be another performative effect of ironic literary language. Davies means, I suppose, that Conrad's irony fortifies the reader against being taken in by the various illusions with which his fictitious characters are bewitched. Irony, it may be, also fortifies the reader to be able take without flinching the dismaying political and psychological insights his novels express. In addition, however, if irony has a performative as well as cognitive dimension, this means the pervasive irony in Conrad's discourse gives it its power to change the reader's political beliefs and actions. This happens, for example, through a pitilessly ironic revelation, in a fictive rendition such as *Heart of Darkness* or *Nostromo*, of the evils of imperialism, colonialism, and economic exploitation of "third world" countries by those of

---

62. Laurence Davies, "'The Thing Which Was Not' and The Thing That Is Also: Conrad's Ironic Shadowing," in *Conrad in the Twenty-First Century: Contemporary Approaches and Perspectives*, 223–37.

63. de Man, "The Concept of Irony," 165.

the "first world," especially, these days, by the United States. The United States, however, was already Conrad's target in *Nostromo,* by way of the truly sinister American financier, Holroyd. The reader must remember, however, that those who believe they have mastered irony, for example, by knowing "what de Man really means," are certain to be the victims of that irony, especially if they try to act on their presumed understanding. *Nostromo* does not by any means promise that we can ever be free of the sorts of ideologies and secret obsessions that doom the characters in the novel.

Nostromo, after all, tells a story, the story of the founding of a new state, or rather, it tells, side by side, and in alternating segments, the stories of a group of isolated, secret consciousnesses as they participate, in ways that are always ironic and disjunctive, in the founding of a new state. All these stories in the end exist all at once before the narrator's gaze, in a simultaneous spatial array, but, as with a musical composition whose development is latent in the initial juxtaposition of the several themes, that spatial array can only be revealed to the reader in words given bit by bit, in temporal segments, with many back-trackings, foreshadowings, and gaps in space and time. These constant time shifts function to spatialize time.

Nostromo: Not Another Multi-Plotted Novel Like *The Last Chronicle of Barset*

My initial choice of *Nostromo* was motivated by the sense that with so many characters and such a large "canvas" it would be a modernist version of the Victorian tradition of large multi-plotted novels, like *Middlemarch* or *The Last Chronicle of Barset,* whereas *Lord Jim,* for example, among Conrad's novels, focuses single-mindedly on a single story, that of the titular hero. That difference might, I thought, make *Nostromo,* like its Victorian predecessors, a "model of community." What could be more likely to be a community than the inhabitants of Sulaco, forced willy-nilly to share the same history? This hypothetical paradigm has turned out to be inapplicable to *Nostromo.* Not only is Sulaco a particularly fragmented and disjointed form of a non-community or unworked community, but also the stories Conrad tells do not in the ordinary sense constitute "plots." Each character, rather, has a separate life-story that evolves, often toward a conclusion in death. Each life-story does this according to its own inner laws. Each is to a considerable degree separate from the life-stories of the others and from the surrounding disaggregated community. Each, nevertheless, is impinged upon and endures in his or her own way the "historical events" that occur in his or her lifetime in Sulaco. That, however, does not prevent each character from remaining more or less immured in his or her own secret and doomed to live out the private destiny that hidden obsession prescribes.

For Conrad, a particular kind of painful isolation, even in the midst of others, is the human condition. That isolation is broken only, unbeknownst to them, by the pitiless clairvoyance of the narrative voice. That voice speaks to the reader for the characters' hidden thoughts and feelings. It betrays their secrets to the world. *Nostromo* is, to a considerable degree, made up of separate segments in which nothing much in the way of forward moving action in some imaginary present takes place. In each segment, rather, the narrative voice hovers over the continually subsisting subjectivity and iterative way of life of one of the characters. The subjectivity is presented as a separate bubble or monad. A basic assumption is that a given character's whole history is continually present to him or her as a major component of any present consciousness.

One example out of many is the initial presentation of Old Giorgio Viola (31–36). This passage gives Viola's whole past life and his present way of life in a totalizing portrait. The pages introducing Viola are something like what used to be called, in the Renaissance, a "character," though with singularity and specificity rather than with the typifying generality of entries in Renaissance character books.

Conrad is also a master of what Henry James called "scenic" presentation—that is, presentation of character through the give and take of dialogue. Examples are conversations between Charles Gould and his wife that punctuate the novel, or her interchanges with Dr. Monygham, or the dramatic scene of Sotillo's interrogation of Hirsch under torture, whom he cannot believe is telling the truth about what happened to the silver. Eventually, he shoots Hirsch while the latter is dangling by his arms from a rafter, when Hirsch spits in his face. This detail has its parallel in similar behavior by the imprisoned Garibaldi, though Garibaldi was not shot for his defiance.

Even though Conrad and James inherit the same repertoire of narrative techniques, Conrad's narrative procedure in *Nostromo* is near the opposite end of the spectrum from James's formal strategy. An extreme example in James is one of his most formally rigorous novels, *The Awkward Age*. It was written just a few years before *Nostromo* and published in serial form in 1898–99. *The Awkward Age* consists almost entirely of dialogue. It has an absolute minimum both of narrator's commentary and of what James calls "going behind," that is, direct presentation of the characters' subjectivities. In *Nostromo*, Conrad presents some dialogic scenes, as I have said, but the dominant narrative mode is an extravagant "going behind." Form follows function, in fiction as in architecture. James's goal in *The Awkward Age* was to dramatize the conflicts among people as they try to figure out what the other is thinking from what he or she says. Conrad's goal in *Nostromo* was to show the way each person is isolated from the others and lives imprisoned in his or her own subjectivity. In *Nostromo*, a hidden single-minded obsession determines behavior for each character. That obsession clashes discordantly with the secret motivations of his or her fellows. Conrad, like James, chose the mix of narrative conventions most in consonance with what he wanted to show of the human condition.

The Violas

The characters' isolation is easiest to see in some of the "minor" characters, that is, characters that are treated with less amplitude than that accorded the major characters. Old Giorgio's wife, for example, dies in the midst of the Monterist revolution, just as Garibaldi's wife had died in the woods from exhaustion during one of Garibaldi's campaigns for freedom, and just as Conrad's mother had died from the effects of the exile imposed by the Russian authorities on her husband, Conrad's father, for his political activities. What even Teresa Viola's husband does not understand about her, though Dr. Monygham glimpses it, is that she is secretly motivated by a love for Nostromo that is something more than motherly and by a fervent desire to have Nostromo become the husband of one of her daughters. "Old Giorgio," the narrator says, was "in profound ignorance of his wife's views and hopes" (281).

Old Giorgio Viola himself, as the narrator never tires of telling us, is "an old Garibaldino" entirely preoccupied with his past as a soldier in Garibaldi's revolutionary army fighting in Montevideo and then in Italy, by his adulation of Garibaldi, whose portrait hangs in his house, and by his grief that the cause of Italian and South American liberty has been betrayed by reactionary counter-revolutionaries: "This stern devotion to a cause had cast a gloom upon Giorgio's old age. It cast a gloom because the cause seemed lost. Too many kings and emperors flourished yet in the world which God had meant for the people" (35).

Holroyd

Holroyd's motives seem public enough. He wants to make his transnational company ever richer through global economic conquest. He also wants to spread Protestantism everywhere by establishing and endowing churches. He makes no secret of these goals. Why should he? What no one, not perhaps even Charles Gould, fully understands about him is his secret commitment to the San Tomé mine, to what the narrator repeatedly calls its *"imperium in imperio,"* its separate imperial sovereignty in the midst of the state sovereignty that through the vicissitudes of various revolutions rules Sulaco, but does not have sovereignty over the mine.

The impossibility of controlling by political means "material interests," particularly material interests organized globally, is one of the "lessons" of *Nostromo* of most relevance today, in our time of global economic imperialism. A striking example, a decade ago, was the difficulty of keeping the huge conglomerate corporation ADM ("Archer Daniels Midlands"), "supermarket to the world," from becoming a criminal rip-off of world markets. The company conspired to fix internationally the price of the food additives they make that are ingredients of many foodstuffs. Every bottle and can of carbonated drinks has some, as do most cattle feeds. The top executives from all around the world of the various companies involved met in places like a golf resort in Maui or the Marriott Hotel in Irvine, California. At those meetings they connived to fix the worldwide prices of the essential food ingredient lycene and to carve up the global market for it. They formed a secret monopoly in restraint of trade, a criminal offense in the United States. Eventually, they were caught and fined, but only by a series of accidents involving a top executive of ADM who was a congenital liar and cooperated secretly with the FBI investigation, clandestinely taping those meetings, while lying to both ADM and the FBI.

Holroyd is secretly committed not so much to the San Tomé mine as to his backing of Charles Gould and to his faith in Gould's abilities. He keeps his business correspondence with Gould secret from his subordinates in his office, even though there is no particular reason to do so given that the investment in the silver mine is only a tiny fraction of the worldwide Holroyd enterprises. Holroyd is sovereign in his company. He can do what he likes with its money. Nevertheless, Holroyd lives a hidden imaginative life focused on the success of the mine, as Charles Gould understands perhaps better than anyone else.

One passage presents in free indirect discourse Gould's intuition about Holroyd's secret, as well as the narrator's direct and full knowledge:

> The head of the silver and steel interests had entered into Costaguana affairs with a sort of passion. Costaguana had become necessary to his existence; in the San Tomé mine he had found the imaginative satisfaction which other minds would get from drama, from art, or from a risky and fascinating sport. It was a special form of the great man's extravagance, sanctioned by a moral intention big enough to flatter his vanity. Even in this aberration of his

genius he served the progress of the world. Charles Gould felt sure of being understood with precision [by Holroyd] and judged with the indulgence of their common passion. (421)

In the end, of course, the mine wins out. It is flourishing at the end of the novel in the momentarily peaceful new state. The mine is now once more sending its constant flow of silver ingots up the coast to San Francisco and making the rich Holroyd and his company even richer. Holroyd's imaginative investment has paid off, at least for the moment, though at the end of the novel the narrator reports that peaceful Sulaco and the smooth working of the mine are already endangered by labor unrest and by the beginnings of labor organization against the exploitation of the mine workers. This may lead ultimately, Conrad hints, to a new cycle of violent revolutions or perhaps to foreign invasions like the United States invasions of or interventions in Latin American countries.

Pedrito Montero

A savagely ironic and farcically comic version of the Conradian law that says each person is motivated by some hidden obsession is Pedrito Montero. He is the guerilla bandit who invades Sulaco on behalf of his brother's take-over of supreme power in Costaguana. Though no one knows it, this miserable personage—greedy, lazy, stupid—is secretly living in a dream world. That absurd fantasy is motivated by popular histories he has read about the French Second Empire and by his desire to recreate its sovereign pomp for himself in Sulaco. This idea is so unlikely and so nutty that it has led everyone, including Charles Gould's astute political agent in the Costaguana capital of Santa Marta, completely to misunderstand him by assuming that his motivations are sane.

> His ability to read did nothing for him but fill his head with absurd visions. His actions were usually determined by motives so improbable in themselves as to escape the penetration of a rational person. . . . [Pedrito Montero] had been devouring the lighter sort of historical works in the French language, such, for instance, as the books of Imbert de Saint Amand upon the Second Empire. But Pedrito had been struck by the splendor of a brilliant court, and had conceived the idea of an existence for himself where, like the Duc de Morny, he would associate the command of every pleasure with the conduct of political affairs and enjoy power supremely in every way. Nobody could have guessed that. (430–31)

Conrad has great ironic fun with the wretched Pedrito, but a serious argument lies behind the fun. Pedrito exemplifies the way big political events that cause a lot of suffering are brought about by the absurd illusions of those who act to bring about those events. When he was president, George W. Bush, our Pedrito Montero, may have been motivated (who knows?) by an illusory image of himself, based perhaps on his playing of video games (which we know he did) rather than on reading light histories. He may have imagined himself as George W. Bush in a flight jacket, commander-in-chief of the world's greatest military power, taking over the evil-doing countries of the world, one by one, until he reigns in sovereign supremacy over the whole shebang. In fact he was the mere tool of the "special interests" that paid for his campaigns. He was a blind agent of global capitalism and of a neo-conservative agenda whose ideology he probably did not understand. Bush was in his illusions not all that different from Pedrito Montero. Of Pedrito's strange and absurd secret dreams of "enjoy[ing] power supremely in every way," like the Duc de Morny, dreams that nobody could have guessed, the narrator says: "And yet this was one of the immediate causes of the Monterist revolution. This will appear less incredible by the reflection that the fundamental causes were the same as ever, rooted in the political immaturity of the people, in the indolence of the upper classes and the mental darkness of the lower" (431). Far from holding that the effects of global imperial capitalism are straightforward and inevitable results of ideological mistakes, Conrad dramatizes the considerably more disquieting insight that world-changing historical events happen by way of unpredictable and absurd secret obsessions that "nobody could have guessed."

Emilia Gould

Emilia Gould's secret is easy to identify. She loves Charles Gould with all her heart, loves him enough to have come with him to all the dangers and uncertainties of Sulaco and of her husband's project to start up again the Gould Concession. Her secret is the deep sorrow of her gradual discovery that the mine has corrupted Charles Gould, that he loves the mine more than he loves her, and that the mine has come more and more to stand like a great wall of silver between them. All her compassionate care for the poor, the destitute, the old of Sulaco, and all her radiant kindness and gracious hospitality to the important people who come to her receptions, political and business associates of her husband, people it is important for him to have on his side, for the sake of the mine, are displacements of her frustrated love for her husband, her anxiety for what he has become and for the danger he is in. Of her forlorn solitude and estrangement from her husband she can of course say nothing to anyone. It is her version of the impenetrable secret each character in *Nostromo* carries locked within his or her breast.

The last extended inward presentation of Emilia Gould shows her sitting motionless in her garden after hearing that her husband will spend the night at the mine. She sits lost in the desolation of her solitude. It is a solitude in the midst of people, servants, friends, all the comforts of a wealthy home, but it is as desolate as the literal solitude in his rowboat that leads Decoud to kill himself:

> Mrs. Gould's face became set and rigid for a second, as if to receive, without flinching, a great wave of loneliness that swept over her head. And it came into her mind, too, that no one would ever ask her with solicitude what she was thinking of. No one. No one, but perhaps the man who had just gone away [Dr. Monygham]. No; no one who could be answered with careless sincerity in the ideal perfection of confidence. . . . An immense desolation, the dread of her own continued life, descended upon the first lady of Sulaco. With a prophetic vision she saw herself surviving alone the degradation of her young ideal of life, of love, of work—all alone in the Treasure House of the World. The profound, blind, suffering expression of a painful dream settled on her face with its closed eyes. In the indistinct voice of an unlucky sleeper, lying passive in the toils of a merciless nightmare, she stammered out aimlessly the words:
> "Material interests." (582–83)

The Secret as a Linguistic Mistake

I have used the Freudian word "displacement." As modern structuralist Freudians such as Lacan have shown, the two key terms Freud uses for the dreamwork, "condensation" and "displacement," correspond to two figures of speech, those porcelain dogs, *chiens de faience*, of modern rhetorical theory, as Gérard Genette calls them: metaphor and metonymy. In trying to satisfy her love and compassion for her husband by way of her compassion for the sufferings of the common people, Emilia Gould has made the linguistic mistake of taking a trope literally, in this case identifying two adjacent objects of compassion. What else can she do? Her capacity for love and compassion must express itself somehow. *Nostromo* can, like Proust's *À la recherche du temps perdu*, be defined as an elaborate analysis through many different examples of the way person-to-person and person-to-community relations are governed by the penchant human beings have for making the elemental mistake of taking a fictive tropological identification as though it were literally true. It is like trying to grow grapes by the luminosity of the word "day." This, according to Paul de Man, is the essence of ideology: "What we call ideology is precisely the confusion of linguistic with natural reality, of reference with phenomenalism."[64]

Conrad says repeatedly that the characters' obsessions are "illusions," a different one for each person. What generates or constitutes those illusions? The cause in each case is a different version of the aboriginal error of taking a figure of speech literally and then acting on that mistake, perhaps, most often, by uttering some performative speech act, like the Monterist *pronunciamento* of independence from the Blancos and the foreign exploiters, or like Decoud's declaration of love for Antonia, or like a promise to do something, such as Nostromo's promises to take the lighter full of silver to safety or to ride to Cayta to get Barrios to bring his troops by ship to turn the tide against the Monterist revolution.

Dr. Monygham

A striking example of this linguistic confusion is Dr. Monygham's identification of Mrs. Gould and the mine. Dr. Monygham has two secrets. He was a military doctor in an English regiment before coming to Sulaco. His first and primary secret is his hidden and undying shame at having, years before the primary action of the novel begins, betrayed his English code of honor by breaking under Guzman Bento's crippling torture and "confessing" to a whole set of so-called crimes against the state that he had not committed. The abiding remorse for this self-betrayal has left him embittered and cynical, as unable as Decoud to believe that political motives can be other than selfish and fraudulent. He is disliked by the local people, considered to be *loco,* and to have the evil eye, as he limps around town with his medicine bag in his hand and a sneer on his face.

Dr. Monygham's second secret is much more recently generated. He admires and loves Emilia Gould with a hidden and hopeless passion. He will do anything to protect her. He sees her as the embodiment of the mine and acts to save the one by saving the other. He has identified part with whole, a synecdochic mistake, or he has confused one thing, Mrs. Gould, with what is beside it, the mine, a metonymy mistake: "As the dangers thickened around the San Tomé mine, this illusion [the mine 'presenting itself' in the person of Emilia Gould] acquired force, permanency, and authority." This figurative

---

64. de Man, "The Resistance to Theory," 11.

transference, says the narrator, makes Dr. Monygham "extremely dangerous to himself and to others" (482).

He is dangerous to himself and to others because it is always dangerous to act on the basis of assumptions that have no counterpart in the material world. An ideology, it may be remembered, is the confusion of a linguistic formulation with a real state of affairs, as Marx, Althusser, and de Man in their different ways aver. As long as my ideological aberration remains secret and I do not act upon it, all may be well, though my secret confusion might appear ridiculous or insane if it were revealed. If I act in the real world on the basis of my illusion, however, I may do much mischief because I have not seen the true state of things correctly.

The possibility that he may act on his erroneous reading of the world is what makes Dr. Monygham extremely dangerous to himself and others. His strange mistake or illusion, identifying Emilia Gould's safety with the safety of the mine, combined with his first secret, his shame at his dishonoring cowardice, motivates Dr. Monygham to play his part in the dramatic events that lead to the defeat of Sotillo and Montero. Singlehandedly, and with great difficulty, he persuades the now disillusioned Nostromo to try to recover his sense of himself by making his famous four-day ride to Cayta to tell Barrios the situation and to come back with him by boat to take over the town for the Separatists and Blancos, thereby saving the mine and, with it, Emilia.

Even more dangerously, to himself and others, Dr. Monygham makes use of his evil reputation in the town to persuade Sotillo, who is maddened with greed for the silver that he believes must be still hidden somewhere, that he has come to betray Gould by telling Sotillo that the silver has been sunk in the harbor to be recovered later. The time Sotillo spends fruitlessly dragging the harbor, in increasing rage and frustration, gives Nostromo time to get to Barrios. It gives Barrios time to enter the harbor just as Sotillo is about to hang Dr. Monygham by the derrick on the afterdeck of his ship. The rope is around his neck. He is saved in the nick of time, in a highly cinematic scene. Dr. Monygham is lucky enough to live on in the new Republic still sustained by the hidden treasure of his secret love for Emilia, whereas those in the novel who attach themselves to literal treasure are not so lucky: "Dr. Monygham had grown older, with his head steel-grey and the unchanged expression of his face, living on the inexhaustible treasure of his devotion drawn upon in the secret of his heart like a store of unlawful wealth" (*N* 563). This sort of comparison between one secret and another occurs fairly often in the discourse of the narrative voice. In this case, Dr. Monygham's living on the hidden treasure of his love for Emilia Gould is like Nostromo's "getting rich slowly" as he recovers the silver one bar at a time from the island where it is hidden.

Monygham's role in the founding of the new Occidental Republic of Sulaco is a good example of the dismaying law defining what actually brings about political events that *Nostromo* everywhere exemplifies. Dr. Monygham does not care a damn about creating the new state or about the silver mine. He loves Emilia. He wants only to save and protect her. This leads him to perform actions that have important unintended political consequences. His actions, based on a linguistic mistake, bring about a true historical event, the founding of a new nation state. This is a quite different account of politics from the one that we in the United States are taught, for example, about the founding of the United States. A group of heroic and courageous patriots, we are told, got together and signed the Declaration of Independence, as written by Thomas Jefferson and amended by others in the group of revolutionaries. Their single-minded goal was to establish a new democratic country, the United States of America. If Conrad is to be believed, political change does not happen that way. It is the result of a set of independent actions, each based on secret fallacies. The actors do not intend the result they achieve. Those actions bring about a political result through a series of more or less farcical accidents, contretemps, and misunderstandings.

Linguistic Confusions That Have Results

A similar analysis as that for Dr. Monygham can be made of the illusions of all the main characters. Gould, for example, has confused making the mine work efficiently with a dream of justice and prosperity. The two have nothing to do with one another. The good working of the mine is completely indifferent to the justice or injustice of the political order within which it operates. It does not need anything but the efficient working of its machinery of extraction. When Gould says he pins his faith on material interests and believes they will bring law, order, and justice at last to Sulaco, he confuses one kind of order with another. It is a tropological mistake.

Decoud identifies the fulfillment of his love for Antonia, one way of making her happy, with another way of making her happy, that is, fulfilling her political hopes, modeled on those of her father, Don José Avellanos, by getting Sulaco declared an independent country. The two kinds of fulfillment of desire are quite different, but Decoud confuses them.

All of the characters' secrets, their hidden primary motivating illusions, can be shown to be versions of this kind of error. Taking a farfetched metaphorical similarity seriously, Pedrito identifies the pomp of the Duc de Morny with the grandeur he thinks he can get as the ruler of Sulaco, that miserable, tiny, out of the way, insignificant province. That is why he is so bitterly disappointed and angry when he finds that the mob has totally trashed the *Intendencia,* leaving him to sleep on a camp bed, eat on a deal table, and sit on a hard wooden chair, not on the cushioned throne he had imagined.

Nostromo is perhaps the most confused of the lot. In his vanity, he makes the elemental linguistic mistake of confusing the worth he has in other people's eyes with his actual worth. It is the reverse of the error that attributes a value to the silver that it does not have in itself, but has only because other people invest it with the power to have exchange value or to be coined into money. Nostromo *is,* he thinks, what he is in other people's eyes, as he rides around town on his gray mare in his silver-buttoned outfit accepting the adulation of all the populace and flirting in public with whoever is his mistress of the moment. He is the "incorruptible Capataz" and, though he is a Man of the People, he has performed many daring acts on behalf of the Blancos and for the rich foreigners who are exploiting Sulaco. Sulaco comes, after the Separation, to be called in an article in the London *Times,* so Captain Mitchell tells visitors, "the Treasure House of the World" [537, 541].

When the most dangerous and daring act of Nostromo's life fails, or seems to have failed, in the supposed sinking of the lighter full of silver, and everyone thinks he is drowned, Nostromo swims alone back to shore to hide in the ruined fort at the harbor entrance. He then has an experience of disillusionment that changes his life. After fourteen hours of sleep, he wakens like the healthy animal he has always been and then, so to speak, falls for the first time into self-consciousness:

> Handsome, robust, and supple, he threw back his head, flung his arms open, and stretched himself with a slow twist of the waist and a leisurely yawn of white teeth; as natural and free from evil in the moment of waking as a magnificent and unconscious wild beast. Then, in the suddenly steadied glance fixed upon nothing from under a forced frown, appeared the man. (458)

Now that his vanity cannot any longer be appeased by having his high opinion of himself reflected in the eyes of others, Nostromo suddenly becomes "nothing" in his own eyes. At the same time everything around him changes its aspect and becomes emptied of the meanings it once had:

> The thought that it was no longer open to him to ride through the streets, recognized by everyone, great and little, as he used to do every evening on his way to play monte in the posada of the Mexican Domingo; or to sit in the place of honor, listening to songs and looking at dances, made it appear to him as a town that had no existence. (463)

Nostromo's disillusionment takes the form of a sudden political conversion. He feels that he has been "betrayed" by the rich foreigners and that they have simply used him for their own ends without really caring about him at all. The narrator's analysis of Nostromo's change, which is no less than a total inner convulsion, goes on for many subtle pages, but the essence is given in an early passage in the sequence:

> The confused and intimate impressions of universal dissolution which beset a subjective nature at any strong check to its ruling passion had a bitterness approaching that of death itself. And no wonder—with no intellectual existence or moral strain to carry on his individuality, unscathed, over the abyss left by the collapse of his vanity; for even that had been simply sensuous and picturesque, and could not exist apart from outward show. . . . The capataz de cargadores, in a revulsion of subjectiveness, exasperated almost to insanity, beheld all his world without faith and courage. He had been betrayed! (466, 467)

Central in the narrative voice's account is its stress on the way Nostromo gains a new kind of subjectivity. He begins to *think*. His inner life almost begins to approach Martin Decoud's exacerbated skepticism.

Conrad's goal in this segment is to explain how Nostromo the incorruptible (in this like silver) gets corrupted. He steals the silver, a bar at a time, from Great Isabel Island, getting rich slowly, after he realizes that with Decoud almost certainly dead no one but he knows where the silver is buried. Conrad's desire to account for the transformation of a good man into a thief, the reader will remember, was the original germ of the novel. The whole enormous novel was written as it were backwards. Once Conrad transformed imaginatively the historical source in a truly bad man who has stolen a lot of silver into the idea of a good man who comes to do that, he had a lot of explaining to do and a lot of what might be called "contextualizing" and explanation of antecedent circumstances. As a result, the novel got longer and longer. The immediate explanation for the theft is that Nostromo loses his loyalty to the ruling class. This happens because he suddenly gains insight into the way he and the whole working class in Sulaco have been mercilessly exploited.

Unlike Decoud, however, who loses all his illusions, Nostromo reconstructs his vanity, out of his disillusionment, differently from its original form. He now satisfies his vanity by his sense that he is betraying the rich as they have betrayed him. He speaks to Giselle of the theft as a "revenge" for his "betrayal" by the rich (604), though on his deathbed he says to Mrs. Gould, "I die betrayed—betrayed by—" "But," says the narrator, "he did not say by whom or by what he was dying betrayed" (623). In fact he has become as much a slave to the silver as Charles Gould is. Nostromo's slavery to the silver corrupts him in more than superficial ways. His vanity is still satisfied by the admiration of everyone, but for the first time he has a secret. That secret now makes his distinction from others, his singularity, but having this secret makes all his public behavior now a sham in his own eyes and takes all the joy out of it. The narrator says:

> A transgression, a crime, entering a man's existence eats it up like a malignant growth, consumes it like a fever. Nostromo had lost his peace; the genuineness of all his qualities was destroyed. He felt it himself, and often cursed the silver of the San Tomé mine. . . . [The building of the lighthouse on the Great Isabel] would kindle a far-reaching light upon the only secret spot of his life, whose very essence, value, reality, consisted of its reflection in the admiring eyes of men. All of it but that; and that was beyond common comprehension, something that stood between him and the power that hears and gives effect to the evil words of curses. It was dark. Not every man had such a darkness. And they were going to put a light there. (585–86)

The words "power" and "darkness" here refer to Nostromo's ideological illusions, not to something in which the narrative voice believes. Nostromo, like Hardy's Henchard, believes he "must be in Somebody's hands."

The long coda of the novel dramatizes Nostromo's courtship of Giorgio Viola's daughters and his death at Giorgio's hands when Giorgio mistakes Nostromo for an unwelcome suitor for his younger daughter. In this double courtship Nostromo finds the ultimate and ultimately deadly satisfaction of his vanity. He is loved, so he thinks, by both Linda and Giselle. He has his choice between them. Consistently in this novel, Conrad calls loving and being loved another form of the illusion that all men and women must dwell in if they are not to suffer Decoud's fate. Love can be "a most splendid of illusions," but it can also be "an enlightening and priceless misfortune" (573). Emilia's love for her husband, Decoud's for Antonia, Viola's wife's infatuation with Nostromo, and Linda Viola's passion for Nostromo are analogous to Dr. Monygham's devotion to Emilia. None of these loves is satisfied or leads to happiness. Like Nostromo's captivation by the silver, Dr. Monygham's secret love-life makes him extremely dangerous to himself and to others, as do the loves of the other characters.

Love and the silver are, it happens, metaphorically identified in the novel, in another example of the inveterate linguistic mistake that causes so much grief in this novel. Viola and his daughters have by the end of the novel become keepers of the newly built lighthouse on the Great Isabel, which just happens to be the island where Nostromo and Decoud have hidden the silver. Just as Nostromo is supposed to be engaged to the elder sister, Linda, but actually wants to marry the younger sister, Giselle, in another metonymical substitution or displacement of desire, so he uses his apparent courtship of Linda as an excuse for going to the island both to meet Giselle secretly and, even more surreptitiously, to take away another few bars of the silver so he can go on getting rich slowly. The townspeople know he goes to the island, and they even know that he comes back often after midnight, but they mistakenly think he must be meeting Giselle. Old Viola mistakenly shoots Nostromo, whom he loves as a replacement for his son who had died in infancy. Viola shoots Nostromo in the dark because he takes him for the good-for-nothing "mozo," Ramirez, who wants Giselle. This is another mistake in "reading the signs." He is not so wrong after all because Nostromo is indeed after Giselle and is betraying his promises to Linda and to her father to marry Linda, not Giselle. What Nostromo really wants is neither girl. He wants the silver. He is as much a captive of the treasure as Gould is or as those dead-alive gringos on the Azuera are in the prophetic folk story told in the first chapter.

The complex series of condensations and displacements of this last episode provides one more allegory of the way the lives of all the characters in *Nostromo* are what one might call allegories of reading, or rather of misreading. Whether it is dramatizing love or politics or the disastrous development of "material interests," *Nostromo* is always really about reading—that is, it is about the "incorrigible" (582)[65] penchant human beings have to take the sign for the reality and to act fatally on the basis of that mistake, or to make unjustified substitutions and posit unjustified equivalences.

Nor is it possible, alas, to cure human beings of their illusions. If one is exposed another takes its place, just as the correction of one linguistic mistake is itself another linguistic mistake. Paul de Man elegantly formulated this disquieting feature of "ideology critique" in "Allegory of Reading" (*Profession de foi*):

> Deconstructive readings can point out the unwarranted identifications achieved by substitution, but they are powerless to prevent their recurrence even in their own discourse, and to uncross, so to speak, the aberrant

---

65. Conrad underlines this word by repeating it several times in the passage speaking for Emilia Gould's sadness toward the end of the novel: "The word 'incorrigible'—a word lately pronounced by Dr. Monygham—floated into her still and sad immobility. Incorrigible in his devotion to the great silver mine was the Señor Administrador," and so on (582). "Incorrigible" names the impossibility of curing people of their ideological infatuations either with someone they love or with "material interests."

exchanges that have taken place. Their gesture merely reiterates the rhetorical defiguration that caused the error in the first place. They leave a margin of error, a residue of logical tension that prevents the closure of the deconstructive discourse and accounts for its narrative and allegorical mode.[66]

One resists believing what de Man says here. This is especially true of what he says about my "powerlessness" to avoid doing what I clearly understand is a mistake. Surely he must be wrong! Nevertheless, Conrad's inability ever completely to untwist unwarranted identifications and expose illusions by a cool-headed analysis might account for the great length of *Nostromo,* or even for the length of this chapter, that tries to account for *Nostromo.* Both of us are trying, always unsuccessfully, to "get it right," to do a complete untwisting. That, it may be, accounts for our use of different sorts of a "narrative and allegorical mode," instead of crisp conclusive formulations. In the terms provided by my epigraph from de Man at the start of this chapter (another distressing counter-intuitive formulation; surely he must be wrong!), I have attempted to do poetics and hermeneutics, rhetorical analysis, and the recapitulation of meaning, at the same time. I have ended up, however, like de Man himself, primarily concerned with meaning, not with how meaning is expressed. I have done a bit of poetics here and there, but it does not mesh well with my hermeneutical account of Conrad's meanings.

Decoud

I have left Decoud for last because he is perhaps the most powerful rendition of the theme that all the characters dramatize—that is, the fatality that lies in belief. Decoud is initially presented as a total skeptic whose Parisian education has left him viewing all the commitments of his Sulaco countrymen with savage ironic scorn. He believes in nothing. Nevertheless, he has been enticed into returning home from Paris with the cargo of modern rifles that are decisive later on in Barrios's easy defeat of the Monterists. His motivation is his memory of Antonia Avellanos, whom he knew when she was hardly more than a child being educated in Paris. She has inherited from her father, Don José, a fanatical idealistic commitment to the Blanco, that is, the conservative, cause. Decoud does not care a bit about the Blanco cause, but the one break in his skeptical detachment is his passion for Antonia. He imagines that if he can satisfy Antonia's political aspirations by establishing Sulaco as a separate state

---

66. Paul de Man, "Allegory of Reading (*Profession de foi*)," in *Allegories of Reading* (New Haven: Yale University Press, 1979), 242.

then she will marry him and with him leave the wretched Sulaco for good. It is he who has supported the Blanco cause, though totally disbelieving in it, as the editor of the Sulaco newspaper, the *Porvenir* (the *Future*). He has repeatedly called Montero in the *Porvenir* a *"gran' bestia,"* thereby making himself a man marked for execution if the Monterists take over Sulaco. That is why he flees with Nostromo in the lighter full of silver and why Nostromo leaves him behind on the Great Isabel after they bury the silver there. His life is in danger unless he hides himself.

Before Decoud flees, however, he writes the *Pronunciamento*, which is the basis of the Separatist counter-revolution. He is the Thomas Jefferson of Sulaco, the author of its Declaration of Independence. It is he who first has the idea of separation and who succeeds in persuading Charles Gould, Dr. Monygham, Don José, Antonia, Emilia Gould, the chief railway engineer, and others that separation is the way to go. The irony is that he does not believe in separation or in any other political action. He just wants to marry Antonia and then leave Sulaco forever. He thinks successfully proclaiming separation is the best way to win Antonia. It is another case of displacement. This is another striking example in the novel of the way political consequences are brought about by actions that have entirely different goals.

The separatist proclamation, authored by Decoud, is a felicitous performative, like the American Declaration of Independence. After Decoud's death and the success of the separatist movement he is revered as the father of his country by everyone, including the perpetually bereft and forlorn Antonia, widowed without ever having been married. Decoud intended his speech act, the proclamation, to have one result, the winning of Antonia. Like many other speech acts in the novel, and like so many performative utterances in the real world, it misfires. A current example would be George W. Bush's declaration at the beginning of May 2003 that hostilities in Iraq were at an end and the war was over ("Mission Accomplished!"), whereas the war kept on unabated, whatever he said. The United States had many more casualties after Bush's declaration than in the period after the invasion began and before he said the war had accomplished its mission. (Note the quasi-religious term.) United States soldiers were still in 2013 being killed or wounded in Iraq and Afghanistan. Speech acts, such as Decoud's proclamation, or Bush's, have a distressing way of making something happen all right, but not what the one who uttered or wrote it intended.

The extended account of what drives Decoud to suicide is one of the most powerfully dramatic episodes in *Nostromo*. As the narrator says, Decoud is killed by solitude. As day follows day and he is still left alone with the silver on the Great Isabel, eating little and sleeping almost not at all, Decoud loses all sense of his individuality and all sense of the reality of Sulaco affairs, even of his love for Antonia. Language ceases to have meaning and becomes a senseless material sound. Nothing is left but what the narrator sometimes, in fulfillment of Conrad's impressionist commitment, wants the reader to believe is all that is really there, pure meaningless sensations. The usual sense of one's individuality, Conrad is showing, depends on being an active part of a community:

> Solitude from mere outward condition of existence becomes very swiftly a state of soul in which the affectations of irony and skepticism have no place. It takes possession of the mind, and drives forth the thought into the exile of utter unbelief. After three days of waiting for the sight of some human face, Decoud caught himself entertaining a doubt of his own individuality. It had merged into the world of cloud and water, of natural forces and forms of nature. In our activity alone do we find the sustaining illusion of an independent existence as against the whole scheme of things of which we form a helpless part. Decoud lost all belief in the reality of his action past and to come. On the fifth day an immense melancholy descended on him palpably. He resolved not to give himself up hopelessly to those people in Sulaco, who had beset him, unreal and terrible, like jibbering and obscene specters. He saw himself struggling feebly in their midst, and Antonia, gigantic and lovely like an allegorical statue, looking on with scornful eyes at his weakness.... He beheld the universe as a succession of incomprehensible images.... The silence, remaining unbroken in the shape of a cord to which he hung with both hands, vibrated with senseless phrases, always the same but utterly incomprehensible, about Nostromo, Antonia, Barrios, and proclamations mingled into an ironical and senseless buzzing. (556, 557–58)

Then, after Decoud weights his pockets with four bars of the San Tomé silver, rows his small boat out into the gulf, and shoots himself so that he sinks into the sea, the narrator comments: "A victim of the disillusioned weariness which is the retribution meted out to intellectual audacity, the brilliant Don Martin Decoud, weighted by the bars of San Tomé silver, disappeared without a trace, swallowed up in the immense indifference of things" (560), just as Nostromo, a few sentences later, is described as "the magnificent capataz de cargadores, victim of the disenchanted vanity which is the reward of audacious action" (560–61). Both audacious thought and audacious action victimize and ultimately destroy those who perform them. If you want to go on living, you had better have some ideological illusions that make you like your neighbors. Those illusions, however, are extremely dangerous to you and to your neighbors, as in the case of Dr. Monygham's love for Emilia Gould and his confusion of her with the silver mine.

Just as Othello, for example, would have fared better had he been in Hamlet's situation, or Hamlet in Othello's, the situation in each case bringing out the tragic flaw, so another person, Nostromo for example, or Charles Gould, or Dr. Monygham, could have endured that solitude and silence in the midst of the Golfo Placido without yielding to it. Such a person would have been sustained by his sense of himself and by his secret obsession, whatever that might be. Decoud's radical skepticism, so close to Conrad's own, has no such consoling illusion. Therefore he is destroyed, or is driven to destroy himself. What happens to Decoud is striking confirmation that Conrad, like T. S. Eliot, believed that humankind cannot bear very much reality. We are kept in life only by some secret saving illusion that forms the ground or substance of each person's selfhood or "individuality." Alas, because, as their name implies, those illusions do not correspond to things as they are, they are in the end destructive, too, as destructive, almost, as Decoud's exceptional entry into a state of mind almost without any illusions at all. Illusions, too, make men or women extremely dangerous to themselves and to others.

Decoud's suicide draws its importance, among the interwoven iterated "parts" in Conrad's multipart invention, from the way it demonstrates that it is an error to believe that Conrad recommends a thoroughgoing skepticism and detached observation, to "look on and never make a sound," as Heyst, the protagonist of Conrad's *Victory*, says of his resolution to remain a spectator during his travels (*V* 153). Both Heyst and the narrative voice of *Nostromo*, of course, make lots of sounds in the way of words. Skepticism like Decoud's is deadly. It leads to an ignominious and inglorious death that is in some ways farcical, absurd, whereas Nostromo's death, for example, and even Señor Hirsch's, and Teresa Viola's, and Giorgio Viola's, have something defiant and downright courageous about them.

No Transcendent Ground in *Nostromo*

The forlornness of the characters in *Nostromo*, the way each lives imprisoned in a private ideological illusion, is made even more forlorn by the almost complete absence, so far as I can see, of the "metaphysical" dimension that is so important in *Heart of Darkness*. The characters of *Nostromo* do not even have the somber consolation of having confronted a transnatural antagonist force. In *Heart of Darkness*, this antagonist is experienced as a mysterious personage hidden behind visible appearances, as an implacable force with an inscrutable intention that obscurely governs their lives. The characters in *Nostromo* have brought their trouble on themselves, collectively, or have been subject to those outside economic forces that Conrad calls "material interests." All the "metaphysics of darkness" seems to have vanished from Conrad's work in the few short years between *Heart of Darkness* and *Nostromo*.

Decoud is driven to suicide by "solitude," solitude total and absolute, not by a confrontation with some version of a spooky force such as the one that destroyed Kurtz in *Heart of Darkness*. Decoud comes to share rather in the superficial material vision the narrative voice has in the opening pages of the novel and throughout. The reader is left at the end of *Nostromo* back with the endless indifferent succession of days and nights, showers and sunlight, over the Golfo Placido. In an analogous "material vision," today's climate change is seen by many as inhuman, mechanical, without concern for the future of the human species, or for any other organic species: coral, or fish, or migrating birds. If you shift to a worldwide civilization powered by coal, gas, and oil, that will put a lot of carbon dioxide and methane in the air. Global warming will inevitably follow, with melting glaciers, coastal flooding, wildfires, stronger and more frequent storms, and so on.

The sad implication of *Nostromo* is that, for Conrad, at that moment of his writing at least, only some ideological illusion or other can hold my sense of my personality together and protect me from the suicide-inducing emptiness of what Conrad calls "solitude." Conrad also shows, however, that the secret obsessions governing a given person's decisions and behavior are also a kind of self-destructive madness. On the one hand, speaking of Nostromo, the narrative voice says, in an oracular generalization, "Each man [sic] must have some temperamental sense by which to discover himself. With Nostromo it was vanity of an artless sort. Without it he would have been nothing" (461), just as Decoud becomes nothing in the absence of *his* saving focus, his love for Antonia. On the other hand, such an obsession is a kind of madness. The narrative voice, for example, reports Emilia Gould's thoughts about her husband, as she has come to understand him and fear for him. She watches him as he sits in abstraction, writing in his mind the letter he will send to persuade Holroyd that "the San Tomé mine is big enough to take in hand the making of a new state" (423):

> Mrs. Gould watched his abstraction with dread. It was a domestic and frightful phenomenon that darkened and chilled the house for her like a thundercloud passing over the sun. Charles Gould's fits of abstraction depicted the energetic concentration of a will haunted by a fixed idea. A man haunted by a fixed idea is insane. He is dangerous even if that idea is an idea of justice;

for may he not bring the heaven down pitilessly upon a loved head? The eyes of Mrs. Gould, watching her husband's profile, filled with tears again. (422)

For Conrad, human beings are caught between two insanities, Decoud's suicidal insanity of seeing everything with skeptical clarity, unsupported by any remaining egotistical illusion, as opposed to Gould's insanity of being "haunted" by a fixed idea, or Dr. Monygham's dangerous confusion of the mine with Emilia Gould, or Nostromo's vanity that reconstructs itself even after his disillusionment. Even an ideal of justice turns ultimately against the one who is haunted by it. Illusion destroys integrity, as Nostromo's incorruptible integrity is destroyed when his vanity fails him and he comes to think that the rich have used and betrayed him. For Conrad, in the end, history is not made by the implacable impersonal forces of global capitalism, but by innumerable individual acts, motivated most often by idealistic secret obsessions. These bring about changes that are absurdly incongruous with the intentions that motivate them.

Edward Said, in his fascinating interview about Conrad, given just a few months before he died, after praising *Nostromo* with generosity and insight, marks out succinctly his difference from Conrad:

> Oh, I have a great contempt for such policy-intellectuals. [He means the sort of "experts" from the government or from conservative (or even liberal) think-tanks who are lobbyists or who appear on television or radio talk-shows.] I learned that all from Conrad. That if you get involved in the machine, as he calls it in a famous letter [to Cunninghame Graham, cited earlier], or, say, in something like the mine in Costaguana, there's no escape. What you must try to do is to maintain division [I suppose he means some distance, some detachment]: of corruption; of power, leading to all sorts of dark places; and from becoming part of it oneself. And also to be able to do what Conrad did aesthetically, which is to stand outside and to say: Well, yes, those things are happening. But there are always alternatives. But the big difference between Conrad and me in the end—and this is true of *Nostromo* as well as *Heart of Darkness*—is that politically for Conrad there are no real alternatives. And I disagree with that: there's always an alternative.[67]

Said seems here to grant Conrad a belief that there are always non-political alternatives. Things might have turned out differently. It is just that for Conrad there are no political alternatives, just an endless series of fortuitously

---

67. Kaplan, Mallios, and White, "An Interview with Edward Said," 292.

created corrupt and unjust regimes. Said, on the contrary, believed that there are always political alternatives—for example, ways to solve with justice the Israeli-Palestinian conflict that Said was as completely invested in as old Giorgio Viola was in the lost Garibaldi cause. Such stubborn political optimism was one of Said's most admirable traits.

I agree that Conrad is different from Said. His reasons for being less optimistic are not that he cannot imagine political alternatives, but that any political alternative will, in his view, become corrupted and unjust, corrupted not by the Juggernaut of global capitalism as a form of historical or materialist determinism, but by the "incorrigible" flaws in human nature shared by those who have devised and carried out the alternatives. The chief flaw in human nature is the need each human being has to believe in some illusion to save himself or herself from the madness of suicide. Every such illusion, without exception, Conrad believed, also ultimately turns into some form of dangerous madness. It becomes a secret insanity dangerous to others, dangerous to oneself, as Nostromo's frustrated vanity leads him to his death.

Nostromo ultimately reveals itself to be not so much a political novel, as it is usually taken to be, as a psychological novel, or a novel about the way human psychology can be shown to determine political history through a series of absurd linguistic mistakes, when you get down to the fine grain of the way material events actually happen.

Another, and final, way to put this would be to say that *Nostromo* is a covert rhetorical analysis. It is a deconstruction before the fact, in the guise of a psychological and political analysis, of the way interpersonal and political actions are governed by linguistic errors of which the actors are not aware and can only be made aware of by some form of suicidal insight. What they *are,* their secret singularities, is those errors. *Radix malorum cupiditas non est sed lingua.* Without language, however, human beings would be nothing. Language gives human beings the incorrigible habit of ascribing fictitious value to material things, of which ascription cupidity is one signal form. Without these linguistic mistakes or illusions, human beings would dissolve into that solitude and silence within which Decoud imagines himself suspended, as from a long cord hung from the sky over the Golfo Placido, before he shoots himself.[68]

---

68. Decoud succeeded in this better than did Conrad himself, who, absurdly or perhaps unconsciously/deliberately, botched his suicide attempt in 1878. He was in despair over debts he could not repay. He shot himself in the chest, *durch und durch,* through and through, as his Uncle Tadeusz Bobrowski wrote in a letter, without damaging his heart or any other vital organ. Watts, *Joseph Conrad: Nostromo,* 8. If his aim had been "better," we would not have *Nostromo, Lord Jim,* or *Heart of Darkness,* or any other of Conrad's fictions. That would be an irreparable loss about which we would know nothing.

Either way we human beings, according to the evidence provided by the narrative voice in *Nostromo*, have had it. Is it better not to know and to live on in an illusion that makes one extremely dangerous to oneself and to others, or is it better to know and to be led to a self-destroying emptiness, silence, and solitude? That is a hard judgment call to make, though Conrad's people do not, of course, have the chance to choose with a clear head one or the other fate. Nor does *Nostromo* choose between them. It exposes pitilessly the consequences of happening to go either way.

To return in conclusion to my topic of the individual's relation to community: Neither of these ways is anything more than the non-relation of an inauthentic selfhood to an unworked community. That is true unless one judges, as one plausibly might, Decoud's insight and literal *sein zum Tode*, being toward death, to be a hyperbolically ironic version, before the fact, of Heidegger's resolute *Dasein* bent on fulfilling its "ownmost" possibilities of being and as a result dying its own death. I see no evidence, however, that Conrad had anything like Heidegger's belief in a Being that is ground for everything, including the underlying ground for each person living with his or her fellows, each *Dasein* as *Mitsein*. For the Conrad of *Nostromo* there is only the immense indifference of things, the silence and solitude of the Golfo Placido and of the distant Cordillera.

INDEX

Achebe, Chinua: "An Image of Africa," 93, 96, 169
affect, 165–69
Afghanistan, 183, 185, 213, 217, 253
Africa/African, 17, 75, 77, 82, 90, 93, 94, 102, 104, 105, 107, 113, 114, 116, 117, 119, 120, 159, 160, 169, 193, 207
Agamben, Giorgio: "The Muselman," 160
aletheia, xiii, 85
allegory, allegorical reading, 75, 111, 120, 128, 129, 135, 163–65, 193, 199, 212, 221, 222, 251–52, 254
Althusser, Louis Pierre, 246
analepsis, 162, 204, 205
Anderson, Benedict: *Imagined Communities*, 208
antithesis, xiii, 85
apocalypse, apocalyptic reading, xii–xiii, 74–87, 91, 103–5, 109, 111, 112, 113, 118, 164, 165
Argentina, 215
Aristide, Jean-Bertrand, 215
Aristotle, 186, 197; *Poetics*, xxii, 68, 146, 223
Arnold, Matthew, 236; "The Study of Poetry," 236
Arthur Daniels Midland, 218, 241
Augustine, Saint, 158; *Confessions*, 125
Austen, Jane, 190; *Northanger Abbey*, 168
Austin, J. L., xix, 93n5, 118, 167n14; *How to Do Things with Words*, 92–93, 92n4; "Other Minds," 167; "Pretending," 167

Bach, Johann Sebastian, 182, 185, 227–28, 234–35; *The Goldberg Variations*, 235; *The Well-Tempered Clavier*, 235
Bal, Mieke, 162n7
Baudelaire, Charles, 28
Bechtel, 218
Bedford, Errol, 167
Belgium/Belgian, viii, 17, 93, 97, 110, 114, 159, 161, 168, 169
Bell, Michael: "Modernism, Myth and Heart of Darkness," 170
Benjamin, Walter, 164, 172; "Critique of Violence," 141n18; *Ursprung des deutschen Trauerspiels*, 164n9
Berthoud, Jacques, 192; *Joseph Conrad: The Major Phase*, xx, 175n5
Blanchot, Maurice, 208; *The Writing of the Disaster*, 170
Bobrowski, Tadeusz, 258
Bolívar, Simón, 211–12
Bonaparte, Louis Napoléon, 234
Bonaparte, Napoléon, 234
Bonney, William W.: *Thorns & Arabesques: Contexts for Conrad's Fiction*, viii
Booth, Wayne C.: *The Rhetoric of Fiction*, 162
Brazil, 215
Brontë, Emily: *Wuthering Heights*, 57n1, 58
Brooks, Cleanth: *The Well-Wrought Urn*, xn6
Browning, Robert: *The Ring and the Book*, 69
Brussels, 96
Burke, Edmund, x, x–xin8, 145

Bush, George H. W., 216
Bush, George W., 185, 215, 216, 217, 230, 243, 253

Caminero-Santangelo, Bryon James: "Failing the Test: Narration and Legitimation in the Work of Joseph Conrad," 127n7
Camus, Albert, 5
Cape Horn, 181, 219
capitalism, xiv, 89, 96, 109, 116, 118, 119–21, 185, 186, 201, 202–24, 231–34, 240–42, 243, 257, 258
Carlyle, Thomas, 9
Castor: *The Iliad*, 236
catachresis, xiii, 85, 106, 133, 145, 160, 162, 165, 195
Catholicism, 154, 194, 208, 215
Celan, Paul: "Aschenglorie," 89; "*Niemand/ zeugt für den/Zeugen* Paul Celan, Aschenglorie," 160
Central America/Central American, 179, 205, 211, 222
Certeau, Michel de, 192
Cervino, Dominic, 185
Chamfort (Sébastien-Roch Nicolas), 43
Chatman, Seymour, 162n7
Chechnya, 213
Cheney, Dick, 185, 216, 218, 220
Chile, 215
China/Chinese, xx, 99, 136, 220
Clytemnestra, 236
Cohen, Tom: "Toxic Assets: de Man's Remains and the Ecocatastrophic Imaginary (an American Fable)," 197n31
Cohn, Dorrit, 162n7
Colebrook, Claire: "The Geological Sublime," 193n25, 196
Coleridge, Samuel Taylor, 59, 163; "Letter to Joseph Cottle, 1815," 59n4, 60; "The Rime of the Ancient Mariner," 67
Colombia, 179, 220
colonialism. *See* imperialism
confession, 90, 95, 112, 125–26, 139, 148, 152, 179, 245
Congo, 8, 75, 80, 81, 86, 89n2, 93, 96, 97, 110, 114, 159, 161, 168, 169
Conrad, Joseph: *Almayer's Folly*, xx, xxi, 23, 188; *Chance*, 9, 13, 16, 19, 29, 68, 173, 206; *The Collected Letters of Joseph Conrad*, xxi, 12, 13, 14, 15, 19, 21, 27, 28, 29, 60, 97, 97n10, 98, 111n18, 212, 224; "The End of the Tether," 101; "Falk," 14; *Heart of Darkness*, xii–xiv, xvii, xx, xxi, 1, 2, 6–31, 33, 35, 42, 61, 72, 74–87, 88–121, 125, 129, 134, 156–71, 177, 178, 183, 193, 194, 202, 235, 237, 255, 256, 257, 258; *Lord Jim*, ix, x, xi, xii, xiv, xix, xxi, 1, 10, 11, 12, 16, 29, 30, 31, 57–73, 115, 124n5, 125, 207, 238, 258; *The Mirror of the Sea*, 97, 189, 198; *The Nigger of the "Narcissus*," 9, 11, 19, 127, 140—"Preface" to, 20, 31, 70, 78, 110, 122, 184; *Nostromo*, xiv–xv, xvii, xviii, xxi, xxii, 1, 2, 3, 10, 11, 26–27, 35, 115, 172–259—"Author's Note" to, 173–80, 173n3, 189, 190, 211, 228–29, 233; *Notes on Life and Letters*, 97; *An Outcast of the Islands*, 15, 23; "An Outpost of Progress," xxi; *A Personal Record*, 10, 13, 19, 97, 180, 181, 215; *The Rescue*, 10, 11, 18, 19, 20, 21, 22, 24–26, 27, 115; *The Secret Agent*, 16, 22, 27, 31–59, 237; "The Secret Sharer," 102, 122–55; *The Shadow-Line*, 18, 19, 20, 21, 22, 127; "To-morrow," 174; "Author's Note" to '*Twixt Land and Sea*, 136; *Typhoon*, 2–3, 10, 15, 26, 127, 174; *Typhoon and Two Other Stories*, 173, 174; *Under Western Eyes*, xx, xxi, 10, 11, 27, 123n3; *Victory*, xx, 26, 255; "Well Done!," 9; *Within the Tides*, 19—"Author's Note" to, 19; "Youth," 101; *Youth and Two Other Stories*, 101—"Author's Note" to, 101
Conrad in the Twenty-First Century (Kaplan, Mallios, White), 172, 182
Coppola, Francis Ford, xii; *Apocalyse Now*, xii, 74, 103, 183
Crane, Stephen, 184, 225; *The Red Badge of Courage*, 184
cultural studies, 165, 183, 197
Cunninghame Graham, R. B., 12, 61, 175, 179, 201, 209, 212, 221, 222, 257
Curle, Richard, 97
Cutty Sark, 136

Dan, Shen, 162n7
Dante Aligheri: *Letter to Can Grande*, 164
darkness, the, 5, 6–56, 71, 83, 84, 106, 107, 110, 116, 157, 193, 256
Daudet, Alphonse, 184
Davies, Laurence: "'The Thing Which Was Not' and The Thing That Is Also: Conrad's Ironic Shadowing," 237–38

Declaration of Independence, The, 247, 253
Deconstruction, vii, xi, xv, xviii, 251
Deleuze, Gilles: *Logique du sens,* 58n2
de Man, Paul, 86, 145n20, 246; "Allegory of Reading," 251–52; "Autobiography as De-Facement," 160; "The Concept of Irony," 186, 237–38; "Conclusions: Walter Benjamin's 'The Task of the Translator,'" 172; "Phenomenology and Materiality in Kant," 145n20, 193n25, 195, 196–202; "The Resistance to Theory," 245; "The Rhetoric of Temporality," 164
Derrida, Jacques, x, xi, 88–89, 93, 93n5, 94, 95, 98, 99, 118, 120, 134, 138, 139, 164–65; *Acts of Literature,* 98n11, 99; *Donner le temps: 1. La Fausse monnaie,* 138; *L'écriture et la différance,* xin9; *Force de loi,* 141n18; "Fourmis," 134; *De la grammatologie,* x, xi; *Passions,* 118, 138; *The Politics of Friendship,* 208; *Spectres de Marx,* 93; "D'un ton apocalyptique adopté naguère en philosophie," 84n3, 164–65; *Le Voix et la Phènoméne,* xin9
Descartes, René, 99–100
Diagesis, 162, 163, 223
Dickens, Charles, xin8, 5, 16
Dickinson, Emily, 99
Diderot, Denis, 157
Dostoevsky, Fyodor, 5, 125

Eastwick, Edward B.: *Venezuela,* 175, 179, 209, 221
Eliot, George, 5, 65; *Middlemarch,* 66, 166, 238
Eliot, T. S., 4n3, 32, 255
Empson, William: *Seven Types of Ambiguity,* x
Engels, Friedrich. *See* Marx, Karl
England/English (British), 5, 6, 8, 13, 32, 57–58, 62, 88, 96, 99, 109, 114, 117, 129, 134, 140, 150, 153, 154, 160, 178, 184, 200, 201, 207, 209, 210, 211, 216, 217, 227, 229, 233, 245
Enron, 185, 218, 219
ethical turn, xviii
Europe/European, x, xx, 5, 8, 10, 22, 75, 91, 99, 100, 102, 104, 105, 107, 108, 109, 114, 115–16, 117, 119, 133, 160, 168, 184, 209, 210, 214, 215, 218, 225
Eurydice, 29, 83

fable, 128, 191, 212, 215, 221, 233
Fastow, Andrew, 185
Faulkner, William, 47, 204, 225
Federal Bureau of Investigations (FBI), 241
feminist studies, 93, 130, 183
Fernández, Ramón: "L'Art de Conrad," 17n19
Feuerbach, Ludwig Andreas von, 93, 93n5
fidelity, 9–11, 19, 32, 61, 62, 108, 140
Flaubert, Gustav: *Salammbô,* 28
Fleishman, Avrom: *Conrad's Politics: Community and Anarchy in the Fiction of Joseph Conrad,* 175n5; "The Symbolic World of *The Secret Agent,*" 37n31
Fluor, 218
Ford (Hueffer), Ford Madox, 184; *Portraits from Life,* 89n2
Forster, E. M.: *Howards End,* 110n17, 207
France/French, viii, xi, 17, 104, 181, 183, 210. *See also* French Revolution, the; French Second Empire, the; Paris
Frankenstein (Shelley), 197
free indirect discourse, 205, 211, 232, 233, 241
French Revolution, the, 43
French Second Empire, the, 242
Freud, Sigmund, 21–22, 130, 131, 134, 169, 244; "Das 'Unheimliche,'" 129, 130, 149–51

Galatians, Book of, 214
Garibaldi, Giuseppe, 210, 227, 239, 240, 258
Garnett, Edward, 27
gender studies, 183
Genette, Gérard, 244; "Discours du récit," 162, 204
Geneva School, viii
Germany/German, 164, 184, 196, 210
Gide, André, 5
Gothic literature, 168
Gould, Glenn, 234–35
Greek literature, 99, 163, 164
Guerard, Albert: *Joseph Conrad,* 28
Guetti, James, ix; *The Limits of Metaphor,* ix
Gulliver's Travels (Swift), 177, 200

Hagan, John, Jr.: "The Design of Conrad's *The Secret Agent,*" 46
Haiti, 215
Halliburton, 185, 218, 220

Index

Hamacher, Werner, 120; "Lingua Amissa: The Messianism of Commodity-Language and Derrida's Specters of Marx," 93

Hampson, Robert: "Conrad's Heterotopic Fiction," 185, 192; *Joseph Conrad: Betrayal and Identity,* 175

Hardy, Thomas, xi, 5; "In Front of a Landscape," xvi; *The Mayor of Casterbridge,* 176, 250; *The Return of the Native,* 107, 182, 183, 187, 193; *Tess of the d'Urbervilles,* 57n1; *The Well-Beloved,* 57n1

Harper's Magazine, 136n13

Haverson, John: "The Original Nostromo: Conrad's Source" (with Watt), 176

Hawthorn, Jeremy, 223n54

Hawthorne, Nathaniel, 99

Hay, Eliose Knapp: "Joseph Conrad and Impressionism," 184; *The Political Novels of Joseph Conrad,* 175n5, 192

Hector, 236

Hegel, Georg Wilhelm Friedrich, 100, 105, 198

Heidegger, Martin, 158, 163, 164n8, 170, 173–74, 197, 203, 208, 259

Helen of Troy, 236

hermeneutical reading, 129–36, 252

hermeneutics, 76, 172

Hoffmann, E. T. A.: "The Sandman," 151

Hölderlin, Friedrich, 196, 197

Homer: *The Iliad,* 236; *The Odyssey,* 162, 163, 223

Hopkins, Gerard Manley, 174

Horror Stories (magazine), 168

Hussein, Saddam, 213, 216

Husserl, Edmund, viii; *Cartesian Meditations,* 166

imperialism, xiv, 6, 8, 9, 17, 19, 58, 75, 85, 89, 93, 94, 96, 99, 100, 105, 109, 110, 113, 114–16, 117–18, 119–21, 129, 133, 134, 140, 144n19, 158, 159, 169, 173, 175n5, 185, 201, 202–24, 227, 231, 232, 233, 237, 240–42, 243

impressionism, 19–20, 184, 198, 203–4, 205, 221, 225, 254

Iraq, 159, 183, 185, 213, 216, 217, 224, 229, 253

Ireland/Irish, 184

irony, x, xiii, xiv, 13, 15, 27, 34, 35–36, 37, 72, 79, 105–6, 81, 83, 85, 86–87, 95, 101, 105, 109, 113, 115, 117, 119, 123, 126, 133, 137, 139, 157, 167, 169, 174, 177, 179, 184, 186, 188, 191, 200, 201, 210, 211, 220, 227, 231, 234–38, 242, 243, 252, 253, 254, 259

Israel, 258

Italy/Italian, 210, 227, 240

James, Henry, 3, 175, 187, 188, 204, 239; *The Ambassadors,* 187–88; *The Awkward Age,* 239–40; *The Golden Bowl,* 188; "The New Novel," 13, 68, 173, 206; *The Wings of the Dove,* 105, 188

James, William, 3; *The Varieties of Religious Experiences,* 2

Jameson, Fredric, 207, 213, 221

Jefferson, Thomas, 247, 253

John the Baptist, 119

Joyce, James, 184

Kafka, Franz, xix, 184; *The Castle,* xixn28

Kant, Immanuel, xiii, xv, 145n20, 193, 193n25, 194–202; *The Critique of Judgment,* 145, 194–95, 202; *The Critique of Practical Reason,* 202; *The Critique of Pure Reason,* 202; *Logic, Werkausgabe,* 197n34; "On the Presumed Right to Lie Out of Love for Humanity," 91, 95

Karl, Frederick, 75

Kellogg, Robert, 162n7

Kierkegaard, Søren, 86, 105, 122, 175, 237

Kimbrough, Robert, 96

Kingsley, Charles: *Westward Ho!,* 8

Korzeniowska, Ewa, 240

Korzeniowski, Apollo, 240

Kosovo, 213

Lacan, Jacques Marie Émile, 129, 130, 158, 244

Lacoue-Labarthe, Philippe: "The Horror of the West," 156–71; *L'imitation des modernism,* 157; *Typographie,* 157

Lawtoo, Nidesh, 164; "A Frame for 'The Horror of the West,'" 170; *Conrad's Heart of Darkness and Contemporary Thought,* 156

Lay, Kenneth, 185

Leavis, F. R.: *The Great Tradition,* 112, 223n54

Leda, 237

Leopold II of Belgium, 89n2, 93, 114, 117

Levi, Primo: *The Drowned and the Saved,* 160

Lévinas, Emmanuel, 208
Lingis, Alphonso, 208
London, 33, 35, 36, 37, 38, 39, 40, 42, 46, 50, 51, 55, 160, 188, 218
London, Bette, 93
Longinus, 145n20
Lord of the Rings (film), 183
Lothe, Jakob, 162n7, 205
Lukacher, Ned: *Daemonic Figures,* 154
Lyotard, Jean-François, 145n20

Mallarmé, Stéphane, 183
Mallios, Peter Lancelot: "Untimely *Nostromo,*" 175n5
Mann, Thomas, 5, 184; *Doktor Faustus,* 6; *Death in Venice,* 94–95
Martin, Wallace, 162n7
Marx, Karl, Marxism, 34, 35, 93, 93n5, 121, 233, 246; *The Communist Manifesto* (with Engels), 74, 231; *Das Kapital,* 186; *Eighteenth Brumaire,* 234; *The German Ideology,* 186
Masterman, G. F.: *Seven Eventful Years in Paraguay,* 175, 179, 209, 221
materiality, 22, 46, 136, 145, 147, 181, 186, 197–202
Matthew, Book of, 74–75, 111, 128–29, 222
Meinam, River, 122, 133, 143
Melville, Herman, 99; *Benito Cereno,* 70; *Billy Budd,* 141
Meredith, George, 5
metaphor, xi, xvii, 16, 18, 32, 59, 60, 70, 76, 77, 78, 81, 106, 130, 146, 191, 244, 247, 250
metonymy, 76, 244, 245, 251
Mexico, Gulf of, 175–76, 178
Miller, J. Hillis: *Ariadne's Thread,* xv, xviii; "Cold Heaven, Cold Comfort: Should We Read or Teach Literature Now?," xix–xx; *Communities of Fiction,* 172, 208n46, 209␣8n49; *The Conflagration of Community,* xiv; "Conrad's Colonial (Non)Community," xv, 172–259; "Conrad's Secret," 102, 122–55; *The Ethics of Reading,* xiii, xvii, xviii; *Fiction and Repetition,* xii, xvi, xviii, xix, xixn26, 57; "Foreword" to *Conrad in the Twenty-First Century* (Kaplan, Mallios, White), 172; *The Form of Victorian Fiction,* 65; "Franz Kafka and the Metaphysics of Alienation," xviii; "Geglückte und misslungene Sprechakte in Kafkas *Der Process,*" xix; "The Geneva School," ix; "*Heart of Darkness* Revisited," xii, xiii, 74–87, 156–71; *An Innocent Abroad,* xix, xxn31; "The Interpretation of *Lord Jim,*" ix–x, xi, xii, 57; *The J. Hillis Miller Reader,* xn8, xin10; *The Linguistic Moment,* xin11, xiiin12; "The Linguistic Moment in 'The Wreck of the Deutschland,'" xin11; "The Literary Criticism of Georges Poulet," ixn3; "*Lord Jim*: Repetition as Subversion of Organic Form," xii, xixn26, 57–73; "'Material Interests': *Nostromo* as a Critique of Global Capitalism," xiv, 172; *Narrative Ethics,* xix; *On Literature,* xiv, xv; *Others,* 89, 105n15, 110n17, 122, 146n21; "Philosophy, Literature, Topography: Heidegger and Hardy," 187n17; *Poets of Reality,* viii, ix–x, 4–56; *Reading Narrative,* xv, xviii; "Should We Read *Heart of Darkness,*" xiv, xvii, xx, 88–121, 122; "Should We Read or Teach Literature Now?," xix, xx; "Text; Action; Space; Emotion in Conrad's *Nostromo,*" xv, 172; "Theory in the Development of Literary Studies," xn6; *Thinking Literature across Continents,* xix, xixn29, xixn30, xxn31; *Thomas Hardy: Distance and Desire,* xi; *Topographies,* xv, xvi; "Topography and Tropography in Thomas Hardy's 'In Front of a Landscape,'" xvi; "Yeats: The Cold Heaven," xxn32
mimesis, 59, 98, 100, 109–12, 148, 162, 163, 170, 180, 186
modernism, 129, 170, 183, 186, 198, 204, 205, 207, 211, 222, 223, 238
Monsanto, 218
Montevideo, 240
Moore, Marianne, 148n23
Morny, Charles Auguste Louis Joseph, Duc de, 242, 243, 247
Moscow, 213
Mudrick, Marvin: "Conrad and the Terms of Modern Criticism," 146
Muecke, D. C., 237
Mullaney, Steven: "Reforming Resistance: Class, Gender, and Legitimacy in Foxe's *Book of Martyrs,*" 154n27
Murdoch, Rupert, 220

Murfin, Ross C.: *Conrad Revisited: Essays for the Eighties*, xii; "Introduction" to *Heart of Darkness*, 161n6
Musil, Robert, 184

Nancy, Jean-Luc, 168, 208, 215; *La communauté désoeuvrée*, 212–13; *Corpus*, 165
Napierski, Stefan, 28
narrative ethics, xv, xviii, xxi
narrative theory (narratology), xv, xviii, xix, xxi, 162, 162n7, 164, 170
Nazism, 121
New Criticism, x, xin10, xv, xviii
New Historicism, 130, 187
New York, 218
Nietzsche, Friedrich Wilhelm, 157, 170
Nietzschean repetition xii, 58n2
Nihilism, viii–ix, 5–7, 59

Obama, Barack, 230
objectivity, ix, 7, 13, 48, 96, 143, 148, 149, 169, 201, 203
Odysseus, Ulysses, 162, 163, 223
Oedipus, 163
Orpheus, 29, 83

Páez, Ramón, 179
Palestine, 258
Panama, 215, 220
parable, parabolic reading, xiv, 74–87, 111, 120, 128–29, 143, 164–65, 191, 212, 213, 221–22, 223
"Pardoner's Tale, The" (Chaucer), 191, 233
Paris, 218, 221, 252
Parry, Benita: *Conrad and Imperialism*, 175n5; "The Moment and Afterlife of *Heart of Darkness*," 185
Pater, Walter, 184
Phelan, James: *Living to Tell about It*, 162
Phenomenology, viii, xin10, xv, xviii, 166
Plato, 101, 157, 161, 162, 163, 195; *The Republic*, 162, 223
Platonic repetition, xii, 58n2
Poe, Edgar Allan: "The Purloined Letter," 142
Poland, 180, 189, 194
Pollux (*The Iliad*), 236
postcolonial criticism, 130

Poulet, Georges, viii–ix, x, xi
Powhatan, 220
Prince, Gerald, 162n7
prolepsis, 162, 204, 205
prosopopoeia, xiii, 85, 106–8, 159, 187
Protestantism, 154, 217, 229, 240
Proust, Marcel, 5, 173, 183; *À la recherche du temps perdu*, 108, 162n7, 244

realism, 57, 74, 75, 110, 161, 163, 221, 222, 228, 236
Renaissance, 99, 221, 239
Revelation, Book of, 31, 82, 91, 113, 164
rhetorical reading, 130–55, 162, 170
Rhodes, Cecil, 89n2
Rimbaud, Jean Nicolas Arthur, 157
Rimmon-Kenan, Shlomith, 162n7
Robbe-Grillet, Alain: *Jalousie*, 203
Rochère, Martine Hennard Dutheil de la: "Sounding the Hollow Heart of the West: X-rays and the technique *de la mort*," 170–71
Romans, Book of, 75
romanticism, ix, 4–5, 63, 198
Rome/Romans, 114, 117, 160, 218
Ross, Stephen: *Conrad and Empire*, 175n5
Rousseau, Jean-Jacques, 199; *La nouvelle Héloïse*, 101
Roussel, Royal, viii; *The Metaphysics of Darkness*, viii
Royal, Nicholas, 205
Rumsfeld, Donald, 216
Russia/Russian, 157, 240
Rwanda, 213

Said, Edward, 172, 182, 185, 221, 227, 257–58; *Culture and Imperialism*, 94
Saint-Antoine, 178
Saint Armand, Imbert de, 242
San Francisco, 215, 217, 218, 219, 242
Sartre, Jean-Paul, 21, 98
Schelling, Friedrich Wilhelm Joseph, 149, 163–64, 165
Schiller, Friedrich, 198
Schlegel, Friedrich, 86, 105, 237
Schmitt, Carl, 230
Scholes, Robert, 162n7

Scott, Nathan A.: *The Tragic Vision and the Christian Faith*, xviii
Sedgwick, Eve, 108
Shakespeare, William, 100, 154; *Hamlet*, 165, 190, 255; *Othello*, 255
Sherry, Norman, 75, 135; *Conrad's Eastern World*, 69, 75, 126n6, 128n8, 136
Siam, Gulf of (Thailand), 122, 133, 143
"Sir Gawain and the Green Knight," 148
Socrates, 101
South Africa, 1, 89n2, 94, 99
South America/South American, xv, 175, 176, 179, 183, 185, 186, 189, 207, 209, 211, 214–15, 219–21, 223, 229, 240
Spain/Spanish, 131, 178, 188, 209, 210, 214, 232
Staten, Henry: "Conrad's Dionysian Elegy," 171
Stevens, Wallace, xvi, 4n3, 77; "Large Red Man Reading," 7; *The Necessary Angel*, 4; "A Primitive Like an Orb," 58, 112
subjectivism, subjectivity, 5, 6, 13, 16, 68, 72, 99, 100, 122, 145n20, 147, 166, 169, 205, 206, 227–30, 232, 239, 240, 249
sublime, xv, 145–46, 148, 166, 193n25, 194–202
Sydney, Sir Philip: *The Defense of Poesy*, 195–96
Symons, Arthur: *Notes on Joseph Conrad*, 97, 111
synecdoche, xiii, 76, 85, 137, 245

Texaco, 218
Thackeray, William Makepeace, 97; *Henry Edmond*, 57n1
Thames, River, 51, 89, 96, 103, 104
Thomas, Dylan, 4n3, 21
time, 43–44, 47, 49, 50, 54, 55
topography, 181, 189, 190, 192, 193, 201, 221
T. P.'s Weekly, 228
Tremolino, 180
Triana, S. Perez: *Down the Orinoco*, 175
Trilling, Lionel: *The Liberal Imagination*, 32n30
Trollope, Anthony, 5, 65, 190; *The Last Chronicle of Barset*, 66, 238

Tudor, Mary, 154

United States (America), x, 5, 93, 94, 99, 100, 116, 159, 183, 185, 187, 207, 210, 215, 217, 218–20, 221, 222–24, 229–30, 238, 241–42, 247, 253
Uruguay, 215

Valéry, Paul, 183
Venezuela, 176, 179

Wagner, Richard, 236
Warminski, Andrzej, 193n25, 194–202
Warren, Robert Penn: "Introduction" to *Nostromo* by Joseph Conrad, 178
Watt, Ian, 81; *Conrad in the Nineteenth Century*, 69, 75; *Joseph Conrad: Nostromo*, 175n5
Watts, Cedric T., 175n5; *Joseph Conrad: Nostromo*, 175n5, 176n6, 178, 192, 192n24, 221, 231, 258n68; *Joseph Conrad's Letters to Cunninghame Graham*, 175n5
Weiskel, Thomas, 145n20
Wells, H. G., 31
Williams, Frederick Benton (H. E. Hamblen): *On Many Seas: The Life and Exploits of a Yankee Sailor*, 176
Williams, Raymond: *The Country and the City*, 209
Williams, William Carlos, 4n3; *Selected Essays*, 148n23
will to power, 6, 7, 146, 147, 158
Woolf, Virginia, 184, 204; *Between the Acts*, 57n1; *Mrs. Dalloway*, 57n1, 207
Wordsworth, William, 195, 197; "Lines Written a Few Miles above Tintern Abbey," 196; "Preface of 1815," 146n21

Yeats, William Butler, 4n3; "The Circus Animals' Desertion," 228; "The Cold Heaven," xix–xx
Yee, Kevin, 139n17

Zeno, 47

THEORY AND INTERPRETATION OF NARRATIVE
James Phelan, Peter J. Rabinowitz, and Robyn Warhol, Series Editors

Because the series editors believe that the most significant work in narrative studies today contributes both to our knowledge of specific narratives and to our understanding of narrative in general, studies in the series typically offer interpretations of individual narratives and address significant theoretical issues underlying those interpretations. The series does not privilege one critical perspective but is open to work from any strong theoretical position.

Reading Conrad, J. Hillis Miller, Edited by John G. Peters and Jakob Lothe

Narrative, Race, and Ethnicity in the United States, Edited by James J. Donahue, Jennifer Ann Ho, Shaun Morgan

Somebody Telling Somebody Else: A Rhetorical Poetics of Narrative, James Phelan

Media of Serial Narrative, Edited by Frank Kelleter

Suture and Narrative: Deep Intersubjectivity in Fiction and Film, George Butte

The Writer in the Well: On Misreading and Rewriting Literature, Gary Weissman

Narrating Space / Spatializing Narrative: Where Narrative Theory and Geography Meet, Marie-Laure Ryan, Kenneth Foote, and Maoz Azaryahu

Narrative Sequence in Contemporary Narratology, Edited by Raphaël Baroni and Françoise Revaz

The Submerged Plot and the Mother's Pleasure from Jane Austen to Arundhati Roy, Kelly A. Marsh

Narrative Theory Unbound: Queer and Feminist Interventions, Edited by Robyn Warhol and Susan S. Lanser

Unnatural Narrative: Theory, History, and Practice, Brian Richardson

Ethics and the Dynamic Observer Narrator: Reckoning with Past and Present in German Literature, Katra A. Byram

Narrative Paths: African Travel in Modern Fiction and Nonfiction, Kai Mikkonen

The Reader as Peeping Tom: Nonreciprocal Gazing in Narrative Fiction and Film, Jeremy Hawthorn

Thomas Hardy's Brains: Psychology, Neurology, and Hardy's Imagination, Suzanne Keen

The Return of the Omniscient Narrator: Authorship and Authority in Twenty-First Century Fiction, Paul Dawson

Feminist Narrative Ethics: Tacit Persuasion in Modernist Form, Katherine Saunders Nash

Real Mysteries: Narrative and the Unknowable, H. Porter Abbott

A Poetics of Unnatural Narrative, Edited by Jan Alber, Henrik Skov Nielsen, and Brian Richardson

Narrative Discourse: Authors and Narrators in Literature, Film, and Art, Patrick Colm Hogan

An Aesthetics of Narrative Performance: Transnational Theater, Literature, and Film in Contemporary Germany, Claudia Breger

Literary Identification from Charlotte Brontë to Tsitsi Dangarembga, Laura Green

Narrative Theory: Core Concepts and Critical Debates, David Herman, James Phelan, Peter J. Rabinowitz, Brian Richardson, and Robyn Warhol

After Testimony: The Ethics and Aesthetics of Holocaust Narrative for the Future, Edited by Jakob Lothe, Susan Rubin Suleiman, and James Phelan

The Vitality of Allegory: Figural Narrative in Modern and Contemporary Fiction, Gary Johnson

Narrative Middles: Navigating the Nineteenth-Century British Novel, Edited by Caroline Levine and Mario Ortiz-Robles

Fact, Fiction, and Form: Selected Essays, Ralph W. Rader. Edited by James Phelan and David H. Richter.

The Real, the True, and the Told: Postmodern Historical Narrative and the Ethics of Representation, Eric L. Berlatsky

Franz Kafka: Narration, Rhetoric, and Reading, Edited by Jakob Lothe, Beatrice Sandberg, and Ronald Speirs

Social Minds in the Novel, Alan Palmer

Narrative Structures and the Language of the Self, Matthew Clark

Imagining Minds: The Neuro-Aesthetics of Austen, Eliot, and Hardy, Kay Young

Postclassical Narratology: Approaches and Analyses, Edited by Jan Alber and Monika Fludernik,

Techniques for Living: Fiction and Theory in the Work of Christine Brooke-Rose, Karen R. Lawrence

Towards the Ethics of Form in Fiction: Narratives of Cultural Remission, Leona Toker

Tabloid, Inc.: Crimes, Newspapers, Narratives, V. Penelope Pelizzon and Nancy M. West

Narrative Means, Lyric Ends: Temporality in the Nineteenth-Century British Long Poem, Monique R. Morgan

Understanding Nationalism: On Narrative, Cognitive Science, and Identity, Patrick Colm Hogan

Joseph Conrad: Voice, Sequence, History, Genre, Edited by Jakob Lothe, Jeremy Hawthorn, James Phelan

The Rhetoric of Fictionality: Narrative Theory and the Idea of Fiction, Richard Walsh

Experiencing Fiction: Judgments, Progressions, and the Rhetorical Theory of Narrative, James Phelan

Unnatural Voices: Extreme Narration in Modern and Contemporary Fiction, Brian Richardson

Narrative Causalities, Emma Kafalenos

Why We Read Fiction: Theory of Mind and the Novel, Lisa Zunshine

I Know That You Know That I Know: Narrating Subjects from Moll Flanders *to* Marnie, George Butte

Bloodscripts: Writing the Violent Subject, Elana Gomel

Surprised by Shame: Dostoevsky's Liars and Narrative Exposure, Deborah A. Martinsen

Having a Good Cry: Effeminate Feelings and Pop-Culture Forms, Robyn R. Warhol

Politics, Persuasion, and Pragmatism: A Rhetoric of Feminist Utopian Fiction, Ellen Peel

Telling Tales: Gender and Narrative Form in Victorian Literature and Culture, Elizabeth Langland

Narrative Dynamics: Essays on Time, Plot, Closure, and Frames, Edited by Brian Richardson

Breaking the Frame: Metalepsis and the Construction of the Subject, Debra Malina

Invisible Author: Last Essays, Christine Brooke-Rose

Ordinary Pleasures: Couples, Conversation, and Comedy, Kay Young

Narratologies: New Perspectives on Narrative Analysis, Edited by David Herman

Before Reading: Narrative Conventions and the Politics of Interpretation, Peter J. Rabinowitz

Matters of Fact: Reading Nonfiction over the Edge, Daniel W. Lehman

The Progress of Romance: Literary Historiography and the Gothic Novel, David H. Richter

A Glance Beyond Doubt: Narration, Representation, Subjectivity, Shlomith Rimmon-Kenan

Narrative as Rhetoric: Technique, Audiences, Ethics, Ideology, James Phelan

Misreading Jane Eyre: *A Postformalist Paradigm,* Jerome Beaty

Psychological Politics of the American Dream: The Commodification of Subjectivity in Twentieth-Century American Literature, Lois Tyson

Understanding Narrative, Edited by James Phelan and Peter J. Rabinowitz

Framing Anna Karenina: Tolstoy, the Woman Question, and the Victorian Novel, Amy Mandelker

Gendered Interventions: Narrative Discourse in the Victorian Novel, Robyn R. Warhol

Reading People, Reading Plots: Character, Progression, and the Interpretation of Narrative, James Phelan

www.ingramcontent.com/pod-product-compliance
Lightning Source LLC
Chambersburg PA
CBHW030108010526
44116CB00005B/152